WORKS ISSUED BY
THE HAKLUYT SOCIETY

———

COMPASSING THE VASTE GLOBE
OF THE EARTH

SECOND SERIES
NO. 183

CAPTAIN JAMES COOK
Reproduced as the frontispiece of HS Extra 43 of 1988

COMPASSING THE VASTE GLOBE OF THE EARTH

Studies in the History of the Hakluyt Society 1846–1996

With a complete List of the Society's Publications

Edited by

R. C. BRIDGES
and
P. E. H. HAIR

Throw back the portals
which have been closed
since the world's beginning
at the dawn of time.

(*From Richard Hakluyt's dedication
to his translation of Peter Martyr*)

THE HAKLUYT SOCIETY

LONDON

1996

ISBN 0 904180 44 1
ISSN 0072 9396

Typeset by Waveney Typesetters, Norwich
Printed in Great Britain at
the University Press, Cambridge

SERIES EDITORS
W. F. RYAN and SARAH TYACKE

British Library Cataloguing-in-Publication Data
A catalogue record for this book is
available from the British Library

Published by the Hakluyt Society
c/o The Map Library
British Library, Great Russell Street
London WC1B 3DG

CONTENTS

Part IV
EPILOGUE

Appendices

LIST OF ILLUSTRATIONS

PREFACE

The present volume forms part of the Celebration of the one hundred and fifty years of the Hakluyt Society, founded in 1846 to publish scholarly editions of 'Voyages and Travels'. Moreover, by enabling us to look back over that period and consider many achievements and developments, the volume helps members to prepare the Society for a new century and a new era. During its long life the Society has continued to pay tribute to its eponymous forbear of four centuries ago, Richard Hakluyt, and in many aspects it has carried forward his pioneering researches. But it has not failed to recognise changing times, changing views of the past, and changing demands, both academic and public.

We trust that a volume of historical essays will appeal to members of the Hakluyt Society, in that it gives them a time-perspective on the present society, in part through biographical studies of past leading figures. But it should also appeal to a larger readership, inasmuch as it attempts to relate the history of the Society to a larger history, that of the British nation, and hence, indeed, also that of the world. For *The Vaste Globe of the Earth*, with its encountering cultures, often first disclosed to each other, in their complexity and fascination, by *Voyages and Travels* – whether to their individual gain or loss – is today a world bound together as never before.

On behalf of the Council of the Society, we thank the editors and contributors.

C. F. BECKINGHAM (*President 1969–1972*)
GLYNDWR WILLIAMS (*President 1978–1982*)
D. B. QUINN (*President 1982–1987*)
HAROLD SMEDLEY (*President 1987–1992*)

Part I
PROLEGOMENA

Foreword

The Hakluyt Society: from Past to Future

FOREWORD

The title of this volume is taken from a sentence in the 'Epistle Dedica-torie' of Richard Hakluyt's *Principall Navigations* (1589). Applied there to contemporary English overseas endeavour, the phrase is equally appli-cable to the past, present, and intended future action of the Hakluyt Society, in making available, in English, a global range of 'Voyages and Travels'. It thus provides an appropriate title for a volume designed to commemorate one hundred and fifty years of that activity.

The shape of the volume is intended to encourage appreciation of the Society's history and reflection on its meaning. We believe that the Society has been a notable element in British scholarly endeavour and a body which may claim some modest success in contributing to under-standing of the modern world. In the first part of this volume we present an analysis of the editorial and publication work of the Society, which is, of course, its whole *raison d'être*. Part II consists of original biographical studies of four notable figures who established and led the Society in the nineteenth century. In Part III there are shorter and more personal studies of three men who, in different ways, perpetuated and developed the Society in the present century, their lives and careers described by distinguished living members of the Society who knew and worked with them. Part IV of the volume takes the form of an Epilogue. Here the editors point to the wide historical contexts within which the Society has operated and suggest the ways in which the activities of the Society have both reflected these contexts and exerted some influence on their development. The final part, although labelled 'Appendices', is an integral part of the volume, inasmuch as it com-prises basic information about the progress of the Society, especially through a detailed listing of all the Society's publications.

The biographical essays are limited to deceased figures. One absent figure is Eila Campbell, who died while this volume was in prepara-tion. Her name appears on no title-page, yet her influence on the Society in recent decades was considerable – as an Honorary Secretary, as series editor for many volumes, and as a decisive voice in Council.

*   *   *

In the notes to the essays, Hakluyt Society publications are further identified by the numbers given in the Listing on pp. 248–302 below, e.g., HS 15, HS 2/93, HS Extra 34.

The illustrations are taken largely from past Hakluyt Society volumes and have been chosen to reflect something of the range both of published editions and of what has been considered appropriate illustrations. A number of the illustrations also relate to specific editorial work noted in the essays. A number of the illustrations also relate to specific editorial work notes in the essays. Portraits of three leading Victorian figures and of Sir William Foster appeared in the centenary volume (HS 2/93), and portraits of three more Victorian figures (with one repeated) can be found on p. 70. The generous supply of maps in past volumes (the 'more important maps' listed in the centenary volume) is here weakly represented. Being commonly of large size and in fold-out form, the maps do not lend themselves to suitable reproduction within the present format, regrettably.

We thank the Council of the Society for inviting us to edit this volume. We express our obligation to the contributors for their labours in preparing their essays and their patience and forbearance in accepting our editorial interventions. Our principle has been to keep the text of essays 'readable', while including in notes, even if lengthy, not only the necessary evidential references but also such material and argument relating to complex or marginal issues as can assist the scholar to assess the weight of generalisations proffered in the text. We express our gratitude to our Series Editor, Sarah Tyacke, and the Society's design consultant, Stephen Easton, for their tactful guidance. Mrs Dorothy Middleton, the late Professor Eila Campbell and Dr W. F. Ryan were encouraging in the early stages of the project; and we thank the Royal Geographical Society and its then Director, Dr John Hemming, for the permission to use the Society's archives granted to ourselves and other contributors. For preliminary advice on the issue of a commemorative volume we thank Mrs Fiona Easton; for the expert preparation on p. 141 Mrs Sandra Williams; and for much of the photographic work Mike Craig and the photographic service of the Queen Mother Library of the University of Aberdeen. We are grateful for the assistance in procuring illustrations of Mrs Ann Shirley, Tony Campbell, Richard Bingle, and Anthony Farrington; and for permission to use illustrations we thank the British Library, the Wellcome Institute Library, and the Royal Geographical Society, all of London. Finally, we acknowledge the support of the Library and the Department of History and Economic History of the University of Aberdeen, and the Library and the Department of History of the University of Liverpool.

R.C.B., P.E.H.H.

MANDEVILLE'S TRAVELS
First page of the Paris MS. (Bibliothèque Nationale, Nouvelles Acquisition
Françaises 4515).
Reproduced as the frontispiece of HS 2/102 of 1953.

6

THE HAKLUYT SOCIETY

FROM PAST TO FUTURE

P. E. H. Hair

The Hakluyt Society, which is established for the purpose of printing rare or unpublished Voyages and Travels, aims at opening by this means an easier access to the sources of a branch of knowledge, which yields to none in importance, and is superior to most in agreeable variety. The narratives of travellers and navigators make us acquainted with the earth, its inhabitants and productions; they exhibit the growth of intercourse among mankind, with its effects on civilization, and, while instructing, they at the same time awaken attention, by recounting the toils and adventures of those who first explored unknown and distant regions.

(From a statement of the aims of the Hakluyt Society, as intermittently included in the printed volumes 1849–1895.)[1]

The 281 volumes produced by the Hakluyt Society in its Ordinary Series between 1847 and 1995 – the first 100 volumes in a First Series issued up to 1898, the remainder in a Second Series from 1899 onwards – represent, because of multi-volume works, some 220 separate editions. In addition, the Extra Series, published in the present century, comprises 44 volumes and one portfolio of charts, and represents a further 11 editions.[2] The very first publication was a reprint of a single

---

[1] The statement of aims which includes the quoted passage, and which derived from the first Honorary Secretary, William Desborough Cooley, was replaced in 1896, probably on the initiative of the recently-installed Honorary Secretary, William Foster, by a different statement, part of which still appears, only marginally altered, in the annual 'List of Publications in Print' (for a passage from this, see p. 8, note 3 below). For the inclusion of the statement of aims in certain volumes, see p. 15 below.

[2] This essay depends largely on an examination of the set of 281 Ordinary Series and 45 Extra Series volumes. Such long series provide enough material for a whole thesis on scholarly techniques and cultural attitudes over the period; my own examination has been a mere skimming through the volumes, in an attempt to identify some of the trends and provide examples. Hence I am aware, not only of topics I ignore or cannot adequately handle (such as the development of illustrations, maps and book design), but also of generalisations offered which may well be not verified by closer study. In particular, any attempt I

seventeenth-century printed work in English, relating to an English venture, with exiguous scholarly apparatus.[1] The Society has progressively taken a wider view of its responsibilities.[2]

The history of HS editing

Mere reprints of early English works soon became uncommon, and almost all works contained fuller scholarly apparatus.[3] Editions of

---

make to assess the importance of individual editions must be subject to the more informed views of regional specialists. I regret too that I have been unable to look into the biographies of the hundred and more scholars involved other than in a handful of instances, and have generally had to rely on what they give away about themselves in the course of their editing, or in a few instances on information in the essays that follow in the present volume.

[1] C. R. Drinkwater Bethune, ed., *The Observations of Sir Richard Hawkins Knt., in his Voyage into the South Sea in the Year 1593 . . .*, London, 1847 (HS 1). HS numbers refer to the Listing of Hakluyt Society volumes on pp. 243–302 below: in the present essay, because of the number of citations, hereafter works are normally cited only by the HS number. The total of actual volumes in the Ordinary Series is one less than the number given in the text, 281, since in 1910 a number was given to a portfolio of maps (other portfolios of maps in this series have been included in the number of the volume to which the maps relate). Whereas many editions have comprised more than one volume, HS 49 and 79 each comprised two separate editions. As for the Extra Series, discounting HS Extra 1–12, 14–33, 37 and 38 as not being initiated by the Society, and noting that HS Extra 36 and 39 account for two volumes each, the original editions comprise 13 volumes and one portfolio of charts, representing 8 editions.

[2] For earlier discussions of the history of the Society, see William Foster, 'The Hakluyt Society, 1846–1946. A Retrospect', in Edward Lynam, ed., *Hakluyt & his Successors*, 1946 (HS 2/93), pp. 143–70; Edward Lynam, 'The Present and the Future', in ibid., pp. 173–89; G. R. Crone, '"Jewells of Antiquitie": the Work of the Hakluyt Society', *Geographical Journal*, 128, 1962, pp. 321–4; G. S. Dunbar, 'Societies for the History of Discoveries', *Terrae Incognitae*, 6, 1974, pp. 65–71; Helen Wallis, 'The Great Publications Societies', in Germaine Warkentin, ed., *Critical Issues in Editing Exploration Texts*, Toronto, 1995, pp. 109–24; and especially Dorothy Middleton, 'The Hakluyt Society (1846–1923)', *Annual Report* [for 1984], Hakluyt Society, pp. 12–23 (also in a slightly different form, with a beginning date amended to 1847, in *Geographical Journal*, 152, 1986, 217–24). There are also useful references in Loren Pennington, 'Secondary Works on Hakluyt and his Circle', in D. B. Quinn, ed., *The Hakluyt Handbook*, 2 vols, single pag., 1974, pp. 576–610 (HS 2/144–5). I am indebted to a number of members of Council and officers of the Society, past and present, for supplying me with information about the recent inner history of the Society, as well as for their expert advice on desirable future editions.

[3] Whereas the Annual Report of the Society, issued to all members, now contains a brisk and updated summary of the aims (as cited in the text hereafter), the List of Publications in Print, also issued to members, still records a longer version of 1896 (see p. 7, note 1), which includes the following sentence of splendidly Victorian flavour. 'Works of this class are of the highest interest to students of history, geography, navigation and ethnology, and many of them, especially the spirited accounts and translations of the Elizabethan and Stuart periods, are admirable examples of English prose at the stage of its most robust development.' At the genesis of the Hakluyt Society there were influences from earlier literary texts societies, as noted on pp. 61, 63 below. In 1953 the 'Elizabethan or Jacobean flavour' of early translations was still commended as a reason for reproducing them in a modern edition (HS 2/106). For more on early translations, see p. 13, note 2 below.

single printed works have, however, continued to the present day, although from an early date mostly with ancillary documentation from manuscript sources: the second volume initiated this category of publication. Collections of material from a variety of sources of more or less equal value, printed and manuscript, began with the fourth volume and eventually became another significant category: the term 'collections' first appeared in a title in 1914. The most regularly occurring among the printed sources set alongside manuscript sources have been Hakluyt and his successor Purchas, followed by Ramusio, the Churchill collection, and the Calendars of State Papers, their accounts being thus augmented or in some instances corrected. Documents from manuscript sources (the definition necessary because early editions used the term 'documents' to include printed sources) increasingly became the major texts in editions. Editions in which the base work is a single hitherto unpublished manuscript began with one in 1866 and continued with others in 1882 and 1887–1889.[1] For long these formed a small proportion of editions but latterly have become common. Collections wholly or largely of previously unpublished archive documents (as distinct from a single manuscript) began with a 1914 edition by Zelia Nuttall and continued in the inter-wars editions of Irene Wright and the more recent editions of David Quinn, Kenneth Andrews, and others of the 'Quinn school'.[2] In the nineteenth century editorial search for and discovery of hitherto unknown archive material was almost always limited to investigations in British repositories such as the British Museum, Public Record Office and India Office, any original material from foreign archives having been searched for and discovered by local scholars, albeit usually at the request of the HS editor. As late as 1932 a North American scholar asserted that British editors failed to undertake, personally, extensive searches in foreign archives.[3]

Certain features of editions began commendably early: the second volume had an original index, the third a map, and the fourth a translation of a transcribed foreign manuscript.[4] Illustrations in various

---

[1] The editions are HS 35, 65, 74–8.

[2] Note that 'Translated from original Spanish manuscripts' in the title of some earlier works meant translated from modern printed editions of manuscript sources (e.g. HS 47 of 1873, an edition by Markham).

[3] Irene Wright, *English Voyages to the Spanish Main*, 1932 (HS 2/71); as Kenneth Andrews noted in 1959, Wright 'worked with unflagging zeal that rich quarry of information in Seville hardly touched until then by writers on English maritime history' (HS 2/111).

[4] Indexes have been varyingly comprehensive. A few nineteenth-century ones are patently slight and inadequate, and Professor Loren Pennington, who has worked through all the indexes, tells me that in general they are disappointing. My impression is that one of the limited merits of Markham's many editions is their above-average indexes.

technical forms – some illustrations more decorative than relevantly informative – were soon occasionally inserted, and after about 1880 regularly inserted.[1] The size of editions expanded. The first two-volume edition appeared in 1851 and 1852; the third, two volumes issued both in 1866, achieved a bumper 947 pages.[2] Two-volume editions became common from the 1880s. A three-volume edition was published in 1887–1889, and another was issued in a single year, 1896; a number of such editions have followed since.[3] A four-volume edition appeared 1875–1884, and two have been published in recent decades. Publication of a six-volume edition took from 1907 to 1936 to complete; a five-volume edition, begun by one editor in 1958, will probably be completed by a successor editor in 1997.[4] In 1871, 1896, and several more times up to the 1940s members received over one thousand pages for a one-guinea subscription.[5]

In recent times, tight printing schedules tend to make authors scurry through proofs to produce over-hasty indexes: some very recent indexes have been produced mechanically and show it. A few twentieth-century editions credit an individual other than the editor for the index (e.g., HS 2/5), but it may be doubted whether all earlier editors did the work themselves. Mrs Alison Quinn was outstanding as an indexer and her model index for the 1965 facsimile reprint of Hakluyt's *Principall Navigations* was awarded the Wheatley Medal of the Library Association.

[1] Early illustrations consisted mainly of coats of arms, portraits, manuscript pages and topographic and naval engravings. A 1901 edition of accounts of the Solomon Islands was the first to contain a series of ethnographic photographs (HS 2/7–8). Coloured illustrations, produced by various means, very occasionally appeared in editions from the 1850s, normally only one per volume; colour photographs have been introduced in recent times but only very sparingly. The nineteenth-century editions of early printed works normally failed to reproduce the original illustrations, or at least most of them, which reduced the value of the editions. Several editors, e.g. Markham, and later Foster, seem to have been reluctant to introduce illustrations, and a substantial proportion of pre-1945 editions had either no illustrations or none other than maps. The largest number of illustrations, some 150, appeared in an enthralling 1975 edition, Terence Armstrong's 1975 *Yermak's Campaign in Siberia* (HS 2/146). To date, most illustrations in the Ordinary Series have been reproduced from published works, and the number of previously unpublished illustrations, few in the nineteenth century, has increased only to a limited extent in the twentieth, despite decreasing labour and cost in obtaining and reproducing them. But in the Extra Series most of the material in the volumes of Cook charts was previously unpublished.

[2] HS 10, 12; 36, 37. The 1914–1915 updated version of the 1866 edition was slightly longer (HS 2/37, 38).

[3] The first two-volume edition was by Major, the then Honorary Secretary; the bumper edition was by Yule, a member of Council and later president; the first three-volume edition was also by Yule, who added two volumes of annotation to a first volume by another editor whose scholarship he seems to have distrusted (HS 74, 75, 78). The four-volume edition and the 1896 three-volume edition were respectively HS 53, 55, 62, 69, and 92–94.

[4] The six-volume edition was HS 2/17, 35, 45, 46, 55, 78; the forthcoming five-volume one is HS 2/110, 117, 141, 178.

[5] However, such good years were often the result of material accumulating, and hence

Whereas Richard Hakluyt concentrated on assembling material relating to English ventures and hence largely in English, the Society from the start looked further afield – perhaps surprisingly. One of the Society's earliest decisions was to select as the emblem on each of its volumes a logo of Magellan's ship, the 'Victoria', presumably symbolising its intention of intellectual circumnavigation.[1] Its second volume commemorated a non-English voyager, Columbus (although this was possibly a gesture of invitation to anglophone North America); and over two-thirds of the First Series volumes related to foreign activities, Spanish ones being well to the fore, partly as a result of the editorial enthusiasm of Clements Markham. The present century has seen a slightly larger proportion of editions devoted to English ventures, helped by William Foster's series of editions on individual East Indian voyages (and encouragement of others to work in this field), while the dominance of Spanish among the foreign-language sources deployed

---

came after thin years (e.g. 1865). Apart from editions being of very varying lengths, the Society has never been able to even out publication to a fixed number of volumes each year. Even in the nineteenth century there were odd years without any publication, while in the 1970s the subscription year date and the actual publication date grew apart by as much as six years (note also the date of the editor's introduction) – thereafter the subscription year date was not shown on volumes. The explanation for delays given in the 1977 annual report is of interest: 'the principal reason . . . is that in order to satisfy the editorial standard of the Society a dozen years may elapse between the acceptance of a proposal and the publication of a volume. The editors are in many cases holders of academic appointments; they can give only their spare time to the Society's publications; some projects founder by the way. When an editor delivers his typescript it is examined by experts on behalf of the Society; their findings may lead to a further delay. When a volume is finally ready for publication it would be unfair to the editor to hold it back for very long. For this reason two or three volumes may be published at short intervals; and then a long interval before the next volume.' For a further explanation of the 1970s delay, see the essay by Strachan below, especially p. 128. As for the one-guinea subscription, while it represented good value for most of the period, in 1849 the Council apologised to subscribers, confessing that only two volumes for one guinea was 'inadequate' ('Annual Report' in HS 5).

[1] It might, however, be argued that it was the scope of British imperial activities at the time that encouraged the Society to take the world as its oyster. A possibly related influence was the emphasis on 'geographical material' in the Society's aims and its close connection with the Royal Geographical Society and geographers, a feature which predicated an extension over world space. More specifically, Roy Bridges shows below that Cooley, the founder of the Society and first Honorary Secretary (1847–1849), originally intended to call the new body the 'Columbus Society' and favoured international coverage (p. 68). Although the Society has consistently declared a major concern for 'geography', it is arguable that as academic history has extended its base to world history, and as academic geography has moved away from mere physical and taxonomic description to study of environmental and cultural process, the value of the HS volumes lies nowadays – and perhaps for long has lain – as much in the study of 'change over time' as that of 'change over space'. Yet it is worth noting that as early as 1852, the annual report noted 'the warm interest shown at the present day for all matters affecting geographical discovery and *the world's history* [my emphasis]'.

11

has been somewhat reduced, Portuguese texts gaining ground and Dutch, French and Latin sources becoming more common.[1] About one tenth of all editions include translations of sources in more than one language, a proportion that has not greatly increased in the present century. Modern editors tend to offer material from only two or three foreign languages and an 1857 edition which claimed sources in Latin, Persian, Russian and Italian represented a geographical spread of languages hardly again matched.[2] If this concern for foreign-language texts represents some divergence from Richard Hakluyt's own concern, the Society has nevertheless paid tribute to the master, and made his texts very much more accessible, by being associated with reprints of *Principal Navigations* in 1903–1905 and of Purchas's *Hakluytus Posthumus* in 1905–1907, by publishing an edition of *Divers Voyages* in 1850, by publishing facsimile reprints of *Principall Navigations* in 1965 and of the manuscript *Western Planting* in 1993, and by producing, as a guide to the texts, a *Hakluyt Handbook* in 1974.[3]

When Richard Hakluyt, recording English voyages, had to use foreign-language material he normally gave the reader an English translation, as well as the original or, more often, instead of it. The Society has followed suit by normally publishing texts only in English, foreign-language sources being offered in translation. However, editions which include the original foreign-language text as well as the translation have appeared very occasionally, the most recent in 1968.[4] In the mid-Victorian period chunks of Latin, Italian and French sometimes turned up in appendices, and very occasionally a passage within a translation was allowed to remain in the decency of its original language, Latin or

[1] Among the other languages occasionally translated into English in Hakluyt Society editions have been German, Greek, Catalan, Danish, Russian, Icelandic, Arabic, Turkish, Chinese, Ethiopic, and an unspecified Indian 'vernacular' (HS 2/22). For an earlier comment on the range of languages translated, see C. F. Beckingham, 'Arabic texts and the Hakluyt Society', *Annual Report* [for 1979], Hakluyt Society, p. 1.

[2] But, as pointed out in Beckingham, 'Arabic texts', p. 1, the Persian text was translated from a French version. A recent edition includes material extracted from texts in Latin, Greek, Arabic, Russian and Icelandic, but only the texts in Latin, Russian and Icelandic were translated especially for this volume. As not uncommonly in recent editions, the title-page named the separate translators as well as the editor (HS 2/167).

[3] Two of Hakluyt's separately published translations were also reprinted, the account of Florida by the 'Gentleman of Elvas' in 1851 (HS 9) and the account of 'The Discoveries' by Galvão in 1862 (HS 30).

[4] The earliest editions with a text in the original language as well as a translation were published in 1847 (Columbus's letters in Spanish: HS 2), 1862 (Galvão in Portuguese: HS 30), 1866 (Odoric in Latin and Italian: HS 36, 37), and 1872 (*Le Canarien* in French: HS 46). In the present century the Spanish texts of a previously unpublished journal of the Quiros voyage and again of Columbus's letters have been included in editions (HS 2/64, 65, 70), as have the Portuguese text of Tomé Pires (HS 2/89, 90), the French text of Mandeville (HS 2/101, 102), and the letters of Leichardt in German (HS 2/133–135).

in one instance Turkish.[1] In the nineteenth century the translation offered was not uncommonly an existing one, usually one contemporary with the foreign source, hence in practice often an Elizabethan or Jacobean translation – justified at the time on literary as much as on historical grounds. In the present century it has become uncommon to reprint early translations, or at least to offer them without a running commentary of original corrections, thus rendering them more adequate.[2]

The range of editions

The 1847 constitution of the Society laid down that the publication of sources was to be, chronologically, only up 'to the circumnavigation of Dampier', that is, up to c.1700. This limitation, not lifted until 1903, meant that the First Series concentrated heavily on sixteenth- and early seventeenth-century sources, backed up by a scatter of texts from earlier periods. This concentration remained in the Second Series but was reduced, partly by the inclusion of more late seventeenth–century texts, and only slowly and gradually by the inclusion of even later texts. The first edition to penetrate beyond 1700 was in fact HS 11 of 1852 (contrary to the then limitation), but the next not until HS 2/32 of 1913. Of the first hundred editions of the Second Series only seven involved the eighteenth century; to date the total approaches a score. The first edition to penetrate into the nineteenth century was HS 2/52 in 1925; HS 2/91

---

[1] In his editions of 1869 (HS 42) and 1874 (HS 52) H. E. J. Stanley included an appendix of documents in Portuguese; and the appendices to the four-volume edition of Albuquerque's *Commentaries* by W. de Gray Birch included extracts from sources in Latin and Portuguese (HS 62, 69). The Lord's Prayer in Armenian and Tatar was supplied in 1879 (HS 58). As regards decency, in 1848 Major reported that there were 'passages unfit for publication in Herberstein's *Russia*', a work he was editing as HS 10 and 12 (Middleton, 'Hakluyt Society', p. 12; also p. 96 below). How much silent or oblique censorship has been exercised in HS editions is uncertain but it is unlikely that much has occurred in the present century.

[2] In 1873 a 'quaint old translation' was preferred to a modern one (made by a member of the British Museum staff) 'on account of its interest as English of the time of Edward IV' (HS 49); and in 1892 an ancient translation was again preferred on the grounds that 'the somewhat archaic form of the language used in it seems to be in keeping with that of the original letters, and to give them a character and flavour which would be wanting in a modern translation' (HS 84). (For the source of this literary consideration, see p. 8, note 3 above.) The argument is not entirely without merit, provided that the ancient translation is checked and revised. But statements in 1855 and 1880 that 'it seems on the whole to be a very exact translation' (HS 18), or is 'on the whole creditable and trustworthy' (HS 60), are not reassuring, and in many instances no critique and correction of the early translation was included in the edition. A foreign editor who took over an edition in 1885 remarked bluntly that the ancient translation his predecessor had used and he was annotating was 'poor' and he supplied corrections (HS 71), while 1896 editors promised that 'any vital defects will be pointed out' (HS 92): see also HS 2/9 of 1902.

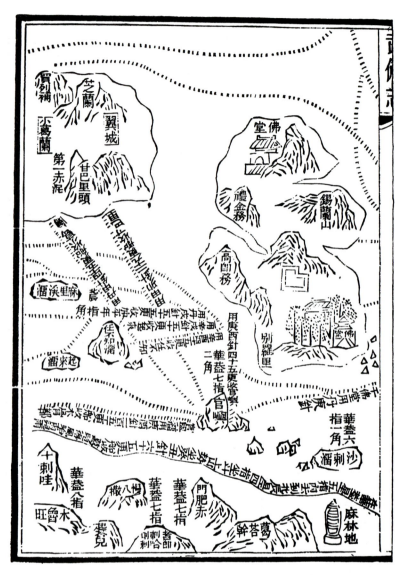

CHINESE MAP OF THE INDIAN OCEAN
(the sea minimised between the land-masses of Ceylon, India, and East Africa).
Based on fifteenth-century exploration, as recorded in Mao Yüan-i's *Wu-pei chih* of 1621.
Reproduced in HS Extra 42 of 1970.

14

reached 1821, HS 2/116 1830, HS 2/133–135 1848, and HS 2/169–170 1854; while an edition to appear in the anniversary year deals with the 1880s. However, the Extra Series – whose recent concentration on Cook material has enlarged the eighteenth-century score – with a 1969 edition reached the 1880s earlier. Thus, the weight of HS publications has been only marginally spread beyond the period of Richard Hakluyt's principal interest, roughly 1450–1615.[1] No doubt the process of chronological advance will continue, not least since there must be some exhaustion of texts of the 'Hakluyt period'.[2] And perhaps twenty-first century publications will include accounts of latterday exploration even beyond the confines of Hakluyt's globe.

The aim of the Society as stated in the 1847 prospectus was to publish 'the more rare and valuable voyages, travels, and geographical records, from the early period of exploratory enterprise to the circumnavigation of Dampier, and to promote knowledge of these matters'.[3] Today this aim is expressed in an extended and slightly more outward-looking definition – 'to advance education by the publication of scholarly editions of records of voyages, travels and other geographical material of the past, and to promote public knowledge of these matters'.[4] The Hakluyt Society is the oldest society devoted to this category of publication but today not the only one. Closest to it in aim is the Linschoten Vereeniging, founded in 1909; but the global coverage of this society's many excellent editions is limited to Dutch voyages and these are

---

[1] As will be shown more fully in the forthcoming *Purchas Handbook*, Hakluyt collected texts up to his death in 1616, the unpublished material passing, by gift or purchase, to the younger scholar, who published them, or extracts from them, in 1625. Texts from earlier than the 'Hakluyt period' have occasionally been edited. The medieval texts mainly relate to pilgrimages to the Holy Land or missions to Central Asia, but include Mandeville and the account of the almost certainly fictitious voyage of the Zeno brothers, as well as the account of the remarkable land travels of Ibn Baṭṭūṭa. The first text in even earlier history was that of Cosmas, edited in 1897, and two texts on the 'Erythraean Sea' were published in the 1980s (HS 98, 2/151, 172). As the editor of one of the latter remarks, few historically significant Graeco-Roman texts of the kind appropriate to Hakluyt Society publication remain to be translated into English.

[2] In 1946 Lynam wrote – 'Personally I see no reason why we should not publish narratives of every age right down to the present time' (adding discreetly, 'or so far as the Copyright Laws allow'): Lynam, 'Present and Future', p. 189.

[3] A slightly diffent wording appeared in the 'Laws of the Hakluyt Society' agreed in 1847 and printed in the 1849 and later volumes, and this included, after the records of voyages and travels, those of 'naval expeditions'. When the 'Laws' became 'Rules' in 1931 and were revised in 1980 (see the Annual Report for 1979) the slight rewording included the omission of 'naval expeditions', probably out of deference to the Navy Records Society. However, this was long after the founding of that society in the 1890s, a move which in fact caused a dispute between the Secretary and the President of the Hakluyt Society (Foster, 'A Retrospect', p. 157).

[4] The phrase 'to advance education' was introduced in the 1980 revision of the 'Rules'.

published exclusively in Dutch.[1] Lacking the global coverage of the Hakluyt Society are a small number of regional societies, such as the Champlain Society of Canada and the Van Riebeeck Society of South Africa, although of course such societies also publish source material not pertinent to the aims of the Hakluyt Society.[2] Global coverage and publication in English therefore represent the unique distinction of the Society. The outstanding value of its past publications to scholars across the world has been expressed by very many of these, and is indeed without contradiction.[3] The Society's record of scholarly achievement has been built up by the labours of generations of both volume editors and the Society's officers, including its own series (i.e. general) editors. Like the volume editors, the series editors have been and are voluntary scholars, labouring without payment.[4] Only because of the security of the Hakluyt Society's past reputation is it profitable to turn, later in this essay, to a consideration of its present situation and its future.

The context

In 1946, at the centenary of the Society, aspects of its history were ably sketched, in an essay contributed to a commemorative volume, by Sir William Foster.[5] This drew attention to the changes in the world between 1846 and 1946, one minor symptom of which was the growth

---

[1] The foundation of the Linschoten Vereeniging in 1909 was formally welcomed by the Hakluyt Society.

[2] The series *Fontes Historiae Africanae*, which is sponsored in Britain by the British Academy, also produces edited translations of historical texts, to date principally on North and NE Africa, some of which come close to being HS material.

[3] Two recent tributes will suffice. 'Rappelons aussi les remarquables traductions critiques de textes portugais, publieés par la Hakluyt Society de Londres où nous relevons les noms de Charles Raymond Beazley, Edgar Prestage, E. G. Ravenstein et George H. T. Kimble ... Ce sont là des ouvrages sérieux, malgré leur ancienneté' (Joaquim Barradas de Carvalho, *Á la spécificité de la Renaissance Portugaise* ..., Paris, 1983, p. 14). 'This book owes much to the Hakluyt Society, whose publications have been indispensable' (opening sentence of the Preface in Philip Edwards, *The Story of the Voyage: Sea-narratives in Eighteenth-century England*, Cambridge, 1994).

[4] For a list of the Society's editors, entitled Honorary Secretaries, see p. 316. In 1946 Lynam stated that 'our editors, with two exceptions, have never received any reward for their labours' (Lynam, 'Present and Future', p. 185). This was not strictly correct since editors, both volume editors and series editors, have latterly received, and presumably always have received, a number of free copies of any edition on which they had worked. As regards monetary reward, the identity of the two exceptions is not known. An extraordinary hangover from nineteenth century notions is that until the 1990s the series editors, announced in the Society's reports misleadingly as merely its 'Honorary Secretaries', were not identified in the publications they had seen to press, other than by a passing reference in the Acknowledgements.

[5] Foster, 'A Retrospect'.

in Hakluyt Society membership – never exceeding 330 in the nineteenth century, by the end of the Second World War it had climbed to 1,000. Fifty years on, membership has more than doubled (and the annual subscription, miraculously held at one guinea from 1848 to 1954, apart from a five-year lapse 1910–1915 when it stood at one guinea and a half, is now £25). Even more significantly for the Society's future, the world within which the Society operates has again changed, indeed has changed vastly, in certain pertinent aspects perhaps more so than in the whole previous century. A straw in the wind is the more globally-spread membership; another is that whereas Foster listed the members of the British nobility who for a century had patronized the Society and been its vice-presidents, in recent decades the Council has not included a single peer (and there are few in overall membership), the titles of traditional aristocracy being replaced by the titles of modern academia.[1]

The centenary appraisal of the Society's achievements was largely just, but essentially self-congratulatory and therefore bland.[2] Although the first 1946 essayist, the historian J. A. Williamson, managed to conclude with a groan about 'State capitalism, the mechanized society, and the erosion of liberty which have characterized the first half of the present century', the volume did not address itself to the global ambience of the previous one hundred years, and its tone was therefore implicitly approving of the process of history which had produced Richard Hakluyt and thereafter the British Empire.[3] Foster, Williamson,

---

[1] In fairness to the Victorian peers, it should be added that several of them edited HS volumes. The Society has also totally lost, not only from its from its Council but even from membership, the Anglican bishops and clergy who were fairly prominent at the start, perhaps because Christian missionaries have worked out their role as pioneer explorers. As regards the incoming academics, their presence has in the present century (until perhaps recently) strengthened one aspect of the Society that deserves further investigation elsewhere, in studies of the mechanisms of British intellectual history: the extent to which the Society has from the start been essentially a London society. Attention to English and other travel records centralized at the British Museum, Public Record Office and India Office, all in London, gave such advantages to London-based scholars that not even Oxbridge, let alone provincial Red Brick, could play other than a relatively minor role in Society affairs. Even the advent of microfilming of records, allowing more provincial scholars, as well as more overseas scholars, to edit away from London, has only marginally affected the capital's decisive weight.

[2] Lynam, *Richard Hakluyt & his Successors* (HS 2/93), 1946.

[3] In 1916, the President of the Society enlisted Hakluyt in the 'great brotherhood' of 'empire builders': Albert Gray, *An Address on the Occasion of the Tercentenary of the Death of Richard Hakluyt*, 1917 (HS OB 3). The late Helen Wallis, commenting on Crone's account of the early years of the Society (see p. 8, note 2 above), referred engagingly to 'the founding fathers with their sturdy patriotism and their sometimes delightful touches of amateurism' (*Annual Report* [for 1983], Hakluyt Society, p. 20). In 1902 an editor drew a contrast between the ignoble aims of the sixteenth-century Portuguese activities in Ethiopia and the noble aims of the British 1867 expedition to that land (HS 2/10), although it was a Portuguese editor who in 1944, rather too late, hailed the English as 'the

and the other essayist, Edward Lynam, had all been born in the time of British imperial advance, just as very many of the first century of editors had been officers – often very distinguished officers – of the colonial empire. This category of editors was in particular dominated by retired officers of the Indian Civil Service – which explains the contemporary concentration of publications on Asia.[1] *Tempora mutantur.* It is probable that the present writer will be the last president of the Society to have spent part of a career in a British overseas colony.[2]

In 1946 the volumes of the Hakluyt Society were widely used by

---

principal heirs of the great Portuguese Eastern Empire' (HS 2/89). In 1943, William Foster allowed himself to write of Asian lands 'overwhelmed by the yellow flood of Japanese invasion' (HS 2/88).

[1] Many of the first century of editors had served in India, in a civil or military capacity, – a few were still resident there – and hence were interested in editing texts involving that part of Asia: some added to on-the-spot knowledge and linguistic capacity considerable research into written sources after they returned to Britain. A number of other editors worked in the India Office, for instance, Markham and Foster, and texts deposited in that Office generated many editions. Bolton Glanvill Corney, who edited with distinction texts on the Pacific (HS 2/13; 2/32, 36, 43), served for decades in the British islands of that ocean as a medical officer (see the reference in HS 2/52). Other editors had visited outlandish parts of the world in semi-imperial capacities. Markham frequently drew attention to his travels in the Andes in the 1850s and 1860s (e.g., HS 33, 47), on the latter occasion collecting plants for British India, and he accompanied the British military expedition to Ethiopia in 1867–1868 and wrote triumphantly about it (Middleton, 'Hakluyt Society', p. 17; and pp. 173–6 below). Burton typically began an 1874 introduction – 'It was my fate during nearly three years . . . to endure exile as H. B. M.'s Consul for the port of Santos' (HS 51). Editors kept an eye on their intellectual colonies. In Markham's edition of a volume on Peru issued in 1883, and apparently written during a recent war between Chile and Peru, he inserted a dedication in enthusiastic tribute to the Peruvian general (HS 68). In 1925, V. T. Harlow, editor of seventeenth-century texts on the English in the Caribbean, in his Preface beating a drum for Imperial History got perilously close to beating a drum for the Empire (HS 2/56). Presumably because British India predated British sub-Saharan Africa and was more intensively administered, and also because Africa had fewer English records of the 'Hakluyt period', the latter area failed to produce any number of colonial administrators who later became HS editors (although latterly several have become prominent Council members and officers): however, if academic service in these colonies in their latter days were to count as crypto-imperial (as some would have it), a handful of editors so indicted would include the present writer.

[2] The retreat from empire (at least by Europeans), seems to have reduced the number of editors whose principal claim was that during their careers they had become closely acquainted with the relevant overseas locality. Thus, two 1990 editors noted that their nineteenth-century predecessor had had the advantage of 'long periods of travel' in the research area (HS 2/173). (In 1902 it was remarked that – 'Translators without special local knowledge have ever laid themselves open to the scoffer': 2/10). If this is a serious loss, it can be compensated for by the recruitment of impatriate editors. Yet many excellent recent editions have been the work of editors who have never visited the locality. On the other hand, the editions of David Quinn on early English colonisation of North America have been informed by his elaborate on-the-spot reconnaissances (as recounted in his autobiographical piece in C. H. Clough and P. E. H. Hair, eds, *The European outthrust and encounter: the first phase c.1400–c.1700*, Liverpool, 1994, pp. 3–26).

historians but mainly to narrate and implicitly to approve the alleged achievements of European out-thrust to other continents. Hereafter they will no doubt be still more widely used, but most probably often to claim and to illustrate alleged human and environmental disasters caused by European out-thrust and cultural encounter. What was too loudly trumpeted as praiseworthy is now not uncommonly seen as contemptible; what was considered positive and a global gain is widely – if equally facilely – interpreted as negative and a loss for humankind. The attention of the Society was in 1983 perceptively drawn to this burgeoning *zeitgeist*, in the address to the Society's annual general meeting by H. C. Porter; and something of the current pessimistic tone of the relevant historiography can be further illustrated by the opening remarks of the introduction to an edition of 1989. 'The survival of the wilderness of Amazonia and its remaining aboriginal inhabitants hangs in the balance . . . the rich plant and animal resources of the region are threatened with obliteration by the demands of material progress . . . [while] concerned people . . . throughout the world struggle to avert this human and environmental tragedy.'[1] Intercultural encounter in the past appeared again, albeit in somewhat less apocalyptic terms, in an extremely well-received edition of 1988, whose preface concluded – 'proud men of two cultures [European and Inuit] . . . at first antagonistic, they at the end proved to themselves and to one another that the human spirit can be both generous and genocidal. Today we can all take heart in reading what came about improbably from 1852 to 1854 at Point Barrow.'[2] In more general terms, recent decades have witnessed a 'translation of the study of exploration history and its writings from the genres of national epic and/or scientific reportage, to those of cultural analysis',[3] at least to some extent and in certain quarters.

Again, the chronological advance into the nineteenth century has inevitably led editors to consider how the activities of that century produced the power dispositions of the twentieth century: thus, a Canadian editor of 1973 sketched the confrontation of three imperial advances – those of Spain, Russia and Britain – which resulted in the political shape of the present-day North Pacific.[4] Perhaps even more fundamentally, the terms 'discovery' and 'exploration' commonly used

---

[1] H. C. Porter, 'The Tudors and the North American Indian', *Annual Report* [for 1983], Hakluyt Society, pp. 1–13; Lorimer, *Amazon* (HS 2/171), opening of Preface.

[2] Bockstoce, *Rochfort Maguire* (HS 2/172, 173).

[3] From the opening paragraph of the editor's 'Introduction' to Warkentin, *Editing Exploration Texts*.

[4] Gough, *With Beechey*, 1973 (HS 2/143).

in the past by editors can nowadays be subject to radical onslaught.[1] Yet if current critical appraisal of the Society's past editions shows that here and there they tended to smack of imperial triumphalism and contemporary political correctness, leading to exaggerated claims of European cultural impact and achievement overseas (although on occasion there were dissenting voices), it is possible to have confidence in global scholarship and believe that, in time, the same degree of critical appraisal will eventually detect that the negative aspects of the historical process now stressed have also been exaggerated, similarly for ideological and 'racist' advantage.[2] Meanwhile the Society must continue to serve scholarship by multiplying, widening, and deepening its critical editions of primary sources.

A critical appraisal

In general, the scholarly quality of editions has improved over time.[3] While the scholarly know-how of a few of the Victorian editors was remarkable and has seldom been surpassed, in the present century factors such as better cataloguing, easier travel, and technological advance – notably microfilming, electronic communication and word-

---

[1] Whereas the 'exploration' of the Antarctic continent and much of the Arctic region involved humanity going where no-one had gone before, the exploration of inhabited regions of the globe was no more than (and no less than) merely 'European exploration'; similarly, the 'Discoveries' were mainly of lands already known to the inhabitants. However, latterday criticism of these terms is only partly justified. Historically, 'exploration' and 'discovery' meant more than merely travel by Europeans or Euro-Americans to regions unknown to them, since each term normally referred only to such travel as defined geographical features and produced overall accounts of a kind which added to the sum of knowledge that was already accessible to all humanity, via literacy. Thus, that Africans lived in those parts and made use of the waters does not lessen the 'discovery' of the sources of the Nile. The aims of the Hakluyt Society, in the form cited at the head of this essay, while not including the term 'discovery', referred to 'those who first explored unknown and distant regions', and it was clearly assumed that 'voyages, travels, and other geographical material' were primarily accounts of topographical and cultural 'exploration'. Yet mitigation of the charge of Eurocentricity can be read into the claimed justification for study of these records: 'they exhibit the growth of intercourse among mankind', that is, they document what is now termed 'encounter'.

[2] A remarkably early dissenting voice was an Argentinian guest editor, Luis L. Dominguez, who in 1891 laid out an argument much pursued a century later, to the effect that 'cannibalism' was a myth invented by Europeans to justify conquest of non-Europeans (HS 81). Even earlier, Clements Markham's editions on Peru, with their sympathy for the Inca and their criticism of the Spaniards, can be interpreted as foreshadowing late twentieth-century 'anti-colonialism'. However, they can can be equally plausibly interpreted as a revival of the *Leyenda Negra* of the sixteenth and seventeenth centuries, a piece of English nationalist mythology and propaganda.

[3] 'The editorial standards of the Society are now impressively high, and the scholarship displayed by the editors in their introductions and notes is outstanding and truly appreciated' (Dunbar, 'Societies', p. 66).

NORTHERN HUNTSMEN
From the sixteenth-century Latin account of the 'Northern Peoples' by Olaus
Magnus.
Reproduced in HS 2/182 of 1996.

processing – have revolutionised the accessibility of historical documentation; and for this reason alone standards of editing have had to
rise.[1] Moreover, there has come about a growing appreciation of the
importance of context.[2] Without going to the extremes of deconstruc-
tionist theory, it may be said that historians have become more aware
of the difficulty of assessing a text without comprehensive knowledge
of the situation of its production and in particular of the mindset of its
author. Since in practice the latter is frequently impossible to ascertain –
and especially so in respect of authors of much earlier times such as
those favoured in Hakluyt Society editions – there is more caution in
drawing firm conclusions from texts than was formerly the case. Hence
editorial comments tend to be more nuanced, or alternatively, to be
limited to the most specific, factual and 'objective' points. As regards
Richard Hakluyt's own editions, the obscurity of both the context of
their publication and the circumstances of Hakluyt's collection and
selection of items, has been a little lessened by E. G. R. Taylor's 1935
edited collection of documents on the two Hakluyts, by the introduction

---

[1] See the introduction to HS 2/165 of 1984 for references to the essential use of
microfilm. The advent of electronic networking of scanned or computerised copies of all
surviving historical documentation will no doubt enable twenty-first century scholars to
achieve even higher standards and draw attention to the limitations of present work.

[2] Although it is unlikely that the issue of contextualisation was ever totally unappreci-
ated – certainly Cooley was aware of it – it was left to G. R. Crone in 1962, in virtually
the first critical overview of the Society's productions, to specify 'the problem of putting
Hakluyt's writings not in some framework of antiquarian isolation but in the matrix of
men and ideas in which they had come forth' (Crone, '"Jewells of Antiquitie"', pp. 121–
4).

by D. B. Quinn and R. A. Skelton to the 1965 reprint of *Principall Navigations*, and by the *Hakluyt Handbook* of 1973, as well as by the independent studies of G. R. Parks.[1]

With more knowledge has come the need to repeat certain early editions. Some of the nineteenth-century ones – like a few of the later ones – were, even by contemporary standards, poor: Markham's *The Hawkins Voyages* of 1878, although itself an extended version of the very first volume of 1847, was one such. Even what was probably the most scholarly early edition, Yule's *Cathay and the Way Thither* of 1866, could be usefully updated in 1913–1916, and presumably should now be further updated. Many earlier editors did not, perhaps could not, make use of all extant versions of an account, document or map, and therefore their editions had an inadequate base. Because the twentieth century has extensively investigated and recorded archives and libraries across most of the world, it is plausible that, at least for the period before 1700, almost all surviving texts, archive documents, and maps are now known and accessible.[2] Additional versions of material can therefore be deployed to improve earlier editions, and so far this has been done in the case of about a dozen early editions; it should proceed further.[3]

Updated revision has also been done, in the course of a number of editions, for some of the accounts edited, published, or passed on to Purchas, by Richard Hakluyt, one or more manuscript versions enabling

[1] E. G. R. Taylor, ed., *The Original Writings and Correspondence of the two Richard Hakluyts*, 2 vols, London, 1935 (HS 2/76, 77); D. B. Quinn and R. A. Skelton, eds, facsimile reprint of Richard Hakluyt, *Principall Navigations ... (1589)*, with scholarly apparatus and an index by Alison M. Quinn, 2 vols, Cambridge, 1965 (HS Extra 39); Quinn, *The Hakluyt Handbook*. Professor Quinn has contributed further thoughts on the character and career of Hakluyt in D. B. and A. M. Quinn, *Discourse of Western Planting*, London, 1993 (HS Extra 45). For Parks, see Pennington, 'Secondary Works', p. 585.

[2] 'Almost all' does not preclude the exceptional recovery of a notable source. In relation to the eighteenth century, a striking instance of late recovery of a source has latterly occurred. The Society published between 1955 and 1967 the massive and apparently definitive edition of the journals of the Cook voyages, edited by J. C. Beaglehole (HS Extra 34–36; but later published, in 1982, in four volumes (HS 2/152–5), the additional and recently-uncovered journal of Johann Reinhold Forster, in English, a major source apparently unknown to Beaglehole. On this recovery, and for another recently-discovered journal currently being edited for the Society, see Wallis, 'Great Publications Societies', p. 120.

[3] Recent examples of very profitable re-editing include the 1953 updating of an 1849 edition (HS 6, 2/103), the 1961 updating of an 1881 edition (HS 64, 2/114, 115), the 1971 updating of an 1868 edition (HS 19, 2/88) and the 1990 updating of part of a 1900 edition (HS 2/4, 2/173). In a few instances later editors have detailed the weaknesses of earlier editions: a notable example is Professor Cummins' critique of a nineteenth-century edition by H. E. J. Stanley, where biographical information throws light on the context of Stanley's editing (HS 2/140). Earlier it had been noted, in respect of another edition by Stanley, 'his almost complete failure to annotate the text' (HS 2/114).

the printed text to be confirmed or amended (but such revision has often appeared in works independent of the Society). However, it would seem that Hakluyt's accounts were often written in a single manuscript and that their printing regularly led to the destruction of the manuscript; hence, in many instances only the printed version survives.[1] Use of Hakluyt's accounts by scholars could be greatly aided by two projects which the Society might care to encourage, perhaps even organise. First, the preparation of a checklist of the accounts, with the most recent studies of each listed, including any or every edition of a particular account. Secondly and more ambitiously, the preparation, by a collective of scholars, of a fully edited version of *Principal(l) Navigations*.[2]

Of Clements Markham, whose many editions in 29 volumes appeared between 1859 and 1923 (the last published posthumously), Foster, Markham's later successor as Honorary Secretary of the Society, noted that 'he thought it unnecessary for an editor to undertake elaborate researches ... on his view the narrative was the thing'.[3] Readability

---

[1] Or more correctly, often two printed versions, since commonly a text in the second, 1598–1600 edition is not precisely the same as its original in the 1589 edition. Earlier scholars tended to ignore the differences; thus, in 1942 J. W. Blake published extracts from the second edition (in his excellent *Europeans in West Africa, 1450–1560*: HS 2/86–7) without comparing them with the same material in the first edition. This was no doubt partly because of the rarity of the first edition, a difficulty overcome by the Society's publication, in the Extra Series in 1965, of a facsimile of the first edition. It may be added that Hakluyt himself, when he borrowed the accounts of two English voyages to Guinea first printed by his predecessor, Richard Eden, did not borrow these directly from Eden's volume of 1555 but from the revised and enlarged version of 1577 produced by Richard Willes, where the accounts were slightly abbreviated.

[2] The Society planned an edited reprint of *Principal Navigations* (i.e. the 1598–1600 second edition) at the beginning of the twentieth century. But the editing was to be limited to minimal annotation, a short introduction, mainly bibliographical, and indexing. The project was abandoned when it was discovered – an extraordinary lack of communication somewhere – that the publisher MacLehose of Glasgow had a reprint in hand, albeit unfortunately an unedited one (Foster, 'A Retrospect', p. 162). However, C. R. Beazley had already begun work for the Society and his edition of the earliest travels documented in *Principal Navigations* appeared in 1903, separately, as *The Texts and Versions of John de Plano Carpini and William de Rubruquis . . .*, 1903 (HS Extra 13). In fact, contrary to the limitations which had been laid down, this is a very comprehensive edition, much on the lines of that now suggested. Beazley's edition was later accounted part of the 'Extra Series' when this term was invented, and was indeed the first genuinely Hakluyt Society work in this series; however, the volume itself contains no reference to it being in a separate category, although the category was presumably introduced with this volume.

[3] Foster, 'A Retrospect', p. 156. This was an echo of an earlier difference of opinion, when J. A. Froude attacked the Society, basically for publishing scholarly rather than popular editions (see in the essay by Campbell below, pp. 96–7). Markham's publications were translations of printed editions of Spanish texts, albeit in certain instances of texts recently discovered in archives by Spanish scholars. Exceptionally, one edition claimed to be of 'an original and unedited manuscript' (HS 29), but Markham had not himself

rather than scholarship has been a priority of a number of later editors, and given the very wide range of members' interests, so that a reader whose interest would lead him to study a work on North America might only glance at a work on Guinea, readability is not altogether to be dismissed as an aim in editions. It is not clear to what extent, and by whom, the nineteenth-century works were read, but judging by the membership lists many subscribers had very general interests and limited specialised knowledge, and might be characterized – or caricatured – as either intrepid travellers or armchair readers in Piccadilly clubs.[1] Probably a number of gentlemanly subscriptions were merely to provide library wallpaper.[2] In the twentieth century the educated reading public has grown apace, and overall grown more serious, so that today many subscribers to the Hakluyt Society obtain the volumes chiefly if not wholly for reading pleasure, wishing to gain information about the world at large, or in order to derive inspiration from the deeds of those in the past who, daring to go on 'voyages and travels', sometimes

---

discovered the manuscript although he certainly inspected it in situ. (Curiously, no transcript is mentioned: if one was made it may not have been made by Markham himself – alternatively, he may have translated direct from the manuscript.) A later Secretary also criticised Markham by inference: 'occasionally there has been too long a sequence dealing with the same region . . . South America under the early Spanish is an example, brought about by the unavoidable necessity of accepting works offered rather than the works most desirable' (Lynam, 'Present and Future', p. 187). But Markham's editions were 'offered' by the current Secretary or President!

[1] The nineteenth-century statement of aims of the Society referred to the early subscribers as those with 'acquirements, taste and discrimination . . . who feel an interest in the same pursuit'. It is perhaps not altogether misreading Victorian language to suggest that this hints that the interest of many subscribers was of a somewhat dilettante nature, and it is certainly likely that this was the case with many of the early readers of Hakluyt Society volumes. This probably explains why features of a number of early editions gave them a *belles-lettres* rather than a scholarly flavour. Texts were often considered to 'speak for themselves', a view that has merit inasmuch as it lessens the danger of anachronistic editorial interpretation, but demerit in that it dodges the issue of editorial selectivity and exposes the text to anachronistic reader interpretation. Fulsome dedications were sometimes included – 'a privilege of authorship not yet entirely obsolete' wrote an editor in 1882 (HS 65). Digressions were tolerated: Markham included a long poem written at Cuzco by a travelling companion (HS 47) and, perhaps more relevantly, a 'Note on Ancient Ynca Drama' (HS 68), and Stanley, editing De Morga on the Philippines, included a list of parochial clergy in 1867 (HS 39). Illustrations, particularly dubious portraits and samples of manuscript text, were often more for entertainment than scholarly illumination. However, the idiosyncrasies of editors have never been entirely eliminated, and there may well have been some loss when editions became more rigorous and less personal.

[2] 'The Society's conception of the national past had pronounced ideological overtones, and its membership were busy to a remarkable degree about the present business of empire and exploration' (Francis Spufford, in *Times Literary Supplement*, 4817, 28 July 1995, p. 14). Research into the membership, not yet undertaken, may prove this judgement exaggerated.

survived appalling and unpredictable circumstances.[1] To overlook the interests of such general readers would be fatal to the future of the Society, not least because of their contribution to its finances.

Nevertheless, the twentieth century has seen the growing dominance of specialist consumers of Hakluyt Society material, largely academics, either as subscribers reading their own volumes or as non-subscribers reading in university and other libraries whose membership of the Society they encourage and support. As academics, and despite sharp regionalisation of geographical and historical expertise, they expect the highest contemporary standards of scholarship even when editions do not fall within their own geographical or otherwise specialist field of interest. It follows that latterly most editions are the product of detailed researches and include extensive scholarly apparatus.[2] In 1946 Lynam was not altogether happy about these developments and suggested that 'a few of our recent editors have done a little too much . . . introductions and footnotes are designed to instruct and interest the reader . . . the over-erudite or over-enthusiastic editor may need sometimes reminding that a true scholar never bores or bewilders his readers'.[3] While the message was well-meant the notion of over-erudite scholars and easily bored readers was even then outdated and certainly inappropriate for the future.

The faults of some of the past volumes are transparent. Apart from the use of non-primary or limited sources, the nineteenth-century volumes often failed to make clear from the start – from the first reference preferably – precisely what sources were being deployed, and their bibliographical descriptions of these sources were at times inadequate.[4]

---

[1] This was very much a pre-1914 theme: 'There can be no question that a study of the heroic deeds of explorers, [and] the contemplation of their high qualities . . . excite a feeling of sympathy which is ennobling to those who are under its influence, and is an education in itself' (C. R. Markham, *Address on the Fiftieth Anniversary of the Foundation of the Society . . . Revised on the Occasion of the Sixty-fifth Anniversary*, 1911 (OB 2), p. 15).

[2] Crone argued that early editors tended to be amateurs and antiquarians, but both terms are weasel words and many early editors were rather more than Crone implied (Crone, '"Jewells of Antiquitie"', p. 322).

[3] Lynam, 'Present and Future', p. 188.

[4] An irritating feature of many nineteenth-century editions is that the text or texts being edited are named only in the course of a lengthy introduction, and at times without an adequate bibliographical description. (But worse, one late twentieth-century edition forgot to include a reference to the printed work whose translation was presented.) Commendably, recent editions, if they do not begin by noting the source or sources being edited, tend to include a separately-signalled section doing this; and in 1940 David Quinn began the scholarly practice, when listing documents on the Contents page(s), of supplying an exact reference for each item. In the early decades, Major, working from the British Museum, set a good example by supplying exact bibliographical descriptions, and a number of later Victorian editors were as careful. An extraordinary feature of the editions of the 1900s and 1910s was the inclusion of long bibliographies for several of the

The editor of Galvão in 1854, admittedly using an earlier translation (actually Hakluyt's), apologised for 'possessing only a slight knowledge of the Portuguese language ... he has to plead that the work was considered to be of great interest and that no-one else seemed inclined to undertake the labour'.[1] The view in the past seems often to have been that any translation was better than none, which from the point of view of the Society's subscribers was perhaps correct, but with the advance of close regional scholarship critique of earlier translations – and of translations in general – has begun to appear.[2] The scholarly apparatus accompanying an English text or translation has at times been very thin.[3] Although an Introduction has always been included, its length and value have varied greatly. Many nineteenth-century introductions were long but consisted merely of a potted biography, a summary of the text, and a discourse on the general historical background. The nadir was reached with Markham's later publications which were basically a translation from an accessible printed text with a chatty introduction and hardly any apparatus other than an index.[4]

---

territories discussed (Abyssinia, Spitzbergen, Easter Island, Canaries, Peru, Mexico: HS 2/10, 11, 13, 21–23). Since British Museum call numbers were supplied, these bibliographies were apparently produced by British Museum staff: in lists in contemporary prospectuses, some of the bibliographies were credited to Basil H. Soulsby, Superintendant of the Map Department. A Markham edition of 1873 included a list of manuscript journals of English East-India voyages held in the India Office (HS 56), hence many of those edited a generation and more later by William Foster and others: this was a forward-looking research exercise, presumably to be credited to Markham himself.

[1] The present writer is not entirely unsympathetic, having made exactly the same plea himself; and in fairness the editor, despite his linguistic incapacity, took the trouble to compare the translation with the text, pointing out omissions and additions.

[2] For a recent general criticism of translations of historical texts, see Beatrix Heintze, 'Translations as Sources for African History', History in Africa, 11, 1984, pp. 131–161; and for the case for the continuing need for translations, see my comments in Adam Jones and Beatrix Heintze, European Sources for sub-Saharan Africa before 1900: Use and Abuse, Stuttgart, 1987, pp. 41–42.

[3] The balance between text and apparatus cannot, however, be prescribed. Whereas, on the whole, in HS volumes the text takes up more space than the apparatus, there have been many instances of the opposite position, possibly sometimes by editorial over-indulgence, but most suitably in other instances. Of the latter, the nineteenth-century classic is the Yule edition of Cathay and the Way Thither (HS 36, 37), while a recent example, where the editorial contribution much outweighs pagewise the documents of the text, is the late Raymond Fisher's 1981 study of Semen Dezhnev and his pioneering passage around the NE tip of Asia (HS 2/159).

[4] Yet students who cannot read Spanish continue to find these volumes useful. It must, indeed, be acknowledged that Markham was a tireless translator from Spanish. But 'difficulties in translation were solved by Gordian methods' (Foster, 'Hakluyt Society', 156). For severe and seemingly justified criticism of Markham as a translator, see the articles by Bailey W. Diffie and others cited in the essay by Ann Savours below, p. 166, note 1; p. 185, note 3. Diffie argues that Markham was not merely careless but ideologically disposed to slant his translations in an anti-Spanish direction.

The amount of textual apparatus in editions is not necessarily an index of scholarship, since some texts call for less explanation and contextualising than others, and since succinct apparatus may represent meticulous research. Yet there can be no reasonable doubt that certain editions, not all in the distant past, have carried too skimpy an apparatus for the intellectual comfort of the reader. It appears that the Society has generally given volume editors a very free hand in deciding the amount of relevant apparatus. Before the 1960s the Society's own editors exercised some general control, it is true, but the extent seems to have varied between the individuals involved, perhaps because the duties of the office were never laid down.[1] It is also true that there were presidents who intervened and took a hand in the rewriting of editions, notably Yule in the nineteenth and de Beer in the twentieth century.[2] Guidelines to volume editors – excellent and helpfully detailed guidelines – issued in 1958 called for 'common sense and an imaginative appreciation of the readers' convenience' when preparing apparatus, and footnotes were to be 'as concise as possible', although the latter recommendation was related specifically to the practicality of the printing cost of footnotes.[3] Unfortunately we lack records of the process by

---

[1] Foster believed that Markham 'took very seriously his duties as general superintendant of the works in progress' and cited an editor (S. P. Oliver, editor of HS 82) who noted that 'the secretary of the Hakluyt Society has obligingly revised, suppressed, altered, and added to many of the editor's original notes' (Foster, 'A Retrospect', pp. 156–7). 'Obligingly' sounds sarcastic, and that Markham let this pass into print may indicate rather less oversight of editions.

[2] Some of the interplay between volume and general editors in fairly recent times was described by the late Eila Campbell (in a letter to me of 23.4.1994) in the following terms. 'Until the middle fifties most volumes were edited [solely] by their proposers. A serious backlog developed through editors falling behind with their commitments: the Society had no sanctions and for good or bad reasons some editors were very resistant to appeals for them to get on with their work and deliver their volumes. Eventually the Council decided to abandon some volumes and to find new editors for others. Before about 1960 editors tended to be enthusiasts (not all energetic enthusiasts!) but not necessarily scholarly (although some were): from the 1960s editing was more scholarly. The Joint Secretaries [E.C. herself 1962–1983, and Terence Armstrong 1966–1990] initiated the practice of monitoring editors' progress and – in so far as we could – pressurizing them to keep to their dates ...'. I am further informed that since the 1960s the Society's editors have not only regularly intervened themselves but have not hesitated to call up the assistance of expert members of Council to assist in the revising of certain of the offered editions.

[3] 'Hints to Editors' had been first issued by Foster in 1929; the 1958 version, 'Guide for Editors', the work of Crone, Skelton and Quinn, was revised in 1975, when it was said to be 'founded on principles of common sense in book-construction and of respect for the reader's convenience and the Society's purse' (from the Preface by de Beer). New guidelines taking into account up-to-date technology and bibliographic convention were issued by Dr Ryan in 1993: these are without reference to any prescribed overall shape of an edition, thus conforming to what one suspects was actual practice in the past, a pragmatic approach, each edition being considered on its merits and according to its actual needs.

which most editions of dates earlier than the reach of presentday living memory came out in the form they did, and in many instances cannot assess the extent to which the volume editor consulted or was advised by the Society's editor(s).[1] Nor is it easy to assess the extent to which a volume editor of many decades ago, working on a specialised topic, fulfilled his scholarly duty by deploying all the most appropriate elements of contemporary knowledge.[2] Despite this latter uncertainty, it is nevertheless probably fair to judge that the success of volume editors in the past was distinctly variable.

Three nineteenth-century editions with full, not to say, massive scholarly apparatus, were Yule's *Cathay and the Way Thither* of 1866, Brown's 1896 edition of Leo Africanus, and the 1896 and 1899 edition of Zurara's chronicle of Guinea by Beazley and Prestage.[3] This amount of scholarly apparatus was fairly exceptional in the First Series. Several editions made do with only an exiguous introduction. Burton's 1874 introduction to Hans Staden's account of his captivity in Brazil c.1550 was lengthy and very readable, but idiosyncratic (if typical of its author), in that it referred largely to Burton's own travels and observations in the same region three centuries later. Early introductions often took the form of a long and discursive account of the historical background to the material, but as time advanced the narration of general history was left to other writings and the introduction focused on the edited text or texts, the immediate context and the problems of comprehension and interpretation.[4]

Modern editions call for a close analysis of the text or texts, which is

---

[1] But for fraught relations between one series editor and certain volume editors, see the essay by Quinn below; and for the Society's difficulties with some early editors, see the essay by Campbell below. The latterday experience of the editors of 2/175–176 may, however, be memorialized, not least since the edition took twenty years to complete. The late Dr Terence Armstrong, a long-serving series editor, and his successor, Dr Will Ryan, displayed exemplary patience and understanding, while providing guidance on request and permitting a flexible interpretation of the guidelines to meet the peculiar form of the specific edition.

[2] The present writer has a very limited knowledge of the range of Victorian editing of historical texts. But for meticulous contemporary scholarship and attention to detail I would judge, for instance, an 1854–1855 edition by an 'amateur antiquarian' in the Camden Society series (John Webb, *A Roll of the Household Expense of Richard de Swinfield, Bishop of Hereford*) well above the level of a substantial proportion of nineteenth-century Hakluyt Society editions.

[3] HS 36–37 (enlarged in HS 2/33, 37, 38, 41), 92–93, 95, 100. Curiously, the extensive notes of the Zurara edition were mainly drawn from a much earlier French edition by the Portuguese scholar, Visconde de Santarém.

[4] A feature of modern scholarship has been the revelation of the distance between the primary source – in the case of HS material what the traveller instantly noted in his journal, diary or letters – and the version he later wrote up for printing and public consumption. Comparison of consecutive versions of 'observation' is therefore commonplace in historical studies. However, such comparison is ruled out in many HS editions because the only extant source is a single printed text.

normally best catered for in scholarly annotation. While it is the case that there can be no overall rule about the extent of annotation; that certain texts are appropriately served by other than extensive annotation; and that a primary judgement about the extent must be left to the editor of a volume, there can be no doubt that the annotation of too many HS volumes has been inadequate.[1] Volume editors have not been helped by a recurrent appeal on the part of the Society's officers and Council urging volume editors to minimise annotation, partly to save printing costs, partly in the interests of subscriber 'readability'.[2] The comment of the Society's Secretary in 1946 on 'over-erudite' editors has been cited above. It may be allowed that the elimination of the florid digressions of some of the Victorian editions was no great loss to scholarship; and that drawing a line between the relevant and irrelevant depends mightily on the viewpoint – which for the Society's own editors must include the practical and financial viewpoint. Further, a few editors have been incapable of producing the necessary annotation, for reasons acceptable or otherwise. But there remain one or two plaintive references in editions to the minimalising of annotation, apparently against the editor's better judgement.[3] Appendices have occasionally

---

[1] Explanations have sometimes been offered. 'A book like this offers unlimited temptations for annotation; and I fear that in some cases I have extended my notes beyond reasonable limits' (HS 2/19). In fact, this editor over-resisted temptation, in my view. An interesting excuse for too little scholarly apparatus was made in 1881 by Stanley, otherwise a reasonably good editor for the time. 'Some years ago a rather savage criticism of the publications of the Hakluyt Society complained of the excessive length of their introductions. [The complainant was Froude – see Major's riposte in HS 43.] This one is much shorter than it should have been, not in deference to the critic, but because the researches necessary for doing justice to the work of Alvarez have been interfered with and prevented by other less agreeable occupations; but the delivery of the volume could be delayed no longer, and the members of the Society are entreated to excuse its brevity' (HS 64). An earlier edition by Stanley had gestated from 1851 to 1868.

[2] Or as one editor put it in 1948: 'Believing that footnotes serve chiefly to distract the reader from the thread of the story ...' (HS 2/98). At the extreme of the demand for readability, a review appearing in the journal *Cruising* criticised the 1992 edition of an account of Guinea based on two eighteenth-century slaving voyages on the grounds that, for the cruising interest, a good story had been 'spoiled by academic interference'. The printing costs of setting footnotes can hardly have mattered in the nineteenth century, or mattered much before the mid-twentieth century, although the mere length of footnotes no doubt affected volume costs. But thereafter there was economy in endnotes: on the whole the Society resisted a shift to endnotes, except in instances where the nature of the text justified this, and the recent movement to printing photographically from pre-formatted copy has removed the additional cost of footnotes.

[3] For instance, 'In preparing the footnotes I have endeavoured to comply with the canon now recognised by the Society, that notes should be confined to such particulars as are necessary to elucidate the text' (HS 2/66) – a complaint only by inference. It has been remarked elsewhere (my comments in Heintze and Jones, *European sources*, p. 44) that distinguished editors should not have to apologise – 'We have regretfully felt obliged to provide more and longer notes than are usual in the Society's volumes' (HS 2/114).

replaced annotation and in many instances supplemented it, often help-fully and nearly always interestingly, not least when on bizarre and unexpected topics. A list of appendices might have some value.

While particular editions may have had very obvious defects, from the beginning of the Society higher standards of editing were displayed by a progressively increasing number of editors. Subject to the limita-tion that exact assessment of the standard and value of editions ranging over many centuries and much of the globe can only be supplied by specialists in specific regions and specific fields of history,[1] the following

[1] I can comment authoritatively only in respect of the relatively few editions dealing with pre-1700 West Africa, and I cannot say whether this critique is of a fair sample of all HS editions. The section on West Africa in the 1896 edition of *Leo Africanus* (HS 92–3) has been largely outdated in respect of its annotation by a 1956 French translation which has reasonable Africanist annotation. The 1896 edition of *Zurara* on Guinea (HS 95, 100), a good translation albeit in Victorian mock-medieval English, has been outdated in respect of its apparatus, not so much by subsequent Portuguese editions as by an excellent French edition and translation of 1960 which deploys both a critique of the text and Africanist annotation. The 1937 edition of the western Africa section of *Pacheco Pereira* (HS 2/79) remains the only English translation, but better Africanist annotation is provided in a 1956 Portuguese/French edition of the Guinea section. The 1937 edition of *Cadamosto* (HS 2/80), which included sections of Barros and Diogo Gomes (a Latin text), again remains the only English translation but is marred by errors and lacks Africanist annotation: for the text of Cadamosto, scholars now consult an Italian variorum edition of 1966 or an Italian text plus Portuguese translation of 1948, although these lack Africanist annotation, a situation amended to a limited extent in a French translation of 1994. For *Diogo Gomes*, scholars consult a Portuguese/French edition of 1959, with fairly good Africanist annota-tion. Thus, all four HS editions of foreign-language texts on West Africa remain useful principally for their English translations, and almost all need new editions which supply up-to-date Africanist information (for more details, see P. E. H. Hair, 'The early sources on Guinea', *History in Africa* 21, 1994, pp. 87–126). Extracts from later Portuguese chronicles and other Portuguese sources are supplied in translation in Blake's 1942 collection of material on Europeans in Guinea up to 1560 (HS 2/86, 87), which also includes English and in translation Castilian (but not French) source material: in its day this edition did much to open up a new field of history to anglophone historians. Although most of the material is from printed works rather than from archives, although the Hakluyt extracts are from the second rather than the first edition, and although the annotation is limited and the Africanist information now outdated, Blake's work has, nevertheless, for half a century been an essential handbook for students of the relevant history and has been much praised by Portuguese historians. Turning to editions of English texts, all of which mention West Africa only incidentally, one weakness of the 1878 edition of the Hawkins voyages (HS 57) was Markham's lack of acquaintance with contemporary knowledge of West Africa; while even the 1959 and 1977 editions of the Fenton voyage (HS 2/113, 147), otherwise excellent, concentrate annotation on the European at the expense of the African aspect. African studies having advanced from a low base only during the latter half of the present century, earlier editors can be largely excused for their Eurocentric approach. The first HS edition to be annotated by profes-sional Africanists appeared only in 1992 (HS 2/175, 176). While there remain foreign-language texts on this region which need to be introduced to anglophone students by translations, it is likely that scholarly new editions of the foreign-language works noted above will be annotated against the text in the original language, hence the edition may well appear in that language rather than in English.

past editions (up to the 1960s) would seem to be worth drawing attention to as outstanding in one respect or another. In the earliest period, Major's editions stood out for their overall scholarly treatment: three editions with extensive annotation later in the century have been noted above. In the present century, Professor Pennington has highlighted David Quinn's *Roanoake Voyages* of 1955 for its contribution to Hakluyt studies, and it is arguable that this work set new standards of editing, by its collation of all available texts, its comprehensive inclusion of relevant archive material, and by its attention to specialised aspects of the accounts such as their vernacular vocabularies.[1]

However, some elements of Quinn's wide-ranging and meticulous apparatus had appeared earlier. For instance, Markham took some pains over vernacular vocabulary (particularly of course Quechua); among others who did this were Satow in 1900 editing a voyage to Japan and Ravenstein in 1901 editing travels in Angola. Extensive archive documentation was provided by Corney in 1913 in respect of Spanish Tahiti, by Zelia Nuttall in 1914 in respect of Drake's circumnavigation, and by Irene Wright in 1929, 1932 and 1951 in respect of the Spanish Caribbean – all recovering material from Spanish archives. Dutch archive material was translated by De Villiers in 1906 and 1911.[2] As we have seen, Major and later British Museum staff, followed in the 1890s and early decades of the present century by Foster and others researching at the India Office, published original manuscript texts in English from British archives. Among other instances of editorial good practice, an edition of 1867 included a report on 'relics' of the Frobisher expeditions recovered archaeologically; and an edition of 1891 included a great deal of learned annotation on the natural history.[3] The many editions which consisted mainly of reprinting rare early prints were for long useful, but have recently tended to lose their value since scholars can easily obtain facsimile reprints or microfilms – although more easily in the case of English early prints than in the case of, say, Portuguese early prints. The scholarly apparatus of a few elderly and apparently outdated editions may nevertheless retain some value today: for instance, the 1879 annotation by Telfer and Bruun of Schiltberger's fifteenth-century travels, Dames' 1918 editing of Duarte Barbosa, and Jane's 1930 and

---

[1] Pennington, 'Secondary Works', p. 587; Quinn, *Roanoake Voyages* (HS 2/104–5).

[2] HS 2/5; 6; 2/32, 36, 43; 2/34; 2/62, 71; 2/19; 2/26, 27. Irene Wright also contributed Seville archive material for 2/111 (1959).

[3] HS 38 ('relics discovered by Mr Charles F. Hall of Cincinnati' – actually recovered before he knew of the Frobisher accounts in Hakluyt); HS 82–3. In recent times the Society has insisted on the scientific identification of all natural history items mentioned in a text.

1933 comments on Columbus's letters.[1] Finally, it has to be recognised that many editions now superseded by later ones published elsewhere, or in other languages, represent texts which either were first put into print, or first exposed to critical analysis, in a Hakluyt Society publication.

The geographical range, past and future

The geographical distribution of the over-200 Ordinary Series editions is of some interest. Leaving aside nearly one third of the editions which are more general, for instance, voyages to two or more Outer Continents or circumnavigations, rather over fifty editions are concerned solely with the Americas, as against rather under fifty with Asia (including the Middle East): and some forty are divided between Africa and the Pacific (including Australasia). Perhaps more telling is a regional break-down. Of the works on the Americas, two thirds deal with Latin America and the Caribbean (boosted by Markham's output on Peru), the remainder being divided between the Arctic Approaches (i.e. the North-West Passage) and the rest of North America. The vast majority of the works on Asia deal with either India (or neighbouring Persia and Ceylon) or the Far East (mainly China and Indonesia), the remainder dividing between the Middle East and Central Asia/Siberia. A handful deal with Europe (including Russia): no work deals largely with the final landmass, Antarctica.[2] Two general limitations should, however, be borne in mind. First, following Hakluyt, the Society tended to see exploration in terms of 'voyages', with land travels of less relevance. Secondly, the Society avoided texts printed by the current commercial publishers of travel accounts, even when the accounts were incomplete and unedited, partly for copyright reasons.

The relatively few works on North America south of the Arctic and west of early English settlement, with only one on the great land travels, can be excused largely by the existence of active publication societies within that region.[3] This does not apply to other 'deprived'

---

[1] HS 58; 2/44, 49; 2/65, 70. The Jane translation of the first letter appeared again, with revisions by L. A. Vigneras, in 1960 (HS Extra 38).

[2] Bellingshausen approached much of the Antarctic coast in 1821 but there is doubt whether he recognised that behind the ice floes lay a continental landmass (HS 2/91–2).

[3] The exception is the 1970 edition by Kaye Lamb (HS Extra 41) which includes an account of Mackenzie's journeys from Fort Chipewyan to the Arctic and Pacific. To compensate, the search for the North-West Passage and early English settlement on the east coast have received fairly intensive attention throughout the history of the Society, the most recent editions on the former being one of 1988 (HS 2/169–70) which discusses the Alaskan Inuit and one of 1994–1995 (HS 2/177, 181) dealing with explorations of Hudson Bay, and on the latter the 1993 edition of Hakluyt's *Western Planting* (HS Extra 45). It might be added that Greenland and Iceland have been relatively neglected.

BLOODLETTING IN CENTRAL AMERICA
From Wafer's *New Voyage* of 1689.
Reproduced in HS 2/73 of 1934.

regions. Most of the works on Africa are on Ethiopia: among the printed works on the rest of Africa that call out for scholarly editing are those of the nineteenth-century explorer-travellers (even when recently reprinted without annotation) such as Barth, Grant, Von der Decken, and not least Livingstone.[1] Several earlier Portuguese works on sub-Saharan Africa are either untranslated or unedited: thus, Dos Santos on East Africa was recommended to the Society for scholarly treatment in 1849 – the translation published independently in South Africa by Theal around 1900 is useful but incomplete and exiguously annotated. The great Portuguese chroniclers of the 'Discoveries' period have fared badly: apart from Galvão, none has ever had a complete English translation, nor for that matter a fully scholarly edition in Portuguese, although extracts from, for instance, Barros and Correa, have appeared in HS editions on Africa and Asia.[2] It is true that these chronicle-histories contain material other than 'voyages, travels, and geographical material', but then so too have many earlier editions. It may be that the Society's remit should now be formally extended to include the concept of immediate cultural encounter resulting from voyages and travels.

On the Middle East, a number of eligible works in various local languages probably require an adequate critical text before translation: the famous eighteenth-century travelbook in Turkish by Evliya Chelebi is an instance.[3] Among many candidates in western languages for re-editing is the 1863 edition of Varthema's travels in the Middle East c.1500.[4] With the worldwide spread of English as a language of communication, new edited translations of early European accounts of India, Indonesia and Japan could usefully be prepared by scholars from those lands. Similarly, local scholars could usefully edit accounts of Russia, Siberia, and Central Asia, although often these were in languages other than Russian: the 1696 work by Witsen entitled *Noord en Oost Tartarye* is one of several works unavailable in English.[5] Travel

---

[1] Only the expeditions to the Niger of Hornemann, Laing, and Clapperton's party, and the Emin Pasha Relief Expedition led by Stanley have been treated in editions (HS 2/123, 128–30; Extra 40).

[2] HS 42, 49, 52, 2/10, 2/86. The lack of English translations was noted by Dames in 1918 (HS 2/44).

[3] On travel literature in Middle East languages and the problems in its deployment, see Beckingham, 'Arabic Texts and the Hakluyt Society', which concludes – 'There is ample fodder for the Society in these three languages [Arabic, Persian, Turkish], but . . . rather indigestible fodder. If they are to deal with it adequately, our editors will need . . . ample time to chew the cud.'

[4] HS 32.

[5] There would seem to be a case for the Hakluyt Society linking up with the Linschoten Vereeniging to publish bi-lingual scholarly texts of Dutch authors, to the advantage of subscribers to each. Indeed, this sort of connection with various foreign societies may be

texts in Chinese, Japanese and other languages of Further Asia equally deserve translating and editing, by, or at least with the support of, indigenous scholars. Among the great sea-explorations inadequately studied in textual terms is Bering's 1728 voyage. Also in the Pacific, one of Vancouver's lieutenants, Broughton, crossed to Japan and Korea and left journals fuller than his printed account. Further afield, there is scope for re-examination of the accounts of Dampier's voyages. Finally, the Society's comprehensive and rewarding attention to Cook in the Extra Series does not entirely compensate for the very few editions on Australasia and the Antarctic in the Ordinary Series.[1]

Adapting to cultural and social change

The circumstances of editors have changed greatly since 1846. In the Victorian era editors tended to be either wealthy gentlemen of leisure, or else civil servants, active or retired, especially a handful of devoted scholars at the British Museum and India Office. Although many had travelled or lived abroad, and several had organized explorations, few were actual 'explorers' in any strict sense; but it was occasionally argued that editions were of practical value for explorers and other travellers in faraway lands.[2] With the extension of higher education and the rise of a

---

the 'European community' way forward. Less ambitiously, the Society might cooperate in editions of appropriate material on Africa with the series *Fontes Historiae Africanae* or with the Van Riebeeck Society. To date the Hakluyt Society has normally ploughed a lonely path and avoided joint editions with other societies.

[1] I am indebted for the above information, and for more than I here cite on the subject of desirable future projects, from Terence Armstrong, Charles Beckingham, Roy Bridges, Andrew David, and Glyndwr Williams. In 1946 Lynam admitted that 'we have done too little justice to the numerous records of travel in the Pacific Ocean, in Africa, and in Asiatic Russia during the eighteenth century', and he drew attention to the contemporary travels recorded in the many English collections of that century (Lynam, 'Present and Future', pp. 188–9). A proposed edition of Malaspina's expedition will, if realised, to some extent remedy the imbalance noted in the text.

[2] The 1865 Annual Report claimed that the HS volumes on the North-West Passage had been helpful to the Franklin Search expedition; the 1867 Report noted: 'Explorers of the Amazon Valley and the region of the Andes are furnished, by Mr Markham, with portable editions of the leading discoverers of former times, whose footsteps they are following.' (For further instances of the practical use of editions, see Middleton, 'Hakluyt Society', p. 16.) In 1946 Lynam categorised past editors as 'many explorers, retired colonial officials, University Professors and Lecturers, specialists in history, historical geography or navigation, and members of the aristocracy' (Lynam, 'Present and Future', p. 186). In fact, while many editors were travellers, hardly any after the mid nineteenth century have been 'explorers'. The late nineteenth-century exploration of Nilotic and sub-Saharan Africa was so publicised at the time, and so appealed to a widening reading public, that the explorers, mainly British, found no difficulty in having their accounts published commercially; and none came forward as HS editors. (An exception to the

BEARDED PENGUIN
Drawn on Cook's second voyage to the Pacific 1772–1775.
The original water-colour drawing in the Natural History Museum, London.
Reproduced in HS Extra 35 of 1961.

class of professional educationalists, modern editors are now most frequently university academics, active or retired, and the practical value of editions is now thought to relate primarily to education and ideological debate. In 1946 Lynam worried that 'University Professors and Lecturers are over-worked by their academic duties and by a multiplicity of committees, while with the cost of living and taxation both almost unbearably high for the middle-classes, every scholar and expert who can find time to write is writing for the publishers'.[1] While it is certainly true that many recent editions have been prepared by retired academics (who also predominate in the academic membership of the Society's Council) and also that is there some evidence that younger academics consider it inexpedient to spend time on preparing edited material, the Society's flow of editions has not slowed down in recent decades.[2]

One explanation is that financial support for extended research and writing was until the 1980s available for British scholars in the humanities within universities and is still to some extent available from various funds and trusts.[3] But another explanation is a shift in the provenance

latter generalisation was Burton but he edited for the Hakluyt Society only a work on Brazil.) The early twentieth century explorations of the Antarctic have been totally ignored by the Society, undoubtedly for the same reasons. Moreover, only after 1903 did the Society concern itself with explorations later than 1700, and then only in a cautious chronological advance.

[1] Lynam boldly suggested that to overcome these alleged difficulties, the Society editor should make the editor some remuneration, 'say the comparatively modest sum of a hundred guineas for each volume' (Lynam, 'Present and Future', pp. 186–7). The idea was not pursued, but it is of some interest that in the 1990s discussion of possible financial support for editors above mere expenses took place in the Council of the Society. An influx of proposals for new editions led to the view that the change was still premature. The Society has, however, helped with editorial expenses, at least in recent times. According to Lynam, 'incidental expenses incurred by editors for typing, photostats, indexing and the like have always been met by the Society' (ibid., p. 186). But the list of eligible items in itself raises doubts about Lynam's 'always', and it is more likely that many nineteenth-century editors were not helped, and did not need to be helped, except perhaps in certain instances with payments to a clerk for preparing an index.

[2] Factors that discourage younger scholars from working on editions, such as the reluctance of certain universities to accept editions as suitable projects for candidates in History for higher degrees, were noted, in respect of one particular field, in a 1986 conference resolution (Heintze and Jones, *European sources for sub-Saharan Africa before 1900*, pp. 15–16).

[3] It is not clear to what extent nineteenth-century and early twentieth-century editors contributed financially to their editions. The Society's published accounts give the impression that volume publication was paid for entirely out of subscriptions, but the exiguous form of the accounts in this period leaves the issue somewhat open: furthermore, there may have been donations from editors to the general funds, conceivably anonymous. What is certain is that, because they were generally more well-off than their modern successors, editors financed their own researches and in many cases their clerical

of the Society's volume editors. Whereas up to 1914 editors were almost exclusively British, thereafter other scholars gradually became involved, very few from continental Europe but an increasing number from other parts of the anglophone world.[1] This has now reached the point where half of the last twenty editions were prepared by scholars other than British, most North American, the remainder Australasian.[2] Although British scholars may regret that funding appears to be more available outside Britain (so that many British editors have worked extensively elsewhere and there is even something of a 'brain drain' of Hakluyt editors), the Society cannot but welcome this extension of interest, concern, and editing activity, an extension both inevitable and in terms of expertise highly profitable, not least because of the new-comers' local knowledge. A Society devoted to global coverage has become less national, more inter-continental. It has, however, as yet, failed to involve in the aspect under discussion that large part of the world where English is now a second language. Only one edition has been prepared by a scholar from Asia or Africa, despite the advantages, first, of a different viewpoint, and secondly, of easier access to local sources (including, where appropriate, non-written sources) reflecting the receiving end of 'exploration and travel' and the other side of 'encounter'.[3] It would seem, in particular, that scholars from the Middle

---

or even research assistance. Odd instances of translators being paid by editors are known, and it is possible that many of the editors explicitly or implicitly credited with translations in fact paid for translating assistance. However, editors who were civil servants were no doubt subsidised, like modern academics, by their departments, in that departmental overheads carried some of the cost of clerical assistance. Editorial acknowledgements of grants from trusts, foundations or other public funds begin to appear only in the 1980s.

[1] A few distinguished foreign, non-anglophone scholars have prepared editions, singly or in collaboration: the Dutchman, G. M. Asher in 1860 (HS 27); the Spaniard, Pascual de Gayangos, in 1868 (HS 40); the Russian, P. Bruun, in 1879 (HS 58); the Dutchman, P. A. Tiele, in 1885 (HS 71); the Argentinian, Luis L. Dominguez, in 1891 (HS 81); and the Portuguese, Armando Cortesão, in 1944 (HS 2/89–90). Among several scholars who promised editions but died before undertaking or completing them was the German explorer, Heinrich Barth. Editorial acknowledgements indicate that a list of the foreign scholars consulted by British editors, often for fundamental advice or assistance, would be very extensive.

[2] The first editor who can be decisively identified as North American was William Woodville Rockhill in 1900 (HS 2/4), followed by Mrs Zelia Nuttall in 1914 (HS 2/4, 34). But the first American editor was an Argentinian (HS 81). An Englishman living at Rio de Janeiro was credited on an 1874 title-page as translator of a text (HS 51).

[3] The volume was Sinnapah Arasaratnam, ed., *François Valentijn's Description of Ceylon*, London, 1978 (HS 2/149). Welcome although it is to find an editor from Asia, the text edited is European (Dutch), and the editor, after working in the universities of Ceylon and Malaya, completed the edition in the U.S.A. Edited translations of English texts on Japan, in Japanese and edited by local scholars, have, I understand, been published in Japan.

East, from the Indian peninsula, and from the Far East (to use Eurocentric terminology) would have much to contribute not only on encounter but also on non-European exploration and travel.
This is not to say that the Society has totally ignored texts emanating
from these regions. As early as 1857 a Persian account was deployed, and
this was followed in 1866 by an extract from the travels of Ibn Baṭṭūṭa:
the notable multi-volume edition of this Arab and North African
author, begun in 1958, is now nearing completion. In 1871 a translation
from the Arabic of the chronicles of Oman was published; an extract
from an Indian source appeared in 1918 and an extract from an Ethiopian
chronicle formed part of a 1954 edition. In the Extra Series an edited
translation of a remarkable Chinese account of fifteenth-century exploration in the Indian Ocean appeared in 1970.[1] In general, however,
the Society has published sources in European languages edited by
'Western' scholars. That European-languages sources form by far the
greater part of humanity's surviving stock of written 'voyages, travels,
and geographical records' is irrefutable, and it also needs to be recognised that individual non-European sources have frequently been edited
either separately or under other auspices, by societies using local languages or specialising in interests other than those of the Hakluyt
Society. Nevertheless, there would seem to be a case for the Society
encouraging and publishing an increasing number of editions of non-
European sources dealing with non-European travels, not least in the
light of the Society's commitment to 'public education' and the more
critical global attitude to European out-thrust.

Another changing feature of the Society relates to 'gender'. Until
very recently women were almost never explorers, that is, they almost
never led explorations, and on the few occasions when they participated
in explorations only from Victorian times did they begin to write up
their own accounts; therefore the exploration accounts published by the
Society have been entirely male productions. But numbers of women
have always been travellers, and at least from the eighteenth century
onwards accounts of travel and cultural encounter by females have been
not uncommon.[2] It is therefore notable that the Society has never

[1] HS 44; 2/44; 2/107; Extra 42.

[2] See Marion Tinsley, *Women into the unknown: a sourcebook on women as explorers and
travellers*, New York, 1989; Jane Robinson, *Wayward women: a guide to women travellers*,
Oxford, 1990. Among the English, note that 'the Wife of Bath' claimed to have travelled
to Jerusalem: Margery Kempe actually did. As to published accounts, the late nineteenth
century saw an outrush of British females travelling 'alone' (i.e. without British male
accompaniment) to outlandish parts and surviving to publish on return: for comments,
see Dorothy Middleton, 'Travel literature in the Victorian and Edwardian eras', *Annual
Report* [for 1980], Hakluyt Society, pp. 8–9.

published any of these, although the reason may well be that the rarity of the more distinguished (or bizarre) accounts, such as those in the eighteenth century by Lady Mary Wortley Montagu and Lady Hester Stanhope, and in the nineteenth by Mary Kingsley, led to their being in due course separately edited and the editions then being snapped up by commercial publishers. The first woman to contribute in any way to the Society's editions was somewhat effusively thanked by her husband, the editor of the sixth volume issued: Mrs Major had contributed five (copied) drawings.[1] The first woman among the scholars working for the Society was one Alice Wilmere, who in HS 23 of 1859 translated and prepared material on a Champlain voyage (since declared a fake), although credit for the overall editing of the volume went to a man.[2] No other female was associated with First Series editions, and in the Second Series the first female name on a title-page did not occur until 1914, Zelia Nuttall having edited an outstandingly important edition of Drake.[3] However, from 1900 female names began to appear in Introductions, the new class of university-educated women supplying what would later be called research assistants. Most notable was Miss Lavinia Mary Anstey who worked on a dozen volumes over a period of thirty years and at last got her name on a title-page, in 1932 and 1936.[4]

From the 1920s on, female editors became less occasional, with half a dozen in the inter-war years, including Dame Bertha Philpott and the formidable Professor E. G. R. Taylor, whose distinguished contributions terminated only in 1963.[5] Since the 1970s one in ten of editions has

---

[1] She also provided drawings in an 1851 volume (HS 10) – see the essay by Campbell below especially p. 105.

[2] The edition supplies no identification of the individuals concerned. Ms Wilmere is credited with the translation, biographical notice and annotation: since the edition consists of no more than these elements, the role of the male editor is unclear. The edition contains several colour illustrations, apparently hand-coloured, the first coloured illustrations in any edition (but a map in HS 13 of 1853 had its sea coloured blue).

[3] Nevertheless, the volume included among its subsidiary material the Laws of the Society, one of which began – 'Gentlemen preparing and editing works for the Society . . .'. Later female editors up to 1930 found themselves similarly addressed as 'Gentlemen'. Equally, a phrase occurring elsewhere in the subsidiary material, 'Gentlemen desiring to be enrolled as members . . .' only in 1928 became 'Ladies and Gentlemen . . .'.

[4] Miss Anstey wound up the six-volume edition and also a two-volume edition begun by Dame Bertha Philpott, when the male editor (her employer?) died (HS 2/68, 78). Other female assistants noted: HS 2/16, 21. In 1920–1921 Lady Goodenough, wife of a member of Council, was credited with translating from Catalan for her husband's edition – incidentally, almost the only work that seems to be far outside the remit of the Society (HS 2/47, 50). That the female assistants were university-educated is an assumption on my part.

[5] Since feminists object to the term 'formidable' as being normally applied only to females it is worth noting that accounts of the Society label thus, apparently with reason, several of the past presidents, all male.

AN ASSAULT ON A VILLAGE
From an account of travels in North East Africa in the 1820s.
Reproduced in HS 2/184 of 1996.

been the work of female scholars, mostly North American, and this too has helped to widen the range of Society editorship, both geographically and in terms of mindset.[1] However, the proportion is still low, relative not only to male editing, but also to the extensive role women have latterly played in the administration of the Society. Since the 1960s one of the two Honorary Secretaries – in practice also the Society's general editors – and its only remunerated administrator have all been women. From each of these individuals the Society has received long, meticulous and absolutely vital service.[2] The account of the Society's activities up to 1923 presented in the 1984 annual report was prepared by Mrs Dorothy Middleton, for over twenty years the representative on Council of the Royal Geographical Society. The subscribing membership of the 1995 Society is, however, 90% male, the membership of

---

[1] Female editors were viewed somewhat quizzically by certain officers of the Society, it would seem, their editions being criticised perhaps over-severely.

[2] The Honorary Secretaries have been the late Professor Eila M. Campbell (1963–1982) and Mrs Sarah Tyacke (1983–1995), now continuing as a series editor; Mrs Alexa Barrow was Administrative Assistant (at first entitled Clerk of Publications and Assistant Treasurer) 1965–1990, and has been succeeded by Mrs Fiona Easton.

the Council 80%; no woman has yet served as President, and to date there have been only three female vice-presidents.[1] To revert to the editorial aspect, it is arguable that a shift in public and academic interest from exploratory achievement to encounter debate may well help to reduce the predominance of male editing, should it turn out that female scholars come to believe that they have more to contribute on a topic, cultural encounter, which regularly and directly involved their own sex, than on another, exploration and navigation, which did not.

Adapting to technical innovation

In the present century occasional bulky, expensive or otherwise unusual editions not included among those due to subscribers, but offered to them at a reduced price and then sold publicly, have formed the Extra Series. The earliest, the multi-volume reprints of Hakluyt and Purchas in the 1900s, were only loosely connected with the Society, having been initiated by a commercial publisher. More recently, editions of Cook journals and Cook charts and the facsimile edition of Hakluyt's 'Western Planting' have been among the works that have appeared in the series, have been widely acclaimed, and have profitably sold.[2] A limitation of this series is that, its account being separate from that of the subscribers' Ordinary Series, the substantial cost of a publication has to be largely recovered before a further publication can be contemplated.

Costs of publishing the Ordinary Series have of course risen greatly in the last fifty years, even relative to inflation. Nineteenth-century prospectuses reckoned that volumes could be produced 'at little more than the cost of printing and paper', but today this basic cost is almost exceeded by the cost of distribution.[3] Cost-cutting measures such as

---

[1] Professor E. G. R. Taylor was the first woman to be appointed a vice-president, in 1956; followed by Professor Eila Campbell in 1983 and Mrs Sarah Tyacke in 1995.

[2] Ordinary Series volumes are also sold to non-members but generate limited income, perhaps because they do not normally appear on bookshop shelves or are otherwise drawn to public attention. Many sell slowly. In the 1940s certain editions from the 1850s and 1860s were still available for sale; in 1996 a work of 1959 is still available. Before reprints became regularly available the Society's annual reports often pointed out that the second-hand value of out-of-print volumes was greater than the original subscription or purchase price (e.g. the 1856 report). For volumes not reprinted the same is the case today.

[3] The quotation is from the same statement of aims as the passage at the head of this essay. Arrangements for publishing, printing/binding and distribution have changed in the last half century. From the early 1950s until 1973 publication and distribution were in the hands of Cambridge University Press, while until the early 1980s composing and printing/binding were undertaken alternately by MacLehose of Glasgow and CUP, the latter then continuing alone and serving to date. (CUP had printed for the Society since 1914, and only four printers had served earlier, with Richards of London printing 1849–

reducing special features of volumes, for instance, pull-out maps and half-tone illustrations printed on different papers to that of the text, and even substituting endnotes for footnotes, have been tried out.[1] Fortunately the recent shift to printing from camera-ready copy produced by computer typesetting techniques has to some extent reversed, or at least slowed down, the trend in overall costs.[2] The first edition to be supplied by volume editors on disc appeared in 1992 and it is presumed that this procedure will now be increasingly followed.[3] In general, the format of volumes has remained admirably, even astonishingly, consistent.[4] Dustjackets, introduced at an uncertain date (library sets of course lack them), were redesigned to look slightly less austere in 1970. Thanks to expert advice on the design side, it can fairly be claimed that recent volumes are both more handsome than most of their predecessors and more user-friendly.[5] Back numbers of volumes were offered to subscribers, first only in a set, then, from the 1850s, individually: in 1867 the whole set could be bought by subscribers for fifteen guineas. The modern reprinting of a large proportion of the earlier volumes was

---

1883 and the Bedford Press 1894–1914.) While CUP was the publisher the title-page of volumes carried the words 'Published for the Hakluyt Society'; previously the title-page read 'Printed for the Hakluyt Society'. Since 1973 the Society has been its own publisher, and since the early 1980s design, composition and distribution have been handled by commercial bodies other than CUP.

[1] For the following information about the more subtle technical changes in the last half-century I am indebted to Stephen Easton, the Society's production consultant since 1984, whose detailed information I abbreviate. Minor economies introduced during 1939–1945 were progressively extended in the immediate post-war decades, for instance, elaborate title-pages and decorative and drop initials were abandoned. Among stylistic changes was a switch from roman to arabic numerals for imprint and subscription years, and a standard typeface was for a time introduced. The embellishment of the inter-war years has not been resumed.

[2] Comparing the costs of two volumes of the same page size published in 1984 and 1994 respectively, printing costs doubled and paper and binding costs rose by 50%, whereas setting costs fell by 65%.

[3] It should be noted, however, that taking some of the responsibility for lay-out and sub-editing away from the printer/publisher, gives extra work to both the volume editor(s) and the Society's series editor(s), and therefore tends to slow down the editing stage of production.

[4] As a reviewer has noted – 'The size, format, and even the colour of the bindings of the Hakluyt Society volumes have not changed over the years' (Dunbar, 'Societies', p. 66). However, in 1946 Lynam recommended changing the light blue of the binding, which quickly fades into a nondescript dull colour, into dark blue (Lynam, 'Present and Future', p. 189). In the set I have examined the very faded dull blue changes into a brighter dark blue in the 1940s, but a lighter blue was introduced in the 1950s and continues to be the colour.

[5] 'The Hakluyt Society, set up to reprint the venturers' narratives for bibliophiles ... [hence], pleasing the collectors of fine books . . .' (Spufford, *Times Literary Supplement*, 28 July 1995, p. 14). The opening assertion is dubious, but the bibliophilic appreciation just.

entrusted to a commercial reprint-publisher in the 1960s, and this and subsequent similar arrangements have on the whole worked satisfactorily. As technology advances, modes of information retrieval multiply. It is likely that by the end of the present decade the Society will be supplying editions in electronic form as well as in book form.

One technical possibility relates to a fundamental aspect of the Society's procedures. As noted above, very many of its past publications were translations without the original text. Yet it is increasingly being realised that in the last analysis translations are always to some extent inadequate to represent the original discourse. Nevertheless, as the range of the Society's publications broadens, and as scholars progressively attempt a global view of past change, it becomes even less likely that there will exist any number of polylinguists who can tackle texts in all the relevant original languages. Translations will become more, not less necessary. Yet the specialist scholar who can read all or most of the languages of any one region will not be satisfied with translations from those languages, at least not without checking the translations against the original texts. The past history of the Society has been dominated by the fact that it has been financially impractical to accompany translations with the original texts. But in future this will not be so. One cheap solution, that of including a microfiche of the original text in a pocket of the volume, has been very occasionally followed by other societies, but is bitterly resisted by librarians and is unhelpful to those readers who wish to consult the text but lack easy access to a microfiche reader.[1] The way forward may lie in the developing ubiquity of personal computers. An original text on disc, probably not associated with the volume but obtainable by concerned scholars on request for a fee, would not only advantage those scholars but would make translators even more careful.[2]

Although primarily a publishing society, over the last one hundred and fifty years the Hakluyt Society has occasionally initiated or participated in other activities, notably commemorative events relevant to the life and career of Richard Hakluyt. Again, its representatives have attended celebrations of societies with related interests, in particular its brother society, the Royal Geographical Society, but also the Navy Records Society and the Society for Nautical Research. Two joint meetings with the Society for the History of Discoveries have been held, one in America in 1986 and another in London in 1987, and a third in

---

[1] A pocket to include a map or maps has, however, been a feature of about a dozen volumes in the present century, and may provide a precedent.

[2] Thought is currently being given to making available to scholars, on disc, for a fee, those published editions which have been submitted and edited on disc.

Newfoundland in 1997 is planned.[1] Further, it has been suggested that, travel costs being out of proportion to the salaries of younger scholars, the Society might advertise its functions (and recruit subscribers) by organising talks and meetings outside London, perhaps particularly in Scotland and in the U.S.A. In the Celebration year of 1996, Hakluyt Society exhibitions are planned in centres across Britain and to some extent across the English-speaking world, a novel activity. In these various ways the Society is emerging from being, in the main, a private and somewhat reclusive association, and is gaining, in the spirit of the times and hopefully with advantage, more of a public image.

Management

Mrs Middleton concluded her survey of the history of the Society up to 1923 with the tag *si monumentum requiris, circumspice*, inviting the reader to contemplate the Society's tangible achievement in the form of shelves of volumes of editions. The present essay has taken up the challenge by analysing the volumes. However, Mrs Middleton began her survey by noting the paucity of the Society's administrative records – the thinness of the Council Minutes, and the careful summaries of the Annual Reports. Inevitably therefore the inner history of the Society tends to be told merely in terms of personalities and institutions – the connection with other institutions, the personalities of its presidents and officers.[2] The Hakluyt Society grew out of the intellectual collective which a little earlier had produced the Royal Geographical Society: for long many individuals were members of both societies and even officers were shared, and since 1872 the Council of the Hakluyt Society has enjoyed the hospitality of the RGS headquarters in Kensington for its Council meetings.[3] Another fundamental connection has been with

---

[1] For an enthusiastic account of the first joint meeting, see the Annual Report for 1986.

[2] Evidence of several of the disagreements which are normal in the stresses and strains of any institution was presented by Foster and Mrs Middleton and is now further investigated in succeeding essays. The first Secretary departed under a cloud. A later Secretary resigned in disagreement with the president over the founding of the Navy Records Society. Throughout the whole of Yule's presidency Council meetings were infrequent and no AGMs were held, and for 1886 there are no Minutes. Foster, when Secretary, found Markham, the President, treating him with arrogant discourtesy (p.c. C. F. Beckingham; p. 197 below). Awkward volume editors have been known to exist (see the account of Skelton's difficulties, pp. 202–3 below).

[3] During the 1870s the second and third Honorary Secretaries of the Hakluyt Society were joint Honorary Secretaries of the RGS, and earlier the President of the Hakluyt Society served terms as President of RGS (see the essays by Campbell and Savours below). But to some extent the Hakluyt Society was established partly out of its founder's dissatisfaction with the RGS (see the essay by Bridges below).

the British Museum, especially with the section now the British Library. Staff of the Museum have served the Society as officers almost uninterruptedly from the start: the Map Department in particular has provided a string of honorary secretaries for the Society.[1] Nearly all the most notable nineteenth-century officers of the Society have been mentioned above, and the following are the subjects of essays later in this volume: Cooley (Honorary Secretary 1847–1849), Major (Honorary Secretary 1849–1858), Markham (Honorary Secretary 1858–1887, President 1889–1909), Yule (President 1877–1889), Foster (Honorary Secretary 1893–1902, President 1928–1945). Three of their recent successors are also memorialized, more briefly, later in the volume.

The Council and officers have always faced two problems, the first finance, the second the even flow of editions. The second problem was, and is, even more fundamental than the first. The Hakluyt Society is in many aspects a very British institution, for better or worse. Although nineteenth-century annual reports included suggestions for future editions and although editors have not infrequently acknowledged that they were encouraged by one or other of the officers to undertake a specific edition, in general the Society sits back and waits for a voluntary, self-appointed potential editor to come forward with a proposal.[2] The Society's stance is thus reactive rather than pro-active, its editions determined by serendipity: it has never systematically determined – although it has at times thought about it – what editions need doing and how this can be achieved. This has meant that editions are turned out higgledy-piggledy by region and period, and because editors take varying unpredictable periods to complete an edition no exact future publication programme can be agreed. Yet it is arguable that the lack of a master plan was in the past realistic. Whether a more planned programme can be achieved in the future is likely to be controversial, partly because it might demand greater financial assets than are at present available, but at least it should prove possible to draw up a list of works within the various fields appropriate to the Society whose appearance in an HS edition would meet the needs of study in each field and whose editing should be actively and urgently encouraged.[3]

---

[1] For the nineteenth century, see the table on p. 141.

[2] The Council does decide whether a proposal is to be approved, after refereeing by peers, and some proposals are turned down, for what seems a good reason, although very occasionally a mistake is made and a fine edition is produced elsewhere.

[3] The list would include those past HS editions which now need re-editing. The suggestion in the text is not original: in 1946 Lynam wrote – 'We have in our publications covered most of the globe and many periods between 1400 and 1700. But we have not covered them systematically. . . . But the moment has come for the Society to survey the whole history of travel and exploration, to draw up a coordinated table of regions and

A prosopographic study of HS editors would occupy an essay in itself. Regularly editors have died when under way with an edition and have had to be replaced, occasionally in a sequence. For other reasons, some works have been completed only after many years, even decades, of gestation. Mrs Middleton has noted that in 1886 Yule proposed an edition of Cadamosto which in the event did not appear until 1937, and I add that the edition was first suggested in 1849. Some proposed and accepted editions have never appeared, but only a few: occasionally Council has insisted that a long-delayed edition be abandoned. It follows that the publication programme is somewhat ad hoc and often slips. 'The publication programme was four years in arrears when he took over and this was reduced to one year' – a tribute in the 1986 Annual Report to Sir Gilbert Laithwaite, president 1964–1969, reflects an ever-recurring situation. Given these difficulties it is a tribute to the past members of Council and the past officers that, with minor and occasional hiccoughs, a flow of editions to subscribers has nevertheless been maintained fairly steadily for one hundred and fifty years – 281 volumes, averaging over one and four-fifths volumes annually and thus approaching the intended figure of two volumes.[1]

The subscriptions of increasing numbers of members have been one factor in making this possible, allied to the voluntary labours of volume editors and the Society's officers and Council. But a third factor has been the skilful management of finances, latterly by honorary treasurers appointed by Council. During the later nineteenth and early twentieth centuries centuries the Society made do with a poorly-paid clerk to keep and calculate its accounts: of course these were relatively simple, while no doubt presidents and honorary secretaries who had formerly administered colonial provinces or civil service departments kept an eye on the humble employee, the Honorary Secretary being held responsible for presenting the accounts. The first Honorary Treasurer was appointed only in 1908 (but he served until 1946). As additional financial regulators, in 1931 Trustees were appointed; while the increasingly complex responsibilities of the day-to-day running of a sales business and the general management of affairs have been latterly entrusted to an

---

periods which we have neglected, and to base our future publications upon that' (Lynam, 'Present and Future', pp. 187–8). Fifty years later, has the moment come?

[1] Although references were made over the years to 'an obligation' to give subscribers two volumes annually, this was never a formal commitment and in 1981, on the grounds that in the past two volumes had at times been provided only by presenting long editions in two parts, it was decided 'to allow the Society to issue a single volume against one year's subscription' (*Annual Report*, 1982). But the Society continues to aim at, and generally achieves, two volumes annually.

Administrative Assistant, its only remunerated officer.[1] In recent decades the Council has regularly included a proportion of members from the world of commerce whose advice on the arcane financial matters of investments to make and taxes to avoid has been invaluable. In the event, Honorary Treasurers have tactfully and successfully steered the Society away from a series of potential cash-flow crises; and since financial risk is associated with administrative decisions, Council has trained itself to weigh practical considerations against academic enthusiasm. Hence, as a knowledgeable past officer has nicely put it in a recent letter – 'Presidents have alternated between academics and "men of affairs", the Society hoping to get, and generally getting, better knowledge on the subject from the former, and greater orderliness from the latter'.

As the Society celebrates its one hundred and fiftieth anniversary only a little way off is the twenty-first century. I borrow the concluding sentence of the account of the Society's first hundred years written by Sir William Foster in 1946 and apply the sentiment to the Society's future, both in its own next one hundred years and in the coming calendar century.

The Society thus starts upon its new century of endeavour under good omens, and I for one am confident that its volumes, in their familiar livery of blue and gold, will render the same good service to the generations of the future that their predecessors have done to the generations of the past.

---

[1] A post served with distinction for one quarter of a century (1965–1991) by Mrs Alexa Barrow, knowledgeable in the ethos of the Society as the daughter of a former Secretary, R. A. Skelton. The forerunners of the post of Administrative Assistant, although with more limited responsibilities, were a Clerk, later Assistant Treasurer, and an Agent: 'our Assistant Treasurer is paid a salary and our Agent a commission' (Lynam, 'Present and Future', p. 185).

Part II

THE NINETEENTH CENTURY: VICTORIAN FIGURES

William Desborough Cooley and the Foundation of the Hakluyt Society

R. H. Major and the British Museum

Henry Yule: India and Cathay

Clements Markham: longest serving Officer, most prolific Editor

THE

HISTORY OF MARITIME

AND

INLAND DISCOVERY.

VOL. II.

H.Corbould del.

F. Finden sculp.

BALBOA DISCOVERS THE SOUTH SEA.

_____ he ran before his companions to the summit of a
mountain, from which he surveyed, with transports of
delight, the boundless Ocean which rolled beneath.
Page 40.

London;
PRINTED FOR LONGMAN, REES, ORME, BROWN & GREEN, PATERNOSTER ROW
AND JOHN TAYLOR, UPPER GOWER STREET:
1830.

Cooley's *History of Maritime and Inland Discovery* (1830–1831).

50

WILLIAM DESBOROUGH COOLEY

AND THE FOUNDATION OF THE HAKLUYT SOCIETY

R. C. Bridges

There can be no doubt that William Desborough Cooley was the originator of the Hakluyt Society. Yet there was doubt on the matter before Sir William Foster's article on the Society's history appeared in the Centenary volume. Foster had examined the Society's archive and quoted a minute of the annual meeting of 1849 which recorded the thanks given to Cooley 'for having planned and originated the Hakluyt Society'.[1] Since the time of Foster's article, a detailed study of Cooley's career and Mrs Middleton's analysis of the Society's records have both followed Foster's lead and made clear Cooley's right to be regarded as the Society's founder.[2] Yet Cooley's actual activities in the period during which he developed the idea of just such a society and while he was the Society's first Secretary have not been previously described. The overall circumstances in which the Society was founded and in which it established itself in its first three years of existence have remained to be investigated. Even the fact that the new body was

---

[1] William Foster, 'The Hakluyt Society. A Retrospect: 1846–1946', in Edward Lynam, ed., *Richard Hakluyt & his Successors. A Volume issued to commemorate the Centenary of the Hakluyt Society*, London, 1946 (HS 2/93), pp. 141–70. Foster quotes (without precisely citing) the Minute of the annual meeting of 9 May 1849; in fact, the minute was a repetition of the phrasing which had been used in the minutes of a Council meeting held on 1 May. One of the (many) oddities in the story is that this same minute was quoted in the Annual Report for 1848 (although it here recorded an 1849 development) which was printed and incorporated in the fifth of the Society's annual volumes. Hence the information about Cooley's role was available in the Society's published output from 1849, had anyone cared to look.

[2] R. C. Bridges, 'W. D. Cooley, the RGS and African Geography in the Nineteenth Century, Part I' and 'W. D. Cooley . . . Part II' *Geographical Journal*, 192, 1976, pp. 27–47, 274–86, on p. 281; Dorothy Midddleton, 'The Hakluyt Society 1846–1923', *Annual Report* [for 1984], Hakluyt Society, pp. 12–23, on p. 13 (Cooley was, however, only temporarily Secretary of the RGS and not an Honorary Secretary). Drawing on Mrs Middleton's work, a recent article has mentioned Cooley as founder, but wrongly assumes that he chose Hakluyt's name for the Society, a point discussed below (Helen Wallis, 'The Great Publication Societies', in *Critical Issues in Editing Exploration Texts*, Toronto, 1995, pp. 108–24).

originally to have been known as the 'Columbus Society' has been forgotten for a century and a half. The present article attempts to remedy the situation, although the many obscurities surrounding both Cooley and the early life of the Society mean that some uncertainties persist. What can be confirmed is that Cooley was indeed the key figure in 1846. Certain other members of the Provisional Council, notably J. E. Gray, Sir Charles Malcolm and Bolton Corney, may also have had significant roles, but Cooley's role was outstanding.

In a study which will centre largely on Cooley and his ideas and activities, a preliminary question to ask is why it was that this man's importance to the Hakluyt Society went unacknowledged for most of the first hundred years of the Society's existence. Even in his excellent article in the Centenary volume, and despite the accompanying contribution by Sir William Foster which outlined the history of the Society, the then President, Edward Lynam, in the course of his discussion of the 1846 foundation chose not to mention Cooley.[1] Again, when in 1948 Robert Fazy interpreted the Society for Orientalist scholars, he mentioned Cooley only once, referring merely to Foster's article.[2] Again, it is surprising that G. R. Crone, a former Secretary, in his retrospective article of 1962 ignored Cooley when he referred to the foundation and the founders.[3] But this writing-out of the founder was in a much older tradition.

In 1896, at the time of the Society's fiftieth anniversary, Sir Clements Markham was President. His address on a commemorative occasion mentioned Cooley only once, in passing, and only as Secretary. Markham's listing and description of the 'distinguished persons' who came together to found the Society on 15 December 1846 did not include Cooley.[4] This can only have been a deliberate omission by someone who must have had at hand the Council lists in the early published volumes, and also, almost certainly, the record books of the Society. Proof that Markham was not unaware of Cooley's importance can be found in his 1891 obituary of R. H. Major, Cooley's successor as Secretary: 'It was Mr. Desborough Cooley who began this work and he was first Secretary ...'.[5] It is possible that Markham, for so long a

---

[1] Edward Lynam, 'The Present and the Future', in Lynam, *Hakluyt & his Successors*, pp. 171–89 – see especially pp. 181–3.

[2] R. Fazy, 'Le centenaire de la Hakluyt Society 1846–1946', *Études Asiatiques*, 1/2, 1948, pp. 1–15, on p. 8.

[3] G. R. Crone, '"Jewells of Antiquitie": the Work of the Hakluyt Society', *Geographical Journal*, 128, 1962, pp. 321–4.

[4] Clements R. Markham, *Richard Hakluyt: His Life and Work. With a Short Account of the Aims and Achievements of the Hakluyt Society*, London, 1896, especially pp. 10–11.

[5] *Proceedings of the Royal Geographical Society* [hereafter *PRGS*], n.s. 13, 1891, p. 489.

dominant figure in the Royal Geographical Society (hereafter RGS) as well as in the Hakluyt Society, even thirteen years after Cooley's death resented the persistent attacks which Cooley had regularly made on the RGS for nearly half a century, and that he was now getting his revenge.[1] An even less charitable view would be that amid all the distinguished members of the literary, geographical and scientific establishments whom he was mentioning, Markham had no wish to include the eccentric and perhaps half-deranged Irishman, whose geographical work, if it was remembered at all, was by the end of the century recalled as something of a joke. Whatever were his reasons, Markham must be accounted in large measure responsible for the later ignorance about Cooley's role in the Society's history.[2] Yet it is easy to see why the ignorance persisted. Cooley did not remain Secretary of the Hakluyt Society for long and hence did not leave a large imprint on its work in quite the way that later secretaries – such as Major and Markham – were to do. As will be seen, his one piece of editorial work for the Society was, frankly, an undistinguished production.[3] Given these factors, one may forgive Markham to some extent, although his failure to acknowledge at least Cooley's direct role in the foundation of the Society is surely a blot on his record. At any rate, largely (one suspects) because the information must have been gathered from RGS sources, none of the major obituaries which appeared on Cooley's death in 1883 referred to his importance in relation to the Hakluyt Society; nor, more significantly still, did the later entry in the *Dictionary of National Biography*.[4]

At the 150th anniversary of the Hakluyt Society it seems appropriate to assess Cooley's importance in the Society's history by asking exactly how he managed to bring about its genesis and birth. A related issue is how this apparently rather odd Irish writer came to be influential enough in 1846 to persuade figures in the literary and scientific establishments to unite around him and do what he wanted. And a final issue is why Cooley threw up the real chance of lasting influence and literary

---

[1] Bridges, 'Cooley', pp. 282–3. Cooley had certainly criticised Markham directly in a publication of 1872.

[2] In Markham's *The Fifty Years' Work of the Royal Geographical Society*, London, 1881, on p. 46, Cooley's role in relation to the Hakluyt Society (and incidentally also to the RGS itself) had been similarly ignored. The centenary history of the RGS, H. R. Mill, *The Record of the Royal Geographical Society*, London, 1930, p. 62, innocently follows the Markham lead.

[3] W. D. Cooley, ed., *Sir Francis Drake his Voyage 1595, by Thomas Maynarde* ... , London, 1849 (HS 4).

[4] *The Athenaeum*, 2889, 10 March 1883, p. 315; *The Times*, 10 March 1883; *PRGS*, n.s. 5, 1883, pp. 232–3; *DNB* (the New DNB entry is likely to repair the omission).

reputation which he had created for himself with the foundation of the Society, by resigning from the secretaryship in 1849.[1]

Cooley's reputation in 1846

William Desborough Cooley was born on 16 March 1795, the son of a barrister father and the grandson of Thomas Cooley, a notable architect who had designed many of Dublin's public buildings. In 1811 he followed his father to Trinity College, Dublin, and in 1816 graduated, after what seems to have been a mainly mathematical training under Benjamin Lloyd. Information on Cooley's life for the first dozen years or so after his graduation has not so far been discovered, but it seems that he first arrived in London in about 1821 and after 1824 resided there permanently. Probably it was in London that he began seriously to take up geographical studies, and he eventually claimed to have drawn up for his own use a catalogue of 7,000 titles of geographical works.[2] By 1830 he was gaining something of a literary and geographical reputation, and he became one of the earliest Fellows of the newly-formed Royal Geographical Society.[3] Two clues to the nature of his career before 1830 have been found. One is his 1835 statement that he had been in correspondence with the West Indies for ten years.[4] The other is the information that can be gleaned from his correspondence with the

---

[1] The account that follows is based in part on the archives of the Hakluyt Society, presently stored in the House of the RGS, Kensingon Gore, London. The materials available are three manuscript items: the Council Minutes from 1847 onwards [hereafter HSCM], the 'Record Book' (a summary of proceedings almost certainly in its early parts compiled by R. H. Major) [hereafter HSRB], and a volume entitled 'Reports of the Hakluyt Society' [hereafter HSRHS]. The last-named has the texts of the Annual Reports for the years from 1849 onwards but also the lists of Council members from 1847 and the texts of brochures which are referred to as 'Lists' from 1850. There was an annual report for 1847, it would seem, as that for 1848 refers to it but no text has been found. The text of the 1848 report was printed and bound in with the fifth of the Society's issued volumes, Thomas Rundall, ed., *Voyages towards the North-West* ..., London, 1849 (HS 5). However, this report incorporates news relating to 1849 about Cooley (see p. 51 note 1 above), news which does not appear in the report in the volume in the archive headed 'Report for 1849'. Also cited in the present essay are relevant items from the manuscript Council Minutes of the RGS [hereafter RGSCM], also stored in the House of the RGS, which have been used with the kind permission of the Director and Secretary, Dr John Hemming.

[2] *Report of the Commission appointed to inquire into the Constitution and Government of the British Museum*, House of Commons Sessional Papers 1850, vol. XXIV, evidence of W. D. Cooley, 4697–749. I am grateful to Tony Campbell for drawing my attention to the fact that Cooley gave evidence to this Commission in 1849.

[3] Bridges, 'Cooley', p. 28.

[4] Review by Cooley of F. J. F. Meyer, *Reise um die Erde*, in *Foreign Quarterly Review*, 15. 1835, pp. 1–48.

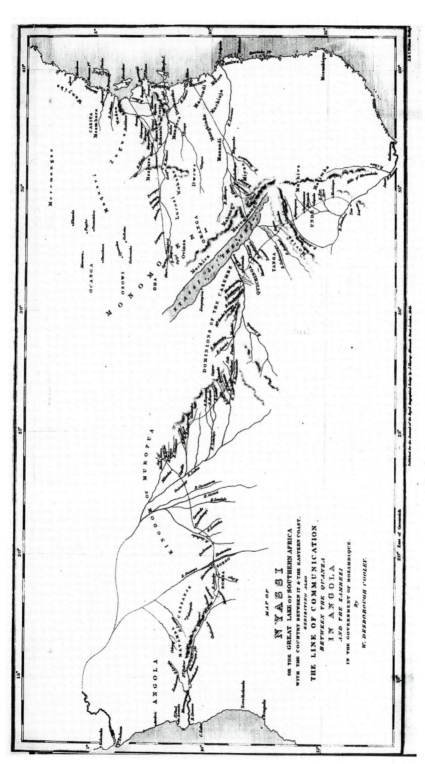

Cooley's map of Central Africa (1845).

editor of the *Edinburgh Review*, Macvey Napier, when Cooley first began to write for that distinguished journal. He talked of the 'absolute necessity of venting [his] spleen . . . on [the subject of] the present state of Ireland', a subject on which he had already written for an encyclopedia. He also mentioned his 'strong tendency to political heresy'.[1] It might therefore be deduced that Cooley was a writer on popular political subjects of the time, such as Catholic emancipation and slave emancipation. However, by 1833 when he joined the *Edinburgh Review*, geographical subjects were clearly taking precedence.

To judge from the character of some of his later writings, the navigational applications of his mathematical training may have had something to do with the direction his interests took, but it is impossible to say precisely why he developed knowledge and expertise in geographical matters. At any rate, Napier seems to have insisted that Cooley write on these rather than political subjects. He must have accepted this instruction since he henceforth built up a reputation in the geographical field alone, there being no evidence of later political writing. The change of direction did not affect his propensity to 'vent his spleen': geographers and explorers were to suffer from his attacks for the next forty years. Cooley first came to prominence in the geographical world by his exposure of the fraud perpetrated by a Frenchman, J. B. Douville, who claimed to have discovered lakes and rivers in the interior of West Central Africa when he had in actuality travelled no great distance into the country behind Luanda. This episode led to Cooley's being elected to the Council of the Royal Geographical Society.[2] A further reason for that election, however, must have been that Cooley was known and applauded as the author of *A History of Maritime and Inland Discovery*, published 1830–1831.[3] This is an impressive work which shows that Cooley had a wide acquaintance with the then existing literature of travel and exploration and that he was capable of sensible judgements; there is, moreover, little of the invective which was to become characteristic of so much of his later writing and which, even in this earlier period, had helped to destroy the career and reputation of Douville.

Maritime and Inland Discovery is the first element in the array of achievements which explains why Cooley was able to do what he did in

---

[1] MS London, British Library, Add. 34616 [hereafter BL, Add. 34616], f. 27, Cooley to Napier, 22 July 1833.

[2] For a full account of this episode, see Bridges, 'Cooley', p. 29. Douville was, in fact, not an entire rogue.

[3] It appeared, in three volumes, as part of *Dr Lardner's Cabinet Cyclopaedia*, London, 1830–31.

1846. It is worth noting what is said in that work on the importance of the subject which was to be central to the Hakluyt Society's concerns.

> The history of the progress of geographical knowledge is calculated more than that of any other branch of learning to illustrate the progressive civilisation of mankind. It has for its object, in some measure, the diffusion of the species, but is more immediately connected with the advancement of navigation and commercial enterprise. . . . In a scientific age the acquaintance with the earth's surface possesses an interest independent of its practical advantages.[1]

Everything, indeed, seems to point to Cooley promoting the idea of the Hakluyt Society because he felt it would hold out both 'practical advantages' and an academic attraction to those with a scholarly and scientific bent.

By the time that he founded the Society, some fifteen or sixteen years later, Cooley had raised his standing to such an extent that his ideas were listened to with considerable respect. Although his association with the *Edinburgh Review* seems to have lasted for only four or five years, he wrote no fewer than eleven long reviews of travellers' and explorers' treatises, and in these he not only analysed the work of each author but also advanced his own geographical theories. In particular, as he said, he was becoming more and more concerned to 'raise the veil' which shrouded the interior of Africa. As a result of meeting in London a Zanzibari merchant, Khamis bin Uthman, and also his Yao slave, and by uniting the information drawn from them with what he had learned from Portuguese sources, ancient and modern, and from other literary evidence, he believed he could see the main details of the interior geography of eastern Africa. 'I will conduct readers to the great inland sea called Gnassa [sic]', he assured Napier.[2] Especially important were the reviews he wrote of an account of Owen's great hydrographic survey of the coasts of Africa, of a work by a former governor of Mozambique, Sebastião José Xavier Botelho, on that territory, and of an account of W. S. W. Ruschenberger's circumnavigation which had included a visit to East Africa.[3] Cooley's views on the works he reviewed were rarely flattering. Privately he told Napier, for instance, that Botelho was 'a political charlatan of the meanest description', and his remarks in the printed review were only slightly more restrained.[4]

---

[1] Ibid., I, pp. 1, 123.
[2] BL, Add. 34616, Cooley to Napier, 9 October 1834; 34717, Cooley to Napier, 23 March 1835.
[3] For a full discussion of these reviews, see Bridges, 'Cooley', pp. 34–5.
[4] MS London, British Library, Add. 34617, Cooley to Napier, 2 July 1836; review of

Perhaps it was this tendency to excessive disputatiousness that led Napier to cease to employ Cooley regularly after 1838. Perhaps, too, Napier knew of the controversy in which Cooley had become involved at the RGS and that made him cautious. Nevertheless, Cooley's standing hardly suffered.

His relationship with the RGS had enabled him to build on contacts with Captain Owen and also with J. B. Emery, the officer Owen had left in Mombasa to command the short-lived British Protectorate there in the mid 1820s, and Cooley actually persuaded the RGS to send an expedition to East Africa in 1834. The chosen traveller, J. E. Alexander, disobeyed his instructions and went elsewhere, much to Cooley's annoyance with both him and the RGS. By this time he was in dispute with the Secretary of the RGS, Captain Maconochie. In December 1835 he accused Maconochie of various rather unspecific failings and these had to be investigated by a special committee. Forty years later, Cooley finally explained his complaint: he accused Maconochie of mishandling his own subscription and other moneys and of participating in some 'doubtful' financial transactions. At the time the committee vindicated Maconochie and in consequence Cooley was obliged to resign the vice-presidency he had been awarded in 1832.[1] Despite these upsets with the RGS in the mid 1830s, Cooley continued to be closely associated with that body and its work, and it was partly as a result of this continuing relationship that his reputation as a geographer increased in the next ten years. This reputation helps to explain Cooley's ability to attract others to the idea of a society publishing accounts of voyages and travels. Yet the legacy of his uneasy or even hostile relationship with the RGS is, as we shall see, equally important in the story of the Hakluyt Society's genesis.

During the late 1830s and early 1840s, Cooley continued to produce some notable scholarly works, including two mathematical texts and an edition of Herodotus with much new annotation, as well as the very scholarly *Negroland of the Arabs*, published in 1841. In this last work he employed his knowledge of Arabic to elucidate the geography of interior West Africa on the basis of extant sources which had hitherto

---

Sebastião José Xavier Botelho, *Memória Estatística sobre os Domínios Portuguezes na África Oriental*, in *Edinburgh Review* 64, 1837, pp. 411–28. Cooley's attack prompted Botelho to write no fewer than 109 pages in reply; he accused his of course unknown critic of 'malicious untruths . . . distorting facts . . . vague assertions' and of resorting to personal invective: S. J. X. Botelho, *Segunda Parte da Memória Estatística . . .*, Lisbon, [?1840].

[1] Bridges, 'Cooley', pp. 30–32; RGSCM, 21 December 1835; W. D. Cooley, *Dr Livingstone and the Royal Geographical Society*, London, 1874, pp. 21–2.

never been properly analysed.[1] Cooley was developing in such works what he called his 'principle of rectification of sources'. This meant that the interpreter of sources must understand not only the language of the original (not to mention any other languages through which the information had been transmitted) but also the theoretical and other preconceptions of the author – a 'contextual' consideration much in favour among scholars 150 years later. Any inconsistencies thus demonstrated needed to be taken into account before a final judgement was formed.[2] Since application of such 'rectification' was not to be confined to ancient sources, contemporary explorers were liable to react with anger when Cooley took it upon himself to 'rectify' their hard-won results. All this indicated that Cooley was developing an intense interest in both modern and ancient geographical source material. He clearly believed that it should all be made available and be properly analysed, in order not merely to gratify purely scholarly interest, but also to meet the highly practical need for the blanks on maps to be filled in.

It was by employing the principles that he had developed that Cooley produced in 1845 an article which was seen at the time as a major contribution to geographical enquiry and which very clearly confirmed his position as an authoritative scholar and an expert on geographical source material, especially where it related to Africa. A fifty-page article with a map, 'The Geography of Nyassi' set out the results of Cooley's investigations and his 'rectifications' of the sources, both old and contemporary, relating to the interior of Eastern Africa.[3] It later became obvious that in the article and map Cooley had made the mistake of conflating the information about Lakes Malawi and Tanganyika and hence had claimed that there was only one lake – a notion which he had first aired in 1835 and to which he tenaciously clung despite the information that eventually came forward from practical

---

[1] W. D. Cooley, *Historical and Cultural Comments on the History of Herodotus . . .*, 2 vols, London, 1844; W. D. Cooley, *The Negroland of the Arabs Examined and Explained . . .*, London, 1841. One drawback to the latter work was that Cooley's sources were all comparatively ancient ones, hence he did not learn about the eighteenth and early-nineteenth century *jihads* which had by 1841 so much affected the disposition of peoples and political jurisdictions.

[2] Ibid. pp. xvii–xxiii.

[3] W. D. Cooley, 'The Geography of Nyassi, or the Great Lake of Southern Africa Investigated; with an Account of the Overland Route from the Quanza in Angola to the Zambézi in the Government of Mozambique', *Journal of the Royal Geographical Society* [hereafter *JRGS*], 15, 1845, pp. 185–235. Cooley was later to extend and elaborate the ideas in this article in a book, *Inner Africa Laid Open in an Attempt to Trace the Chief Lines of Communication across that Continent*, London, 1852. The 1845 map, in part reproduced in my contribution to F. Fernández-Armesto, ed., *The Times Atlas of World Exploration*, London, 1991, p. 199, is here reproduced in full (p. 55).

explorations. Given this error, and quite a few others about rivers and lakes, commentators later in the nineteenth century derided and dismissed Cooley as a charlatan. Yet to continue to do so is to overlook the many virtues of his paper. He identified various African peoples and placed them in more or less their correct positions on the map; he tried to come to terms with the relevant African languages and publicised the growing view that there existed a family of closely related languages in southern Africa, the family which came to be termed Bantu; and he showed how *pombeiros* (mixed race adventurers) from Portuguese settlements, and also Arabs and Swahili from Kilwa and Zanzibar, had begun to penetrate the interior. (Cooley's information on this last point still remains useful for historians.) Since in 1845 there had as yet been no scientific exploratory expeditions to East Africa, Cooley's stock ran extremely high. The President of the RGS praised his article and noted the attention it had commanded outside Britain. Sir Roderick Murchison, then rapidly rising to the position of dominance he was to enjoy in the mid-century geological and geographical world and destined to become the first President of the Hakluyt Society, said that as far as the interior of Africa was concerned it was to Cooley that everyone must look for enlightenment.[1]

To reinforce the point that Cooley did have a considerable reputation in European scholarly circles – even after many of his basic ideas had been discredited – one other much later episode may be mentioned. In 1885, Novo y Colson published a book about the remarkable Malaspina expedition of 1789–1794.[2] He noted that he was accustomed to Spain's achievements being undervalued by non-Spaniards, but when indulging in his favourite reading, which was perusing Cooley's *Maritime and Inland Discovery*, he had come across a too-easy dismissal of the work of Malaspina and his colleagues, and this had encouraged him to respond by writing his book. It was because the name of Desborough Cooley was so 'illustrious and respected' and because he was 'the oracle of many erudite scholars and writers' that his error about the Spaniards' inability to take proper navigational observations at sea needed correction.[3]

[1] R. I. Murchison, 'Annual Anniversary Address to the Royal Geographical Society', *JRGS*, 14, 1844, pp. xiv–cxxviii; Lord Colchester, 'Annual Anniversary Address . . .', ibid., 16, 1846, pp. xxxix–lxxxv.

[2] Don Pedro de Novo y Colson, *Alrededor del Mundo por las Corbetas Descubierta y Atrevida al mando de los Capitanes de Navío D. Alejandro Malaspina y Don José de Bustamente y Guerra desde 1789 á 1794*, Madrid, 1885. I am grateful to Mrs Ann Shirley for drawing my attention to Novo y Colson's work and its references to Cooley.

[3] Ibid., pp. i, ii, v; Bridges, 'Cooley', pp. 28, 285–6. The passage in *Maritime and Inland Discovery* which so upset Novo y Colson was in vol. III, pp. 168–9. He must have been quoting and translating from the original English edition of the book; I have been unable to find any evidence of a Spanish translation although there were versions in French,

Towards the foundation

By the middle of the 1840s Cooley was thus a respected figure with something of a European reputation. When, therefore, he began to promote the idea of an organisation to publish early voyages and travels, he was listened to. Why the idea should have become more widely acceptable in 1846 is a question that has not been considered before. Nor has the exact nature of the impulse which led to the initial meetings been identified, although in 1946 Lynam had some interesting reflections on the issue. He drew attention to the contemporary 'expansion of Britain', with its attendant overseas activities by emigrants, traders, missionaries, scientists and servicemen, and he linked the foundation of the Royal Geographical Society to the concerns of such people and to the interest of their compatriots in them and in the distant lands to which they travelled. The same interest, he seemed to suggest, was one of the reasons for setting up a society which could provide accounts of travel overseas. However, he went on to argue that a revival in the study of history was a stronger reason for the foundation of the Hakluyt Society and he noted the example of the earlier-founded Camden Society in collecting and publishing historical texts and the fact that no fewer than four members of that society were among the founding fathers of the Hakluyt Society. No doubt this influence was important and Lynam may well have correctly judged the later character of the society, but since he did not consider or even mention Cooley, his essay cannot be regarded as definitive on the inception of the society or on the events of 1846.[1]

Pointers to the impulses which led to the foundation of the Hakluyt Society and the reasons for matters being brought to a head in 1846 may be found in the pages of the *Athenaeum*. In the middle decades of the nineteenth century this weekly periodical was a forum for the discussion not only of literary and artistic concerns but also of geographical and other scientific issues. Indeed, in the 1830s Cooley himself was associated with the periodical as some sort of editorial assistant;[2] and much of his controversial writing on Africa was to appear there in the 1850s and 1860s. Already in 1846 the journal did not eschew controversy. An

---

Dutch and Italian, as well as an American issue and a second edition in Britain. Even if there was no translation of his work, Cooley seems to have remained well enough respected in the Spanish-speaking world for him to be given an entry in the *Enciclopedia Universal Illustrado Europeo-Americana*, 15, Barcelona, [c. 1930], p. 318.

[1] Lynam, 'The Present and the Future', pp. 178–83.

[2] L. A. Marchand, *The Athenaeum: a Mirror of Victorian Culture*, Chapel Hill, 1941, pp. 6, 222.

anonymous article appearing on 1 April deplored the poor condition of the country's learned societies and suggested that there was a need for a 'searching inquiry into their constitution and management'. The condition of the Royal Geographical Society was said to be particularly deplorable.[1] Clues within the article make it clear that the writer was Cooley. Confirmation that he had begun a campaign is found in the records of the RGS itself. On 27 April, Cooley and five others invoked a rule of the RGS which stated that if six members forwarded a complaint, the Council had to consider it. The present complainants wanted the general state and efficiency of the Society to be investigated, together with its financial condition. It is significant that among the six complainants, besides Cooley there was another individual destined to become a member of the Council of the Hakluyt Society. This was J. E. Gray, Keeper of Natural History in the British Museum, a naturalist and a Fellow of the Royal Society. Two more complainants, Edward Doubleday, also a naturalist at the British Museum, and the antiquary and frequent writer in the *Athenaeum*, C. Wentworth Dilke, were to become initial members of the Hakluyt Society.[2] As we have seen, Cooley's writings show that he believed that the prosecution of the scientific study of geography required the use of earlier as well as contemporary sources. One of his criticisms of the RGS was that it was doing nothing to assemble these source materials so that current geographical problems could be tackled. The association with him in the events which led to the formation of the Hakluyt Society of at least two professional scientists – and later of a man much concerned with naval survey work, Admiral Malcolm – suggests that Cooley's view struck chords. Thus, it may be suggested that Lynam's emphasis on the predominance of the historical and antiquarian element in the motives for the founding of the Society was a misjudgment.

In response to the prompting of the six complainants, the RGS Council set up a special committee, but then decided what had been done was not constitutional and called a special meeting of the Society. There seems to have been a considerable crisis, with one issue being whether sufficient attention was being paid to Cooley's scholarly work. Eventually the Secretary of the RGS, who had complained of 'foul calumny' in the course of considerable correspondence in the *Athenaeum*, resigned his position. But by early May, in the columns of the *Athenaeum* Cooley was threatening the RGS with the possibility of some new and rival organisation being set up.[3]

[1] *The Athenaeum*, 963, 1 April 1846, pp. 372–73.
[2] RGSCM, 27 April 1846. For Gray, Doubleday and Dilke, see *DNB*.
[3] RGSCM, 30 April, 13 May, 18 May, 25 May, 3 June, 8 June, 20 June, 14 December

Even before the crisis at the RGS, Cooley had been attempting to remedy what he saw as a situation where too few sources of geographical information were being made publicly available. He founded a series called *The World Surveyed in the Nineteenth Century*, which was designed to make available in English the work of distinguished foreign travellers. The only two works to appear were Friedrich Parrot's account of his ascent of Mount Ararat and Adolph Erman's two volumes on his travels in Siberia, both works translated from the German by Cooley himself and published in 1845 and 1848 respectively. Neither made any great impact, and apparently the publisher, Longmans, declined to continue with the series.[1] The project was yet another sign of Cooley's enterprise and his dedication to what in his eyes were the needs of geographical scholarship.

Exactly when in 1846 Cooley took the initiative which was to create the Hakluyt Society is difficult to say. But it must have been at some time in the months between the June meeting of the RGS when new regulations were adopted which, however, failed to meet the complaints of Cooley and his friends, and early December, when the new society project became public knowledge. Within this period, Cooley was presumably in discussion with those individuals who were prepared to respond to his initiative since there are indications that he was prevailed upon to alter some of his ideas. Direct evidence as to what was taking place in these months is, however, lacking; the *Athenaeum*, which had been enthusiastically reporting the debates about the RGS and other learned societies, appears not to have printed anything further about possible new societies between 2 May and 12 December. On the latter date, it announced:

A new society is about to be established in London, under the name of the Columbus Society – somewhat similar, we understand to the Camden, Shakespeare and other literary societies; but the particular rules are not as yet laid down. The object which the Society has in view is the publication of early and rare voyages and travels, both in print and MS. – applicable to all countries and written in all languages: the Society doing as a body what Hakluyt and Purchas were doing individually centuries before. The first general meeting will take place on Tuesday next at the London

---

1846; *The Athenaeum*, 964, 18 April 1846, pp. 395–7; 965, 25 April 1846, p. 425; 966, 2 May 1846, pp. 452–4. A short account of the 1846 RGS crisis, including a reference to a further attack on the Society in September 1846 in the *Pictorial Times* (which sounds like another Cooley diatribe), appears in Mill, *Record*, pp. 55–6. But Mill was apparently unaware of the key function of the *Athenaeum* in the debates and of the leading part played by Cooley.

[1] For details, see Bridges, 'Cooley', pp. 281, 284–6.

Library in St. James's Square, at 2 o'clock; – Sir Roderick Murchison in the chair.[1]

This announcement contains several points of interest. The reference to the literary societies, the stated object of publishing early and rare voyages and travels, and the mention of the analogy with Hakluyt all suggest that Cooley was being pushed further in the direction of setting up an antiquarian society rather than any sort of real rival to the RGS. It seems unlikely that Murchison would have lent his name and influence to the venture had it seemed to threaten the position of the RGS. A recent study of Murchison sees his presidency of the Hakluyt Society as part of his promotion of expansionist and imperial enthusiasm, because 'publishing historical accounts of early geographical discoveries . . . emphasised the causal links between exploration and global power'.[2] Whether or not such an interpretation of Murchison's later role in the Hakluyt Society (which seems in truth to have been very limited) can be justified, it hardly explains what was happening in December 1846. Nevertheless there are indications that Cooley's projected society, despite the statement about its activities being 'applicable to all countries and all languages', was being pushed in the direction of appealing particularly to contemporary feelings about the British marine and imperial heritage.

Comparison between the prospectus of the Columbus Society, which was obviously in the hands of whoever wrote the *Athenaeum* report, and that of the Hakluyt Society helps to elucidate these matters. However, reference to the prospectuses raises puzzling points about the article by Foster in the 1946 Centenary volume. Foster noted the meeting of 15 December 1846 on the basis, as he carefully pointed out, of the evidence of the therefore clearly subsequent Hakluyt Society prospectus. A copy of this prospectus – he added – had been discovered by Mr Skelton in the Library of the British Museum and he supplied the Library call mark.[3] The item so indicated turns out to be one of a number of prospectuses for societies of various kinds projected in the 1840s. These prospectuses seem to have been gathered together and put within hard covers in July 1856 – presumably for the convenience of the Library. The prospectus for the

---

[1] *The Athenaeum*, 998, 12 December 1846, p. 1270.

[2] R. A. Stafford, *Scientist of Empire, Sir Roderick Murchison. Scientific Exploration and Victorian Imperialism*, Cambridge, 1989, p. 24. For a fuller discussion of Stafford's views, see pp. 230–31 below.

[3] Foster, 'A Retrospect', p. 144. No other copy of the prospectus has been found. It is, however, possible that copies will yet turn up, perhaps among private papers.

HAKLUYT SOCIETY.

The object of this Society is to print, in English, for distribution among its members, rare and valuable Voyages, Travels, and Geographical Records—including the more important early narratives of British enterprise.

The highly-prized collections of this kind, made by Ramusio, Hakluyt, Purchas, and De Bry, were all produced between the middle of the 16th and that of the 17th century. Europe still felt, during that period, the emotions awakened by the discovery of a New World, and viewed with pleasure the spirit of enterprise resulting from the impulse of that remarkable event.

The first steps leading to a communication with the inhabitants of strange and distant countries, are naturally those which we regard with the deepest interest. Yet the extension of scientific research into every region of the earth, and the frequent, though less prominent discoveries which affect the channels of commerce, and with them the fortunes of nations, furnish materials of the greatest importance to the history of civilization.

This store of knowledge increases daily. Exploration and discovery advance without intermission; while the general progress of learning throws new light continually on the writings of early travellers.

The publication of Hakluyt's collection may be ranked among the many characteristic distinctions of the age of Elizabeth. That writer had it in view, as he informs us, "for the benefit and honour of his country, to bring Antiquities, smothered and buried in dark silence, to light; and to preserve several memorable exploits by the English nation achieved, from the greedy and devouring jaws of oblivion." But now the time seems to be arrived when the treasures of the older geographical information, may be advantageously reproduced on a plan more comprehensive than Hakluyt's, as well as more in the spirit of an advanced literary age.

COLUMBUS SOCIETY.

The object of this Society is to print for its members a collection of the most rare and valuable Voyages, Travels, and Geographical Records.

The highly-prized collections of this kind, made by Ramusio, Hackluyt, Purchas, and De Bry, were all produced between the middle of the 16th and that of the 17th century. Europe still felt, during that period, the emotions awakened by the discovery of a New World, and viewed with pleasure the spirit of enterprize resulting from the impulse of that remarkable event.

The first steps leading to a communication with the inhabitants of strange and distant countries, are naturally those which we regard with the deepest interest. Yet the extension of scientific research into every region of the earth, and the frequent, though less prominent discoveries which affect the channels of commerce, and with them the fortunes of nations, furnish materials of the greatest importance to the history of civilization.

This store of knowledge increases daily. Exploration and discovery advance without intermission; while the general progress of learning throws new light continually on the writings of early travellers.

The publication of Hackluyt's collection may be ranked among the many characteristic distinctions of the age of Elizabeth. That writer had it in view, as he informs us, "for the benefit and honour of his country, to bring Antiquities, smothered and buried in dark silence, to light; and to preserve several memorable exploits by the English nation achieved when the greedy and devouring jaws of oblivion." But now the time seems to be worldly and advantageously reproduced on a plan more comprehensive than Hackluyt's, as well as more in the spirit of an advanced literary age, so as to commemorate the constant progress of exploration and intercourse, of the study of man, and of physical inquiry throughout the globe.

THE COLUMBUS SOCIETY AND THE HAKLUYT SOCIETY (1846)
The first page of the prospectuses.

Columbus Society is included.[1] It is printed in the same style and on the same sort of paper as that for the Hakluyt Society, and, as will be seen, much of the wording is identical; it is therefore beyond any reasonable doubt that this is the original proposal which attracted those interested to the 15 December meeting. Since the collection of prospectuses had clearly been in Skelton's hands, one must suppose that he did not notice the Columbus Society prospectus and sent only a copy of the Hakluyt Society prospectus to Foster, for it is difficult to believe that so meticulous a scholar as Foster would have failed to note the significance of the former prospectus had he been shown the whole collection. Skelton presumably also failed to notice another interesting item in the collection, a prospectus proposing the establishment of a 'Cabot Society' to publish works 'upon the Maritime History of the British Isles from the earliest times to the present day'. A handwritten note dates this to 1845 but no indication is given as to who was responsible for the prospectus. Its style does not seem quite right for Cooley, who, in any case, wished the British to become aware of foreign sources. Perhaps, however, some of the individuals who transformed the Columbus Society into the Hakluyt Society were associated with this earlier and presumably abortive proposal.

There are further puzzles about the prospectuses which are more directly relevant to the story which follows. It is not absolutely clear when the 'Hakluyt Society' version was produced. Since it records the results of the 15 December meeting and lists a Provisional Council it was certainly produced before the first general meeting of the Society on 4 March 1847 when a permanent Council was elected.[2] The Provisional Council had asked Cooley and Bolton Corney to draw up a 'new prospectus', to which a list of works proposed for publication would be annexed. This prospectus was discussed and amended on 2 March and then approved by the General Meeting two days later.[3] The Society's Minutes do not record the text of what Cooley and Corney produced but it is possible, and perhaps likely, that it was the document which Skelton found and Foster quoted. However, an alternative possibility is that Foster's 'Hakluyt Society' prospectus was produced at some time between the meeting of 15 December and the first meeting of the Provisional Council on 26 January. If this was the case, then the version that Cooley and Corney produced by 2 March was the relatively

---

[1] The call number for the bound collection is 741.k.1. Each item has an identifying number – (7) for the Cabot Society, (11) for the Columbus Society, and (14) for the Hakluyt Society.

[2] HSCM, 4 March 1847.

[3] Ibid., 2 February, 16 February, 2 March, 4 March 1847.

short description of the Society and its aims eventually printed in the fourth of the Society's issued volumes.[1] This would mean that there were three different prospectuses.[2] Be that as it may, the discussion which follows is based on a comparison of the two prospectuses found in the British Library collection. The existence of the two prospectuses, together with yet more evidence from the *Athenaeum*, makes it possible to investigate further the inception of the new Society.

Cooley modified

The first issue to be considered is that of the name. In his *Maritime and Inland Discovery*, Cooley had given a verdict on Columbus which clearly indicated that he thought him to be the most important of the great discoverers. This was both because of the man's 'individual genius and enthusiasm' and because his achievement in discovering the New World was 'superior ... in its important consequences to any other that occurs in the history of man'.[3] Such being Cooley's assessment, it is not surprising that he thought 'Columbus Society' the most appropriate name. The explanation eventually given in the *Athenaeum* for the switch from this name, which clearly was effected at the meeting of 15 December, was that 'Columbus Society' was

> on further reflection, considered to be descriptive rather of a Society established for promulgating fresh geographical discoveries, than of one for printing the labours of early voyagers and travellers; and the name of the Hakluyt Society was therefore substituted in its stead.[4]

This seems a slightly odd argument, but presumably the point that was being made was that Columbus was a doer and Hakluyt a recorder. Interestingly, the *Athenaeum* report goes on to state that the change was made the more easily because 'the Society had been originally so called and the name had given way to Columbus only because of the greater universality of the latter'. It therefore seems that there had been a series of arguments over a name and that Cooley had lost.

The actual reason for the change of name was, almost certainly, that

---

[1] Cooley, *Drake His Voyage*, pp. 1–4.

[2] However, this third document may be what a volume in the Hakluyt Society archives entitled 'Reports of the Hakluyt Society' seems to call brochures or 'Lists'. However, a further point in favour of the third prospectus possibility is that the list of proposed works appears at the end of the description as the Council had directed; in both the Columbus Society and Hakluyt Society versions in the British Library, the list of works comes in the middle.

[3] Cooley, *Maritime and Inland Discovery*, I, p. 381.

[4] *The Athenaeum*, 999, 19 December 1846, p. 1301.

many of those at the 15 December meeting wanted slightly less universality and rather more emphasis on national achievement.

The opening words of the Columbus Society prospectus are as follows:

> The object of this Society is to print for its members a collection of the most rare and valuable Voyages, Travels, and Geographical Records.

The Hakluyt Society prospectus changes this statement, first, in an unimportant way by inserting that the new editions would be in English for distribution among the members, but secondly, by an addition which modifies the thrust of the aims: the general reference to 'geographical records' is qualified by the addition 'including the more important early narratives of British enterprise'. At a later point, Cooley's original prospectus had quoted Hakluyt's own aims, the desire

> for the honour and benefit of his country, to bring Antiquities, smothered and buried in dark silence, to light; and to preserve several memorable exploits by the English nation achieved, from the greedy and devouring jaws of oblivion.

Cooley had followed this quotation by remarking,

> But now the time seems to be arrived when the rich treasures of geographical information already accumulated may be advantageously reproduced on a plan more comprehensive than Hakluyt's, as well as more in the spirit of an advanced literary age *so as to commemorate the achievements of all civilized nations in the career of discovery, and to exhibit the constant progress of exploration and intercourse, of the study of man, and of physical inquiry throughout the globe.* (my emphasis)

The last part of the sentence, which very much represented Cooley's view of what was needed, was omitted from the Hakluyt Society prospectus. Much in the same spirit, the list of records which Cooley had nominated as being suitable candidates for editing and publication was reproduced with only minor changes, but with the significant addition of accounts of Drake's circumnavigation, Frobisher's North-West voyages, the Sherleys in Persia, and the discovery of the Canary Islands, all except the last being 'British heritage' items.[1] Nevertheless, the eventual list contained all the items which Cooley had wanted, the

---

[1] It is of interest that J. A. Froude wrote in 1852: 'It was, therefore, with no little interest that we heard of the formation of a society which was to employ itself, as we understood, in republishing in some accessible form, some, if not all of the invaluable records compiled or composed by Richard Hakluyt' ('England's Forgotten Worthies', *Westminster Review*, n.s. 1, 1852, pp. 32–67, on p. 34). Of course, Froude had particular axes to grind but his assumption about the desirable aims of the Society may have been more widely shared.

majority of these being non-British and including, for example, the travels of Ibn Baṭṭūṭa – a project which no doubt Cooley would have been gratified to know would be realised (or to date almost completely realised), albeit not until 150 years later.

The changes noted so far indicate clearly enough one direction in which Cooley's project was being modified. What seems less clear is whether, at this early stage, it had been decided to make the coverage entirely historical. 'Rare and valuable Voyages, Travels and Geographical Records' could comprehend contemporary or near-contemporary travels like those which Cooley had tried to introduce to English-speaking readers in his *World Surveyed* volumes. However, in the passage quoted above from the Columbus Society prospectus, the reference to the 'rich treasures of geographical information already accumulated', which is somewhat ambivalent on the point, was altered after 15 December to 'the treasures of the older geographical information'. Then, towards the end of the revised document, a resolution passed at the 15 December meeting was quoted, to the effect that the volumes to be distributed to members should include travels dating 'from an early period of exploratory enterprise to the circumnavigation of Dampier.' This formulation was changed, apparently when the laws of the Society were devised by a special Committee, to what appears in the printed version first published in 1849, 'from an early period to the beginning of the eighteenth century'.[1] Thus, during the months of December 1846 and January 1847 Cooley had to modify his ideas in significant ways as the price of bringing the new society into being. Which individual or individuals had been able to prevail upon this distinctly difficult man to accept these changes and yet continue to be associated with the venture as its first Secretary?

At the meeting of 15 December it was Murchison who was in the chair and his influence was no doubt important, even although he had not yet reached the position of eminence and power which he was later to enjoy. Mrs Middleton has implied a special connection between Murchison and Cooley but I have found no evidence of this Murchison attended nine Council meetings up to the end of Cooley's tenure of the secretaryship on 1 May 1849 and some of these, it is true, were important ones. But there were twenty-four other meetings which he did not attend and he missed one of the two general meetings held up to that time.[2] The

---

[1] Hakluyt Society Record Book, p. 1; HSCM, 26 January 1847; Cooley, *Drake his Voyage*, p. 5 (Law I).

[2] Middleton, 'Hakluyt Society', p. 13. Mrs Middleton sees Murchison as important in the affairs of the Hakluyt Society and talks of him, for instance, assembling the first Council. My impression is rather that others took the key initiatives and regarded Murchison as the right person to hold a virtually figurehead position.

William Desborough Cooley c.1870 (top left): Vice-Admiral Sir Charles Malcolm (top right): Henry Yule (bottom left): Sir Clements Markham (bottom right).

definitive motion at the 15 December meeting which led to the setting up of the Society, accompanied by the remit to publish editions of the works of travellers only up to the time of Dampier, was proposed by Dr Andrew Smith and seconded by Sir Charles Malcolm. Dr (later Sir) Andrew Smith was an Army medical officer whose early career was in South Africa and who showed great practical interest in explorations beyond the boundaries of Cape Colony.[1] It seems not inconceivable that Cooley had corresponded with Smith on South African matters and he may have been someone whom Cooley regarded as an ally. In the case of Malcolm the evidence is less speculative. After an impressive early career in the Royal Navy, Malcolm had become commander of the Bombay Marine, a service which later became the Indian Navy. He sent officers on exploratory and surveying expeditions to various parts of the western Indian Ocean, he founded the Bombay Geographical Society, and on his return to Britain in 1838 became associated with the RGS.[2] Maintaining his interest in the coasts around the approaches to India, in the late 1840s he appears to have encouraged and in some way commissioned Cooley to write a paper on 'Regio Cinnamomifera', that is, Somalia.[3] This suggests that he had some regard for Cooley. It was Malcolm who, in the period 1846 to 1849 when the Hakluyt Society was being established, chaired all the 24 meetings which Murchison failed to chair. Patently an important figure (but one whose part in the early history of the Society has not been sufficiently appreciated), it is not hard to believe that his qualities included the ability to keep Cooley in harness.

The other figure with whom it seems Cooley had to work closely in this formative period was Bolton Corney. At the relevant period, this critic, bibliophile and antiquary was associated with the Shakespeare and Camden Societies and was linked in some way to the British Museum Library.[4] At an early meeting of the Hakluyt Society he undertook to edit Middleton's 1604–1606 voyage but the enterprise dragged on for some ten years before eventual completion.[5] Corney

---

[1] *DNB*; for Smith's later controversial career, see John Shepherd, *The Crimean Doctors*, 2 vols, Liverpool, 1991, passim.

[2] *DNB*; C. R. Markham, *A Memoir on the Indian Surveys*, 2nd ed., London, 1878, pp. 13–14, 23; C. R. Low, *History of the Indian Navy*, 2 vols, London, 1877, II, pp. 68–94; for an obituary notice, see R. I. Murchison, 'Annual Anniversary Address to the Royal Geographical Society', *JRGS*, 32, 1852, pp. lxiv–lxv.

[3] W. D. Cooley, 'On the Regio Cinnamomifera of the Ancients', *JRGS*, 29, 1849, pp. 166–91; Bridges, 'Cooley', p. 36; Roy Bridges, 'The Visit of Frederick Forbes to the Somali Coast in 1833', *International Journal of African Historical Studies*, 19, 1986, pp. 679–91, on pp. 680–82.

[4] *DNB*.

[5] See pp. 89–90 below.

seems to have been present at the meeting of 15 December, and he became a member of the Provisional Council, and also (it seems likely) of the Committee which was charged with the task of drawing up the laws that were confirmed when the Provisional Council first met on 26 January 1847. At that meeting Corney, Smith and Cooley were given the key task of producing the list of works to be edited and published, while at the next meeting a week later Corney and Cooley were asked to produce the new prospectus to which the list of proposed publications would be annexed. Thus it is clear that Cooley and Corney must have worked closely together in the first weeks of the Society's existence.[1]

Whoever it may have been who most influenced him, Cooley it was who, from December 1846, had the task of establishing the infant Hakluyt Society on a sound footing. He was, in effect, Secretary and Treasurer. A separate treasurer's office seems to have been envisaged at the inaugural meeting and W.R. Hamilton was designated for the office.[2] But although Hamilton became a member of both the Provisional and the first permanent Council, the Society's records do not give any indication that he ever acted as Treasurer. Instead, subscribers were required to send their one guinea subscriptions to Cooley himself, at his home in King Street. In his original prospectuses Cooley had argued that, given the kind of association he was proposing, members would be able to get volumes at little more than the cost of the printing and paper.[3] No doubt he was somewhat naive about costing and financial matters. Nevertheless, his instinct was right and he established a precedent for which members have had reason to be grateful for 150 years; few would question the contention that, with its academically high-quality editions still handsomely printed and bound, the Hakluyt Society offers better value than almost any other academic publishing society.

Cooley in retreat

The foregoing discussion has covered the initial birth-pangs of the Hakluyt Society. By the General Meeting on 4 March 1847 the Society had a prospectus, a set of laws, a list of works which were to be published, and a constitution providing for a President, two Vice-Presidents, a Secretary and seventeen other members elected annually. Later in the same month, the Council decided on a printing format for

---

[1] Both men suffered from deafness though whether this would have drawn them together it is difficult to say.
[2] *The Athenaeum*, 999, 14 December 1846, p. 1301.
[3] *Prospectus of the Columbus Society*, p. 2; *Prospectus of the Hakluyt Society*, p. 2.

its volumes, although it was not until August 1847 that the famous vignette on the cover of each volume showing Magellan's ship, the 'Victoria', was chosen by Malcolm, Smith, Corney, Captain Bethune, Major and Cooley. (It is not clear which of them had the original idea.) It was also as late as August, surprisingly, that editors were authorised to print introductions. Perhaps this was why the first volume had only seven pages of prefatory and introductory material. Nevertheless, by the end of 1847 that first volume, an edition of an account of the voyage of Sir Richard Hawkins to the South Sea, and a second one, an edition of the letters of Columbus, in this case very substantially introduced and annotated, had appeared.[1] From the distance of 150 years this seems to be very reasonable progress indeed. But already some problems were emerging which, if they were not entirely Cooley's fault, he did not readily overcome. By March 1849 it had become clear to himself and to others that it would be better for him to resign as Secretary.

At the time of the first General Meeting the *Athenaeum* believed that the Society's prospects looked good. It welcomed the first two volumes, while offering certain detailed criticisms. However, by April 1848 it was worried that the first Annual Report showed expenditure to be greater than receipts. It noted that the report admitted that the Society had been set up at a time when the country was 'filled with gloomy apprehensions'; and by March 1847 Britain was indeed suffering 'dearth and famine' and 'commercial embarrassments'.[2] We may assume that Cooley was particularly conscious of the tragic Irish Famine. Whether these general troubles, or the more particular feeling among some subscribers that two volumes was an insufficient return for one guinea, led to the resignation of a number of members which now occurred is difficult to say.[3] In the report for 1848 which appeared in 1849 it was stated that subscribers had expected three volumes a year, and that these would cost about £120 each to print. Hence an annual income of at least £400 was required, whereas only £309 4s 3d had been received in subscriptions.[4] Problems also arose in respect of the agency handling

---

[1] HSCM, pp. 1–9; HSRB, pp. 1–4. Although dated 1847, the second published volume actually appeared a few days into 1848.

[2] *The Athenaeum*, 1011, 13 March 1847, p. 287; 1058, 5 February 1848, pp. 34–5; 1067, 8 April 1848, p. 367. For the complications over the Society's annual reports for the years 1847, 1848 and 1849, see p. 54 note 1 above.

[3] HSRHS, 'Report for 1849'. The report claims 276 members as compared with 247 in 1848, but in the first printed list of members published in the volume issued in April 1849 only 219 are listed. Perhaps, therefore, 28 had resigned before the rise in numbers to 276 began in 1849. However, it is difficult to be precise without knowing the dates to which the list or the claimed numbers relate.

[4] The report was published as preliminary pages to HS 5.

the printed volumes and the delivery of volumes to the subscribers. It was alleged that the chosen agent, Rodd, had entrusted the Society's business to others who neglected it.[1] If this was the case, Cooley ought to have checked the arrangement for himself. But it seems that overall he was beginning to feel pessimistic about the future of the Society. Much later, Markham reported that Cooley threw up his task 'in despair', because he thought that the project to produce narratives of voyages and travels 'must fail through the absence of competent editors in this country, and lack of interest in the subject'.[2] If indeed one of the reasons for Cooley's resignation on 1 May 1849 was that he believed it difficult to find competent editors, it may have been because he was still thinking in the way he had done in 1846 – that what the Society needed was a series of editors capable of analysing a source in detail and comparing it with other relevant sources in order to elicit important geographical information. There is no direct evidence on this point. But something can be said about a crisis which developed in March 1849 and about various other factors which may have contributed to Cooley's difficulties.

Despite his earlier complaints about the book-keeping of the RGS Secretary, Cooley seems not to have kept proper records of all the Hakluyt Society subscriptions.[3] He may have become neglectful in other ways. On several occasions in 1848 the Council Minutes do not report him as present at meetings, although it may be allowed that this may have been only because the presence of the Secretary was taken for granted.[4] It is, however, not impossible that R. H. Major, who first attended a Council Meeting on 16 March 1847, and who was present at almost all meetings up to the time when he officially became Secretary, was already fulfilling some secretarial functions when Cooley was unavailable. In any case, the presence of Major and his patron, Sir Henry Ellis, on the Council was a sign that the Society was coming more and more into the orbit of the British Museum and that this part of the academic and official establishment was taking over responsibility for the Society's activities. There is no sign that Cooley resented this development: when specifically questioned on the point in 1849, he twice insisted that he had always been well and courteously treated by British Museum officials.[5] There may have been other members of the

---

[1] HSRB, p. 4.

[2] Markham included these remarks in an obituary of R. H. Major, in *PRGS*, n.s. 13, 1891, p. 489.

[3] HSCM, 20 November 1849.

[4] Cooley is mentioned as present at only four out of the twenty meetings between December 1847 and his resignation.

[5] See p. 54 note 2 above.

Council whom Cooley found less agreeable. C. T. Beke was a member of the Council by 1849 and Cooley was embroiled in disputes with Beke over questions of East African geography, this being a period when actual observations, including that of snow on the summit of Kilimanjaro, had begun to call into question some of the conclusions of Cooley's 1845 article. Cooley, however, was busily engaged in writing his Somalia article and was preparing his book, *Inner Africa Laid Open.*[1]. These preoccupations must have taken up much of his time, and inasmuch as Cooley's obsessional attitude to problems of East Africa's geography amounted to something akin to mental unbalance, it may well have been that his over-wrought condition was becoming apparent in 1849.

Whatever the reasons, by 1849 Cooley was patently unable to cope with the crisis in the affairs of the young Society he had founded. On 20 February 1849, the Council decided to refer the issue of 'the mode of publication at present adopted by the Hakluyt Society' to a sub-committee of Ellis, Malcolm and, perhaps ominously, Beke. The Annual General Meeting was postponed, and apparently Cooley's draft Annual Report was also referred to the sub-committee. As Secretary, Cooley no doubt participated in the discussions of the sub-committee and he drew up its report. On 20 March the report 'was read, but some expressions in it being objected to, it was not received'.[2] The ostensible subject of debate and discussion was the problem of Rodd's apparent inefficiency in distributing and selling the volumes but it seems almost certain that other issues had come up. Three days after the 20 March meeting, Malcolm, who had been unable to attend, in a letter to Ellis referred to Cooley's 'dispairing' [sic] attitude to the Society. Malcolm seems to have been reacting to what, it would seem, either Ellis, or possibly Cooley himself with whom he had been in contact, had reported – that at the meeting Cooley had acknowledged that he had dissuaded people from paying their subscriptions. Although Malcolm's reaction was in the circumstances mild, he clearly now thought that Cooley should resign for the good of the Society, and he wondered whether such a 'delicate business' meant that the President ought to become actively involved. He also thought that a paid secretary would have been desirable had the Society been able to afford it.[3] In the event,

---

[1] Bridges, 'Cooley', pp. 40–41; *The Athenaeum*, 1119, 7 April 1849 p. 357; 1125, 19 May 1849, p. 516, etc.

[2] HSCM, 20 February, 5 March, 12 March, 20 March 1849.

[3] MS Edinburgh, National Library of Scotland, Acc. 8589, Malcolm to Ellis, 23 March 1849. The letter was noted in Middleton, 'Hakluyt Society', p. 13. Other documents in this collection relate to much earlier periods of Malcolm's career.

the President did appear at the meeting of 3 April which set aside the sub-committee report and instead ordered that Rodd appoint a collector, that he set up arrangements with country booksellers, and that he deal with subscriptions more expeditiously.[1]

The crisis was resolved in part because Rodd promptly died and so a new agent had to be found.[2] But it was also because, on 1 May, Cooley himself resigned. The Council Minutes provide the following statement.

> The Council having considered the desire more than once expressed of Mr Cooley that a person be found to occupy the post of Secretary which he retires from on account of [his deafness *crossed out*] the state of his health – resolved that the cordial thanks of the Council be given to Mr Cooley not only for his able services as Secretary, but also for having planned & originated the Hakluyt Society. In expressing their deep regret at losing the services of Mr Cooley, the Council hear with pleasure that Mr Major will accept the office.[3]

It would be wrong to regard this statement as merely formal and perhaps even hypocritical, although it obviously leaves out much of the story. The deleted reference to deafness is probably significant; the affliction does seem to have begun to isolate Cooley more and more, and doubtless this contributed to his increasingly unreasonable behaviour over geographical questions.[4]

Before he resigned, Cooley had prepared the one volume he was to edit for the Society. Later there was to be some thought of his editing the travels of Varthema, and then, in 1854, it was stated that he would take on Dos Santos on 'Eastern Ethiopia', but neither project seems to have been pursued.[5] In April 1848 he himself had suggested Drake's last voyage as a subject for an edition, and although the Council responded by suggesting that other items should be added, by July Cooley had prepared the Maynarde account, with a Spanish narrative of the attack on Puerto Rico to accompany it. The whole edition amounted to only 65 pages with no more than three and a half pages of introduction. It is hard to understand why Cooley chose documents which have little or no geographical interest. Perhaps he thought he must pay his tribute to

---

[1] HSCM, 3 April 1849.

[2] Foster, 'A Retrospect', p. 147.

[3] HSCM, 1 May 1849. The latter part of this minute was published in the (so-called) 'Report for 1848' (see p. 54 note 1 above).

[4] Bridges, 'Cooley', pp. 40–4, 282–4. Perhaps an attack of rheumatic fever in 1835 brought on Cooley's deafness; MS London, British Library, Add. 34617, f. 4, Cooley to Napier, 7 February 1835.

[5] HSRHS, Annual Report for 1849, p. 3 (presumably written in 1850); 'Lists' for 1854.

British enterprise, but it is more likely that, given the complaints of subscribers, he wanted quickly to produce what would be, technically, a second volume for 1848.[1] In Cooley's introduction there is some echo of what must have been earlier arguments about the function of the Society. He says that Drake 'is one of the brightest ornaments' in Hakluyt's collection and that a Society continuing and completing the latter's work 'cannot be better employed than in publishing documents illustrating the life and achievements of that distinguished seaman [Drake]'. Yet a little later he notes that Maynarde's account tends to dispel the romance surrounding Drake's name and to remind us 'what sordid motives may be cloaked under the pretence of national glory, and how mistrustfully we ought to listen to the professedly generous instigators of war and rapine'.[2] Although the *Athenaeum* received the edition kindly, later scholars have understandably taken little or no notice of Cooley's edition. Only K. R. Andrews, in a definitive Hakluyt Society edition of the same (and other) documents, bothers to mention it and he says that although Cooley's was the first publication of Maynarde's narrative, there were 'many errors of transcription, a few of which are seriously misleading'.[3]

In memoriam

It is a pity that there is not a Hakluyt Society volume which could serve as a better memorial to Cooley; a pity, too, that there is not much more one can say about his association with the society which he had the wit to set up. He remained a member of the Council until 1858 but seems not to have taken any further active part in its deliberations.[4] No doubt this was mainly because he was so fully occupied in arguing with the explorers of East Africa and with the RGS. He remained a member of the Hakluyt Society and did not, in any of his later writings, criticise it or its officials. While it would be idle to deny that Cooley was self-opinionated, that he became an inflexible and obsessional scholar who often misused his knowledge, and that he was a poor administrator who did not give the Hakluyt Society the best start, he does deserve a rather better reputation than the ridicule or obscurity that has been his lot since his death in 1883. Certain of his writings, notably the *Maritime*

---

[1] HSCM, 18 April, 18 July 1848.

[2] Cooley, *Drake his Voyage*, pp. v, vi. Cooley would appear to have distrusted nationalism, whether Irish or English.

[3] *The Athenaeum*, 1121, 21 April 1849, p. 40; K. R. Andrews, ed., *The Last Voyage of Drake and Hawkins*, Cambridge, 1972 (HS 2/142), p. 85n. The errors are not detailed.

[4] Annual Reports, 1849–1859, in 'Reports of the Hakluyt Society'.

and Inland Discovery, the 1845 article, and his *Claudius Ptolemy and the Nile* of 1854, are worth some attention, while his final work, the *Physical Geography* of 1876, was a useful and sensible text for its day. But above all, at the time of its 150th Anniversary, it seems right that the Hakluyt Society should remember, with a measure of respect, its progenitor and founder.

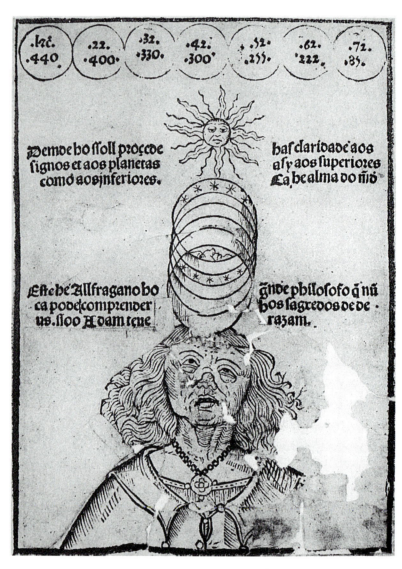

CELESTIAL NAVIGATION
From the *Regimento de Munich*, Lisbon, c. 1495.
Reproduced in HS 2/90 of 1944.

R. H. MAJOR

AND THE BRITISH MUSEUM

Tony Campbell

Richard Henry Major was Honorary Secretary of the Hakluyt Society for all but two of its first twenty years; he was a joint Honorary Secretary of the Royal Geographical Society for fifteen years; he was an active participant in the affairs of the Society of Antiquaries for twenty years; and he was, arguably, the leading figure in Britain in the history of cartography and discoveries. Above all, he was a member of the British Museum Library from the age of 25 until retirement forty years later, as the first and only Keeper of Maps. Despite this impressive range of achievements, Major has attracted no biographical notice since the entry in the original *Dictionary of National Biography*, conveniently published the year after his death. Nor, perhaps, have the similar contributions of the Museum colleagues of Major been given adequate recognition. The previously unremarked scale of their involvement in the early history of the Hakluyt Society is certainly not an isolated instance of the part they played in the intellectual life of the day. The central concern of this biographical memoir is with R. H. Major and the Hakluyt Society. But although it is, for convenience, structured to separate out Major's various professional activities from his private life, the result of this investigation makes the precisely opposite point: that domestic 'trivia' can be as informative as the measured deliberations of a governing body, that any search restricted to formal sources will miss many of the interconnections which help to explain how the intellectual life of Victorian London worked in practice. Like the novels of Major's contemporary Dickens, with their large but finite casts, those who supported Major in his various endeavours will reappear time and again in different contexts.

It is equally inadvisable to try to separate Major's private and Museum lives. It was prior friendship with the Principal Librarian that led to his entry into the Museum; his younger daughter would choose a British Museum Library colleague for her husband, with three others acting as trustees of the settlement; and at Major's death two of that trio would serve as his executors. Nor should the symbiotic relationship between the Museum and the Hakluyt Society be understated. No fewer than twenty-three Museum men were to play a role in the Society during the time of Major's involvement.[1]

The early years

Major was born on 3 October 1818 at 38 Old Street [Road], Shoreditch, where Islington and Hackney meet the City of London. He would spend the next sixty years living in those two inner city boroughs. Richard Henry Major was named after his father, who had married Elizabeth Edge in 1816.[2] The elder Richard Henry was a surgeon, formerly a prize pupil of the celebrated anatomist, John Abernethy, at St Bartholomew's, but he died at the age of 29 when Major was only three. Within less than a year his mother married again, on her twenty-sixth birthday. She and her new husband, Felix Cornuel, apparently abandoned Major and his elder brother Seymour Edward to the care of their paternal grandfather, Joseph. At the latter's death in 1835 the brothers, aged 17 and 16, were left effectively as orphans.[3] Their father had been an only child and their mother, despite producing seven

[1] I wish to acknowledge, with gratitude, the help of the following in the preparation of this essay: Peter Allpress (on bookplates); Christopher Date, British Museum Archives; Roger Evans, Department of Manuscripts, British Library; Paul Goldman, Department of Prints and Drawings, British Museum; P. R. Harris, British Library (retired); Francis Herbert and Paula Lucas, Royal Geographical Society; Seymour E. Major; Seymour Major; T. D. Mathew, Windsor Herald; Bernard Nurse, Society of Antiquaries; Dawn Squires, Archivist, Highgate Cemetery; Dr Andrew Tatham, Royal Geographical Society; Janet Wallace, British Museum Archives; Kay Walters, The Athenaeum.

[2] He was christened at St Leonard's Shoreditch on 29 October 1818; his parents had married on 4 April 1816, at St George's, Hanover Square. Information from a genealogical manuscript with the descendants [hereafter Gen. MS].

[3] See Gen. MS, and *Biography of R. H. Major, F. S. A. &c. From materials supplied by himself at the request of the Author, J. H.*, London (privately printed), 1886, p. 3. The *Biography* is a curious work. There is no copy in the British Library [hereafter BL] or the library of the Royal Geographical Society [herafter RGS]; a photocopy was kindly supplied by a descendant. Published the year after Major had severed all formal links with his professional past, it is effectively an extended premature obituary (for further comment, see p. 138, note 3, below). The effect of Major's father's death on his mentor, Abernethy, is noted in the extracts from Major's lost 'Reminiscences' made by his daughter (MS London, Royal Geographical Society Archives [hereafter RGSA], Correspondence Block 1881–90: 'Evans, I.G.'). (The extracts contain significant inaccuracies: Major's father died in 1822, not 1821; his mother was then 25 not 22. Major clearly did not have access to the more accurate biographical information that was passed down to his brother's descendants.) Regarding addresses, there is a minor confusion in the sources: on entering Merchant Taylors' School in 1832 Major gave his address as that of his birthplace, Old Street Road, but his grandfather, according to his will (proved 1 July 1835), lived at 34 Middlesex Place, Hackney Road.

further children, as the Cornuels moved from one Islington or Hackney address to another, seems to have had no role in the boys' upbringing.[1]

It is reasonable to suppose that Major felt keenly the lack of parents and that Sir Henry Ellis to some extent acted as a substitute father. Their connection goes back, at least, to the four years that Major spent at Merchant Taylors' School. Surprisingly, his elder brother Seymour did not precede him there, nor was there any evident family connection with the school. Sir Henry Ellis, however, was a former pupil of the school, and his brother, the Reverend John Joseph Ellis, taught at the school for forty years, rising to be second master.[2] It is not clear when Major met Sir Henry, described in Major's dedication to his 1851 Hakluyt Society edition of Herberstein as 'his earliest surviving friend'. Taken literally, Ellis's comment in an 1844 recommendation of Major, to the effect that he had known Major 'for the greater portion of his life', should refer to 1831 at the latest, the year before Major went to Merchant Taylors' as a boy of fourteen. If this were the case, it might have bearing on the choice of school. But more plausibly, the two had probably first encountered one another in June 1832 when Major joined the school to which Ellis's own son, Frederick Charles (four years younger than Major), had come the previous December.[3] After Major's death, his daughter would refer to the 'kindness and cordial liking shown him by Mr [sic] and Mrs Henry Ellis and they never ceased to be his true and affectionate friend'.[4]

Proof of the Ellis friendship would come a few years after Major left school but now he was destined to follow his grandfather's wish and enter the Church. That resolve, however, was swiftly set aside 'at the expense of forfeiting a handsome legacy from a great-uncle', and he left

---

[1] Major's own biographical notes make no further mention of his mother after her remarriage, although the choice of a Cornuel daughter as godmother to one of Seymour's children in 1860 shows that some form of contact was maintained. This was after Major's mother's death in 1847 and his stepfather's, apparently in the 1830s.

[2] Charles J. Robinson, *A Register of the Scholars admitted into Merchant Taylors' School from A.D. 1562 to 1874*, 2 vols, Lewes, 1882–3, II, pp. 142, 249; E. P. Hart, *Merchant Taylors' School Register 1561–1934*, 2 vols, London, 1936, entries for the Ellis brothers. Major joined in June 1832 and left in 1836, not 1839 as Robinson states. Major maintained contact with the school, for example attending the 1878 Dinner of the OMT [Old Merchant Taylors, i.e., former pupils] (MS London, British Museum [hereafter BM] Map Department letterbooks, letter to the Dinner Secretary, 14 May 1878). There is a further possible connection between the Ellis and Major families via the parish of St. Leonard's, Shoreditch. Sir Henry wrote a history of the parish (published in 1798); his brother was at some stage 'Lecturer' there; both Major's father and grandfather lived in the parish, and Major was christened at the church.

[3] MS London, BM Archives [hereafter BMA], 'R. H. Major. Testimonials Jan [9] 1844'; Robinson, *Register*, II, p. 248.

[4] 'Reminiscences'.

school, aged eighteen. A biography of Major produced in 1886 'from materials supplied by himself', sketched out his early career as follows:

> He was received as a clerk into an eminent German mercantile house in London, and afterwards into an equally important Spanish house; but, after six years' trial, he found a commercial career entirely unsuited both to his tastes and his capacity, and, contenting himself with having acquired the knowledge of two additional languages and some acquaintance with business details, finally relinquished it.[1]

Shortly after this, at a time when, as Major would later describe his situation, 'I was of no profession, was then entirely unoccupied and had a sufficient income of my own to raise me above anxiety', Robert Bell invited him to come on a Mediterranean cruise. How Major came to know Bell is unclear; Major's later note described his acquaintance with Bell as 'quite new' at that time. However, Bell and his son Robert, then aged thirteen, remained his life-long friends.[2]

The nine-month tour around the western Mediterranean must have been the greatest adventure in Major's life and presumably the longest period he spent abroad. From its anchorage alongside Norris Castle, Bell's 94–ton yacht *Kate*, a well-appointed vessel with a ten-man crew, set sail on 28 August 1842. Major's 300–page journal survives with a descendant.[3] This traces their leisurely course via Cadiz (one month), Tangier, Gibraltar, Ceuta, Algiers, then Tunis, Malta and Sicily (one month at each), the Naples region (almost two months), Pisa, Florence (to which Major was to return to live post-retirement), and then home via Malaga and Gibraltar, where the journal ends on 12 May 1843. Though this is not made explicit, Major may have had a role tutoring young Bob. He was certainly a constant companion to the elder Bell,

---

[1] J. H., *Biography*, p. 3.

[2] From 'Some Incidents in a Yacht Cruize in 1842–43', a two-page note by Major (now with a descendant) written in the 1880s. Bell, a wealthy man, had acquired Norris Castle – a fantasy castle built in 1799 by Wyatville – from its impecunious first owner, Lord Henry Seymour (John Gwilliam, *Norris Castle or Recent Tramps in the Isle of Wight*, London, 1845, sig. D1 verso). The BM letterbooks that document the later part of Major's career show that he stayed at Norris Castle on at least four occasions between 1875 and 1880, for up to six weeks at a time, the last visit a few months before Bell Senior's death.

[3] The manuscript has been kindly made available to the British Library and with permission a copy has been made for the use of researchers. The journal exhibits extensive additions and excisions, and has annotations such as 'new paragraph here' – all of which imply an intention to work it up, perhaps for publication. Once that plan had been abandoned, Major looked to produce extracts from it or perhaps a general summary. A rewritten selection from the Syracuse passage survives alongside the journal, as do the first two pages of an anecdotal summary (covering ff. 48–50), 'Some Incidents in a Yacht Cruize . . .', started post-retirement with the aim of providing amusement. As with most of Major's non-professional writing, none of these schemes was completed.

who clearly valued his linguistic abilities. The German and Spanish Major had learnt as a clerk, added to the Latin, Greek and French he had acquired at school, would later prove invaluable in his Museum and Hakluyt roles. Yet the man who was later to translate the Zeno narrative was at this stage 'ignorant of Italian'.[1]

Bell and Major clearly shared cultural interests. They went to the opera, which Major was able to compare with performances he had heard in Brussels and Paris, and spent most of their time in churches and museums, admiring, most particularly, classical sculpture. Major's journal, as a result, has a ponderous guide-book quality. It does, nevertheless, demonstrate the 24-year-old Major's genuine delight in art and history. The journal was written on the eve of his entry into the British Museum, but its scant references to books would have suggested a corner for him in the Department of Antiquities rather than the Library. His comparison between the Naples museum and the British Museum shows that he was already well acquainted with the latter. Equally, there are no hints of his later interest in cartography and the history of travel and discoveries, although he did remark on a 'good picture of Christopher Columbus' in the Cadiz archives.[2] Happily, the journal is not just one long history lesson. It has anecdote, commentary on local customs and even humour, though of a distinctly forced kind. Bell and Major travelled in style, being entertained by the Governor of Gibraltar and the Bey of Tunis. Sir Thomas Reade, the Consul-General who effected the latter introduction, gave them as a parting gift a gazelle (which later died), ostrich eggs, six special pigeons and a 'box of the most beautiful Carthage Marbles that could be selected'. It was not all ceremony, however, and on leaving Tunis, the cannon that had given the French a 13-gun salute at Algiers were run out against an expected night-time attack – a timely reminder of the dangers attached to a Mediterranean cruise in 1842.[3] As befitted a young bachelor, Major was ready with sweeping critiques of feminine charms: 'the exceedingly pretty faces, figures and dresses' in Cadiz; the Tuscan women, who are 'of middle stature and were it not for bad stays or something of that sort would be well made'; and the brilliant collection of beauty at Malaga, whose 'leer of their dark black eyes is peculiar but they certainly are wanting in the refined grace and easy dignity of the English fair'.[4] Thus

---

[1] 'Journal', f. 51ᵛ.

[2] Ibid., ff. 10, 74ᵛ.

[3] There were threats of a different kind, too: in Cadiz 'enough mire and filth to turn the stomach of an ostrich', while the Neapolitans were 'vermin covered'. Despite this, Bell and Major braved Naples 'to see the process of Macaroni eating which goes on in the streets about 7 o'clock'.

[4] Ibid., ff. 10, 18, 39–40, 73ᵛ, 106, 149ᵛ, 156ᵛ.

did Major return to England with aesthetic sensibilities finely tuned and heart intact.

It was shortly after the return of the *Kate* in the summer of 1843, as Seymour Major was going up to Cambridge (at the mature age of 26) to enter on the career in the Church which his brother had rejected, that the turning-point in Major's career occurred. Despite having had no formal education since school, nor relevant employment, his friend Sir Henry Ellis 'suggested to him that his education and attainments qualified him admirably for the position of an assistant in the British Museum Library', of which Ellis was Principal Librarian (or, in other words, chief officer). On 13 December Ellis recorded in his diary, 'Major dined with us' – presumably the occasion on which the suggestion was made.[1] Suitable references were procured: from Robert Bell on 28 December ('your attainments, capability and high moral worth'); from the Reverend J. J. Ellis ('he shewed great talent and persevering assiduity'); from Sir Henry ('my brother always spoke of him to me as one of his best scholars'); and from J. W. Bellamy, Headmaster of Merchant Taylors' ('he had reached a good place in the Sixth (or Upper) Form ... his talents were good and his principles sound'). Armed with these recommendations, Major duly entered the Museum on 13 January 1844, at the age of 25, as a Supernumary Assistant on '8s 9d a day, no gratuitous holidays and little hope of advancement'.[2]

The Hakluyt Society

Just as Ellis had been Major's route into the British Museum, so he was instrumental in getting Major elected to the Hakluyt Society Council at its first general meeting on 4 March 1847.[3] Ellis, along with John Edward Gray, Keeper of Zoology at the British Museum, had formed part of the eight-man steering group under the geologist, Sir Roderick Murchison. Major might describe Ellis as his 'friend', but, in reality, Ellis was forty-one years older than Major, and the disparity in their positions in the British Museum was the military equivalent of the difference between a general and a captain. Ellis's assistance, acknowledged by Major in the context of his entry into the Museum, can be assumed at many other points in the latter's career. Gray's membership of Council was shortlived but Ellis and Major both served almost up to

---

[1] J. H., *Biography*, p. 3; MS London, British Library [hereafter BL], Add. MS 36653, f. 10.

[2] BMA, 'Testimonials'; BL, Add. MS 36723, f. 510, letter of Major to Panizzi, 18 July 1866.

[3] A wrong date, 1846, is given in J. H., *Biography*, p. 3.

their deaths – giving in total 56 years to the Society and marking the beginning of the strong and continuing links between the British Museum (now British Library) and the Hakluyt Society.[1]

Major threw himself into the Society's affairs with enthusiasm. At the second official Council meeting, on 2 April 1847, he volunteered to translate the letters of Columbus. This was accepted at the next meeting (18 May).[2] On 20 July it was agreed that the original text would be included alongside the translation, a practice that was generally 'abhorrent to the early Councils'.[3] Matters then moved at sufficient speed for the book's publication to be fixed (on 21 December) for 8 January 1848. Nine months from proposal to delivery could well be a Hakluyt Society record. By translating, from both Spanish and Latin, and providing a scholarly introduction, Major was already showing the versatility that would be displayed in the seven further volumes he edited for the Society. He translated from Latin and Spanish select letters of Christopher Columbus (published 1847, revised 1870); from Latin, Herberstein's Russia (1851–2); from French and Italian, material on India in the fifteenth century (1857); from French, Béthencourt's 'Le Canarien' (1872); and from Italian, accounts of the voyages of the Zeno brothers (1873). He edited all these various works, and in addition Strachey's account of Virginia (1849) and accounts of early voyages to Terra Australis (1859). He also wrote introductions to editions of Mendoza on China (1854) and accounts of the Tartar conquest of that land (1855).[4]

The Society's minutes throw no light on the conception of Major's

---

[1] Ellis attended Council until 1864 and died in 1869; Major attended to 1884 and died in 1891. The British Library continues to provide the Society with its postal address.

[2] For Major's request to the RGS to borrow 'Navarrete' in connection with this work, see below p. 109.

[3] G. R. Crone, '"Jewells of Antiquitie": the work of the Hakluyt Society', *Geographical Journal*, 128, 1962, p. 324.

[4] R. H. Major, ed., *Select Letters of Christopher Columbus*, London, 1847 (HS 2), revised 1870 (HS 43) [including Major's reply to J. A. Froude]; *The History of Travaile into Virginia Britannia . . . by William Strachey*, London, 1849 (HS 6) [illustrated by Sarah E. Major]; *Notes upon Russia . . . by Baron Sigismund von Herberstein . . .*, 2 vols, London, 1851–2 (HS 10, 12) [illustrated by Sarah E. Major and W. B. Rye]; *India in the Fifteenth Century . . . from Latin, Persian, Russian and Italian Sources . . .*, London, 1858 (HS 22); *Early Voyages to Terra Australis . . .*, London, 1859 (HS 25); *The Canarian . . . by Messire Jean de Béthencourt*, London, 1872 (HS 46); *Voyages of the Venetian Brothers, Nicoló and Antonio Zeno . . .*, London, 1873 (HS 50). The 1851–2 work was dedicated to Sir R. I. Murchison, and the 1870 work to the Count de Lavradio. The 1859 work was followed in 1861 by a supplementary pamphlet on the 1601 Portuguese discovery of Australia: see p. 99, note 3 below. The introductions were to George T. Staunton, ed., *The History of the great and mighty Kingdom of China . . . by the Padre Juan Gonzalez de Mendoza . . .*, 2 vols, London, 1854 (HS 14, 15); Earl of Ellesmere, ed., *History of the two Tartar Conquerors of China . . .*, London, 1855 (HS 17).

second Hakluyt volume, Strachey's *Virginia Britannia*. However, as the source was a Sloane MS in the British Museum, Ellis's hand can perhaps be detected. Certainly, on 29 November 1849 Major wrote to Ellis about missing biographical details of Strachey – somewhat belatedly since the completed volume was laid on the table at the Council meeting less than three weeks later.[1] Well before the publication of this edition, Major had taken on the office of Honorary Secretary. The 'deafness' of the original Secretary, William Desborough Cooley – coyly toned down in the minutes to read 'the state of his health' – was obviously a contributory factor.[2] So too was the financial crisis surrounding the agency of Thomas Rodd. A subcommittee had been set up in early 1849 (with Ellis as one of its three members) to look into the unsatisfactory distribution arrangements. It is fair to speculate that Ellis had been instrumental in recommending the British Museum's book agent to the Hakluyt Society's founders, and that he felt considerable responsibility when things went wrong. Urgent meetings in March and April 1849 discussed how the relationship might be broken. This duly happened – though not in the way planned – when Rodd suddenly died on 23 April.[3]

In the absence of a surviving job description the responsibilities of the post Major took over on 1 May 1849 must be inferred. Vis-à-vis proposed publications, his role was presumably that expressed at the second Council meeting, when the Secretary was 'directed to report on their respective lengths and such other particulars as were calculated to afford adequate grounds for the decision of the Council'.[4] On the business side it was made plain that the authority transferred from Cooley to the subcommittee was returned to Major, who was requested, at his first meeting as Secretary, 'to make arrangements for the prompt distribution of the Society's volumes'. Two months later, at

---

[1] BL, Add. MS 34577, ff. 582–3; MS London, House of the Royal Geographical Society, Hakluyt Society Archives, Council Minutes [hereafter HSCM], 18 December 1849. The first page of the introduction to the edition explains Major's failure to find out anything about Strachey's life.

[2] HSCM, 1 May 1849. See also the fuller discussion of Cooley's resignation by Bridges on pp. 74–6 above. As a further link between the successive Honorary Secretaries, Cooley had given evidence on the subject of cataloguing to the 1848–9 Royal Commission into the British Museum (*House of Commons, Sessional Papers*, 1850, xxiv, paragraphs 4697–749).

[3] The man who had acted as auction agent for the British Museum, possessing 'probably more bibliographical knowledge of old English literature in particular, and of old books in general, than any other member of the trade' (Robert Cowtan, *Memories of the British Museum*, London, 1872, p. 325), seems not to have been so good with the Society's account books.

[4] HSCM, 20 April 1847.

the last meeting before a four month recess, the Secretary was 'empowered to use his own discretion during the recess in putting in hand any work which might appear to him desirable in the event of too great delay in the progress of the work already in course of preparation'. Clearly the Council now had full trust in their Honorary Secretary – and in Ellis to whom Major would presumably refer any problems. On return from the summer recess, Council was met with disturbing news of a discrepancy between money in the bank and the subscriptions reported by the late Secretary.[1] Happily, such problems were not to recur during Major's tenure.

Once financial control was reasserted, Major was left, as Honorary Secretary, with two perennial difficulties: ensuring a steady flow of published volumes and persuading council members to attend meetings. The dependability Major had shown over the edition of the Columbus letters was no doubt a factor in his later selection as Honorary Secretary. It also provided a clear, early illustration of the scheduling problems from which no subsequent Honorary Secretary of the Hakluyt Society has been free. Major's *Columbus Letters* was the second edition to be published, being preceded by Drinkwater Bethune's edition of Richard Hawkins' *Observations*. Yet neither of these editions had been selected for that honour at the first Council meeting, which had instead intended that John Winter Jones's edition of *Divers Voyages*, the first publication of Richard Hakluyt, should, understandably, be the first publication of the Hakluyt Society, to be followed by Bolton Corney's edition of the account of the second English voyage to the East, the 1606 voyage of Sir Henry Middleton.[2] In the event, those works appeared respectively in 1850 and 1856, as the seventh and the nineteenth publications. The edition of Middleton was in many ways a classic case and, although the Council minutes are disappointingly reticent on most matters, the exasperation with Corney shows clearly through. As the Council fluctuated for ten years between hope and despair the work was included or omitted from the listing of 'works in progress' in the annual reports. In May 1853, Corney agreed to complete the work within three months and it was therefore designated for 1854. Despite this, two years later Major was asked to complete the work, by now partly printed. The following month Major declined and it was agreed to abandon it. This galvanised Corney sufficiently to send a further part, along with more promises. These were renewed some

---

[1] Ibid., 1 May, 17 July, 20 November 1849. On the financial problem, see Bridges, 'Cooley', p. 74 above.
[2] HSCM, 16 March 1847.

months later.[1] Publication was eventually announced in the 1856 Report, two years later than the issue date.

Corney's editing of Middleton was an extreme, but not unique, case of unreliability – one thrown into even sharper focus by the editor's expressed obligation to Major 'for his prompt replies to my inquiries on all occasions'.[2] But some of the other early volumes, for whatever reasons, had an even longer gestation. The three proposals referred, along with Major's Columbus letters, for further consideration at the Society's second meeting were not to appear until the period 1866–1874, under the editorship of Henry E. J. (later Lord) Stanley. Major became a friend of Stanley, who came on to the Hakluyt Society Council for the first time in 1850, and both Major and his elder daughter would later spend time at Stanley's home, Alderley Park in Cheshire.[3] To promise, and be able to deliver, has always been a much prized Hakluyt Society virtue.

Major's other problem, a very real one, was ensuring that at least three people turned out to create a quorum for meetings. Between May 1852 and his resignation six years later, Major missed only one meeting through illness, but Council had regularly to be cancelled for lack of a quorum.[4] 1852 was a particularly bad year with three aborted meetings, leading Council to gather just once between April and December. This might have seemed like bad organisation on the Secretary's part but he had little margin for error, with attendance rarely exceeding half a dozen and four being the norm. The erratic attendance – or more properly consistent non-attendance – of so many Council members affected the efficient running of the Society. On two occasions, decisions were deferred because of the unrepresentative attendance, only for the next meeting to be no better.[5] This lack of practical support inevitably placed a greater decision-making burden on the Secretary, who alone provided any kind of continuity. However, the 1852 appointment of Murchison as a British Museum Trustee may well have provided additional opportunities for informal discussion between the Society's President and its Honorary Secretary.

The Minutes for these early decades – even when taken in conjunction with the annual reports – are in many respects disappointing, providing far less than a full and coherent record of proposed publications

---

[1] Ibid., 17 April, 15 May, 19 June, 20 November 1855.

[2] Bolton Corney, ed., *The Voyage of Sir Henry Middleton* . . ., London, 1856 (HS 19), p. xi.

[3] Major stayed there in September 1870 and again in 1871; his daughter Alice in October 1880 (BM Map Department letterbooks).

[4] The quorum was laid down in 'Law VII' (the 'Laws' first included in HS 4 of 1849): Major was absent in January 1858 (HSCM, 16 January 1858).

[5] Ibid., 18 July 1854, 19 May 1857.

and their subsequent progress.[1] The extent to which Major initiated projects must usually be inferred. Occasionally, the Minutes are explicit, as when he suggested as possible publications Benzoni's *History of the New World* (to be edited by W. H. Smyth as the twenty-first publication) and (during one of his stand-ins for Clements Markham) Galvão's *Discoveries of the World* (edited by Drinkwater Bethune as the thirtieth). In addition, Major was specifically 'empowered to collect geographical tracts or other materials for occasional miscellanies, the publication of which to be subject to future consideration'.[2]

The considerable contribution of British Museum men in the early years of the Society, whether serving on Council or as editors, has not in the past been sufficiently stressed. Major and his colleagues shared their specialist expertise with one another and with outside editors, as a matter of course. William Brenchley Rye thanked Major for assistance with his edition of De Soto and was thanked by Major in turn for help with his Herberstein. The pattern of mutual acknowledgment was rounded off by Major's thanks to Rye and Robert E. Graves for assistance with the second edition of the Columbus letters.[3] Another British Museum editor, William Vaux, acknowledged the 'valuable assistance' of his colleagues, Major and Edward Augustus Bond, and three years later Major used the same terms to thank his 'friend' Vaux.[4] Charles Beke, for his part, thanked Major and Rye for bibliographical help with his edition of Gerrit de Veer.[5] If these were mostly book people, Major was able to turn to his botanical colleague, but also a Hakluyt Society member, John Bennet, for assistance with the 1849 edition of Strachey.[6] Although this might seem like mutual backscratching, it undoubtedly reveals a genuine commitment by Major's colleagues to the aims of the Hakluyt Society.

Many of the texts used for the Society's volumes were based on printed or manuscript sources in the British Museum, as was anticipated in the 1846 Prospectus.[7] An early instance of this was when

[1] See the excellent summary in Dorothy Middleton, 'The Hakluyt Society 1846–1923', *Annual Report* [1984], Hakluyt Society, pp. 12–23.

[2] HSCM, 16 January 1855, 18 February 1861, 21 December 1852. See below, p. 100, for Major's deputising for Markham.

[3] William B. Rye, ed., *The Discovery and Conquest of Florida, by Don Ferdinand de Soto* ... , London, 1851 (HS 9), p. lxvii; Major, *Herberstein*, I, p. cxlvii; Major, *Columbus Letters*, 1870 (HS 43), p. cxli.

[4] William Sandys Wright Vaux, ed., *The World Encompassed by Sir Francis Drake* ..., London, 1854 (HS 16), p. xl; Major, *India in the Fifteenth Century*, p. xc.

[5] Charles T. Beke, ed., *A true Description of three Voyages ... towards Cathay ... by Gerrit de Veer*, London, 1853 (HS 13) p. cxl.

[6] Major, *Virginia Britannia*, p. xxii.

[7] BL, 741.k.1 (14). The three-page prospectus, printed after 15 December 1846, outlines publication plans, based, *inter alia*, on 'Valuable MSS. still remaining unpublished ... all in the library of the British Museum'.

Cooley was given permission to use selected tracts from the British Museum in his edition of Drake's 1595 voyage. It was possibly no coincidence, when, the following month, it was agreed that the Society's volumes should be presented to the British Museum.[1] Council also made occasional formal calls on British Museum expertise. In late 1847, for example, Ellis and Major were asked to 'examine and report on the genuineness of documents proposed to be appended to Raleigh's Guiana' (being edited by Sir Robert Schomburgk). The following month Major was able to report back that they were genuine.[2] Over thirty years later, Major's linguistic experience was invoked in connection with a proposed edition of Almeida's 'Historia Aethiopiae'. He, and Walter de Gray Birch, who would carry active British Museum participation on Council into the 1890s, were asked to report on its feasibility as a publication.[3]

Early membership lists of the Hakluyt Society Council cannot be dated with complete confidence.[4] However, it appears that the original British Museum trio of 1847, Ellis, Gray and Major, were supplemented in 1848 by John Winter Jones, Charles Newton and William Brenchley Rye, and in 1849 by John Holmes. The hand of Ellis can presumably be detected here as well. Besides Major, Ellis and Winter Jones were the only members of this British Museum group to become regular fixtures on the Council (and regular, if intermittent attenders). Newton and Rye failed to come to any meetings during their single year of office, but this needs to be set against the generally poor attendance already described. There is no better illustration of the close links between the British Museum and the Hakluyt Society than the meeting of 16 December 1856. Apart from Major, the participants were only Winter Jones, the Museum's Keeper of Printed Books, and Ellis, the Museum's recently retired Principal Librarian. And what did these three discuss? – the progress of the edition of Fletcher's account of Russia by their Department of Manuscripts colleague, Bond.

The links between the British Museum and the Society from the latter's inception up to 1880 are shown in table form below (p. 141). As

---

[1] HSCM, 19 December 1848, 16 January 1849. It was minuted that the volume was to be 'sent' to the British Museum, but the minute was then altered to read 'presented'. This was shortly before Panizzi's drive to enforce the 1842 Copyright Act.

[2] Ibid., 21 December 1847, 19 January 1848.

[3] Ibid., 9 June 1880. Birch reported back on 14 February 1882.

[4] The printed Council lists were never dated, although when they are found preceding the annual report they presumably represent the following year's Council. The manuscript set in the Society's archives, with handwritten dates, is incomplete. Council lists found at the front of the printed volumes were no doubt those of the current year, but when the issue year and the publication year differed it is unclear to which the list referred.

there indicated, apart from the British Museum men serving on the Council or as editors, a number of others played a role as members of the Society. For example, Edward Hawkins, the Keeper of Antiquities, was a member from the outset until his death twenty years later.[1] Eight colleagues joined during Major's secretaryship, and he must certainly take the credit for some of these recruits. That he was actively prosely-tising – the course he urged on others in successive annual reports – is clearly evidenced by the personal connections he recruited. The Robert Bells, father and son, and Major's wife's uncle by marriage, the solici-tor Thomas Wright Nelson, are examples of these.[2] Another service provided by Major's colleagues – perhaps with a little persuasion – was to attend the annual meeting. The Council preceding the annual meet-ing tended to be no better supported than any other meeting and there must have been a danger of insufficient members for the necessary AGM business. On 21 March 1854, with both Ellis and Winter Jones present, it was 'resolved that Messrs W. B. Rye and C. Cannon be requested to act as Auditors of the accounts of the Society for the past year'.[3] This resolution, bearing as it did the imprint of their Principal Librarian, was obviously not one that Rye or Cannon could refuse. Similar, albeit unminuted cajolement presumably explains why nine-teen of the twenty-four Auditors named in the annual reports between 1852 and 1863 were British Museum men.

It was, however, in the editing of works that the Hakluyt Society most benefitted from its British Museum links. Of the first twenty-five Hakluyt Society publications – roughly coinciding with Major's period in office – no fewer than fourteen had British Museum editors or contributors. To those would need to be added works recorded in the Council minutes as in preparation which, for one reason or another, never achieved publication. Most of the early editions were of texts already in print, but several were based on British Museum manuscripts or included ancillary documentation from such manuscripts. In the table below the 'proposed' date is the earliest official reference to the project, in the Council minutes or annual report, while the 'assigned' date indicates the year that a British Museum editor was apparently chosen for the task. Excluding Major himself, of eleven proposals involving British Museum personnel made in the period 1847–1861, six were achieved by their designated editors. In 1856, one of Major's colleagues

---

[1] Although Hawkins had edited Sir William Brereton's *Travels in Holland* for the Chetham Society in 1844, he did not play an active role in the Hakluyt Society.

[2] Robert Bell (presumably the father) and T. W. Nelson became members in 1849, the younger Bell in 1851.

[3] 'Law V' required the appointment of two auditors.

Nao ſam Paulo.

¶ Viagem & naufragio da
Nao ſam ſPaulo que foy pera a Jndia o anno
de mil ꝛ quinhentos ꝛ ſeſenta. Capitão
Ruy de melo da camara, Meſtre
Joam luys, ſPiloto An-
tonio Dias.

Com licença Jmpreſſo:

THE LOSS OF THE SÃO PAULO OFF SUMATRA IN 1561
Title page of a Lisbon pamphlet describing the disaster.
Reproduced in HS 2/132 of 1968.

from the Department of Manuscripts, N. E. S. A. Hamilton, put forward two proposals, for an edition of material on the 'Dutch in the East Indies' and for an edition of accounts of Hudson's voyages, but he was unable to see either to completion.[1] Hamilton was one of a small British Museum group of editors who resisted joining the Society. Another non-member, Adam White, of the Zoological Department, provided Major with one of his biggest problems. Having signed up White in April 1852 to edit 'a collection of documents on Spitzbergen and Greenland', Major and the Council became increasingly concerned in 1854 at the number of illustrations and their cost. The Society's habit of printing volumes in sections, as text became available, led to a drastic verdict in this case: 'the pages already printed with references to plates to be cancelled'.[2] At an untypical meeting on 18 November 1856, chaired by Winter Jones, three of the four people who had 'offered' to edit or translate were from the British Museum: Hamilton for Hudson, Garnett for Correa's account of Vasco da Gama's voyages, and Cannon for Rozmital's account of his travels through Europe. Sadly for Winter Jones, recently appointed Keeper of Printed Books, none of these three – two of whom were members of his department – managed to complete the promised work. In Garnett's case, the work to which he attached his name had first been proposed in general terms in 1847. Despite its importance, and its repeated appearance among the works 'in progress', enquiries had to be made of Garnett as to his intentions, seven years after the initial offer. No answer is given in the Council Minutes but six years later Henry Stanley saw it into print.[3] Another promising overture on 8 February 1876 was the offer by George Frederick Warner (later to be Keeper of Manuscripts) to prepare a calendar of the manuscript voyages and travels held in the British Museum. However, when, two years later, a reminder was sent, pointing out that any transcription costs would be met by the Society, Warner resisted the bait and withdrew his offer.[4] Besides Major himself, only Winter Jones was able to deliver all he promised.

Filling the role of Hakluyt Society Secretary between 1849 and 1858

---

[1] *Henry Hudson the Navigator: the Original Documents* . . ., London, 1860 (HS 27), was completed by G. M. Asher who explained that Hamilton had 'retired' and gone to the country (p. ccxiv). But there may have been a linguistic confusion here because Hamilton's retirement, on medical grounds, took place only in 1872. Prior to that, he had been responsible, according to the BL Catalogue, for the anonymous *National Gazetteer of Great Britain and Ireland*, 3 vols, London, 1868.

[2] HSCM, 21 November 1854; Adam White, ed., *A Collection of Documents on Spitzbergen & Greenland* . . ., London, 1856 (HS 18).

[3] Ibid., 20 April 1847, 12 January 1863; Henry E. J. Stanley, ed., *The Three Voyages of Vasco da Gama* . . ., London, 1869 (HS 42). Rozmital's travels eventually appeared – in 1957 (HS 2/108).

[4] HSCM, 19 February, 20 May 1878.

did not restrict Major's own activities as an editor. On the contrary, his third work was an ambitious one, the translating and editing, in two volumes, of Sigismund von Herberstein's account of early seventeenth-century Russia. There was no disguising Ellis's hand in this. At a Council meting on 21 March 1848, with Corney's edition of Middleton increasingly despaired of, Ellis proposed an edition of Herberstein to fill the gap. At the next meeting Major agreed to take on this task but – and one senses here that preparing his earlier editions kept him under pressure – 'on the understanding however that he was to be allowed to do it at his leisure'. By now a married man, and with Strachey still to be completed, his delivery of the two volumes of Herberstein for publication three and four years later seems reasonable.[1] But timing was not the only problem. At the following Council meeting Major pointed out that 'there are passages in Herberstein's commentaries which seemed to him unfit for publication and which made him doubt the expediency of translating that work'. Major was told to confer with the elder states-man, Ellis, 'as to the possibility of modifying those passages in such a way as not to impair the value of the work considered as a faithful picture of the age and nation which it describes'.[2]

In 1852, the publication year of the second Herberstein volume, Major suffered the only serious academic attack of his career. Writing in the *Westminster Review*, James Anthony Froude, supposedly discussing three of the Society's early publications, launched into a general attack on the Hakluyt Society's editors and their style of editing. With the exception of Sir Robert Schomburgk, 'we are obliged to say that they [the editors] have exerted themselves successfully to paralyse whatever interest was reviving in Hakluyt, and to consign their own volumes to the same obscurity to which time and accident were consigning the earlier editions'. Major's edition of the Columbus letters was not listed at the head of the review essay; nevertheless Froude made fun of Major for, sup-posedly, apologising 'for the rudeness of the old seaman's phraseology'.[3]

---

[1] HSCM, 21 March, 18 April 1848. The Herberstein volumes have publication dates of 1851 and 1852 but were probably published only a few months apart, since the preface to the first volume notes that the second was 'already at press'. Despite proposing the Herberstein project, Ellis never edited a volume for the Hakluyt Society, although in 1851 he prepared Sir Richard Guildford's *Pylgrymage* for the Camden Society.

[2] HSCM, 16 May 1848.

[3] [J. A. Froude], 'England's Forgotten Worthies', *The Westminster and Foreign Quarterly Review*, n.s. 2/1, July and October 1852, pp. 32–7, with the reference to Major on pp. 35–6. Of perhaps ten volumes published by the time he was writing, Froude selected for detailed comment Bethune's *Hawkins* (HS 1), Schomburgk's edition of Raleigh's *Guiana* (HS 3), and Rundall's *North-West Voyages* (HS 5). On this affair, see also William Foster, 'A Retrospect', in Edward Lynam, ed., *Richard Hakluyt & his Successors*, London, 1946 (HS 2/93,) pp. 148–50.

Coincidentally, these supposed scruples had, unstated, echoes of the qualms Major had actually had about Herberstein's language. Major's greater complaint, however, was that the volume most castigated, the edition of Richard Hawkins's *Observations*, was, in the bibliographical description at the beginning of the review, wrongly attributed to himself as editor. Since the comments on this edition were introduced by a reference to the name of the actual editor, Drinkwater Bethune, Major can be accused of over-reacting. Fifteen years later, goaded by a reprint of Froude's essay, Major responded again in an exchange of letters with Froude in the *Athenaeum*.[1] The unsatisfactory nature of Froude's reply led Major, at the urging of 'some of the leading members of our Council', to reprint the *Athenaeum* correspondence in the preface of his 1870 revised edition of the Columbus letters. With a final swipe at the 'mischievous effect of a savage criticism, built up on the critic's own blunders', Major allowed himself the last word. Froude was closer to the mark with his general criticism about the 'long laboured appendices and introductions', where 'we have found what is most uncommon passed without notice, and what is most trite and familiar encumbered with comment'.[2] It was precisely these ancillary elements which Major himself considered so valuable, even if he felt it necessary to defend their length on more than one occasion.[3] This is clear from the way he singled out for special mention in his description of Herberstein the account of the visits of earlier travellers and the 'list of all publications prior to the year 1550 which in any way referred to the countries described in Herberstein's work'.[4]

Major's next two acknowledged contributions to Hakluyt Society volumes involved the less onerous preparation of introductions: for the two volumes of an edition of Mendoza on China, and for an edition of the accounts of the Tartar conquest of China, the latter editor being the Earl of Ellesmere, chairman of the 1847 Royal Commission into the British Museum. Both works moved smoothly from proposal to publication, in 1853 and 1854 respectively. In the following editions with which he was connected, Major was the sole contributor, though not necessarily from the outset. His next work, on India in the fifteenth

---

[1] J. A. Froude, *Short Studies on Great Subjects*, 2 vols, London, 1868, II, pp. 102–13; *The Athenaeum*, 2072, 13 July 1867, p. 52; 2073, 20 July, p. 82; 2074, 27 July, p. 115.

[2] Froude, *Short Studies*, p. 113.

[3] See the introduction to his *Early Voyages to Terra Australis* (HS 25), pp. cxviii–cxix; and the preface to *Voyages of the … Zeno* (HS 50), defending an introduction that was twice the length of the original text.

[4] Major, *Notes upon Russia* (HS 10), p. cxlvii. In the 1851 Annual Report of the Society, Major gave due credit to his Museum colleague Rye for 'most valuable assistance' with both these additional elements in the edition.

century was, like the Tartar volume, one of the 'miscellanies' which he had been empowered to put together at the Council meeting in late 1852. Announced as in preparation in the 1853 Annual Report, it was originally assigned to Winter Jones, but his appointment to the keepership of Printed Books in April 1856 forced him to give it up. In spring 1857 Major 'volunteered' to see the task through. This was not to be the only external event affecting this volume. The last of the trio of translators, Count Wielkovsky, former Secretary of the Russian Legation in London, had by then died helping Russian wounded in the Crimea, although, fortunately, he had been able to finish his part before his recall from London. Major's magnanimous tribute to Wielkovsky gives no hint that their two countries had so recently been at war.[1] The work was tabled as 'complete' on 21 December 1857 and issued to subscribers for 1857, a year made momentous for India by the Mutiny. Major translated two of the four narratives, Winter Jones providing one of the others.

The conception of Major's next assignment, an edition of early voyages to Australia, can be formally dated to 16 January 1855, when he proposed publication of a selection of early Spanish documents on the discovery of the southern continent.[2] Surprisingly, what would prove to be one of his more influential publications, initiating the debate about a pre-Dutch discovery of Australia, was not originally assigned to him. A mere four months later, at the desperate Council meeting where Corney's Middleton was apparently abandoned, we learn of Drinkwater Bethune's involvement – only because he was to be asked to relinquish it. This he duly did at the next meeting, yet there is no formal record of its transfer to Major. However, it seems safe to assume that when it reappeared in the Council Minutes in May 1856, with the working title '[Early] Indications of Australia', it was Major's responsibility. The book was to be dedicated to Murchison and it must therefore have been this work that Major referred to obliquely as 'my

---

[1] Major, *India in the Fifteenth Century* (HS 22), pp. i–iv.
[2] HSCM, 16 January 1855. However, on two later occasions Major indicated what might be a slightly earlier conception for this work. In about June 1861 he sent a letter to the Ethnological Society (R. H. Major, 'Native Australian traditions', *Transactions of the Ethnological Society of London*, 1, 1861, pp. 349–53) describing how he had 'purposely kept [the edition] open for six or seven years, in order to allow myself the fullest chance of embodying in my introduction all the information I could possibly gather respecting the earliest discoveries' (p. 353). Later again, in 1872, he described having had 'this subject of Australia before my thoughts for nearly twenty years' (R. H. Major, 'Further facts in the history of the early discovery of Australia – supplementary facts', *Archaeologia*, 44, pt. 2, 1873, p. 240 – the paper summarised, *Proceedings of the Society of Antiquaries of London* [hereafter *PSAL*], 2nd series, 5, 1872, p. 291; *Proceedings of the Royal Geographical Society* [hereafter *PRGS*], 16, 1872, pp. 352–5).

forthcoming, or rather promised, book', in a letter to Murchison of 29 January 1856, in which he asked permission to dedicate the selection to him.[1] As work proceeded on the volume over the next three years, one of Major's greatest difficulties was settling on a suitable title. The 1856 Annual Report billed it as 'A collection of documents on the early discoveries in Australia': the following year's report reduced this to 'Early discoveries of Australia', but before the eventual title ('Early Voyages to Terra Australis') was arrived at, Major had also toyed with 'Australia Praedicta'. As he explained in a letter to Lord Broughton, this was intended to indicate how the early discovery presaged the eventual British colonisation.[2] In the face of general resistance, he dropped the suggestion.[3] On publication of the work, it was agreed to present copies to each of the Australian colonial governors in the (possibly pious) hope 'that the attention of the Colonists may be directed to the objects of the Hakluyt Society'.[4] One thinks irresistibly of Mr Micawber, by then well established in Australia.

By the time this edition appeared, Major was no longer the Society's Honorary Secretary, having resigned the previous year after giving nine years of highly effective service. As with his entry into the Society, the cause lay in the British Museum, although this time the decision was forced upon him. The hard-driving Principal Librarian, Sir Anthony Panizzi, who had succeeded the easy-going Ellis in 1856, wished his officers to concentrate their efforts inside the British Museum, the focus for his own unrelenting energy. In March 1858, he requested information about the external commitments of his officers. In reply, Major felt 'bound to admit that my time and attention have been occasionally occupied with the affairs of the Society during the hours allotted to Museum duties'. He then made the still-relevant point about the need for a curator to have scholarly expertise, stressing the complementarity of his two roles. His Hakluyt Society activities, he wrote, had been 'similar to and often identical with those which the

---

[1] BL, Add. MS 46127, f. 172.

[2] HSCM, 3 April 1858; BL, Add. MS 36472, ff. 219–20.

[3] HSCM, 7 May 1861. The constantly changing title clearly confused Clements Markham who, on his return from a long trip to South America, in discussing Major's 1861 coda to the work described it as a supplement to the 'Early Indications of Australia'. The supplement comprised a letter to Ellis previously communicated to the Society of Antiquaries (summary *PSA*, 2nd series, 1, p. 351; in full, 'On the discovery of Australia by the Portuguese in 1601, five years before the earliest hitherto known discovery with arguments in favour of a previous discovery by the same nation early in the sixteenth century', *Archaeologia*, 38, pt. 2, 1860 [1861], pp. 438–59 [paper read to the Society of Antiquaries, 7 March 1861], Portuguese version, Lisbon, 1863). It was 'now distributed to the Members of the Hakluyt Society' – a typical example of Major's scholarly recycling.

[4] HSCM, 21 November 1859.

nature of my Museum duties required me to be acquainted with'.[1] Despite this, and despite Winter Jones's observation that much of Major's own time had been given to the Society, Major felt it would be expedient to resign his secretaryship. This he did at the annual meeting on 1 April 1858.

The resignation did not, however, take immediate effect. The next two Council meetings were aborted for lack of a quorum, and this ensured that nothing happened through the early summer. On 19 July, Major was asked to sound out the 28-year-old Clements Markham of the India Office as his successor. This bore fruit, and after taking the minutes of the November meeting Major handed over to Markham. Thus began a long association between the two men, who would later be joint Honorary Secretaries of the Royal Geographical Society (RGS). But Markham's succession was not without its complications. Within a year he was off on an eighteen-month journey, with Major filling the breech and agreeing 'to perform all the ordinary duties of the Secretary'.[2] This happened again between October 1865 and April 1866. On the third occasion, however, when Markham was absent with the Abyssinian Expedition of 1867–1868, there was no mention of a substitute. By then, Major was preoccupied with the RGS, where Markham's absence left him shouldering the Honorary Secretary burden alone, but he stepped in unofficially and took the minutes twice more.[3] Although the flow of volumes to subscribers was maintained, the lack of a clear hand on the helm and the irregularity of meetings showed a temporary loss of direction. This is clearly seen in the annual reports for this period, which actually appeared in the sequence: 1866, 1868, 1869, 1867.[4]

Convention demanded that a fulsome tribute be made to the nine years of Major's official secretaryship (1849–1858). But in regretting 'the loss of the services of a gentleman who for so many years has devoted himself to the best interests of the Hakluyt Society and has contributed so largely to its success', the Council was doing him no more than justice.[5] The Hakluyt Society had originally aimed to publish

---

[1] Quoted in Edward Miller, *That Noble Cabinet: a History of the British Museum*, London, 1973, p. 267.

[2] HSCM, 21 November 1859. Major took the minutes between 20 February 1860 and 18 February 1861.

[3] Ibid., 3 December 1867, 26 May 1868.

[4] The 1867 report appeared in HS 38 which has 1867 as the publication date, but is out of chronological order, HS 37 having the publication date 1869. Moreover, the British Museum date stamps indicating receipt of this volume and the volume immediately preceding it are as follows: HS 37, publication date 1869, containing the 1869 report, date stamp July 1869; HS 38, publication date 1867, containing the 1867 report, date stamp November 1869.

[5] HSCM, 1 April 1858.

three titles per year but, after a sticky start that saw just three titles issued to subscribers in the first two years, Major managed to maintain an overall rate of two per year, in the process setting a target for his successors.[1] It would be wrong to measure Major's contribution in purely quantitative terms. He was equally concerned with the maintenance of scholarly standards and went to considerable trouble to assist the Society's editors. G.M. Asher was one of a handful of foreigners who gave their services to the Society. He was worried that his edition of Hudson's voyages would be let down by his English, which 'difficulty could never have been surmounted without the extreme kindness of the editor's friend, Mr R. H. Major, who has examined every line of the present book before it was sent to the press'. In addition, Major took upon himself 'the tedious and ungrateful task of correcting the extracts from Purchas'.[2] Thirty years later Markham was to corroborate this picture of helpfulness and modesty, attributing the Society's early success to Major's 'unequalled knowledge of the subject, to his wide acquaintance with fellow labourers in the same field of research, to his readiness to impart his own stores of knowledge to others, and not least to his generous sympathy in the work of editors'.[3]

At the meeting in July 1868, after Major had taken the minutes for the last time, it was agreed that he should prepare a revised edition of his Columbus letters, by then out of print. Subscribers receiving this second edition as the sole volume for 1870 would probably have paid more attention to the frontispiece than would a modern reader. Garish to our eyes, this was a chromolithographed copy of the St Christopher detail from the Juan de la Cosa world map, supposedly a portrait of Columbus himself. Yet chromolithography offered the Hakluyt Society the first opportunity of including complex coloured illustrations.[4] It did not come cheap, costing the considerable sum of £24 10s.[5] As a comparison, the simple outline maps in the Australian edition cost £7 10s

---

[1] The 1848 annual report, in discussing the parlous finances, noted costs per volume and annual costs 'as the Subscribers will expect to receive annually at least three of these [volumes]'. The original prospectus had unwisely drawn parallels with similar societies that produced four to six volumes annually.

[2] Asher, *Hudson* (HS 27), p. ccxiv.

[3] Clements R. Markham, 'Obituary of R. H. Major, F. S. A.', *PRGS*, n.s., 13, 1891, p. 490.

[4] Major, *Columbus Letters*, 1870 (HS 43); Norton Shaw, ed., *Narrative of a Voyage . . . By Samuel Champlain*, London, 1858 (HS 23), had contained ill-registered coloured lithographs, which were far less sophisticated than chromolithography.

[5] HSCM, 2 May, 18 July 1870; Major, *Columbus Letters*, 1870 (HS 43), p. lxxxix. Nor was the chromolithograph readily procured. Major thanked his late friend, the former Portuguese Ambassador, Count de Lavradio, for obtaining the 'colour photograph' (given the date, presumably a hand-coloured photograph) on a visit to Madrid. The chromolithograph was prepared in Berlin.

each for lithographing and printing.[1] Since the Béthencourt portrait of two years later also cost £7, there is a suspicion that the Council, with Major's friend Stanley in the chair, was turning a blind eye to their former Secretary's extravagance.[2] Markham was certainly unclear of the technological advance involved, referring, as he disbursed the cheque, to an 'engraving'.[3]

If the Australian work had had as many successive names as a Transylvanian town, Major's next work for the Society, an edition of Jean de Béthencourt's 'Le Canarien', had as many potential editors. Described as 'Bontier's History of the Discovery of the Canary Islands', it was already under consideration at the time of the 1846 Prospectus. It was referred to intermittently thereafter until, in early 1858, for some inexplicable reason, Bolton Corney was requested to undertake it. Memories were surely not short enough for the Middleton fiasco to have been forgotten in the course of just two years. Stranger still, Markham, the newly-appointed Secretary, was called to take action in similar terms a year later – perhaps Major had diplomatically 'forgotten' to carry out the original instruction.[4] When next heard of, in 1861, the edition was to be suggested to Dr Charles Beke. This clearly fell on stony ground because two years later Sir Charles Nicholson was proposed instead. The 1863, and two subsequent, annual reports transferred editorship to Captain J. G. Goodenough. By the time the project reappeared in the minutes it was for the Council to learn that a naval appointment was forcing Goodenough to give up the work.[5] He accordingly handed over the half he had done to Markham. Another of Markham's intermittent foreign absences intervened and it was a further two years before the work resurfaced. Payment was then sanctioned for the remaining translation and the uncharacteristically absent Major was asked to edit the work.[6] By that stage, Major had already briefly considered Béthencourt's part in the discovery of the Canaries, in his study of 'Prince Henry' published the previous year.[7] Even if the 1869 Annual Report's

[1] HSCM, 20 May 1856, 'Estimate of Messrs Day & Son for tracing, reducing and lithographing two maps for "Indications of Australia" at £4 each and printing 500 copies of each at 4/- per 100 was accepted'. However, Major was capable of economising. On 3 December 1867 he was given permission to re-use these two maps in his forthcoming study of 'Prince Henry the Navigator'.

[2] HSCM, 28 February 1872; the portrait was for his 1870 *Canarian* (HS 46).

[3] HSCM, 18 July 1870. *Columbus Letters* appeared late in 1870, probably in mid-November, when the British Museum Map Department letterbooks record the separate despatch of seven 'books'.

[4] HSCM, 15 February 1858, 21 February 1859.

[5] Ibid., 7 May 1861, 3 June 1863, 21 March 1867.

[6] Ibid., 15 March 1869.

[7] R. H. Major, *The Life of Prince Henry of Portugal, Surnamed the Navigator; and its results:*

prediction of completion 'before the end of the present year' proved over-optimistic, events now moved steadily and confidently towards publication in 1872, twenty-six years and at least five potential editors after it had first been proposed.

With his final work for the Society, an edition of the Zeno voyages, Major showed how straightforward the production of a volume could be, given determination and undivided control. Proposed in late 1872, the edition was completed in early 1874, and issued as one of three volumes for 1873.[1] This brought to an end Major's editorial work for the Hakluyt Society. There is no clearer indication of the importance that he himself attached to this contribution than the fact that over half of his authorised biography discussed his work for the Society, summarising the biographical details of the subjects' lives and proudly recording the length of Major's various introductions.[2]

Marriage

Just a fortnight after his Columbus proposal had been accepted for publication Major was married, on 3 June 1847, to Sarah Elizabeth Thorn, aged 33 and hence four years Major's senior.[3] Sarah Thorn was

---

comprising the Discovery, within One Century, of Half the World ... with New Facts in the Discovery of the Atlantic Islands ... and the History of the Naming of America ... illustrated with Portraits, Maps, etc., London and Berlin, 1868, version in Portuguese, Lisbon, 1876, facsimile reprint, London, 1967, pp. 145–6. Major summarised his book in *Edinburgh Review*, 128, July–October 1868, pp. 200–36. Major was certainly responsible for introducing the inappropriate epithet 'Navigator' into the English language and hence into a great deal of later historical writing up to the present day, but earlier German scholars had described Prince Henry as 'Seefahrer' (e.g., Johann E. Wappaüs, *Untersuchungen über die geographischen Entdeckungen der Portugiesen unter Heinrich dem Seefahrer*, Göttingen, 1842).

[1] HSCM, 10 December 1872. The speed was despite its being 'a troublesome task' (J. H., *Biography*, p. 11). Council decided on 20 January 1874 to add a sketch map of Greenland to the work, and the 1874 annual report described it as already issued. The BM date stamp gives a receipt date of February 1874.

[2] The relative downplaying of the British Museum and RGS in the biography might point to the unknown author's being more associated with the Hakluyt Society.

[3] The church Major married at, St Stephen's, was a stone's throw from Sarah's home at 4 Albion Place, just south of Canonbury Square, Islington. Major's newly ordained brother, Seymour, conducted the service. Sarah had been christened on 20 March 1814 at St Gregory by St Paul, London. Even though apparently an only child, she brought with her the appurtenances of a family: uncles, aunts, cousins, and a pair of living, and present parents. Major moved from De Beauvoir Square, Hackney (at his entry into the British Museum in January 1844, he was living at 5 Park Place, De Beauvoir Square, and at his marriage he was registered as of the parish of St John Hackney) to join Sarah and her parents in the house he would not leave until 1881. Over the next twelve years 4 Albion Place saw the successive deaths of Major's parents-in-law, Henry and Elizabeth Thorn (in 1853 and 1859 respectively), and the births of his two daughters, Alice Elizabeth (1849) and Sarah Isabelle (1853).

an established artist. In the period 1838–1848 she exhibited 39 pictures at the Society of British Artists, the British Institution and the Royal Academy (seven subjects).[1] The absence of information about these in the Courtauld Institute's Witt Library suggests that they are neither to be found in public galleries nor much regarded today. But Sarah Thorn should not be dismissed as just another lady of independent means dabbling in art. The domestic subjects of her paintings suggest senti-mentality to us but they matched the early Victorian mood. She may well have been quite successful.[2] Having exhibited nothing in the year of her marriage, Sarah's last recorded painting, 'Portrait of an infant' (1848), presaged the birth of her own first child in the following February.

At about this time – in a move that would have relevance for the Hakluyt Society – she abandoned painting for etching. Since her output as a printmaker has not been commented upon in art cata-logues, our knowledge of her etched work comes entirely from a group of thirteen impressions now in the British Museum.[3] These comprise four architectural scenes, three assured illustrations for an apparently unrealised edition of de la Motte Fouqué's 'Undine', and illustrations for two of Major's Hakluyt Society editions. Whether or not it was at Major's instigation, the first Hakluyt Society volume to

---

[1] Confusingly for the biographical dictionaries, she exhibited as two different indi-viduals, Thorn and Major: see Algernon Graves, *A Dictionary of Artists Who Have Exhibited Works in the Principal London Exhibitions from 1760 to 1893*, 3rd ed., London, 1901, and the more detailed catalogues of the separate institutions there referred to. Separate entries under Major and Thorn also appear in Christopher Wood, *The Dictionary of Victorian Painters*, 2nd ed., Woodbridge, 1978.

[2] A contemporary small reproduction survives of 'The sisters; or, the lecture un-heeded', an oil she exhibited at the British Institution in 1844. For this genteel, if dull, canvas, roughly four feet square, she received £30 – not far off a quarter's salary for her husband-to-be in his first year at the British Museum. This painting, one of a tiny handful by lady artists, was selected by a member of the Art-Union of London from the many hundreds on public exhibition that year. Members of this body drew annually for the chance to select a work from one of their main exhibitions. The Witt Library holds the reproduction, described as from the 'London Art Union Prize Annual 1845'; the BL has the unillustrated *Catalogue of the Pictures, &c. Selected by the Prizeholders in the Art-Union of London 1844*, her picture No. 25.

[3] Most of Sarah's unpublished etchings were donated to the Museum as a group on 7 August 1880, a few months before her husband's retirement – clearly a tidying up operation. But two of the three architectural scenes, Hearn and Dorking, had been presented earlier, in 1851–2, one of them being based on a sketch by Major himself – which suggests that he did have distractions from his intellectual labours. Other examples of these scenes were possessed by British Museum colleagues, William H. Carpenter, Keeper of Prints and Drawings, and Edward Hawkins, Keeper of Antiquities, from whom they were purchased posthumously (BM, Prints and Drawings 1867.3.9.1795, 1868.8.8.13264). The donated etchings are held in the Department of Prints and Draw-ings (which, unlike the Library, remains a part of the British Museum): BM, Prints and Drawings, c.5*.

use, in the pre-photographic era, commissioned reproductions of original plates was his edition of Strachey's *Virginia Britannia* (1849). To illustrate this, Sarah produced five copies of the De Bry Indian engravings, for which she was duly thanked by Council in November 1849 – though naturally, as the Secretary's wife, not paid.[1] Major provides his own explanation at the end of his introduction, in a tone that jars on modern ears but would have raised no eyebrows at the time:

> He also felt it to be only a just expression of gratitude to his wife, to acknowledge here her kind aid in supplying the illustrations, – a "labour of love" which it is hoped that the reader will criticise with a lenient eye, as they are her first efforts at etching, and would for that reason not have been made in connexion with a work like the present, but from a natural desire to share in the Editor's labours, and an earnest wish to add, in however feeble a manner, to the interest of the narrative.

This account of Sarah's new role, as Major's assistant, accords with what her younger daughter would write after her mother's death in 1890, that Sarah, 'who before her marriage had been devoted to painting ... after her marriage ... was always, as long at least as I can remember her, busied with working with him in whatever occupied his home hours'.[2] Despite Major's apologies on his wife's behalf, the *Virginia* illustrations were professionally done and, not surprisingly, Sarah was called upon to assist again with his 1851–1852 edition of Herberstein. This time she provided the frontispiece portrait of the author and a striking illustration of armed horsemen, both included in the first volume. This was her last Hakluyt Society contribution because the frontispiece portrait for the second volume was provided instead by Major's Library colleague and exact contemporary, William Brenchley Rye.[3] Major's future work for the Society would not call for reproductive illustrations until the reissue of his Columbus letters in 1870.

[1] 'Thanks to Mrs Major for her kindness in etching the Strachey illustrations and a copy of the book to be presented to her' (HSCM, 20 November 1849).

[2] RGSA, Correspondence Block 1881–90, 'Evans, I.G.', 'From my Father's Reminiscences'. Major's later dedication to his 'honoured and beloved wife' in an 1877 work presented the partnership in a different light, attributing the idea of a book on 'Henry the Navigator' to a suggestion made by Sarah thirty years before, that is, if the number be taken literally, in the year of their marriage (R. H. Major, *The Discoveries of Prince Henry the Navigator, and their Results; being the Narrative of the Discovery by Sea, within One Century of more than Half the World ... Illustrated with Portraits, Maps etc.*, London, 1877 – a popular version of the 1868 *Prince Henry*).

[3] Rye's etchings were privately printed in 1857 (see *DNB*). It is not clear why Major handed the task to another, since Sarah's work was superior, but the decision was taken early enough for him to be able to thank Rye in the first volume for the frontispiece to the second (Major, *Notes upon Russia*, I (HS 10), p. cxlvii).

RUSSIAN HORSEMEN
Etching by Sarah Major for her husband's edition of Herberstein, copied from
the original publication of 1571.
In HS 10 of 1851.

Whether the couple met through an interest in art is not known but it
seems possible.[1] That Major maintained the interest in art he had shown
on the Mediterranean voyage is demonstrated by his membership of the
Arundel Society (by 1866).[2] An alternative explanation for the first

---

[1] Major's brother, Seymour, was a watercolourist, and a number of his works survive
in the family. Further evidence of Major's connection with the world of art comes from a
recommendation on his behalf, dated 19 December 1854, to the Society of Antiquaries by
Henry Shaw, an architectural draughtsman, engraver, illuminator and antiquary, on the
basis of 'personal knowledge'.
[2] Another artistic link came via the 'landscape engraver' Thomas Jeavons, one of the
trustees of the will of Major's grandfather, Joseph Major. (Most of the biographical
dictionaries of artists give Jeavons a birth-date of 1816, but as his earliest work dates from
1830, or possibly even 1822, this is implausible.) Jeavons would have needed to maintain
contact with Major until at least the latter's twenty-first birthday in 1839. In fact, a single
entry in the Hakluyt Society Council minutes indicates that their connection was evidently maintained long after that date. Besides Augustus Petermann (compiler of the
maps) a 'Mr Jeavons' was thanked in 1853 for work on Beke's De Veer (Beke, *Three*

meeting of Major and Sarah Thorn might be that Major's Library colleague, John Winter Jones, was the matchmaker. Certainly Sarah's father's will, drawn up just two years after the Major marriage, lists his 'friend' Winter Jones as an executor in the event of his wife's predeceasing him.[1] At the death of Sarah's mother in 1859 the house at 4 Albion Place became Major's. With the property inherited from his father-in-law added to his grandfather's inheritance, Major was now comparatively wealthy.[2]

Involvement in other Societies

Comfortably off and with his family complete, in the mid 1850s it was time for Major to think of extending his scholarly reputation. This he did by offering himself for election to the Society of Antiquaries. Then as now, the Antiquaries played a central part in London's scholarly life. With Major's mentor, Ellis, serving as an officer of the Society for over forty years, it is hardly surprising that he was put up for fellowship. His Museum colleagues and Hakluyt Society collaborators, William Vaux and John Winter Jones, were already FSA. Of the five who signed his application 'from personal knowledge' on 9 December 1854, three were Museum men: Ellis, by then the Society's Director, and two from the Department of Antiquities, Edward Hawkins and Samuel Birch (respectively Keeper and Assistant Keeper). The artist Henry Shaw and the Antiquaries' Treasurer, Peter Levesque, were the others. Major knew Levesque well from Hakluyt Society Council meetings, at which he had been an unusually assiduous attender.

Major wasted no time and within a month of his election had read the first of a succession of papers that would be spread over the next eighteen years.[3] During that period he also served on the society's

---

Voyages ... towards Cathay ... by Gerrit de Veer (HS 13): HSCM, 19 April 1853). The most likely explanation for this is that Major, using his power of patronage as Honorary Secretary, commissioned his grandfather's friend to produce the unsigned copies of the engravings that had illustrated the original text.

[1] Henry Thorn's will was made on on 1 August 1849. Winter Jones, who was also to be an executor of Major's mother-in-law's will ten years later – and described again as a 'friend' – also lived in Islington, at 24 Stonefield Street.

[2] Henry Thorn had owned a hosiery and merino manufactury in Ludgate Street since at least 1814 (*Holden's Annual Directory*). Mrs Thorn's effects were valued at up to £8000. To put this into perspective, it was twelve times Major's annual salary when he retired as a Keeper. The house at 4 Albion Place (redesignated 96 Canonbury Road in 1863) was spacious enough for the 1851 census to list three (unspecified) servants and the 1871 census to list a cook and a housemaid (Albion Place was missed off the 1861 census).

[3] Major read papers or contributed 'remarks' on the following subjects: the supposed

Council on four separate occasions.[1] When Major came onto the Council for the first time, in 1859, Hawkins was one of those elected with him, and Winter Jones one of those standing down. Major's first paper, on the supposed city of Vineta near the mouth of the Oder, which he identified as Wollin, was an excursion into twelfth-century archaeology, linguistics and toponymy. This was followed by a six-year gap, despite an appeal in October 1856 from the Society's Director, Ellis, then recently retired from the British Museum, that Major, one of its 'ablest members', should come up with a suitable subject. Given that Major was then working for the Hakluyt Society on both his India and Australia volumes, it is hardly surprising that he was unable to help Ellis overcome a lack of Fellows prepared to 'bestir themselves to contribute at meetings'.[2] The papers that followed – many of which coincided with a lull in Major's Hakluyt Society activities – were mostly directed towards unravelling the discoveries of America and Australia. They are more conveniently treated in the general discussion of his historical writings below.

Although Major had joined the Royal Geographical Society in 1845, it was a further twenty years before he became active in its affairs.[3] His fellowship application was signed by the President, Roderick Murchison, as 'having personal knowledge of the Candidate'. Later, Major would serve Murchison as Secretary of both the Hakluyt Society and RGS. Major's relationship with the RGS did not, however, start auspiciously. In July 1846 he wrote to Colonel Jackson, the Honorary Secretary, objecting strongly to the decision to charge compounding members like himself for the Society's journal. Referring to the 'injustice of the resolution', and the 'infringement of the private rights of property' that he considered it to constitute, he refused to pay. The Council was then in recess for the summer. By the time it reconvened in November it was informed of four other complaints besides Major's.[4] The Council

---

city of Vineta (1855), the discovery of Australia (1861); the 'Leonardo' mappemonde (1864); a MS study of Vespucci (1865); a globe cup (1869); the 'true date of the English discovery of the American continent' (1870); 'further' facts on the discovery of Australia (1872); 'supplementary' facts on the discovery of Australia (1873); the Fra Mauro world map (1873). All were published in *Archaeologia* or *PSAL*. Most are discussed below: the others are 'Remarks on the supposed city of Vineta . . . in a letter to Sir Henry Ellis, K.H., Director', *Archaeologia*, 36, pp. 85–94 [letter dated 10 February 1855, paper read 15 February 1855]; [on the 'Saggio di un elegio istorico di Amerigo Vespucci'], *PSAL*, 2nd series, 3, 1865, p. 38; [on a cup, in the form of a globe, found in Lancashire c. 1819], ibid., 4, 1869, pp. 335–7.

[1] 1859–61, 1863–5, 1867–9 and 1873–5.
[2] BL, Add. MS 70842, f. 140.
[3] J. H., *Biography*, p. 3. His membership application is not dated.
[4] RGSA, Correspondence Block 1841–50, 'R. H. Major', 4 July, 6 July 1846; RGS

minutes ignore the moral issue and throw no light on how an accommodation was reached. Within a year, however, Major was asking for, and being granted, an extended borrowing period because 'it is necessary that I should have Navarrete constantly by me', a reference to Major's work on the Columbus letters volume for the Hakluyt Society.[1] This was again the case when Major approached the RGS in 1856 with a request to borrow more books than the standard allowance, in connection with another forthcoming Hakluyt Society publication, this time on India.[2] The internal reason for agreeing to this request, that 'he will probably be able to promote the interests of the society', underlines the symbiotic relationship between the two societies Major was to serve so loyally. Major tells us in the authorised biography that Murchison, then serving the third of his four terms as RGS President, had offered him the Honorary Secretary's post as early as 1857. Reasonably enough, Major had turned it down, citing 'official duties, together with the editorial and other responsibilities of the secretaryship of the Hakluyt Society'.[3] Eight years later, however, he felt able to accept the post.

Markham's absences had led Major temporarily to take up the Hakluyt Society reins in 1859 and again in 1865. On the second of these occasions (October 1865 to April 1866) he agreed to deputise for Markham as a joint Honorary Secretary of the RGS as well, a post to which Markham had been appointed three years earlier. On 13 November 1865 it was 'Resolved that Mr R. H. Major be invited to attend the Council meetings and to act as Secretary in the absence of Mr C. R. Markham and Mr Laurence Oliphant'.[4] Whereas Hakluyt Society meetings were intermittent during Markham's absences, the RGS Council maintained a punishing schedule of fortnightly meetings. For the two months before Oliphant's return, Major was carrying out the duties of three Honorary Secretaries and running two societies. By the time he was formally appointed a joint Honorary Secretary of the RGS

Council Minutes, 9 November 1846. One of the others was John Edward Gray, the British Museum's Keeper of Zoology and a member of the original Hakluyt Society Council. See Bridges, 'Cooley', above, for these disputes at the RGS. If Major and Cooley were involved in the same campaign, then Major was in a sense involved also in the inception of the Society he was destined to administer from 1849.

[1] RGSA, Correspondence Block 1841–50, 'R. H. Major', 17 July 1847. The reference is to Martín Fernández de Navarrete, *Colección de los viajes*, 5 vols, Madrid, 1825–37. This supplied the Spanish text for most of the documents Major used.

[2] RGSA, Correspondence Block 1851–60, 'R. H. Major', 15 March 1856.

[3] J. H., *Biography*, p. 10.

[4] RGS Council Minutes, 13 November 1865. Major attended for the first time on 27 November.

in succession to Oliphant in May 1866, Markham had returned, no doubt to Major's great relief. Once more Major was serving Murchison, who, for the last nine years of his life again combined the presidencies of the two societies. With this trio in charge at the RGS, it is hardly surprising that the older Society readily agreed to the Hakluyt Society holding, for the first time on 2 July 1872, its meetings at the RGS headquarters – where the Council has gathered ever since.[1]

During Major's fifteen years in the RGS post, he was to work with seven presidents. His role was largely an advisory one, with the day to day work carried out by the assistant secretary, H. W. Bates.[2] Nevertheless, despite the fact that within less than a year of the RGS appointment Major would be embroiled in setting up and then running the newly created Map Department in the British Museum, he was an assiduous attender at the meetings of Council and of the numerous special committees. In early 1867, for example, he was at the RGS on average once a week. Besides his administrative role, Major found time to deliver four papers to the RGS and, representing his final published work, a flurry of letters in 1883. Again, these are discussed below as part of his overall output.[3] The ill health that led to Major's resignation from the British Museum caused him to relinquish the RGS secretaryship in the following year, 1881. For three years he served as a Vice President, after which he returned to Council for a final year. By the summer of 1885 his retirement from professional life was complete.[4]

If Major had initially sought favours from the RGS, he made up for it a hundredfold in the services he provided in return, in particular as midwife to three separate RGS catalogues. The year before he became an Honorary Secretary a catalogue of the library had been published,

[1] Ibid., 11 March 1872, resolved that the Hakluyt Society might meet whenever the 'room is not required for the Meetings of the Council or a Committee'.

[2] Major's assistance to Markham has been considered as 'in the main consultative' (Hugh R. Mill, *The Record of the Royal Geographical Society 1830–1930*, London, 1930, p. 102). Yet a letter from Major to the then President, Sir Henry Rawlinson, showed him proposing a solution to the vexed question of presidential expenses (RGSA, Correspondence Block 1871–80, 'R. H. Major', 28 September 1875).

[3] Major read papers or 'remarks' contributed on the following subjects: the map of Africa published in Pigafetta's 'Kingdom of Congo' in 1591' (1867), the landfall of Columbus (1871), the first discovery of Australia (1872), the lost colony of Greenland (1873), a 1591 map of the African lakes (1874). All were published in the *Journal of the Royal Geographical Society* [hereafter *JRGS*] or *PRGS*, as were five letters in 1883. Those not discussed below are: 'On the map of Africa published in Pigafetta's "Kingdom of Congo" in 1591', *PRGS*, 11, 1867, pp. 246–51; [on the Lopez-Pigafetta map of the African lakes], ibid., 18, p. 147; 'Geographical Department, British Museum', ibid., new monthly series, 5, 1883, pp. 294–6; [letters on Greenland and Iceland], ibid., pp. 294–6, 408–9, 473–5, 725–8.

[4] He attended the RGS Council for the last time on 8 June 1885.

arranged in the traditional alphabetical author sequence. However, since 1850, Council had decided that the library's catalogue should be provided with a geographical index and active steps were taken in the late 1860s to produce such a 'classified catalogue'.[1] Major was involved in these discussions from 1867 onwards, and when it was clear that J. H. Lamprey, the Librarian, was having difficulties, Major and the cartographer Alexander G. Findlay were asked to take charge. For five years the Library Committee had been grappling with delays and its own indecisions on both the supplement and the geographical index, until finally, in June 1869, it was agreed that 'Mr Evans be employed during the recess in preparing the Alphabetical Index of places'.[2] Godfrey Matthew Evans was a colleague of Major's, an Assistant in the Department of Printed Books.[3] Major's choice was a good one and Evans duly completed both works for publication in 1871: the five-year author supplement (1865–70) and – what had now become a separate volume – a cumulative Classified Catalogue of the RGS Library, to December, 1870. This latter comprised simplified forms of the author entries arranged in an alphabetical geographical sequence. Evans's preface uninformatively described this catalogue as having been 'made upon a plan'. In fact, its headings and cross-references exactly mirror those of Major's own (then unpublished) catalogue of the printed maps in the British Museum, as can be seen from its 1885 printed form.

Evans was Major's protégé when he started work for the RGS in 1869. By the time the work was complete, Evans was Major's son-in-law. It is hardly fanciful to think that the RGS catalogue was the unlikely matchmaker between Evans and Major's younger daughter, Sarah Isabelle, whom Evans married in 1870 when she was aged 17. The couple set up house next door to the Majors. As an Assistant, Evans was not well paid and the £175 he was awarded by the RGS was little short of his annual salary.[4] Altogether, he had considerable reason to be grateful to his new father-in-law. Sadly, any further collaboration there might have been between Major and his son-in-law neighbour was cut short by the latter's early death in 1877, leaving the 24-year old Sarah Isabelle with two young children. When, in 1881, the Majors moved to Kensington, the Evans's went with them.

If Major's stamp was on the geographical index to the library catalogue,

[1] RGSA, Catalogue Committee, 20 January 1859, referring to the 1850 rule.
[2] RGSA, Library Committee, 16 April 1869, 25 June 1869.
[3] G. M. Evans joined the British Museum as a Transcriber in 1856 and was promoted to Assistant in 1862; his brother, Charles John, joined the Museum, as an Assistant in the Department of Printed Books, in 1858.
[4] RGS Library Committee, 26 May 1871.

he was also involved in the RGS's equally innovative map catalogue. The idea of such a publication had been mooted back in the 1850s.[1] It was not until 1878, though, when Council constituted a subcommittee of the Library and Maps Committee to pursue the matter, that the project was officially constituted. The group comprised Major, Markham and James Fergusson, the architectural historian and longstanding Council member. As published in March 1882, *The Catalogue of the Map Room of the Royal Geographical Society* was prepared, as it explained, in accordance with (unspecified) instructions handed down by the subcommittee in June 1878. In fact, the published catalogue is closely based on a surviving manuscript catalogue in two volumes, drawn up in or before 1866.[2] Unless Major had been privately consulted about the original arrangement, he cannot take any credit for the catalogue's structure. Nevertheless, it is worth noting that, while the British Museum Library was the first great national collection to print its own map catalogue (in 1885), the RGS – partly through the agency of the British Museum's Keeper of Maps – was the second institution in this country to achieve that distinction.[3]

While the trio of learned societies – Hakluyt, Antiquaries and Royal Geographical – occupied most of his attention, Major did play a part in other organisations as well. The 'F. R. S. L.' he was proud to place after his name referred to the Royal Society of Literature. He joined this in 1860, no doubt at the instigation of the Secretary, his British Museum colleague Vaux, and he would later serve on its Council for several years.[4] Another appointment of which he was proud was his election in 1870 to the Athenaeum Club.[5] But clearly less to Major's liking than the intimate world of London's clubs and societies was the hurly burly of national and international conferences. The British Association for the Advancement of Science met annually but Major appears to have attended on just two occasions. In 1866 he was elected a member, in time to serve as one of several secretaries to the Geography and Ethnology

---

[1] For example, Major's British Museum predecessor, William Hughes, made the suggestion in a letter to the Secretary in 1854 (Francis Herbert, 'The Royal Geographical Society's Membership, the Map Trade, and Geographical Publishing in Britain 1830 to ca. 1930', *Imago Mundi*, 35, 1983, p. 71).

[2] It was referred to at a committee meeting on 5 March 1866.

[3] The first was the India Office Library (now part of the British Museum's successor institution, the British Library), its catalogue compiled by none other than the RGS's former map curator, Trelawney Saunders, under the direction of none other than Clements Markham, the Honorary Secretary of the Hakluyt Society.

[4] J. H., *Biography*, p. 9. Vaux was a fellow Hakluyt Society editor and an FRGS.

[5] On 16 May 1870. He was proposed by Murchison, the current RGS President, and seconded by Rawlinson, Murchison's successor. He thereafter gave the Athenaeum as an alternative address in the Society of Antiquaries membership list.

Section at the Nottingham conference (along with his RGS colleagues
Markham and Bates) and to deliver a paper on the fourteenth-century
discovery of the Madeira group.[1] Major was listed with his title as
Honorary Secretary of the RGS, to which he had been appointed a few
months earlier. Since he had never attended these annual conferences
before, it is highly likely that he was made to feel that, as a senior figure
in the RGS, his presence was required. If this was the case, it did not
take him long to find the will to resist. He next attended in 1870, the
year that saw the revised edition of his Columbus letters for the Hakluyt Society, when he delivered a paper on the Columbus landfall to the
Liverpool meeting.[2] Major's regular trips abroad during the periods of
British Association conferences explains some of his absences but he
was no more assiduous in attending international meetings. He sent his
regrets to the first International Geographical Congress, held at
Antwerp in 1871. This was despite the fact that he, like Livingstone,
was a member of the Comité d'Honneur, and despite his being in
nearby Ostend at the time, presumably on holiday. He did attend the
second conference, at Paris in 1875, but the proceedings record no
measurable contribution by him, not even when one of the sessions was
devoted to the discovery of Australia.[3] Nevertheless, Major's de-
briefing letter to the RGS President, Sir Henry Rawlinson, voted it a
great success, on the grounds that he had been invited to the Elysée
dinner.[4] On that ceremonial note ended Major's last official trip abroad.

Major's Writings

Major seems to have found conferences uncongenial, preferring to
broadcast his latest views and discoveries via papers to learned societies
and through the pages of their journals. Given his habit of using

[1] R. H. Major, 'On priority in discovery of the Madeira group', Report of the Thirty-
sixth Meeting of the British Association for the Advancement of Science; held at Nottingham in
August 1866, London, 1867, 'Report – 1866', p. 112.
[2] R. H. Major, 'The Landfall of Columbus', abstract in Report of the Fortieth Meeting of
the British Association for the Advancement of Science, Held at Liverpool in September 1870,
London, 1871, 'Report – 1870', pp. 171–2. Besides providing an opportunity to publicise
his forthcoming volume, the conference also meant he could stay beforehand with his
friend Lord Stanley. (The British Museum Map Department letterbooks record that
Major was written to at Congleton, Cheshire, not too far from Liverpool, on 13
September and again the next day, the opening day of the conference.) An added spur
could have been the fact that Murchison, still President of the RGS, was that year's
president of the Section.
[3] The 1871 conference was held 14–22 August; he was at Ostend and Spa 2–30 August.
For the 1875 session, see Congrès international des sciences géographiques tenu à Paris . . . 1875.
Compte rendu des séances, 2 vols, Paris, 1878–80, II, pp. 512–25.
[4] RGSA, Correspondence Block 1871–80, 'R. H. Major', 28 September 1875.

multiple publishing routes to explore a given topic, and then often returning to it some years later, it is convenient to look at his more significant output topic by topic. The analysis that follows does not, however, attempt to be exhaustive. Major's most important contributions concerned the discovery and early mapping of America and Australia respectively, fourteenth century exploration in the North Atlantic, and – his single most important work – the life of Prince Henry of Portugal, 'Henry the Navigator'.

The events surrounding the discovery of the New World provided Major with his most abiding interest. He returned to two aspects of the story repeatedly throughout his working life: the bibliographical details of Columbus's earliest published letters about his discovery, and the modern identity of the first landfall. It is no coincidence that his first and last publications should have discussed the landfall issue. The long introduction to his first venture into print, the 1847 edition of the Columbus letters for the Hakluyt Society, touched on both these favoured themes. To take the landfall first, Major followed the theory of Martín Fernández de Navarrete – the source equally for most of the Spanish texts he used – that Guanahani represented Great Turk. Twenty-three years later he had reason to change his mind, announcing his new decision in a paper read to the 1870 British Association meeting at Liverpool. He there 'had the honour of proving for the first time that the first anchorage of Columbus in the New World was off the S.E. point of Watling's Island'. The new theory was elaborated in his revised edition of the Columbus letters, in a paper to the RGS on 8 May 1871, and finally reaffirmed in the last of his letters to the RGS, in 1883.[1] However much Major's theories might fluctuate, he was never in doubt as to their absolute certainty. Given his hope in 1870 that his argument 'will finally settle this much vexed question', he would certainly have been surprised to see the debate still raging in the quinquecentennial issue of the leading history of discoveries journal.[2]

The other aspect of the American discovery to which Major returned repeatedly was the bibliographical analysis of the first four Columbus letters. A mere four pages in the first edition of the Hakluyt Society volume, this had expanded to thirty-five by the time of the second. 'In this he proved that an edition, printed by Stephen Blannck at Rome, in

---

[1] Major, *Columbus Letters*, 1847 (HS 2), p. liii; abstract, *Report . . . British Association, 1871*, 'Report – 1870', pp. 171–2; Major, *Columbus Letters*, 1870 (HS 43), pp. lviii–lxiii; 'The landfall of Columbus', *JRGS*, 41, 1871, pp. 193–210 (summary *PRGS*, 15, 1871, pp. 210–11); 'The landfall of Columbus', *PRGS*, new monthly series 6, 1884, pp. 42–3.

[2] Major, *Columbus Letters*, 1870 (HS 43), p. lx; *Terrae Incognitae*, 24, 1992.

1493, and which had previously stood fourth in priority, was the real *editio princeps'* – it was so stated in the authorised biography. The enlarged bibliography was later published separately, without its antecedents being acknowledged.[1]

The nineteenth-century history of cartography was much concerned to establish the priority of discoveries. As befitted a pioneer in this field and a librarian, Major was also keen to determine cartographic and bibliographical 'firsts'. A good example of this was his Society of Antiquaries paper in 1864 on the subject of a series of hand-drawn globe gores in the royal collection at Windsor. Major assigned these to Leonardo da Vinci and, dating the gores to 1513–1514, considered them to present the earliest cartographic evidence of the name 'America'. When the separately published version of the Antiquaries paper was acquired by the British Museum Map Room in 1904, the catalogue entry noted dismissively that the gores were 'proved not to be by [Leonardo's] hand'. More recent scholarship is less certain but inclined to dispute both the attribution and the early date.[2] Cartographic doubts were expressed more quickly. In a postscript dated less than a year later and issued with the original paper, Major sought to rebut the claim by Friedrich Kunstmann that a printed map by Stobnicza antedated the Windsor globe gores. Major was sceptical about the very existence of the Stobnicza map. As it happens, both scholars were wrong. The map exists but names the new continent Terra Incognita, not America. The subsequent discovery of 'America' on two earlier printed maps – a Ptolemaic world map possibly dating from 1507 and the Waldseemüller wall-map clearly dated that year – have rendered that particular argument irrelevant.[3] On 'the true date of the English discovery of the American Continent under John and Sebastian Cabot' Major has been

[1] Major, *Columbus Letters*, 1847 (HS 2), pp. ii–vi; *Columbus Letters*, 1870 (HS 43), pp. cviii–cxlii; J. H., *Biography*, p. 4; *The Bibliography of the First Letter of Christopher Columbus, describing his Discovery of the New World*, London, 1872 [limited edition of 75 copies, 50 for sale], reprinted Amsterdam, 1971.

[2] R. H. Major, 'Memoir on a Mappemonde by Leonardo da Vinci; being the earliest map hitherto known containing the name of America; now in the Royal Collection at Windsor; in a letter addressed to Augustus Wollaston Franks Esq., Director', *Archaeologia*, 40, 1866, pp. 1–36 [paper read to the Society of Antiquaries 26 May 1864, summary *PSAL*, 2nd series, 2, 1864, p. 417]; Justin Winsor, *Narrative and Critical History of America*, 8 vols., Boston and New York, 1889, II, p. 124 (citing J. P. Richter, 1883, as doubting the attribution); [Mario Baratta, et al.], *I manoscritti e i disegni di Leonardo da Vinci publicati dalla Reale Commissione Vinciana sotto gli auspice del Ministero dell'Educazione Nazionale. I disegni geografici conservati nel Castello di Windsor. Fascicolo Unico*, Rome, 1941, pp. 14–16, 32, 33; *British Museum. Catalogue of Printed Maps, Charts and Plans*, London, 1967, vol. 9, col. 511.

[3] *Archaeologia*, 40, 1866, pp. 37–40; Rodney W. Shirley, *The Mapping of the World: Early Printed World Maps 1472–1700*, London, 1993, nos 26, 33, 35.

better treated by posterity.[1] His contention that the English should accept a loss of three years over the Cabot voyage, through a misreading of the 1497 manuscript date as 1494, is now conventional wisdom.

As far as the history of cartography is concerned Major made his biggest impact with his claim for a Portuguese discovery of Australia, though here again he was obliged to change his mind. It was well known that the Dutch had outlined most of the Australian coast, in a series of voyages from 1606 onwards. The hypothesis revived by Major pushed the first landfall back some three-quarters of a century, and transferred the honour to Portugal. The claim, a reworking of those made previously by, inter alia, Alexander Dalrymple (1786) and Barbié du Bocage (1807), first appeared in his 1859 Hakluyt Society volume on early voyages to 'Terra Australis', but was elaborated and modified in papers and publications for the Hakluyt Society, the Society of Antiquaries, and the RGS over the next fourteen years. The thesis was to depend, for the most part, on cartographic evidence, to which, as is explained below, Major was probably alerted by Ellis.

In 1859, Major was able to identify six charts showing 'Java la Grande', a large and incomplete landmass to the south of Indonesia. Because of the charts' corrupted Portuguese toponymy, and other documentary evidence, he concluded that it was 'highly probable that Australia was discovered by the Portuguese between the years 1511 and 1529, and, almost to a demonstrable certainty, that it was discovered before the year 1542'. Two years later, on 1 March 1861, Major returned to the topic, sending a letter to Ellis, which was read at the Antiquaries' meeting on 7 March. Two-thirds of this was a recapitulation of the earlier statement, and it is instructive to read Major's own justification for what would become a pattern of repetition in his writings: 'for brevity's sake I have omitted the minuter details, and in some cases remodelled my language; but that, where no advantage was to be gained thereby, I have not pretended for the mere sake of appearance to alter the language in which I had written before. Such a proceeding seemed to me to be disingenuous and therefore unworthy'.[2]

The gist of the new matter, and the point of the paper, was to

---

[1] R. H. Major, 'The true date of the English discovery of the American continent under John and Sebastian Cabot: a letter addressed . . . to C. S. Perceval, esq.', *Archaeologia*, 43, 1871, pp. 17–42 [paper read to the Society of Antiquaries, 5 May 1870, summary *PSAL*, 2nd series, 4, 1870, p. 484].

[2] Major, *Early Voyages to Terra Australis*, p. lxiv; Major, 'On the discovery of Australia', p. 440. As stated on p. 99, note 3 above, an essentially unaltered 'Extract' from the 1860 article was issued to Hakluyt Society members that same year as a supplement to *Early Voyages*. The date of the original letter was omitted at its first appearance but inserted in the 'Extract'.

announce the discovery 'within the last few days' of a manuscript
mappemonde in the British Museum. This bore a legend attributing the
discovery of Java la Grande [i.e., Australia] to Manoel Godinho de
Erédia in 1601, five years before the earliest known Dutch contact.
Although this new evidence pointed to a date sixty years later than
Australia's 'certain' discovery by the Portuguese, Major considered the
British Museum chart to be important for fixing the 'earliest known
voyage to Australia by which a date and the discoverer's name can be
attached', and further proving that this had been 'made by the Portuguese'. The map in question, which Major appreciated was a recent
copy, had, as he explained, been acquired by the British Museum in
1848. That it needed 'discovery' by Major some thirteen years later is a
reflection of three circumstances: the size of the Michelena collection of
which it was a part; that Major had no jurisdiction over manuscript
maps; and that the published catalogue description – surprisingly for a
world map, under 'America' – made no mention of Erédia or of the
1601 inscription.[1] Major considered that the British Museum mappemonde was based on one drawn about 1620 by Erédia himself. By
the time his book on 'Prince Henry' appeared in 1868, with a broadly
unaltered account of the Erédia story, Major had discovered, 'from a
letter addressed to Navarrete by the Vicomte de Santarem in 1835', that
the Erédia map was based on one drawn in the seventeenth century by
the Portuguese chartmaker, João Teixeira. Subsequent research has
confirmed this.[2]

Major's attempt to unearth aboriginal traditions of early European
discovery, the prompting of a letter to the Ethnological Society of
London in 1861, brought no apparent response.[3] The next development
on the Erédia front occurred in March 1872, when Major was able to
read a paper to the Society of Antiquaries with 'further facts' on the
matter. This announced two additional discoveries: first, that Ruelens,
Librarian of the Royal Burgundian Library in Brussels, had found
Erédia's original report to Philip III, dated 1613. This Major rushed to

---

[1] BL, Add. MS 17647A; *Catalogue of the Manuscript Maps, Charts and Plans and of the
Topographical Drawings in the British Museum*, 2 vols, London, 1844; vol. 3 printed 1861
but not released, III, p. 448. The catalogue description was probably made by John
Holmes, although it was not printed until shortly after his death and might have been the
work of his Keeper, Sir Frederick Madden, who saw the third volume of the catalogue of
manuscript maps through the press.
[2] Major, *Prince Henry*, pp. 442–7, specifically p. 442; Armando Cortesão and Avelino
Teixeira da Mota, *Portugaliae monumenta cartographica*, 6 vols, Lisbon, 1960, IV, pp. 43,
116–18, where it is treated as a late eighteenth or early nineteenth century copy of a chart
in an atlas by João Teixeira of about 1630.
[3] Major, 'Native Australian traditions'.

communicate, before having seen a transcript. He noted that Ruelens had sent this to him in November 1871; in fact it formed the substance of a paper presented by Ruelens, the preceding August, to the International Geographical Congress at Antwerp, which Major did not attend.[1] The second new piece of evidence concerned the 1531 double-cordiform world map of Oronce Finé that had just been purchased by the British Museum. Major was evidently the first to write about this map. He concluded that, while providing further confirmation of an early discovery of Australia, its toponymy pointed to Provence, not Portugal. In defending his early concentration on Portugal, Major was able to point out that the French had never claimed Australia for themselves. He ended by hoping for documentary corroboration but not by means of an 'infamous French forgery'.[2] To proceed further, Major needed to see the text of the Erédia report. In his annual presidential address to the RGS on 27 May 1872, Rawlinson reported that Major was still hoping that the Portuguese minister in Brussels would be able to publish the document.[3] Following an alternative tack, Major wrote to the Antiquaries on 25 June to ask if they would pay for it, since the Portuguese had decided the expense was too great. These efforts proved successful.[4] On 9 January 1873 Major returned to the Society of Antiquaries to share 'supplementary facts' with them. Sadly, it *was* an infamous forgery he had to announce, though Portuguese rather than French. Armed with a transcription, he was able to show, largely on linguistic grounds, that Erédia's report to the king, and hence the related map, recounted imaginary discoveries.[5] A few years later Major had his last word on the subject, ending his abridged Prince Henry with the following declaration: 'I repeat that I am not ashamed that with the amount of evidence that then lay before me I believed him [Erédia]; but I am very happy in the thought, that, so soon as the field of evidence was enlarged, it was I, who alone had been responsible

---

[1] Major, 'Further facts', p. 234; *Compte-rendu du Congrès des Sciences Géographiques, Cosmographiques et Commerciales tenu à Anvers du 14 au 22 Août 1871*, 2 vols, Antwerp, 1872, II, pp. 513–25.

[2] Major, 'Further facts', pp. 237–41; Shirley, *World Maps*, no. 66.

[3] *PRGS*, 16, 1872, p. 352.

[4] MS London, Society of Antiquaries, letter from Major to the Secretary, 25 June 1872; J. H., *Biography*, p. 9 ('The Chevalier d'Antas, the Portuguese Minister in Brussels, obligingly supplied Mr. Major with an extract of that portion with which he was immediately concerned').

[5] Note, however, that more recent opinion considers that Major's 'grotesquely exaggerated repudiation . . . discredited Erédia's modest but real claims as a well-informed cosmographer' (O. H. K. Spate. 'Luso-Australia: in maps and verse', *Revista da Universidade de Coimbra*, 27, 1979, also Série separatas 124, Centro de Estudos de Cartografia Antiga, Lisbon, 1979, p. 222).

for its promulgation, that had the good fortune at once to detect the imposture'.[1]

If Erédia proved to be a red herring, the debate about a sixteenth-century European discovery of Australia remains lively today, with the Portuguese position having been restated by the late Helen Wallis and a claim for a still earlier French encounter made by Elizabeth Bonner – these reflecting, respectively, Major's early and final positions. There have, however, been forceful dissenting voices.[2]

The other main geographical focus for Major was the Atlantic: Portuguese discoveries in its central section and Italian towards the north. His first foray into the exploration of the central Atlantic took the form of a paper at the Nottingham meeting of the British Association. Using the Medici Atlas in Florence, on the basis of its supposed date of 1351, he showed that the Madeira group had been discovered in the early fourteenth century by Genoese in the service of Portugal.[3] Much of Major's most celebrated work, the study of 'Henry the Navigator', continued in like manner, assigning a new, earlier discoverer to the various Atlantic island groups. Ironically, given the effect that winter cold had on Major's health in the latter part of his life, most of the writings from his last decade of literary activity concerned the frozen north. The commentary he prepared for his final Hakluyt Society volume in 1873, an edition of the accounts of the fourteenth-century voyages of the Zeno brothers to the 'Northern Seas', opened up to renewed historical scrutiny documents whose significance, and indeed authenticity, are still matters of debate. Although claims that the manuscripts were fraudulent had been made as early as 1830, Major championed the Zeno story with vehemence. While discussion continues to centre today on the Zenos' 'Frislanda', identified by Major as the Faeroes, he recognised the greater interest in the restated argument for a pre-Columbian Norse discovery of America, and accordingly delivered

---

[1] R. H. Major, 'Supplementary facts in the history of the discovery of Australia', *Archaeologia*, 44, 1873, pp. 242–58 (summary *PSAL*, 2nd series, 5, pp. 386–7); Major, *The Discoveries of Prince Henry*, p. 310, an appendix (pp. 301–10) restating the earlier arguments.

[2] Helen Wallis, ed., *The Maps and Text of the Boke of Idrography. Presented by Jean Rotz to Henry VIII, now in the British Library*, Oxford, 1981, pp. 58–67; Helen Wallis, 'Java la Grande: the Enigma of the Dieppe Maps', in Glyndwr Williams and Alan Frost, eds, *Terra Australis to Australia*, Melbourne, 1988, pp. 39–81; Elizabeth Bonner, 'Did the French Discover Australia? The First French Scientific Voyage of Discovery, 1503–1505', in David W. Lovell, ed., *Revolution, Politics, and Society: Elements in the Making of Modern France*, Canberra, 1994, pp. 40–8; Stuart Duncan, 'Shaving with Ockham's Razor: a Reappraisal of the Portuguese Priority Hypothesis', *The Globe: Journal of the Australian Map Circle*, 39, 1993, pp. 1–9 (including a discussion of the toponymic analysis made by W. A. R. Richardson).

[3] Abstract in *Report . . . . of the British Association . . . 1866*, 'Report – 1866', p. 112.

that section of his commentary as a paper to the RGS.[1] Victor Emmanuel
II clearly overlooked this slight to Italy's most famous son in awarding
Major a knighthood for the main substance of the Zeno voyages edition. It is doubtful if any other Hakluyt Society volume has been
accorded an equivalent honour.

Major was in many ways a pioneer in the history of discoveries and
in many respects courageous – if sometimes foolhardy – in defending
the positions he adopted. As a geographical historian he had a number
of advantages: a command of the relevant European languages, ac-
quaintanceship with all the leading figures in the history of discoveries
and its related field, and, in the British Museum, many of the original
manuscripts from which new evidence could be culled. Given that the
subject has been largely defined since by the Hakluyt Society, in
Major's time much that was fresh could still be found. Because he
wrote in an age that had yet to value the footnote, establishing the
originality of a fact or a theory in his writings would demand a large-
scale exercise in literary archaeology.[2] Yet Major's repeated claims, for
example in his *Prince Henry*, that such and such a navigator was 'now
first shown' to have been its first discoverer, seem well-founded. That
Major's name appears infrequently in footnotes today is because most
of the positions he established have either become recognised fact or
have been overtaken by new and conflicting evidence. Either way, he
tends to be ignored more than he deserves. Much of today's discussion
on the discovery of Australia or discoveries in the Atlantic owes an
unacknowledged debt to Major. Alternatively – and the signs are
already there – he will be demonised for the supposed sin of projecting
Victorian Britain's imperial ambitions onto a largely mythical, half-
English 'Prince Henry'. To be forgotten may be a greater tragedy than
to be misunderstood.

In his own day, Major certainly did not go unrecognized, at least

---

[1] Major, *Voyages of the . . . Zeno* (HS 50); R. H. Major, 'The site of the lost colony of
Greenland determined and pre-Columbian discoveries of America confirmed, from 14th
century documents', *JRGS*, 43, 1873, pp. 156–206 (summary *PRGS*, 17, 1873, 312–21).
Major had put this view, based on Rafn (1837), in his first work, the 1847 edition of the
Columbus letters: for a contemporary assessment of the argument and Major's place in it,
see Winsor, *America*, I, pp. 94–6, also a supportive report, probably by the editor
Clements Markham, in *Ocean Highways: the Geographical Review*, n.s. 1, 1873, 171–3. A
resumé of the introduction to the Hakluyt Society volume appeared in *Proceedings of the
Massachusetts Historical Society*, 13, 1875, pp. 352–66, and was published separately;
similarly an Italian translation, 'Del viaggi dei fratelli Zeno, dissertazione di R. H. Major',
Archivio Veneto, 7, 1874, pp. 301–28; 8, 1875, pp. 262–304, was also published separately.
Major defended his identification of 'Frislanda' in R. H. Major, 'Zeno's Frislanda is not
Iceland, but the Faroes; an answer to Admiral Irminger', *JRGS*, 49, 1879, pp. 412–20.

[2] Though much of the same ground was gone over, with exhaustive bibliographical
precision, by Justin Winsor.

abroad. The history of cartography, particularly where it ventures into questions of priority in geographical discovery, runs the risk of being consumed in the fires of nationalism. Major, however, was almost invariably acting as advocate for other nations.[1] He was duly rewarded by the crowned heads concerned. The first of these, following Major's claim for a sixteenth-century Portuguese discovery of Australia, was the Knighthood of the Tower and Sword, presented to him by Pedro V of Portugal in 1861. This was upgraded by his successor Luís I – in the wake of Major's 1868 study of the Infante D. Henrique, alias Prince Henry – from Knighthood to Officer. As an exceptional mark of favour, the Collar of the Order was sent to Major in gold.[2] At some unspecified later date he was made a Knight Commander of the Order of Santiago (St James of the Sword) by the same monarch.[3] With an unfortunate sense of timing, the Emperor of Brazil, Dom Pedro II, in an act of solidarity with Portuguese royalty, created him a Knight Officer of the Rose of Brazil in 1873, the year in which Major transferred the honour of Australia's first discovery from Portugal to France.[4] Had Napoleon III been still on the throne, Major might have expected recognition from Paris.[5] As it was, the French were by then into their Third Republic and Major's final award would come instead from Italy.

[1] If we discount the honorary Englishman, Cabot, whose American discovery he anyway diminished by moving it three years later. The claim of the Englishman, Robert Machin, to have discovered Porto Santo and Madeira in 1418 was substantiated in Major's *Prince Henry* (chapter V), only for the honour to be reassigned in Chapter VIII to the earlier voyage of Jean de Béthencourt, whose account Major would later edit for the Hakluyt Society. However, a recent Portuguese historian has argued, citing Major at length, that discovery by Machin is 'not to be lightly dismissed' (Armando Cortesão, 'A história de descobrimento das Ilhas de Madeira por Roberto Machin em fim do século XIV / The story of Robert Machin's discovery of the Madeira Islands in the XIV century', *Revista da Universidade de Coimbra*, 23, 1973, pp. 394–409, also Série separatas 85, Agrupamento de Estudos de Cartografia Antiga, Junta de Investigações do Ultramar, Coimbra, 1973).

[2] Following Major's Society of Antiquaries paper (which had been translated into Portuguese), 'the late King Dom Pedro V. who had been intending to give him a decoration in recognition of his previous work on "Early Voyages to Terra Australis" (1859), then said, "Now Mr. Major shall have the Tower and Sword", that being the highest Order the King had to confer; and accordingly he bestowed on him the Knighthood of that Order' (Cowtan, *Memories*, p. 379). The insignia of the decoration survive with a descendant. *Prince Henry* also had a Portuguese translation. On the Portuguese and the following awards, see Peter Allpress, 'A Much Decorated Geographer – R. H. Major', *Journal of the International Map Collectors' Society*, 50, 1992, p. 39.

[3] J. H., *Biography*, p. 10.

[4] Major wrote to the Brazilian Legation on 5 May 1873, presumably in connection with this.

[5] Apart from Major's attempt to claim French discovery of Australia, he wrote a popular note on on an explorer of North America who worked for France: R. H. Major, 'Verazzano', *Pall Mall Gazette*, 26 May 1876, reprinted *Geographical Magazine*. 3, 1876, pp. 186–8.

In 1874, as stated above, Victor Emmanuel II appointed him a Knight Commander of the Crown of Italy, in recognition of the previous year's Hakluyt Society edition of the Zeno voyages.[1] Major was the classic case of 'a prophet without honour in his own country'. It is doubly ironic that he should have received no formal recognition at all in Britain, while being honoured in two southern European countries he had probably not visited during his British Museum career.[2]

Within the British Museum

The British Museum formed the bedrock of Major's life, giving him academic status and the opportunity, already described, to play an active role in London's learned societies. Major joined the Museum in early 1844 to fill a vacancy caused by the 'retirement' of William Hughes, the map cataloguer.[3] Major took over Hughes's responsibilities. These related to maps in the Department of Printed Books, but not, confusingly, to those in the Department of Manuscripts. A distinction, on the basis of medium, between printed and hand-drawn maps is understandable, if, for modern users, unhelpful. But enforcement of the twin principles of departmental autonomy and the integrity of collections blurred a division that was supposedly defined by subject expertise. The most notable contradiction was the presence of several thousand manuscript maps in what then formed the bulk of the cartographic

---

[1] J. H., *Biography*, p. 13. In due course, the insignia of these foreign knighthoods were incorporated into Major's own coat of arms, with its motto '*Deus anchora major*'. The arms were Gules an Anchor Argent on a Chief Or three Roses Gules, with the crest of a Greyhound's Head couped Gules collared and ringed Or (letter from T. D. Mathew, Windsor Herald, 15 July 1994). The arms had been confirmed to a Hampshire Major family in 1628, as Major learnt on a visit to the College of Heralds in 1861. (A copy of the sheet on which Major set out the genealogy of his ancestors was kindly supplied by a descendant.) Thereafter, he used the arms on letters, even on occasions those written from the British Museum, for example, a letter to Panizzi on his retirement, 18 July 1866 (BL, Add. MS 36723, ff. 510–11). Two versions of Major's bookplate have been identified, the first showing the insignia of his Portuguese knighthood of the Tower and Sword, the later version adding his three subsequent knighthoods. Examples of both versions are held by a descendant, the earlier form in a copy of Major's *Canarian* of 1872. On the later version, see Allpress, 'A Much Decorated Geographer', and Peter Allpress, 'Bookplates of Unusual Characters: 15. Richard Henry Major', *Newsletter of the Bookplate Society*, 14, no. 4, 1992, p. 40. (Allpress kindly drew my attention to an example of the early form in the British Museum, Prints & Drawings, Franks no. 19539.) A frontispiece coat of arms from an unidentified quarto work in the possession of a descendant also apparently dates from the 1860s and here the arms of Major, 'by whom this Plate is Presented to the Work', are impaled with those of Thorn, his wife's family.

[2] Certainly the trips recorded in the British Museum Map Department letterbooks during his keepership (1867–80) involved northern Europe only.

[3] Hughes would go on to have a distinguished career as a prolific cartographer, atlas editor, map engraver and Professor of Geography at King's College, London.

holding of Printed Books, namely King George III's Topographical Collection, colloquially known as 'K.Top'. By an amazing coincidence, the Maritime equivalent of K.Top., viz., K.Mar., retained by the Admiralty when K.Top. was presented to the British Museum in 1828, was transferred to the Museum as a result of negotiations begun and finished in the week preceding Major's arrival. Here again there were hand-drawn items, which were retained with the rest of the collection in Printed Books. It was only during the brief period of Major's keepership that a single map expert had general responsibility for the Museum's collection of maps. This explains why Major was not involved in the publication of the catalogue of manuscript maps, the work largely of John Holmes in the Department of Manuscripts. The first two volumes of this catalogue appeared in the year of Major's arrival, the last was delayed until 1861 – and then printed but not published.[1] In confirmation of what were evidently good relations between Holmes and Major we can cite their joint service on the Hakluyt Society Council. Major may have had nothing to do with Holmes's first period of service (1849–50) but his recall in 1853 during Major's secretaryship would surely have been unthinkable if their complementary roles in the British Museum had created friction.

Major joined the British Museum Library as a cataloguer, with the status of Supernumerary Assistant. A description written fifteen years after Major's arrival explained that below the Keeper there were two Assistant-Keepers and 25 'so called "assistants" who are gentlemen of education and acquirements, chiefly employed in making the catalogue'.[2] Winter Jones's account of 1851 went more into specifics, mentioning Major by task, if not by name.

> . . . for the purpose of forming the catalogue, several gentlemen possessing linguistic qualifications are employed in the library. All are linguists to a considerable extent, some possess this accomplishment in a more than ordinary degree . . . One cataloguer attends solely to Chinese books . . . a fourth devotes his attention to the maps.[3]

Despite these skills and the apparent delegation of responsibility, the cataloguer 'is required, in common with the whole of the Assistants, daily to enter in a diary the business upon which he has been engaged;

---

[1] See p. 117, note 1 above.

[2] *English Cyclopaedia*, London, 1859, column 376. In 1847, there were 15 Supernumerary Assistants arranged by order of initial appointment. Major was no. 6, with, immediately below him, Cannon, Porter and Lardner (all members of the Hakluyt Society), J. B. McCaul, who would later take a 'sketch portrait' of Major, and, at no. 14, J. F. von Bach (another Hakluyt Society member).

[3] *North British Review*, 15, 1851, p. 175.

this diary is inspected and signed periodically by the senior officer of the Department, and by him transmitted to the Principal Librarian'.[1] Linguistic ability Major certainly possessed, as he demonstrated, not least in his work for the Hakluyt Society, throughout his career. Two of his early forays into translation are interesting because of the lurking presence of Panizzi, his Keeper. In 1852, Major translated from French a speech by the Italian statesman, Count Cavour. Panizzi was closely associated with Cavour, who tried to entice him back to Italy. Although there is nothing to link the work directly with Panizzi, the use of William Pickering as printer (Thomas Rodd's successor as British Museum agent) is revealing. The second work, this one undoubtedly carried out at Panizzi's direction, and on Cavour's behalf, was a translation, done from Italian in 1858, of a 'private and confidential' matter relating to the Council of Diplomatic Law of Sardinia and Piedmont.[2] This time there were three others to share the load, all of whom had served under Panizzi as Keeper of Printed Books, Charles Cannon, Campbell Clarke and Richard Garnett.

No collection is of much use without a catalogue. It could certainly be argued that Major's greatest legacy – and one that does not even bear his name – was the continuing catalogue of the printed maps in the Department of Printed Books which he produced. The quantity of entries he created is staggering. His predecessor, Hughes, claimed to have catalogued 'the greater number' of the '15 or 16 thousand maps' then in the Library.[3] The annual statistics, however, credit him with far fewer than 5,000 catalogue entries during his tenure (1841–1843). Yet, during the 37 years that Major was responsible, directly or indirectly, for printed map descriptions, the annual reports chronicle 200,000 main and cross-reference catalogue slips, at an annual average of well over 5,000. Where title slips were originally simple hand-written affairs, copied out neatly by 'transcribers', the development in 1850 of the Wedgwood or 'carbonic' process, which produced three further carbon copies, allowed a second copy of the map catalogue to be produced, for use in the reading room. Since the catalogue was a classified one, in this case by means of a system of geographical headings devised by Major,

[1] 'Names and Salaries' (8 May 1860) (*House of Commons, Sessional Papers*, 1860, xxxix, part 1, p. 300). The quoted job description, for George Bullen, applied equally to Major.

[2] Count Benso di Cavour, *A Speech on the Treaty of Navigation and Commerce between Sardinia and France*, London, 1852 [translated from French]; Consiglio del Contenzioso Diplomatico, *Private and Confidential. The Council of Diplomatic Law, having taken into consideration the following matter ...* [the seizure of the *Cagliari*, etc.], London, [1858] [translated from Italian]. One of Major's later efforts was [Emile Banning], *Africa and the Brussels Geographical Conference*, London, 1877 [translated from French].

[3] Herbert, 'The Royal Geographical Society's membership', p. 71.

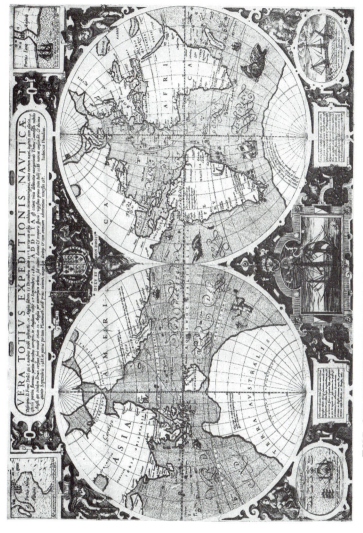

THE CIRCUMNAVIGATIONS OF DRAKE AND CAVENDISH
The Hondius map of 1595, with an inset of 'New Albion.
Reproduced in HS 16 of 1855.

125

new entries had to be interpolated in the appropriate place.[1] As a result, the next thirty years saw a continuous process of revision and re-arrangement of the contents of what became four copies of the catalogue, as the initial 57 volumes grew to well over 300.

The maps situation was a relatively small-scale reflection of a similar problem affecting the printed book catalogue, and the same solution was adopted in each case. Printing the catalogues had been discussed in the British Museum for decades, but resisted, because the supplements that would necessarily result were felt to be less convenient for use than a cumulated manuscript catalogue. With the appointment in August 1878 of a new and reforming Principal Librarian (Bond), who was convinced of the necessity for moving to print, events moved fast.[2] By early 1880, all new book descriptions were being printed, under the supervision of the man who would be Major's successor, Robert K. Douglas. As far as maps were concerned there are hints that Major may not have welcomed the introduction of printing, no doubt realising that to reduce 323 manuscript volumes to print would involve sacrifices, as proved to be the case. In November 1879 he was instructed by the Trustees to prepare a 'scheme for indexing or abridging the catalogues', and in the following month a sum was set aside for the task. But within a fortnight Major was struck down with an extended bout of the illness that would end his Museum career ten months later. Despite his return to work in May, four months before his retirement, it seems that none of the necessary work for preparing the map catalogue for print was carried out during his keepership. Douglas's introduction to the two-volume catalogue, dated November 1885, noted that it was being issued to the public 'within little more than four years of its inception'. Major, it should be noted, had retired a full five years before. Nevertheless, virtually all the matter in the 1885 catalogue had been prepared during Major's time. Since the 1967 successor to that work was essentially an expanded version of the 1885 publication, and since the 1967 work in turn is currently being converted to machine readable form, the labour on which Major spent most of his working hours is being given renewed relevance. By contrast, much of his historical writing has passed into obscurity.

Essential as a catalogue undoubtedly is, it, in turn, is dependent on a programme of acquisitions. As far as antiquarian material is concerned, both operations require a knowledge of the history of cartography. Despite his map responsibilities, Major seems to have come to that

---

[1] The two-volume classification, in Major's hand, survives in the BL Map Library.

[2] Richard Garnett, 'Printing the British Museum Catalogues' [an essay originally written in 1882], in *Essays in Librarianship and Bibliography*, London, 1899, pp. 73–4.

subject relatively late. There is a simple, internal explanation for this. Until John Holmes died in service in 1854, he was the British Museum's acknowledged cartographic expert, as his unpublished note-books reveal.[1] The first evidence of Major's interest in early maps is to be found in his discussion of the Dieppe School charts in his 1859 Hakluyt Society edition, a work that had become Major's editorial responsibility by at least 1855, or, in other words, by the year following Holmes's death. Ellis seems to have encouraged Major in this interest, directing him, in a letter of that year, towards 'portolani' [i.e. early sea charts] as a suitable subject for a Society of Antiquaries paper.[2] It is fair to assume that, had he survived, Holmes would have carried out this investigation himself, and Major's blooding on manuscript maps would have been delayed.

A policy of acquiring historical cartographic materials had only been introduced in the late 1830s and few such items were purchased before Major's arrival.[3] Some of these had come via the bookseller Rodd, who was later to serve, unhappily, as the Hakluyt Society's agent. Since acquisitions were the direct responsibility of a Keeper, Major would have had little opportunity to display any expertise in this direction until he himself became a head of department. His time as Keeper he recorded in print as follows.

> On the 16th of January, 1867, the geographical collection of the British Museum was created a separate department, of which Mr. Major was appointed keeper. . . . In 1880 his state of health induced him to resign the Keepership of the Department of Maps and Charts in the British Museum, which, under his charge, had become the finest cartographical and topographical collection in the world.[4]

These two separated sentences, from the fourteen pages of his author-ised biography, are all the comment Major thought fit to make on his keepership. This is, to say the least, surprising. The 'duties incidental to his official position' – principally, acquiring material and making it accessible through a catalogue – receive no mention. That the creation of a separate department of 'Maps, Charts, Plans and Topographical Drawings' should be considered at all, required the joint resignations,

[1] BL, Add. MS 20751–3, 20774.
[2] BL, Add. MS 70842, f. 140, Ellis to Major, 16 October 1856 (i.e., a few months after Ellis's retirement). In a later, undated letter (presumably written between March 1858 and December 1859), Ellis questioned Major specifically about 'manuscripts which will throw light upon the maritime exertions of the Dieppois' (ibid., 70842, f. 143).
[3] On this, see Philip J. Weimerskirch, *The 1981 AB Bookman's Yearbook. Antonio Panizzi and the British Museum Library*, Clifton, N. J., 1982, pp. 93–9.
[4] J. H., *Biography*, pp. 10, 14.

in 1866, of Sir Anthony Panizzi and Sir Frederick Madden. It is no coincidence that the proposal to establish the map keepership was put to the Trustees the month after Madden's departure.[1] The warring champions of the book and manuscript collections could never have agreed on a department that inherited some of the functions of each. With the giants gone, their replacements were three of Major's Hakluyt Society colleagues, Winter Jones (now Principal Librarian), Bond (Keeper of Manuscripts) and Watts (Keeper of Printed Books). Only Watts objected but he was overruled by the Subcommittee on Printed Books and Manuscripts.[2] Clearly, a large consideration in establishing a map department was that in the 48-year old Major there existed a suitable Keeper. Panizzi and Winter Jones had both considered him to be one of the most able men on their staffs, although the fiercely antagonistic Stefan Poles put this down to Major's being 'an intimate friend of Mr Jones, if, at least, such address as "my dear Dick" implies intimacy'.[3]

Any assessment of Major's legacy must consider both the printed and manuscript material he acquired, since, uniquely in the Museum's history, he was responsible for both. The most accessible source of information is the summary listing in successive annual reports. From this we learn of the important acquisition, made the year following Major's appointment, of the library of Philipp Franz von Siebold, including 92 Japanese maps. Von Siebold, who died in 1866, had long been a member of the Hakluyt Society. In 1850, during Major's secretaryship, he had offered to let the Society use his Tasman manuscript.[4]

When Major submitted his annual account of acquisitions for 1878, two of the three he itemised were photographic reproductions. This might seem strange until it is realised how long it took for the 1820s invention of photography to become a standard aid to research, and commonplace as a means of book illustration. Writing in 1884, Richard Garnett appreciated the 'public benefit to be derived from cheap reproduction and unlimited multiplication with infallible accuracy of historical documents'. But, when commenting again fifteen years later, he

---

[1] BMA, C.11072, 13 October 1866.

[2] BMA, SC 1414, 30 October 1866.

[3] Miller, *That Noble Cabinet*, p. 271; Stefan Poles, *The Actual Condition of the British Museum: a Literary Expostulation*, London [published by the author], 1875, p. 29. The idea that Major was known as 'Dick' in the Museum is somewhat surprising, given the formality of his letters to close colleagues of long standing. Even his brother Seymour wrote to him as 'Richard' (letter with a descendant).

[4] HSCM, 18 June 1850. The von Siebold collection is now split between the Map Library and what is now the Oriental and India Office Collections, but will be reunited in the new 'St Pancras' British Library building.

lamented that 'not a single step has been taken'.[1] The Museum's failure to establish a photographic service by the end of the century puts in context Major's active interest in the medium from the mid-1860s. Seeking a photographic copy of a portrait of 'Prince Henry the Navigator' in the Bibliothèque Impériale for the biography that he would publish three years later, and using Panizzi as an intermediary, in June 1865 Major contacted Prosper Merimée.[2] He had perhaps been hoping to cut through the red tape, but the message came back that he should write directly to the library. Nevertheless, Merimée wrote to Panizzi in November with the message that he had acquired Major's photograph and sent it on.[3] The next recorded indications of Major's interest in photography date from 1869. The 'colour photograph' of the Juan de la Cosa map, which he acquired from Madrid, has already been referred to.[4] In that same year Major obtained the first in a succession of facsimiles of early charts and world maps that led Cowtan, writing in 1872, to hope that 'money will be made available to build up a facsimile collection of all early manuscript mappemondes'.[5] Major had embarked on this course in 1869 by acquiring a full-size photographic copy of the 1459 Fra Mauro map in Venice.[6] When, in April 1873, Baron Heath presented another version of these prints to the Society of Antiquaries, Major was invited to 'say a few words' at the 8 May meeting. After analysing the map's content he described other copies, though not the British Museum example of the Heath photograph. He dwelt instead on the Museum's hand-drawn version produced by William Frazer in

---

[1] Garnett, 'Printing the British Museum Catalogues', p. x. The delay was despite the fact that Bond, prior to his appointment as Principal Librarian, had introduced photography in the Department of Manuscripts 'upon an extensive scale' (W. B. Rye, 'Library Memoranda' [a collection of printed extracts, MS documents, photographs, etc, relating to the British Museum Library], BL Cup.407.cc.8, No. 101). This reluctance is also surprising given that the Museum had been farsighted enough to employ Roger Fenton as official photographer in the 1850s (Christopher Date and Anthony Hamber, 'The Origins of Photography at the British Museum, 1839–1860', *History of Photography*, 14/4, 1990, pp. 309–25).

[2] Prosper Merimée, *Correspondance générale*, 17 vols (including supplements), Paris, 1941–64, XII (deuxième série, 6), pp. 455, 573, Merimée to Panizzi, 7 June, 2 November 1865.

[3] The Map Department letterbooks, which start in 1868, show that Major wrote directly to Merimée on 5 May 1869. Merimée's assistance was duly acknowledged when the work appeared three years later (*Prince Henry*, p. xiii). Interestingly, Major describes how the photograph was used to authenticate the hand-drawn copy on which the published chromolithograph was based.

[4] Since colour photography was not generally available at that time, Major was probably referring to a hand-tinted black and white photograph.

[5] Cowtan, *Memories*, p. 380.

[6] This is preserved, with its rollers, in a large box. There is no date stamp but the date '1869' is given on what would appear to be the original printed label.

1804, which had cost the huge sum of £200. Photography was not only much cheaper, it also avoided the inevitable defect of a copy in that 'one could never be sure of the accuracy of the transcription of the words, which in the original are very often abbreviations'.[1] The vital and unique importance of toponymy to cartography has often been a spur to technical advance.

Whether, before 1867, successive Keepers of Manuscripts sought Major's advice about the acquisition of manuscript maps is unclear. Once the separate map department was set up, he was responsible for the selection of manuscript map items, although those illustrating manuscript volumes (like the Psalter Map), or forming part of an archive, remained in the Department of Manuscripts.[2] It has to be said that the purchases of his thirteen-year keepership were disappointingly thin. Since all those acquired by him for the Map Department were returned en bloc after his retirement, the task of reviewing his manuscript maps legacy is straightforward.[3] Among items worth special mention were some early portolan atlases, including a Grazioso Benincasa of 1470; Cook's Newfoundland charts; and a collection of material, some by Livingstone, relating to recent African exploration.[4] All in all, one might conclude in the manner of a school report: some worthy material but few items that now rank among our great treasures.

The same report, under 'relations with colleagues', would comment that Major must have been respected for his reputation as a historian and valued for his dependability. But more than that, these same colleagues were also his friends. This seems clear from the fact that all three trustees of his daughter's marriage settlement were his Printed Books colleagues. These were, respectively, William Younger Fletcher, an authority on bookbindings; Robert Edmund Graves, an art historian; and George William Porter. All three had been members of the Hakluyt Society during Major's secretaryship, but had lapsed thereafter. Further demonstrating how inseparable were Major's professional and private lives, two of the three would be executors at his death in 1891, Porter having predeceased him in 1887. Even without accepting the judgement of the unreliable Poles that 'the Library is managed

---

[1] R. H. Major, 'Remarks on the mappamondo of Fra Mauro', *PSAL*, 2nd series, 6, 1873, pp. 22–32, on p. 32.

[2] The Psalter Map: BL, Add. MS 28681.

[3] BL, Add. MS 31315–383, 31863–5.

[4] The Benincasa is Add. MS 31318; the Newfoundland charts are Add. MS 31360; and the African material is Add. MS 31356. The three numbers previous to the 1470 Benincasa, 31315–7, were donated by the Lords of the Admiralty on 18 November 1872. They include a 1469 Benincasa atlas, whose George III Maritime Collection origin (III.1) was not appreciated.

'THREE SEVERAL SORTS OF SWINGINGS', IN TURKEY
From an English account of travels 1608–1628 (Mundy MSS, Bodleian Library,
Oxford).
Reproduced in HS 2/17 of 1907.

by a clique of jobbing ignoramuses', a clique there clearly was, with Porter being cousin and Graves godson of the Principal Librarian Winter Jones.[1] The year of his daughter's marriage also saw publication of the second edition of Major's Columbus letters, and its introduction provided him with the opportunity to thank Graves, 'one of the most accomplished of the Assistant Librarians'.[2]

Nevertheless, while undoubtedly being a fully paid-up member of the British Museum 'club', Major was saved from organisational introspection by the range of his outside interests and contacts. The best evidence for these is provided by the letterbooks that survive in the British Library Map Library. Covering the period from 1868 onwards, they list the correspondents to whom Major addressed letters and thus give a tantalising glimpse into his life as a keeper.[3] What gives these entries a deeper value is the promiscuous mingling of the professional and the personal. Among the former can be found most of the significant names in the histories of exploration and cartography. Those with whom Major was corresponding, presumably on map-related matters, included M. A. P. d'Avezac, Guglielmo Berchet, Luciano Cordeiro, Henri Cordier, P. F. E. Cortambert, Cornelio Desimoni, Pascual de Gayangos, Johann G. Kohl, V. A. Malte-Brun, Frederik Müller, Federico Odorici, Ferdinando Ongania, August Petermann, E. G. Ravenstein, Henry Stevens, P. A. Tiele, and Franz Wieser.[4] Several of these feature likewise in the Hakluyt Society Council minutes. Additionally, among the historians of exploration with whom he corresponded are no fewer than fourteen of the Hakluyt Society's editors and translators, and this at least ten years after Major had relinquished the secretaryship.[5] Some of Major's correspondents were no doubt seeking information

[1] Poles, *Actual Condition,* pp. 18–19. Rye's 'Library Memoranda' conveniently assembles photographs of the Printed Books people, among them Cannon, Fletcher, Major, Panizzi, Porter, Rye and Winter Jones (nos 148, 151).

[2] Major, *Columbus Letters,* 1870 (HS 43), p. cxli.

[3] No copies of the letters remain in the Museum (or Library) archives, with one traced exception, but there is a dated record of every recipient, usually with their address and sometimes with a note of an accompanying 'Prince Henry' or another of Major's writings. The exception is Major's letter to John Barrow of 29 April 1874 about acquiring Lady Franklin's autograph for the daughter of Commendatore Negri Cristoforo (BL, Add. MS 35308, pp. 400–01).

[4] Many of these individuals are listed in Wilhelm Bonacker, *Kartenmacher aller Länder und Zeiten,* Stuttgart, 1966. Kohl, some years earlier, had offered to edit for the Hakluyt Society a series of the maps referred to by Richard Hakluyt (HSCM, 19 May 1857). Wieser's correspondence with Major in 1875 no doubt related to the map tracings he donated to the Map Department that November.

[5] George Asher, the Reverend George Badger, John Barrow, Admiral C. R. Drinkwater Bethune, Richard Burton, Admiral Sir Richard Collinson, W. Desborough Cooley, Charles Henry Coote, Pascual de Gayangos, General Sir John Lefroy, Clements Markham, Lord Stanley, P. A. Tiele and Henry Yule.

from him about British Museum documents in connection with forthcoming Hakluyt Society volumes, for example, Henry (later Lord)
Stanley, with whom there was regular correspondence. Other correspondents worth mentioning were the book collectors, the Earl of
Ashburnham, the Earl of Crawford and Balcarres, and Henry Huth;
John Gregory Crace, who catalogued his father's London collection
which came to the British Museum in 1880; the African explorers
Burton and Grant, as well as the Sultan of Zanzibar; and, expressing
broader interests perhaps, Henry Bradshaw and Edward Whymper.
Major also wrote regularly to the *Athenaeum* and on occasion to the
national newspapers.

If this summary list of his correspondents shows Major as a man at
the very heart of his subject, the official log also records letters to his
stockbroker and bank, to a bootmaker and a cabinet-maker, as well as a
steady flow to the various members of his family. When Major was
away from the Museum a stream of letters would follow him, presumably reporting, sometimes daily, on events there. From this correspondence it is possible to trace his movements fairly accurately,
whether these were visits to European libraries, vacations or, as increasingly became the pattern, trips to the coast in search of better health.
Originally recreational, these winter visits increasingly became a life-
line. The first clear sign of the respiratory illness that would eventually
kill him can be seen in letters, dated May 1876, to Bates at the RGS.[1]
Two months were lost in 1877 and then, in December 1879, he had an
extended attack of bronchitis that lasted until the following May. His
subsequent retirement on 9 October, aged 62, can have come as no
surprise to anyone.

Twilight

With Major's departure, the British Museum keepership that had been
created for him thirteen years previously was snuffed out. His successor, Robert K. Douglas, was a distinguished orientalist with no special
interest in maps. Responsibility for the sub-department of maps rested
with Douglas's deputy, Edward D. Butler. Together, they oversaw the
transfer to the Department of Manuscripts of all the manuscript maps
acquired by Major. This was completed in six months, by 30 April
1881.[2]

After retirement, Major seems to have had little further contact with

---

[1] RGSA, Correspondence Block 1871–80, 'R. H. Major'.
[2] Miller, *Noble Cabinet*, p. 267, n. 2.

the British Museum, although he clearly kept up with former colleagues. Since the letterbooks record only a single outgoing letter to him during the eleven years of his retirement, he was evidently not consulted on matters cartographic.[1] Major's only professional activities in this twilight period involved the RGS (as already described) and an annual attendance at the November meetings of the Hakluyt Society in 1882, 1883 and 1884. The spread of his letters for the 1883 RGS *Proceedings* confirms that he was braving the London weather that winter but in January 1884 his health again failed.[2] In 1888, he went to Italy 'with his entire family' – presumably wife, both daughters and the two grandchildren. It was when they were in Florence, in early 1890, that his wife suddenly died.[3] The following year, in mid-May, the Major and Evans families returned to England from Genoa. But within just six weeks Major fell ill and died on 25 June at his Kensington home.[4]

There proved to be one surprising legacy. Left unfinished at his death was what *The Times* obituary referred to as a 'work of scriptural research which will be shortly published'.[5] This forecast proved premature. Major's daughter, Sarah Isabelle, attempted to prepare it for publication but the task proved beyond her and at her death in 1918 she passed it to her children.[6] No trace of it can be found among the

---

[1] A letter of 22 December 1884 to Rye mentions a visit from 'our old friend [Robert] Graves' (Rye, 'Library Memoranda', no. 115). Major was written to on 26 February 1887.

[2] According to his daughter's biographical notes.

[3] On 22 January 1890, at an address given as Lung'Arno no. 22.

[4] His funeral two days later was at nearby St Barnabas, followed by burial in Highgate Old Cemetery, in the Thorn family grave (no. 4953) bought by his wife in 1853, rather than in no. 6649, which he had himself bought in 1855 and where his brother and sister-in-law lay. Consecrated in 1839, Highgate Cemetery was the favoured resting place of Major's British Museum colleagues. The Majors had moved from Islington to 51 Holland Road, Kensington, in 1881.

[5] *The Times*, 29 June 1891, p. 10.

[6] Sarah Isabelle provided more detail in a letter to Bates written three weeks after Major's death. 'My father has left a book of Biblical Research I believe completed – but it will need time to see that it is in condition for production. No arrangements have been made for its publication. My [elder] sister [Alice Elizabeth] and I will have to make this our first business so soon as the most pressing business incident on his death is arranged' (RGSA, Correspondence Block 1881–1910, 'Evans, I. G.', letter to Bates, 13 July 1891). She handed to her children 'all the manuscripts of or appertaining to my father's book which I have endeavoured to edit . . . in the hope that the work may be edited at some future date', and gave express direction that her son and daughter should be 'particularly careful not to destroy any of the manuscripts either of my late father or of myself appertaining to the said book'. She died on 14 April 1918. The manuscript was not referred to in the will of Major's clergyman grandson. This did, however, mention the Society for the Propagation of the Gospel in Foreign Parts, but it could not be found in the Society's archives.

surviving Major papers. We can only guess at the content of this final, unfinished work, but religion was a constant undercurrent to Major's life, even if, as the authorised biography put it, in a surprisingly vehement comment on his decision not to enter the Church: 'there is no event in his life on which he has more frequently and conscientiously congratulated himself'.[1] Major's elder brother was a clergyman and the letterbook record of his keepership notes a stream of letters, some presumably on religious matters, to clergymen and nuns, as well as two to Cardinal Manning, Archbishop of Westminster. The obituary of Major in the *Athenaeum* referred to him as a 'High Churchman' and it is possible that he was linked to the Oxford Movement via his fellow keeper (and Hakluyt Society editor) Vaux.[2]

With the sole exception of Markham, Major's obituarists concentrated on his official persona and writings, offering no observation on his character. In the absence of more intimate documents, such as diaries or personal letters, it is hard to flesh out a convincing portrait of Major the man. From the few remarks we have, Major appears as someone who was thoroughly dependable, who would give generously of his time to others, who was in many ways self-effacing. He was, in other words, the ideal committee member, the one who could be relied upon to attend, the perfect society secretary, knowledgable, meticulous and totally loyal. The judgements passed on him as a young man entering the British Museum sound plausible as comments on his maturity: 'His demeanour invariably respectful, and amiable in his disposition' (J. J. Ellis); 'He is . . . of strict integrity, and mild and docile in his manners' (Sir H. Ellis); 'He applied himself with great steadiness to the work of the School and was very observant of its discipline . . . he secured my approbation and regard by his uniformly correct conduct' (J. W. Bellamy).[3]

'Respectful . . . docile . . . correct conduct' were terms he would have been proud to own to, even if a biographer might wish for livelier qualities. With that sense of status and position to which the Victorians were so attuned, he could expect his wife to abandon a career as an artist to become his assistant, while showing, in turn, what to us is an embarrassingly fulsome respect for Panizzi, his titled or royal

---

[1] J. H., *Biography*, p. 3.

[2] *The Athenaeum*, 3323, 4 July 1891, p. 40. For W. S. W. Vaux, see *DNB*. It may be significant that the daughter of Major's clergyman brother converted to Rome in 1869 (W. Gordon Gorman, *Converts to Rome: a Biographical List of the More Notable Converts to the Catholic Church in the United Kingdom During the Last Sixty Years*, enlarged edition, London, 1910, p. 182 – a reference I owe to P. R. Harris).

[3] BMA, 'R. H. Major. Testimonials Jan [9] 1844'.

contemporaries, and the subjects of his historical studies.[1] Major's support of his Zeno thesis in the face of criticism from Admiral Zahrtmann turned into a personal defence of the veracity of the Zeno brothers' sixteenth-century descendant and chronicler. Major made it plain that he considered it ungentlemanly to throw upon 'an honorable man, occupying no less distinguished a position than that of one of the Council of Ten of the Republic of Venice, a series of aspersions of the most ungenerous character'.[2] It must have been equally hard for those unconvinced of Major's attribution to Leonardo of the globe gores at Windsor to formulate a reasoned response to what was treated as an act of faith, requiring worship, not appraisal. 'In the presence', we read, 'of such a stupendous assemblage of original conceptions from the mind of this one noble monument of God's creative power, what transcendant honour must we own to have been shed upon the glorious country which gave birth to such a man'.[3] When hearts and minds become inseparable in scholarship, when those who disagree with us are not just deluded but morally suspect as well, it is difficult to admit error. When the Godino de Erédia document – on which much of the evidence for a Portuguese discovery of Australia depended – was found to be false, Major, instead of feeling abashed, congratulated himself, 'that it is with my own hand' that the forgery was revealed.[4]

If Major would willingly do battle over academic points, and on matters of principle, this combativeness did not come across in relations with colleagues. Markham's obituary referred to the 'charm of his manners and conversation' and elsewhere to 'his well-known face, so genial and sympathetic'.[5] Major's academic generosity to Hakluyt Society editors has already been remarked upon. In a passage that brings a wry smile to his Library successors, Major thanked Panizzi for enabling himself and his colleagues 'for years to proceed with our work in peace and quietness'.[6] If this suggests an ability to steer a safe course through the various British Museum factions, this is corroborated by Stefan Poles. Although Major was clearly identified in Poles's mind with the camp of his sworn enemy, Winter Jones, and despite considering the new Map Department

---

[1] He wrote to Panizzi, on 18 July 1866, about 'the years during which you have been our honoured guide and chief . . . You have made the grand institution with which we have the honour to be connected unspeakably grander . . . It has always been a matter of pride with me to possess your good opinion' (BL, Add. MS 36723, f. 510).

[2] Major, *Voyages of the . . . Zeno* (HS 50), p. viii.

[3] Major, 'A mappemonde by Leonardo da Vinci', p. 36. There is a similar passage in J. H., *Biography*, p. 10.

[4] Major, 'Supplementary facts', p. 258.

[5] *PRGS*, n.s., 13, 1891, p. 490; 14, 1892, p. 594.

[6] It may be worth noting that the letterbooks reveal Major as corresponding equally with the rival Museum giants, Panizzi and Madden, after their retirements.

'not called for by any public interest', Poles concluded: 'I will not say a word against Mr Major personally'.[1] From such a source, this was high praise indeed.[2]

If Major remains a somewhat shadowy personality, we have a clearer idea of his physical appearance from three surviving portrait likenesses, taken decades apart. In 1850, at the age of 32, he sat for a wax portrait by Richard Cockle Lucas. This shows him in profile, partially bearded.[3] The subsequent portraits are all undated photographs. The first, in the RGS Picture Archive, is a full-length studio portrait, of a kind routinely carried out for RGS Fellows. It probably dates from the 1860s (when Major was in his forties), showing his beard as by now full, dark and bushy. What could well be another pose from the same session is preserved in the albums compiled by his Printed Books colleagues, Robert Cowtan and W. B. Rye.[4] The last photograph (again in the RGS) shows him in his later years, the beard now turned to white. It was this that was reproduced by Justin Winsor in 1889 ('kindly furnished by himself at the editor's request') and, two years later, in the *Illustrated London News* obituary, the only obituary to include a portrait.[5]

The 1890s saw a succession of posthumous biographical notices, including Major's entry in the *Dictionary of National Biography*.[6] It is

---

[1] Poles, *Actual Condition*, p. 29.

[2] One of those whom Poles admired, considering him among the 'great scholars' who had left the British Museum, was the Reverend Joseph Benjamin McCaul (ibid., p. 18). In the possession of a descendant is a four-line verse by McCaul addressed to R. H. Major Esq: 'The Keeper of our Maps: we boast / None manlier, truer, sager. / And all *superlatively* great / Must own you to be Major!'. The verse was endorsed by Major as a 'sketch portrait of me, one of a series taken by him of men in the Museum Library'. McCaul resigned from the Museum to take up the rectorship of St Michael Bassishaw in 1865, so this, with its reference to Major's keepership (beginning 1867), must post-date McCaul's departure.

[3] The Lucas connection is not hard to unravel. Lucas was associated with the British Museum from at least 1845 when he made a model of the Parthenon in wax. In 1849 Madden and his lady sat for their portraits and the following year Panizzi (not to be outshone by Madden), Edward Hawkins and Major himself followed suit (E. J. Pyke, *A Biographical Dictionary of Wax Modellers*, London, 1973, pp. 82, 83). Perhaps Major, as a junior was presumptuous in associating himself with the three keepers. Only a single example of the Lucas portrait of Major is recorded – that purchased for the British Museum in 1927 (reproduced in Lynam, *Richard Hakluyt & his Successors* (HS 2/93), plate VI).

[4] R. Cowtan, an album of *carte de visite* photographs, BM, Prints & Drawings, 1943–11–15–1 (210*.b.ll); Rye, 'Library Memoranda', no. 148. The background is slightly different and Major has a full-length coat but his appearance is otherwise the same. The 'Maull & Polyblank' imprint of the RGS version is missing but this would have been removed when the photograph was trimmed.

[5] Winsor, *America*, I, p. 112; *Illustrated London News*, 4 July 1891, p. 3.

[6] The entry was written by E. J. L. Scott.

perhaps as much a measure of a man's perceived status if he is so treated when still alive, and in Major's case there were several such notices. The first of these was in the 1862 edition of *Men of the Time*. His entry – initially a tribute to his work for the Hakluyt Society – was to be steadily updated through the last thirty years of his life. In 1870, Allibone provided a very brief notice, which was somewhat expanded in a supplement written shortly before Major's death.[1] Major added to these biographical notices a measure of autobiography. Writing to help Markham compose Major's obituary for the *Proceedings* of the Royal Geographical Society, Major's daughter, Sarah Isabelle, revealed that 'in one of the few short intervals of his life when his mind was not engrossed upon some subject of serious interest my father began to write his "Reminiscences" . . . I regret that they were continued only into his schooldays'.[2] Apart from the extract she transcribed for Markham, these 'Reminiscences' seem now to be lost. In 1886, however – and it is strange that Sarah made no reference to this – a small work entitled *Biography of R. H. Major, F.S.A. &c* had been privately printed in London, prepared 'from materials supplied by [Major] himself at the request of the Author, J. H.' – an unidentified individual. Whether or not Sarah had this to hand, certainly no copy is available today in either the British Museum (now British Library) or Royal Geographical Society, to both of which Major might have been expected to have donated a copy. As a result, neither Markham nor the *DNB* was able to give as full and accurate an account as they might have done.[3] The *Biography* is a strange and, it must be admitted, disappointing affair. It is clearly a 'vanity' publication and, if not actually written by Major, has his imprimatur all over it. It is factually accurate but, because of its eulogistic purpose, unrevealing.

Following Major's death, appreciations duly appeared in the publications of the societies he had served.[4] His entry in *Men of the Time* had described him as a 'member of many home and foreign learned

[1] G. W. Moon, *Men of the Time*, 5th ed., London, 1862 – entries were maintained up to the 13th edition of the retitled *Men and Women of the Time: a Dictionary of Contemporaries*, London, 1891; S. A. Allibone, *Critical Dictionary of English Literature*, 3 vols, London, 1859–71, II, 1870, p. 1207; J. F. Kirk, (supplement to Allibone), II, 1891, pp. 1066–7.

[2] RGSA, Correspondence Block 1891–1910, 'Evans, I.G.', letter to Bates, 13 July 1891.

[3] Who was the sycophantic 'J. H.' and why did Major, who was then in London, not present copies to the institutions it describes, or to colleagues? It is particularly surprising that Markham seems not to have had a copy, given its favourable comment on his 'learning, energy, and indefatigable industry' as Major's successor at the Hakluyt Society, and the long supportive quote from Markham on Major's edition of the Zeno voyages (J. H., *Biography*, pp. 4, 13).

[4] Hakluyt Society 'Report for 1891' (in HS 84), pp. 1–2; *PSAL*, 26 November 1891 to 22 June 1893, 2nd series, 14, p. 133; *PRGS*, n.s. 13, 1891, pp. 489–91.

societies', so it is not surprising to find obituaries in Italian and German geographical journals, at least.[1] If the first half of the twentieth century saw a decline in Major's reputation, there are recent indications of his increasing relevance. Around 1945, the *Encyclopedia Britannica* added a note on him, albeit brief and unsigned. More recently still, three of his works have been reprinted.[2] On the other hand, his 1849 edition of Strachey's *Virginia Britannia* and his 1870 *Columbus Letters* were both reissued by the Hakluyt Society this century with fresh commentaries and, in the case of the Columbus, with new translations.[3] Even if J. N. L. Baker's review of the *Prince Henry* reissue noted that 'a number of points of detail, and of a more general nature, which were unknown to Major have been brought to light ... [and] thus in a number of ways Major's work is now out of date', these volumes have been given a new lease of life.[4] Equally, the claim for a sixteenth century Portuguese discovery of Australia, which he was among the first to champion, has been forcefully revived in the writings of Helen Wallis.[5]

Another aspect of Major's continuing legacy can be seen in the two societies he served as Honorary Secretary. His successors have played a regular part in the Royal Geographical Society, as Vice Presidents, as members of the Council or on the Library and Maps Committee. But it is in the Hakluyt Society that the link with the British Museum (and now the British Library) has been so firm and unbroken. A number of Major's successors in the British Museum's Map Room have served as Honorary Secretaries: B. H. Soulsby (1902–1909), J. A. J. De Villiers (1909–1923), F. P. Sprent (1926–1931), Edward Lynam (1931–1945, then President, 1945 until his death in 1950), R. A. Skelton (1946–1966), and latterly, Sarah Tyacke (1983–1995). T. A. Joyce, Deputy Keeper in the Department of Ceramics and Ethnography, held the secretaryship

---

[1] As a 'corresponding member of many foreign learned societies' (J. H., *Biography*, p.14), Major had his death recorded in, for example, brief notes in *Società Geografica Italiana, Bollettino*, serie 3/4, 1891, p. 976; *Geographisches Jahrbuch*, 16, 1893, p. 487.

[2] *Prince Henry* in 1967, the *Columbus Letters* in 1971, and *India in the Fifteenth Century* in 1974.

[3] Louis B. Wright and Virginia Freund, eds, *The Historie of Travell into Virginia Britania (1612) by William Strachey, gent.*, London, 1953 (HS 2/103); Cecil Jane, ed., *Select Documents illustrating the Four Voyages of Columbus, Including those contained in R. H. Major's Select Letters of Christopher Columbus*, 2 vols, London, 1930, 1933 (HS 2/65, 70). The Society has also published L. A. Vigneras, ed., *The Journal of Christopher Columbus*, Cambridge, 1960, which repeats the relevant 1930 text.

[4] *Geographical Journal*, 134, 1968, p. 140. It must be added, however, that *Prince Henry* is now of almost as much interest to historians for its documentation of Victorian attitudes to 'Henry the Navigator' and his supposed influence on early 'Discovery', as for its information on the prince and his actual career. See Peter E. Russell, *Prince Henry the Navigator: the Rise and Fall of a Culture Hero*, Oxford, 1984.

[5] See p. 119, note 2 above.

in the period 1923–1926, thus keeping the post in the British Museum (except for the single year 1945–1946) from 1902 to 1966.

Major's direct bloodline died out with his grandchildren.[1] His effects subsequently passed to the descendants of his elder brother. In a family with an unusually strong sense of its own history, the names of Major's brother, Seymour Edward, have been used for the five succeeding generations; but a second son today bears the names Richard Henry, in honour of his great-grandfather's brother.

The British Library holds little of Major's work. The few letters from him came with the recipients' archives; the Lucas portrait and his publications (other than the Hakluyt Society ones) seem to have been bought. Happily, some of his personal and professional effects survive with his descendants: his insignia of knighthood, the handwritten diary of the 1843 voyage, isolated books from his library and some scattered papers. Sadly, the 'Photographs and Autograph letters etc addressed to R. H. Major', mentioned in Major's grandson's will (drawn up in 1907) are thought to have been sold at auction in the 1930s.[2] Until and unless they are found, the student of Major's life must rely on the limited sources on which this memoir is based.

---

[1] Of his two daughters, the elder, Alice Elizabeth, died unmarried at Nice on 17 March 1906, and the younger, Sarah Isabelle, on 14 April 1918, leaving two children. Both of those, in turn, died childless in South Africa: Major's grandson, the Reverend Godfrey Theodore Major Evans as Dean of Pietermaritzburg on 8 August 1935, and the daughter, Isabelle Major Evans, on 7 May 1941. With her, Major's direct line ended.

[2] Information from a descendant.

BRITISH MUSEUM CONTRIBUTION TO THE HAKLUYT SOCIETY 1846–80
HAKLUYT SOCIETY VOLUME EDITORS

Name	DNB	British Museum Department	Council	Examined Accounts	Society Member	Vol No	Short Title	Proposed	Assigned	Published	Realised Instead By	Other Comments
BACH, Johann F Van		Printed Books			(1849) 54							
BENNETT, John Joseph	x	Botany			(1847) 1849							
BIRCH, Walter de Gray		Manuscripts	1877–92		(1877) 1904+	53	Albuquerque			1875		
BOND, Edward Augustus	x	Manuscripts	1877–80		(1877) 80	20	Fletcher	(1848)	1855	1856		
CANNON, Charles		Printed Books		1854, 1856 / 1861–3	1849 80	2/108	Rozmial		1856		Letts (1957)	Co translator with Major of 'Council of Diplomatic Law' (1858). Left BM 1866.
DOUBLEDAY, Edward	x	Zoology			(1847) 1849							Died 1849
ELLIS, Sir Henry	x	Printed Books	1846–69		1847 69							Died 1869. Major's 'earliest surviving friend'.
FLETCHER, William Younger		Printed Books		1857, 1859, 1861–3	(1855) 64							Trustee of Major's daughter's marriage settlement (1870). Major's executor (1891). Co-translator of 'Council of Diplomatic Law' (1858)
GARNETT, Richard	x	Printed Books		1858, 1860	1857 66							Co-translator with Major of 'Council of Diplomatic Law' (1858)
GRAVES, Robert Edmund		Printed Books		1859	1857 62							Trustee of Major's daughter's marriage settlement (1870). Major's executor (1891). Winter Jones's godson
GRAY, John Edward	x	Zoology	1846–48		1847 55	42	Da Gama		1856		Stanley (1869)	
HAMILTON, Nicholas E S A		Manuscripts			1847 66	27	Dutch in E. Indies / Hudson		1856 / 1856		Asher (1860)	
HAWKINS, Edward	x	Antiquities		1852	1847 66							Recommended Major to Society of Antiquaries (1854). Died 1867
HOLMES, John	x	Manuscripts	1849–50, 1853–54	1853	(1849) 54							In charge of MS maps. Died 1854
LARDNER, Leopold J		Printed Books			(1849) 54							Died 1855
MAJOR, Richard Henry	x	Printed Books / Maps	1847, 1859–91, Hon. Sec. 1849–58		1847 91	2	Columbus	1847		1847		
						6	Strachey	1848	1849	1849		
						10, 12	Herberstein	1852		1851–2		
						14, 15	Mendoza	1853		1853–4		
						17	Tartar Conquerors	1853		1854		
						22	India	1855	1857	1857		
						25	Terra Australis	1855	1855	1859		
							Terra Supplement	1861		1861		
						43	Columbus (ed. 2)	1868	1869	1870		
						46	Bethencourt	1846		1872		
						50	Zeno	1872		1873		
NEWTON, Charles Thomas	x	Antiquities	1848		1847 50							Trustee of Major's daughter's marriage settlement (1870). Winter Jones's cousin. Died 1888
PORTER, George William		Printed Books		1856	1847 51							
RYE, William Brenchley	x	Printed Books	1848	1854, 1860	1847 80	9	Treswell / De Soto	1848	1849	1851		Illustrated vol.2 of Major's Herberstein (1852), assisted with introduction and bibliography
VAUX, William Sandys Wright	x	Coins & Medals				16	Drake	1846	1850	1854		Offered to list MS journals in BM (1876); backed down (1878)
WARNER, George Frederick	x	Manuscripts										
WATTS, Thomas	x	Printed Books		1852		18	Spitsbergen			1855		Died 1869
WHITE, Adam	x	Zoology										
WINTER JONES, John	x	Printed Books	1848–78		(1848) 80	7	Hakluyt	1847	1852	1850		Died 1881
						22	India (part)	1853	1849	1857		
						32	Varthema	1846	1861	1863		

'NORTH APPROACH OF THE GOLDEN PAGODA AT PROME [BURMA] MARCH 1853'
Drawn by Lieutenant Henry Yule.
Original in the Oriental and India Office Collections of the British Library, reproduced with permission.

HENRY YULE

INDIA AND CATHAY

R. J. Bingle

Yule à de solides connaissances scientifiques joignait une forte éducation classique et une grande culture littéraire.[1]

This sentence, which occurs in one of the many tributes paid to Sir Henry Yule after his death, sums up the three strands in Yule's work which form the subject of this brief sketch.[2] The aim is to show the educational background, professional training and practical experience which lay behind the achievements of a man who is remembered today as the editor and translator of three important works for the Hakluyt Society, together with a scholarly edition of *The Book of Ser Marco Polo*, and as the compiler of *Hobson-Jobson*, the only one of Yule's books which is still in print, a century after the date when it was first published.

Yule and India

Henry Yule was born on 1 May 1820 at Inveresk, near Edinburgh, the third son of William Yule and his wife Elizabeth, née Paterson.[3] The Yule family had been tenant-farmers in East Lothian for generations, but Major William Yule (1764–1839) and his brother Colonel Udney Yule (died 1830) left Scotland to serve in the East India Company's Bengal Army. During his twenty-five years in India William Yule saw little active service, and spent his last two years (1804–1806) in diplomatic

---

[1] H. Cordier, 'Le Colonel Sir Henry Yule', *Journal Asiatique*, 8ᵉ série, 15, 1890, p. 244.

[2] I express my thanks to colleagues who have helped me at critical points in the preparation of this essay, namely Anthony Farrington, Ian Baxter, Andrew Cook, Catherine Pickett and Frances Wood.

[3] There is no biography of Yule, but his daughter, Amy Frances Yule [hereafter A. F. Yule, *Memoir*], published 'A Memoir of Colonel Sir Henry Yule, with a bibliography of his writings' in Henry Yule, trans. and ed., *The Book of Ser Marco Polo, the Venetian, concerning the Kingdoms and Marvels of the East*, 3rd ed., revised by H. Cordier, London, 1903.

143

posts as Assistant to the Residents at Lucknow and Delhi.[1] These posts enabled him to acquire a fine collection of 267 Arabic, Persian and Urdu manuscripts which his sons presented to the British Museum in 1847 and 1850. Evidently William Yule was 'no mean Persian scholar: his MSS are full of marginal notes which bear testimony to their attentive perusal by their owner'.[2] However he published only one work, *The Apothegms of Alee*, with an old Persian paraphrase and an English translation.[3] Thus Henry Yule grew up in a military family with firm Indian connections and strong scholarly interests. Yet despite the fact that his eldest brother, George Udney Yule, entered the Bengal Civil Service, and his next brother, Robert Abercromby Yule, was commissioned into the Ninth Lancers, neither India nor the Army figured in Henry's initial choice of career.[4]

Henry went to Edinburgh High School, but left at the age of thirteen to be tutored privately in preparation for Cambridge and a career as a barrister. For two years he studied at the home of the Reverend Henry Parr Hamilton, an eminent mathematician, but in 1835 Hamilton returned to Cambridge as perpetual curate of Great St Mary's. Yule was then sent to be coached by the Reverend James Challis but this lasted only six months, as Challis was appointed Plumerian Professor of Astronomy at Cambridge in February 1836. Although the emphasis at both establishments was on mathematics, Yule apparently preferred Greek plays and German.[5] After a brief period at University College, London, Yule changed his mind about his future career, and applied for a cadetship in the East India Company's Bengal Engineers.[6] The reasons for this decision have never been explained, but both of his elder brothers were in India at this time and perhaps their letters home, which have not survived, persuaded Henry to join them. Nevertheless the letter of recommendation from his former tutor, James Challis, suggests that Yule would have done well at Cambridge.[7] Yule was

---

[1] V. C. P. Hodson, *List of Officers of the Bengal Army 1758–1834*, 4 vols., London, 1927–47, IV, p. 555.

[2] C. Rieu, *Catalogue of the Persian Manuscripts in the British Museum*, 3 vols, British Museum, London, 1879–83, III, p. xviii.

[3] W. Yule, ed., *Apothegms of Alee, the Son of Abo Talib Son in law of the Moslim Lawgiver Mahummid . . .* , Edinburgh, 1832.

[4] A. F. Yule, *Memoir*, pp. 22, 47–8.

[5] C. Trotter, 'Memoir of Colonel Sir Henry Yule, R.E., C.B., K.C.S.I., LL.D.' in *Proceedings of the Royal Society of Edinburgh*, 17, November 1890–July 1891, pp. xliii–lvi, on p. xliv. For Hamilton and Challis, see *DNB*.

[6] London, British Library, Oriental and India Office Collections, India Office Records [hereafter IOR], L/MIL/9/185, ff. 376–85, Cadet Papers 1836.

[7] 'I consider his literary attainments even at present to be of a very high order, and that he shewed decided talents for aiming at great proficiency as well in mathematical as in classical studies' (IOR, L/MIL/9/185, f.383, certificate by Professor J. Challis, 9 September 1836).

examined by the East India Company's Military Committee on 25 January 1837, and entered the Company's Military Seminary at Addiscombe in Surrey on 3 February 1837; his military career had begun.[1]

Addiscombe was a remarkable institution, for it trained all the Infantry, Artillery and Engineer Officers needed for the Company's Armies in Bengal, Madras and Bombay. Cadets were admitted twice a year, were between fourteen and eighteen years old on entry, and usually remained there for two years, or four terms; parents had to pay £30 per year for each cadet.[2] The military aspects of the course included regular drill and parades, but the cadets also received instruction in Mathematics, Fortification, Military Drawing and Surveying, Civil Drawing, Hindustani, French and Latin.[3] Yule's choice of the Engineers was significant, for that branch involved a thorough scientific education, (similar to that required of Artillery cadets but a term longer), and was therefore more demanding than the training provided for Infantry officers. The range of subjects can be seen in the subjects which Yule had to study in the Mathematics class: geometry, algebra, heights and distances, mensuration of solids, mechanics, dynamics, hydrodynamics, fluxion (i.e., differential calculus) and rectifications, and spherical trigonometry. After a slow start in his first term Yule made rapid progress and was second in his class in his second and third terms and top of the class in his final term. It is not surprising, therefore, that Yule passed out in December 1838 as head of his year and first for the Engineers, and received a sword of honour; his general character was praised highly: in study as 'very attentive' and out of study as 'most exemplary'.[4] On leaving Addiscombe Yule and his fellow Engineer officers were sent to the Royal Engineers' depot at Chatham for practical training in surveying to supplement the basic training which they had already received. This involved a period of attachment to the Survey of Ireland, during which Yule was trained to use the magnetic instruments which he was to convey to a new observatory at Aden, on his way to India.[5]

In June 1840 Yule left for India via the 'overland route', travelling by sea to Gibraltar (where a cousin was stationed) and Egypt; he then took the desert route to Suez, and another ship to Aden. There he found that

[1] IOR, L/MIL/9/185, ff. 376, 380.

[2] A. J. Farrington, *The Records of the East India College Haileybury and other Institutions*, HMSO, London, 1976, pp. 114–5.

[3] H. M. Vibart, *Addiscombe, its Heroes and Men of Note*, Westminster, 1894, p. 154.

[4] IOR, L/MIL/9/341, Mathematical Lists and Reports, 1836–51; L/MIL/9/343, 'List of Gentlemen Cadets of the First Class to be brought forward for Public Examination at the East India Company's Military Seminary, Addiscombe, on Tuesday the 11th December 1838'.

[5] IOR, L/MIL/10/32, no. 347, 1843, Bengal Service Army Lists.

his journey was completely useless, for the person who was to have run the observatory was dead, the observatory had not been built, and the instruments had been broken in transit.[1] There was no reason to stay in Aden, and so Yule sailed for Bombay, and finally reached Calcutta on 23 November 1840. Almost immediately he was given leave to go to Mymensingh, to visit his brother George Udney Yule, who was stationed there as Special Deputy Collector. His first official duty was also in Eastern Bengal, 'to survey and superintend the execution of a road from the Cherra coal mines to the Roonah Ghat'.[2] The coal mines were near Cherrapunji, in the Khasi Hills, Assam, reputed to be the wettest place in the world, with an annual rainfall of over 400 inches. The mission was unsuccessful, as the dense forest and deep ravines made road-building impossible, but Yule produced some excellent maps of the area.[3] His first two papers, 'Notes on the Iron of the Kasia Hills' and 'Notes on the Kasia Hills and people', were now written and published.[4] Both papers display the main characteristics which flowered in Yule's later work, namely careful observation and insatiable curiosity about every aspect of any area which he visited. In the papers he described the geography and geology of the Kasia Hills, and the fauna and flora, as well as the customs, language, clothing, diet and beliefs of the inhabitants. His scientific training is evident in his detailed description of the methods used to smelt iron, and his artistic skill in the sketches which illustrated the articles. Yule had made a notable contribution to the study of an area which was not well-known, and in doing so was maintaining an established tradition in the Company's service, the regular contribution of important articles to the *Journal of the Asiatic Society of Bengal*.

On his return from Cherrapunji, Yule was posted to the western frontier of the Company's territories, as Assistant Superintendent of the Delhi Canals, under the direction of Captain (later General Sir) William Baker.[5] This appointment marked the beginning of Yule's involvement in the development of irrigation in northern India, which was to last seven years, interrupted by one period of home leave and three brief periods of active service. Yule's work led to a friendship with Baker, which was to benefit Yule later on, and he made a number of useful contacts with the civilian administrators and fellow Army officers. The

---

[1] A. F. Yule, *Memoir*, p. 8.
[2] IOR, L/MIL/10/32, no. 347, 1843.
[3] A. F. Yule, *Memoir*, p. 8; IOR, X/2188/1–18, 'Survey of part of the Cossya Hills'.
[4] *Journal of the Asiatic Society of Bengal*, 11/2, July-December 1842, pp. 853–7; 12/2, July-December 1844, pp. 612–31.
[5] IOR, L/MIL/10/32, no. 347, 1843.

Delhi canals were originally Mughal creations: they had fallen into disuse during the eighteenth century but one of them had been revived in 1820 to supply fresh water to Delhi.[1] Baker had plans to extend the network of canals, and eventually this became the Western Jumna Canal system. Neither Baker nor his assistants had received training in the design and construction of irrigation canals (it did not form part of the syllabus at Addiscombe) and much had to be learned by trial and error; in some cases expensive corrective work had to be done later.[2] Yule's work was interrupted early in 1843 by an insurrection in the small Indian state of Kaithal, which was situated near the headquarters of the canal works at Karnal in the Punjab. Major (later Sir) Henry Lawrence, who was responsible for the administration of the area, called on Baker and his assistants for military support. There was little for them to do, and no fighting was involved, but Yule met four very able men, Henry Lawrence and his brother John (later Lord Lawrence and Viceroy of India), Sir George Russell Clerk (later Governor of Bombay), and Captain Robert Napier, Bengal Engineers (later Lord Napier of Magdala).[3] Immediately after this excursion, although it was very unusual for a young officer to be granted home-leave in less than three years after he had arrived in India, Yule managed to obtain permission to go home to Scotland to marry his cousin, Anna Maria White.[4] When the couple returned to India in January 1844, Yule was fortunate to be allowed to return to his old post, but less than two years later in September 1845 he was detached briefly to serve on a committee to investigate the causes of an outbreak of malaria in the Karnal area, and along the line of the Delhi canal. The committee's report suggested that the outbreak was not caused by canal irrigation itself, but by 'interference with the natural drainage of the country' and recommended that this should receive greater attention in the design of future canals.[5] Despite these preoccupations, historical geography was never far from Yule's mind, and he found time to write an article on a canal act of the Emperor Akbar.[6]

Before the completion of the committee's report, Yule and the other

---

[1] IOR, MSS. Eur.F.89, Box 2A, no.1/3, Lord Hastings to W. F. Elphinstone, 17 June 1820.

[2] E. W. C. Sandes, *The Military Engineer in India*, 2 vols, Chatham, 1933, 1935, II, pp. 3–4.

[3] R. Bosworth-Smith, *Life of Lord Lawrence*, 2 vols, London, 1883, I, pp. 167–8.

[4] A. F. Yule, *Memoir*, p. 10.

[5] Ibid., pp. 11–12; R. Maclagan, [obituary], *Proceedings of the Royal Geographical Society*, n.s. 12, 1890, p. 100.

[6] H. Yule, 'A Canal Act of the Emperor Akbar, with some Notes and Remarks on the History of the Western Jumna canals', *Journal of the Asiatic Society of Bengal*, 15, 1846, pp. 212–23.

Engineer officers working on the Delhi canals were ordered to join the Army of the Sutlej at the beginning of the First Sikh War. Yule played a minor but important part in the campaign, for his survey of the fords of the Sutlej enabled Sir John Grey's division to cross the river on 10 February 1846 immediately after the battle of Sobraon and to pursue the defeated Sikh army; the Engineers then built permanent bridges.[1] When the army was dispersed Yule returned to his duties at Karnal, but not for long, as in June 1846 he was appointed an Executive Engineer of the northern division of the new Ganges Canal project in succession to his friend and Addiscombe contemporary, Lieutenant (later Lieutenant-General Sir) Richard Strachey, and moved from Karnal to Roorkee where the workshops for the project were situated.[2] The Ganges Canal was the largest irrigation project undertaken by the Government of India, and was more ambitious than the Delhi canals which had introduced Yule to the techniques of building canals. The initial survey was made by Lieutenant-Colonel John Colvin in 1836, but it was Captain (later Colonel Sir) Proby Cautley who in 1840 submitted the first detailed project, with detailed plans and estimates of costs; the project was approved but financial stringency during and after the First Afghan War meant that progress was very slow, and in 1845 Cautley submitted another report.[3] Two years later work began in earnest. Yule was responsible for the massive head-works at Hardwar; from there the canal and its main branches stretched for 648 miles to irrigate the Ganges-Jumna *doab*, the area lying between these two great rivers. The canal was opened in 1854 and Yule was among the engineers who were thanked for their services.[4]

Yule's work on the Ganges canal was interrupted and in effect ended by his active service in the Second Sikh War (1848–1849) which

---

[1] *Statement of Services of Lieutenant Colonel Henry Yule of the Bengal Engineers*, [c. 1862], p. 3; Vibart, *Addiscombe*, pp. 487–8. A privately printed 'Statement of Services' was frequently produced by officers at the conclusion of Indian service and contained details of career and commendatory extracts from official documents: the only copy known of Yule's 'Statement' is in IOR, MSS.Eur.F.127/277.

[2] Sandes, *Military Engineer*, II, p. 9.

[3] Ibid., II, pp. 5–8; P. J. Cautley, *Report on the Ganges Canal from Hurdwar to Cawnpore and Allahabad*, Calcutta, 1845.

[4] P. J. Cautley, *Report on the Ganges Canal Works from their Commencement until the Opening of the Canal in 1854*, 3 vols, London, 1860; Yule, *Services*, pp. 5–6. It should be noted that Yule left the project five years before it opened. Like the Delhi canal, the Ganges canal suffered from defects in design which came to light within a few years and had to be rectified at considerable expense (R. B. Buckley, *The Irrigation Works of India and their Financial Results*, London, 1880, pp. 101–2; E. Whitcombe, *Agrarian Conditions in Northern India: Volume 1, The United Provinces under British Rule 1850–1900*, Berkeley, 1972, pp. 81–2).

involved more fighting than the previous war. He was present at Lord Gough's cavalry skirmish at Ramnagar (22 November 1848) and assisted in the crossing of the river Chenab before General Sir Joseph Thackwell's inconclusive action at Sadullapur (3 December 1848), for which he was mentioned in Thackwell's despatch. Yule then examined and surveyed the fords of the Chenab, and was present at the ferocious drawn battle of Chillianwala (13 January 1849), but was not involved in Gough's final victory at Gujerat (21 February 1849) which brought the war to an end.[1] The campaign seems to have damaged Yule's health, for after it he had to spend five months in the hills at Dehra Dun to recuperate, and when this was ineffective, resigned his appointment as Executive Engineer and went home on 'sick certificate' in August 1849.[2] Yule's decision to go home for a long period may not have been based entirely on his own ill-health. His wife had had to leave India four years before, after scarcely two years in the country, because her health had collapsed, and her doctors had told her never to return to India.[3]

Once he was back in Scotland, Yule seems to have recovered his health very quickly, and much of his three years' furlough was spent in professional studies and personal research. He lectured on fortification at the Naval and Military Academy in Edinburgh, and embodied in these lectures a thorough knowledge of the history, theory, and practice of fortification, together with his own experience in the Sikh Wars; his lectures were illustrated with his own detailed drawings of fortifications.[4] The East India Company authorised him to visit ironworks and factories in the North of England, paid his travelling expenses and 'a moderate pecuniary compensation', and he managed to see brick-yards, timber-yards, docks and railway works as well.[5] Yule's historical and geographical interests were also developing rapidly, but he had not joined the Hakluyt Society. According to his daughter (who was born at this time) his serious work on Marco Polo's travels now began.[6] He published a paper on Tibet which discussed the route of the Tsangpo river after it left the Tibetan plateau; some geographers had argued that it flowed into the Irrawaddy, but Yule maintained that it became the Brahmaputra. The point was not settled until long after Yule's death,

[1] Yule, *Services*, p. 3; G. Bruce, *Six Battles for India: the Anglo-Sikh Wars 1845–6, 1848–9*, London, 1969, pp. 251–60, 281–97.
[2] IOR, L/MIL/10/47, no. 347, 1849.
[3] A. F. Yule, *Memoir*, p. 10.
[4] H. Yule, *Fortification for Officers of the Army and Students of Military History, with Illustrations and Notes*, Edinburgh, 1851; French version, Paris, 1858.
[5] IOR, L/MIL/10/53, no. 347, 1852; A. F. Yule, *Memoir*, pp. 13–15.
[6] A. F. Yule, *Memoir*, p. 13.

when F. M. Bailey and H. T. Morshead explored the area in 1913 and proved that Yule's conclusion was correct.[1]

Yule arrived back in Calcutta in January 1853, and was involved immediately in the aftermath of the Second Burmese War and the annexation of Pegu. His interest in fortification had not escaped official attention, and he was sent to investigate the fortifications of the town of An in Arakan, and the passes between Arakan and Lower Burma.[2] A steamer took Yule from Calcutta to Kyaukpyu, and a gunboat negotiated the An river to the military post of Krengyuen, near the town of An. After he had inspected the fortifications of An, Yule faced an arduous journey on foot over the An pass and then south to Prome, where he met Captain (later Lieutenant-General Sir) Arthur Phayre, the Commissioner of Pegu. From Prome Yule travelled east across the Arakan *Yoma* (mountain ridge) to Taungup and the coast. He was back in Calcutta by 1 May, and spent the next four months writing his report and drawing the maps which accompanied it; the report revealed again his acute powers of observation and his interest in the people and places which he visited.[3] Yule's next task was to survey the defences of Singapore, which until 1867 was administered by the East India Company. This he did between September and November 1853, and then wrote an able report, for which he was thanked by the Government of India.[4]

Yule's reward for these travels and reports was twofold: he was promoted to Brevet Captain on 1 December 1853 and appointed Deputy Consulting Engineer in the Railway Department of the Government of India, working for his old senior officer, Major William Baker.[5] This was the beginning of Yule's career in the Secretariat of the Government of India, which was to last, with interruptions, until he left India in 1862. Railways were a completely new area of expertise for Yule, although he had visited railway workshops in England during his leave. His chief contribution to the development of railways in India was to advocate the wide use of metre-gauge lines as feeders to the main trunk routes between the major cities. In this he had the support of his friends

[1] Henry Yule, 'Tibet and the Lamas', *Blackwood's Edinburgh Magazine*, 71, 1852, pp. 335–54; E. D. Morgan, 'Colonel Sir Henry Yule', *Scottish Geographical Magazine*, 6, 1890, p. 94; F. M. Bailey, 'Exploration on the Tsangpo or Upper Brahmaputra', ibid., 30, 1914, pp. 561–82, and *No Passport to Tibet*, London, 1957.
[2] IOR, L/MIL/10/55, no. 347, 1853.
[3] H. Yule, 'Report on the Passes between Arakan and Burma', *Papers on Indian Engineering*, I, 1863, pp. 1–28.
[4] Yule, *Services*, pp. 4, 5; A. F. Yule, *Memoir*, p. 17; IOR, L/MIL/10/58, no. 347, 1854.
[5] IOR, L/MIL/10/55, no. 347, 1853; L/MIL/10/58, no. 347, 1854; Vibart, *Addiscombe*, p. 488. His promotion to Brevet Captain was made substantive on 1 August 1854.

Richard Strachey and C. H. Dickens, but the arguments about the merits of broad-gauge and metre-gauge lines continued for many years.[1] Baker's office was absorbed into the new Public Works Department created in 1854, Baker being appointed Secretary in the Department, with Yule as his Deputy.[2]

Very shortly after this reorganisation Dalhousie despatched Colonel Arthur Phayre on a goodwill mission to King Mindon of Ava, Burma; Yule was appointed Secretary to Phayre and 'was given to understand that one of the chief duties of the office would be the preparation of a narrative of the mission for publication'; in all other respects he regarded the mission as 'a bright and joyous holiday'.[3] The mission left Calcutta in July 1855 by steamer, and made its way by river-steamer up the Irrawaddy to Mindon's capital at Amarapura near Mandalay (29 August 1855). Yule gives a very full account of the progress of the mission, describing the places on the route and the people that he met, with verbatim records of the conversations with senior officials of Mindon's court. In addition to the chronological account of the mission, Yule wrote chapters on Burmese Buddhism, the administrative structure of Burma, and the gradual progress towards the production of a map of Burma. All previous published accounts of Burma were used, and Yule supplemented them with information from Colonel Phayre and other members of the mission, including Thomas Oldham, Superintendent of the Geological Survey of India, who wrote about the coal-mines and oil-wells of Burma.[4] The mission arrived back in Rangoon on 30 October, and Yule resumed his work in the Public Works Department on 1 December 1855.[5] It took Yule a year to write his official report, and two years later an extended version, illustrated with lithographs from Yule's own sketches and some of the earliest photographs of Burma by Captain Linnaeus Tripe, was published in London.[6] This was Yule's first major publication and reflected the characteristics of his previous articles: acute observation, thorough research, good organisation, a fluent style. The result was a volume which provided readers in England with an authoritative and accurate account of Burma

[1] A. F. Yule, *Memoir*, pp. 18, 24–5; H. H. Risley et al., *The Imperial Gazetteer of India, New Edition*, 26 vols, Oxford, 1907–1909, III, pp. 380–3.

[2] IOR, L/MIL/10/58, no. 347, 1854; A. F. Yule, *Memoir*, pp. 18–19.

[3] H. Yule, *A Narrative of the Mission sent by the Governor-General of India to the Court of Ava in 1855, with Notices of the Country, Government and People*, London, 1858, pp. v–vi.

[4] Ibid., chapters 10–12, and Appendix A.

[5] IOR, L/MIL/10/60, no. 347, 1855.

[6] H. Yule, *Narrative of Major Phayre's Mission to the Court of Ava, with Notices of the Country, Government, and People*, Calcutta, 1856; extended version, Yule, *Mission to Ava*, 1858; reprinted, together with Phayre's journal, Kuala Lumpur/London, 1968.

for the first time, and laid the foundations for Yule's later work as a writer on historical and geographical subjects.

A year after his return from Burma, Yule went on leave on 'urgent private affairs' taking with him the draft of his book on Burma. It was still in the hands of his publishers when he returned to India in April 1857, travelling overland with his friend, Colonel Robert Napier; they had reached Aden when they heard of the outbreak of the Indian Mutiny at Meerut, north of Delhi, on 11 May 1857. They hurried on to India, but Yule did not reach Calcutta until 29 June, unaware that his elder brother, Robert Abercromby Yule, had been killed at Delhi on 19 June.[1] Yule was sent to Allahabad on 10 July as Garrison Engineer, and a month later was appointed Extra Superintending Engineer of the North Western Provinces. At Allahabad the first task was to strengthen the fortifications, and then to secure communications with Calcutta.[2] Once this had been done Yule was sent to fortify Rajghat, near Benares, which he did 'in a few weeks, and at a small cost' so that it was 'believed to be impregnable by any number of Native Troops', as his friend Lieutenent-Colonel Richard Strachey put it in a letter of thanks from the Governor-General in Council.[3] When the immediate danger had receded, Yule was summoned back to Calcutta, and he was in a position to officiate as Secretary of the Public Works Department when Colonel William Baker had to go home on sick leave in November 1857.[4]

The time spent by Yule in the Public Works Department from September 1857 until his departure from India in March 1862 was the longest period of uninterrupted work in the whole of his career in India.[5] During it he was made substantive Secretary in the Department, with the rank of Lieutenant-Colonel.[6] Yule's work in the Secretariat brought him into contact with the Viceroy, Lord Canning, and the two became friends.[7] Canning was anxious that the reconstruction which followed the Mutiny should not be retarded by financial constraints, despite financial stringency. This policy was supported by the Secretary of State for India, Sir Charles Wood, and so the Public Works Department

---

[1] A. F. Yule, *Memoir*, pp. 21, 42, note 22; IOR, L/MIL/10/64, no. 347, 1857.

[2] Yule, *Services*, p. 4; A. F. Yule, *Memoir*, p. 21; Vibart, *Addiscombe*, p. 488.

[3] Yule, *Services*, p. 7.

[4] Vibart, *Addiscombe*, pp. 418–19; Yule, *Services*, p. 4.

[5] Apart from a brief period of home leave in 1859, and a sea-voyage to Java in 1860, on account of ill-health (A. F. Yule, *Memoir*, p. 26).

[6] Yule, *Services*, p. 4.

[7] When Lady Canning died on 18 November 1861 and had to be buried on the following day (as was necessary in India), Yule worked through the night superintending the workman who built 'a solid masonry vault' in time for the funeral (A. F. Yule, *Memoir*, p. 27).

had a budget of £4,000,000 per year between 1857 and 1862.[1] Yule had therefore to manage considerable sums, and was congratulated on his success in doing so by the Government of India and the Parliamentary Under-Secretary of State for India; the detailed annual departmental reports and accounts provide ample evidence of Yule's success in managing the department.[2] Two important areas of work occupied much of Yule's time and energy. The first was the construction of permanent barracks for the British troops who were sent to India during and after the Mutiny, the final total being 100,000 men.[3] The second main task was to supervise the rapid extension of railway-building in India. This also had Canning's and Wood's support.[4] The results were dramatic; although only 140 miles of new track were opened in 1858, this rose to 198 in 1859, 213 in 1860, 749 in 1861 and 746 in 1862, making a total of 2,333 miles of route miles open in 1862.[5] The actual construction of railways in India was carried out by private companies, who were guaranteed an annual return of five per cent, and who received compensation from the Government of India if their profits fell below this level. It was an expensive method of financing railway-construction, but brought immense long-term benefits to India, and indeed some immediate benefits, particularly in the relief of the 1861 famine in the North-Western Provinces.[6]

After India

Yule's work as Secretary of the Public Works Department came to an end in March 1862 when he decided to retire and return home. The reasons for this decision lay, according to his daughter, in his increasing ill-health, his 'weariness of India' and the promise that Canning (with

---

[1] R. J. Moore, *Sir Charles Wood's Indian Policy 1853–66*, Manchester, 1966, p. 144.

[2] Yule, *Services*, p. 8; IOR, V/24/3277, 'Report of the Proceedings in the Public Works Department, 1857–8 to 1861–2'.

[3] A. F. Yule, *Memoir*, pp. 21–22. Yule's success in organising this major building project was noted and applauded by Canning in 1859: 'In surmounting these difficulties the intelligence and earnestness of Lieut. Colonel Yule have been the main help of the Government; and the thanks, not only of the Governor-General in Council, but of the English Army in Bengal, are well deserved by him' (Yule, *Services*, pp. 7–8).

[4] M. Maclagan, *'Clemency' Canning, Governor-General and Viceroy of India 1856–1862*, London, 1962, p. 279; Moore, *Wood's Indian Policy*, p. 136.

[5] I. J. Kerr, *Building the Railways of the Raj 1850–1900*, Delhi, 1995, p. 211 (Appendix II, Table 1).

[6] J. M. Hurd, 'Railways', in Dharma Kumar, ed., *The Cambridge Economic History of India, Volume 2*, Cambridge, 1983, pp. 738–41; Maclagan, *Canning*, pp. 279–80. Despite these achievements there remained a number of public works projects, notably in the construction of irrigation works, which were suspended for lack of funds (Moore, *Wood's Indian Policy*, pp. 144–5).

whom Yule travelled home) would help him to secure 'congenial employment'.[1] There was certainly no financial incentive to retire, for he was only 42 and had spent 22 years in India; consequently his pension was calculated at a Captain's rate, and amounted to only £204 per year.[2] Yule's hopes of future work were dashed by Canning's death on 17 June 1862, but he did obtain some official recognition of his services in India by his promotion to Colonel in the same month, and the award of a C.B. in the following year.

After a period of travelling in Germany and Switzerland, Yule decided to move to Italy in the hope that a warmer climate might alleviate his wife's chronic ill-health. They spent a year in Pisa, and then settled in Sicily, at Palermo, in 1864.[3] By this time Yule was already deeply committed to historical and geographical research. Reference has been made to the historical materials incorporated into the articles written in India, and the history of Burma is described in detail in Yule's account of the Mission to Ava, while, as stated earlier, his study of Marco Polo began while he was on home leave in 1850. The first results of his growing interest in medieval historical geography were published by the Hakluyt Society in 1863, as *Mirabilia Descripta. The Wonders of the East*, an edition of a description of 'the East' by a fourteenth-century friar.[4] The research for this edition was probably begun while Yule was still in Calcutta, and the footnotes drew heavily on his experience of living in India. At this time Yule was not a member of the Hakluyt Society and *Mirabilia Descripta* was not among the texts which the Society listed as desirable candidates for editing.[5] It seems likely, therefore, that Yule offered the edition to the Society through a friend, and it may have been published quickly because no other edition was ready, the Society wishing to maintain its admirable objective of attempting to supply its members with two volumes a year.

A more substantial contribution to the Society's publications followed soon afterwards. In the Annual Report for 1865 the Council reported that *Cathay and the Way Thither* was 'in a forward state' and would be delivered as one of the volumes 'for the present year'.[6] In fact Yule's industry meant that the work expanded into two volumes and was only published in 1866. An extended title indicated that it included

---

[1] A. F. Yule, *Memoir*, pp. 25–6, 28–9.
[2] IOR, L/AG/21/11/20, Military Pension Book.
[3] A. F. Yule, *Memoir*, pp. 29–32.
[4] Henry Yule, ed., *Mirabilia Descripta. The Wonders of the East, by Friar Jordanus, of the Order of Preachers and Bishop of Columbum in India the Greater (circa 1330)*, London, 1863 (HS 31).
[5] According to the list in the supplementary material in HS 29 (1862).
[6] Annual Report in HS 34.

an essay 'on the Intercourse between China and the Western Nations previous to the discovery of the Cape route'.[1] This was a work on the grand scale, not only the longest of the Society's editions to date but arguably the most scholarly, Yule's command of sources in many languages being accompanied by sound critical judgements. The two volumes brought together in translation the work of medieval travellers who had received little attention, notably Odoric of Pordenone, and thus enabled many more readers to appreciate their accounts of China. The Society was clearly proud of Yule's work, although he was not yet a member, and the Annual Report for 1867 declared that 'Colonel Yule's laborious and admirably edited work will in future be the standard authority on all questions relating to the early intercourse between Europe and the Far East'.[2] In the opinion of a modern historian of the Society, 'Cathay and the Way Thither is perhaps one of the finest works produced under the Hakluyt imprint'.[3] Yule was proposed for membership of the Council in 1868, and his name appears for the first time in the list of members.[4] His edition was a pioneering study, and was bound to be subject to revision as new information came to light. The task of revision was eventually undertaken by Yule's friend, Henri Cordier, the compiler of a magnificent (and still unsurpassed) bibliography of China.[5] Cordier had returned from China in 1876, and was introduced to Yule by Dr Reinhold Rost, the Librarian at the India Office.[6] In his obituary of Yule, Cordier praised Cathay and the Way Thither and added that Yule had encouraged him to produce his own new edition of the travels of Odoric of Pordenone.[7] Some thirty years later, Cordier was asked by the then President of the Hakluyt Society, Sir Clements Markham, to work on a second edition of Cathay and the Way Thither, probably because he had been responsible for a third edition of Yule's The book of Ser Marco Polo. The Society published the second edition, revised by Cordier and enlarged to four volumes, between 1913 and 1916.[8] This was again the

---

[1] Henry Yule, ed., Cathay and the Way Thither. Being a Collection of Medieval Notices of China ... With a Preliminary Essay on the Intercourse between China and the Western Nations previous to the discovery of the Cape Route, 2 vols, London, 1866 (HS 36–7).

[2] Annual Report for 1867 in HS 40.

[3] Dorothy Middleton, 'The Hakluyt Society 1846–1923', in Annual Report [1984], Hakluyt Society, p. 18.

[4] List of members in the supplementary material in HS 40.

[5] H. Cordier, Bibliothea Sinica: dictionnaire bibliographique des ouvrages relatifs à l'Empire Chinois, 8 vols, Paris, 1878–85.

[6] Yule, The Book of Ser Marco Polo, 3rd ed., revised by H. Cordier, p. vii.

[7] H. Cordier, ed., Les Voyages en Asie au xive siècle du bienheureux frère Odoric de Pordenone, Paris 1891.

[8] Henry Yule, ed., Cathay and the Way Thither ... New Edition, Revised throughout in the Light of Recent Discoveries, by Henry Cordier, London, 1913–16 (HS 2/33, 37, 38, 41).

'AṢAF <u>KH</u>AN. MINISTER OF SHĀH JAHĀN'
Frontispiece of the edition of the travels of Fray Sebastian Manrique 1629–1643:
HS 2/59 of 1927.

longest work that the Society had published to date. The expansion from two to four volumes was justified by Cordier on the ground that a vast amount of new information had come to light between 1866 and 1914, including Aurel Stein's recent expeditions to Central Asia. He was careful to point out that there were few errors to be corrected in Yule's notes; this in itself was a tribute to the soundness of Yule's research.[1]

Yule's next publication brought him to the notice of a wider circle of readers, as it ran to three editions in thirty years. In 1871 he published a new translation of Marco Polo's travels in Asia; a second edition was published in 1875, and a third followed, long after Yule's death, in 1903.[2] Although Yule's attention had been drawn to Marco Polo as early as 1850, the impetus to produce a new edition came from 'the wealth of appropriate material, and the acquaintance with the medieval geography of Asia' acquired during the preparation of *Cathay and the Way Thither*; this, he wrote, 'could hardly fail to suggest as a fresh labour in the same field the preparation of a new English edition of Marco Polo'.[3] The research was based on the resources available in libraries in France and Italy, but Yule obtained much of the additional information which he needed by correspondence with scholars in many countries: missionaries in Southern India, Tibet, and Shanghai, diplomats, and brother-officers in the Indian Army and Indian Political Service.[4] The first edition was well-received and earned Yule the Founder's Medal of the Royal Geographical Society and election as an Honorary Member of several European geographical societies.[5] So many letters were received, particularly from China, that Yule was encouraged to publish a second edition in 1875.[6] In his later years a third edition was considered, but Yule had made no progress with it at the time of his death. A decade later his daughter persuaded Cordier to edit the third edition, and this was published in 1903, prefaced by a long memoir of her father written by Miss Yule. Cordier was able to incorporate a great deal of information into his edition, but altered little else.[7] Yule's edition of Marco Polo was a remarkable example of

---

[1] Ibid., II, pp. xii–xiv.

[2] Yule, *The Book of Ser Marco Polo*, 2 vols, London, 1871; 2nd ed., 2 vols, London, 1875; 3rd ed., revised by Henri Cordier, 2 vols, London, 1903.

[3] Ibid., 1871, I, p. vii.

[4] Ibid., pp. ix–xi.

[5] A. F. Yule, *Memoir*, p. 34.

[6] H. Cordier, *Journal Asiatique*, 8ᵉ série, 15, 1890, pp. 255–6.

[7] He wrote: 'I have suppressed hardly any of Sir Henry Yule's notes and altered but few, doing so only when the light of new information has proved him to be in error, but I have supplemented them by what, I hope will be found useful, new information' (Yule, *The Book of Ser Marco Polo*, 3rd ed., I, pp. ix–x). The list of Yule's writings in this edition was compiled by Cordier and Yule's daughter.

nineteenth-century scholarship, and displays an immense amount of learning in the notes to the text. On the other hand the archaic style of the translation has not worn well, although it was appreciated at the time.[1]

Yule's third and last publication for the Hakluyt Society was his final major work. The late seventeenth-century Bengal diary of William Hedges had been discovered in a Canterbury bookshop by Robert Barlow, a retired Bengal pilot.[2] Barlow made a careful transcription and added a brief introduction and a few notes. The work was accepted for publication by the Council of the Hakluyt Society and sent to the press. When the first proofs appeared, Yule, now President of the Society, was appalled to find that the 'further necessary editing' had not been carried out. He hastily corrected the errors in the proofs and in the transcription, and added extra notes and an index; however, he felt that the volume could still be published as it stood.[3] But he later stated that 'when correcting the proofs I did not consider that the office of Editor had devolved on me, and [I] had not made the research which I have since undertaken'.[4] This later research produced so much new information that two further volumes were needed. The title pages of all three volumes correctly noted that the volumes included 'Copious Extracts from Unpublished Records'. The second volume was published in 1888 and contained documents relating to Job Charnock, the founder of Calcutta, and other East India Company officials; the third volume followed in 1889, and was devoted partly to documents relating to Thomas Pitt, Governor of Fort St George, Madras (and grandfather of William Pitt, first Earl of Chatham) and partly to documents about the early history of the Company's settlements in Bengal.[5] Thus Yule's decision to remedy Barlow's failings as an editor and historian resulted in a major contribution to the history of the East India Company's

---

[1] R. Maclagan, 'Sir Henry Yule', *Journal of the Royal Asiatic Society*, n.s. 22, 1890, pp. 224–5; Trotter, 'Memoir', pp. xlviii–xlix.

[2] Robert Frederick Barlow (c.1818–1900) had served in the East India Company's Bengal Pilot Service 1834–59 (IOR, L/MAR/8/1; L/AG/20/13/19, no. 338). He presented the manuscript to the India Office (IOR, G/40/15).

[3] *The Diary of William Hedges, Esq. (afterwards Sir William Hedges) during his Agency in Bengal; as well as on his Voyage Out and Return Overland (1681–1687) ... Transcribed ... by R. Barlow ... and Illustrated by Copious Extracts from Unpublished Records, etc. by ... Henry Yule*, London, 1887 (HS 74).

[4] Yule, *William Hedges*, I, pp. vii–ix.

[5] Yule, ed., *Diary of William Hedges ... Volume II. Containing Notices regarding Sir William Hedges, documentary Memoirs of Job Charnock, and other biographical and miscellaneous Illustrations of the Times in India*, London, 1888 (HS 75); *The Diary of William Hedges ... Volume III. Containing documentary Contributions to a Biography of Thomas Pitt, Governor of Fort St. George; with Collections on the early History of the Company's Settlement in Bengal; and on early Charts and Topography of the Húgli River*, London, 1889 (HS 88).

activities in Bengal in the late seventeenth century. There is no hint in the editorial matter that Yule contemplated a larger work on this subject, but in any case his declining health would have prevented him from carrying out such a large project.

Italy had provided Yule with plenty of scope for his research, but after his wife's death in April 1875 there was no need for him to make his permanent home there. He moved to London, and found that there was a great demand for his talents. In the autumn of 1875 his old friend and mentor, Sir William Baker, resigned his seat on the Council of India, and Yule was immediately appointed to succeed him.[1] This not only gave Yule an opportunity to influence the Secretary of State for India in the making of British policy in India but also provided him with a useful salary of £1200 per annum. It is difficult to assess the extent to which he exerted direct pressure within the Council as debates were not recorded, but it seems likely that he expressed his views mainly in the departmental committees of the India Office. Yule rarely registered formal minutes of dissent from the Council's decisions, but did so in 1878 when the Council sent a despatch to India approving Lord Lytton's Vernacular Press Act, which curtailed the freedom of the vernacular press in India (exempting English language-newspapers) and imposed severe penalties on printers and publishers of material which the Government of India, or the local authorities, found objectionable.[2] The work of the Council of India did not reduce Yule's literary output: letters to the press, reviews, obituaries of his friends in the Bengal Engineers, articles and addresses poured from his pen. Not all of this

---

[1] A. F. Yule, *Memoir*, p. 38; Yule had remarried in 1877 but his second wife died in 1881.

[2] S. Gopal, *British Policy in India 1858–1905*, Cambridge, 1965, pp. 118–19. Yule objected to the hasty enactment of this important piece of legislation, and to the harsh penalties imposed on Indian newspapers. A few sentences will serve to show the vigour of Yule's opposition to the measure. 'Most of the offending paragraphs quoted by the Government of India are indeed very unpleasant reading. But a considerable proportion of these are only as the Duke of Buckingham has said the utterance of unpalatable truths in strong language. It is not good for us that the utterance of those truths should be suppressed . . . . There is a just distinction between the liberty of the Press and License. But what some supporters of the Act, both in India and in the Council seem to me to have overlooked is that the line between these must be drawn by Law, and its transgression judged by a regularly constituted Court. Where the judgement is arbitrary, and in the hands of the Executive it is idle to talk of the liberty of the Press' (IOR, C/128, Minutes of Dissent by Members of the Council of India 1877–1893, pp. 235, 237–8). The Act was found to be unworkable, and was repealed by Lytton's successor as Viceroy (Gopal, *British Policy*, pp. 119, 144–5). [Yule also took a liberal attitude on certain African issues, being associated, for instance, with H. M. Hyndman in condemning Stanley's 'Bumbirch Massacre' of 1875, and he resigned from the Council of the RGS on the issue: H. Yule and H. M. Hyndman, *Mr. Stanley and the R. G. S. Being the Record of a Protest*, London, 1878. Editors.]

159

was serious, for Yule also composed light verse which he signed 'M.P.V.' or 'Marco Polo Venetus'.[1] He was President of the Royal Asiatic Society in 1886 and 1887, a remarkable honour at the time for a scholar whose expertise was not in oriental languages. In 1883 he was made LL.D of Edinburgh University.

In 1877 Yule's nine-year membership of the Council of the Hakluyt Society was rewarded with his election as President of the Society, an office which he held for twelve years and until a few months before his death in 1889.[2] His term of office was marked by greater supervision of the volumes published by the Society, and a concern for high standards of scholarship.[3] The episode of William Hedges' diary described above seems to suggest that the Council had accepted Barlow's transcript without examining it thoroughly, and Yule became aware of the lack of critical and explanatory matter only when the first proofs reached him. It is to his credit that the final publication was a substantial work of scholarship. This attention to high standards in scholarship was not matched by concern for his administrative duties; it has been noted that Council meetings were held infrequently, and there are no minutes at all for 1886.[4] During most of Yule's presidency the indefatigable Clements Markham was Honorary Secretary and Yule was probably content to entrust organisation of the Society to the younger man, even when this meant bypassing the Council. Nevertheless the standing of the Society remained high, and was certainly enhanced by those publications which reflected Yule's scholarly standards.

In the midst of Yule's official duties and literary work he found time to compile a volume which to some extent stands apart from the general run of his publications. *Hobson-Jobson: being a Glossary of Anglo-Indian colloquial Words and Phrases*, published in 1886, was originally planned jointly with A. C. Burnell, a Sanskrit scholar, but after Burnell's death was continued and completed by Yule. Although seven-eighths of the work was done by Yule, he paid a handsome tribute to Burnell in the preface, named him as his co-author, and included his portrait at the beginning of the volume.[5] *Hobson-Jobson* amounts to some 870 pages, printed in double columns, and is much more than a glossary; after the definition of each word, its etymology, and a discussion of its use, there

---

[1] A. F. Yule, *Memoir*, pp. 41, 49–54 (bibliography).

[2] William Foster, 'The Hakluyt Society. A Retrospect: 1846–1946', in Edward Lynam, ed., *Richard Hakluyt & his Successors*, London, 1946 (HS 2/93), p. 154.

[3] Middleton, 'History of the Hakluyt Society', p. 18.

[4] Ibid.

[5] H. Yule and A. C. Burnell, *Hobson-Jobson: being a Glossary of Anglo-Indian colloquial Words and Phrases; etymological, historical, geographical, and discursive*, London, 1886, pp. vii–viii.

A CANTONESE WAR-JUNK
From the *Ch'ou-hai-t'u-pien*, 1562.
Reproduced in HS 2/106 of 1953.

are copious quotations illustrating the ways in which it was used. Unusual or difficult words allowed Yule to write short essays, for instance, four pages each on 'India, Indies' and 'Tea' and two pages on 'Rupee'. Certain derivations were rejected brusquely in favour of better sources.[1] The chief delight of Hobson-Jobson lies in the large number of quotations used by Yule, for they reflect the range and depth of his reading and his command of a wide range of European languages; he readily acknowledged the help which he had received from scholars of Semitic languages, Chinese and Sanskrit.[2] The tone of Yule's preface suggests that he regarded Hobson-Jobson as something of a *jeu d'esprit*, but it is much more than that, for it summarises the whole range of his scholarly interests, and his affection for India. It has never been superseded.[3]

As his early work in India had shown, Henry Yule was a thoroughly professional military engineer and an able administrator, and he carried the qualities that had produced his success in the military world into his scholarship. In India he had found time to develop his historical and geographical interests, and these flourished after his return to Europe. His three publications for the Hakluyt Society, especially *Cathay and the Way Thither*, together with the edition of Marco Polo and *Hobson-Jobson*, were landmarks in scholarship, all the more remarkable for the fact that the early works were prepared in isolation in Italy, while the later work had to be combined with his active membership of the Council of India and presidency of the Hakluyt Society. As one obituary stated: 'Everything he produced was characterized by thoroughness of investigation and accuracy of detail, and enlivened by a wealth of note and comment that laid all he had to say clearly and completely before the general reader, the scholar and the critic.'[4]

Early in 1889, when Yule had become very weak, he resigned from the Council of India. He was knighted, as a Knight Commander of the Star of India, but died in London on 30 December 1889. On his deathbed he received news that he had been made a Corresponding Member of the Institute of France. Yule immediately dictated a graceful reply in Latin, which served as his valediction:

Reddo gratias, illustrissimi domini, ob honores tanto nimios quanto

---

[1] For instance, in discussing 'Gingham' he sweeps aside the suggestion that the word came from the town of Guingamp in Brittany, or from India, and points to a Javanese origin: "*ginggang*, a sort of striped or chequered East Indian lijnwand", the last word being applied to cotton as well as linen stuffs, equivalent to the French *toile*' (ibid., p. 287).

[2] Ibid., pp. ix–x.

[3] A second edition, edited and enlarged by William Crooke, was published in 1902 (London). This edition was reprinted in 1969 and 1985, and in its Indian edition is still in print.

[4] Maclagan, 'Yule', p. 221.

immeritos. Mihi robora deficiunt, vita collabitur, accipiatis voluntatem pro facto. Cum corde pleno et gratissimo moriturus vos, illustrissimi domini, saluto. Yule.[1] [*I thank you, most distinguished masters, for the honours you have paid me, which are as excessive as they are unmerited. Since my strength is failing, and my life is ebbing away, you must accept the will for the deed. With a full and most grateful heart, I who am about to die salute you, most distinguished masters. Yule.*]

---

[1] A. F. Yule, *Memoir*, p. 45.

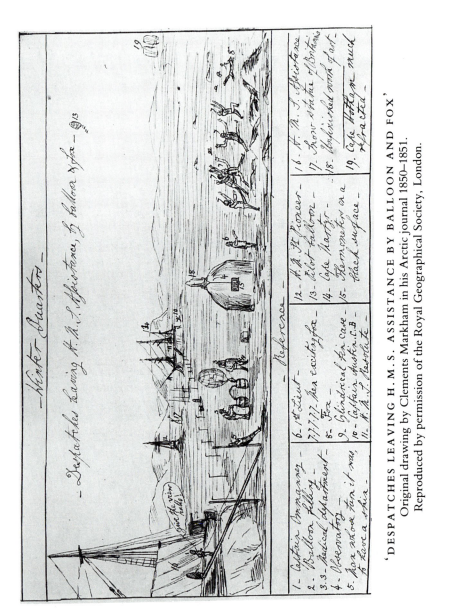

'DESPATCHES LEAVING H.M.S. ASSISTANCE BY BALLOON AND FOX'
Original drawing by Clements Markham in his Arctic journal 1850–1851.
Reproduced by permission of the Royal Geographical Society, London.

CLEMENTS MARKHAM

LONGEST SERVING OFFICER,
MOST PROLIFIC EDITOR

Ann Savours

Clements Robert Markham (1830–1916) served the Hakluyt Society for twenty-eight years as Honorary Secretary and then for nearly twenty years as President, while he edited for the Society some thirty volumes, the first published in 1859, the last in 1923.[1] He was the dominant figure in the middle period of the history of the Society. Yet it is difficult to assess his exact role, although there can be no doubt that his personality carried the Society forward, after its early decades, through to the end of the nineteenth century. Apart from the evidence of his posts and of his editions, the Society's records reveal little about the man. This may well be because the Society involved only a small part of his multifarious activities – in this he was not, of course, alone among the Society's Victorian leaders. He was, for instance, a joint Honorary Secretary of the Royal Geographical Society for twenty-five years (1863–1888) and President for twelve (1893–1905). In the Hakluyt Society he was admired, patently for his energy and tenacity, but not, perhaps, invariably respected.[2] The annual report for 1886 announced his resignation as Secretary with only a reference to his length of service and no other commendation; yet the 1889 report stated that 'shortly before his death he [the then president, Colonel Yule, a distinguished scholar] sent for Mr Clements Markham, and expressed the wish that he should succeed him in the office'.[3] Markham's own scholarship may

---

[1] For information on Clements Markham and assistance in the preparation of this essay my thanks are due to Mr Peter Wordie, Dr Peter Blanchard, Dr Nigel Allan, Dr Michael Barkham; to the following staff of the Royal Geographical Society: Dr John Hemming, Ms Paula Lucas, Mr Francis Herbert, Ms Janet Turner, Ms Lisa Monk, and Mr Ted Hatch; to Mr and Mrs F. Markham, the Reverend Canon Gervase Markham, Sir Laurence Kirwan, Mr Anthony Payne, Mrs Setitia Simmonds, Dr Andrew S. Cook, Dr and Mrs D. Pratt; and to the editors of the present volume.

[2] See, for instance, the comment on Markham by Foster, p. 197 below.

[3] It is perhaps doubtful whether Yule and Markham had worked together closely during the time they were respectively president and secretary, but no doubt Yule had

have stretched over too wide a range of subjects and as an HS editor he has been severely criticised.[1]

But this range was related to the aspects of Markham's character which made him a 'workaholic' – with a great penchant for travel, which travels he recorded assiduously, and with an inveterate urge to write on many other matters. Yet, in the circumstances of the period, he practised both activities with considerable distinction. Apart from his HS editions, he published almost 30 books – some travelogues describing his own expeditions to foreign parts, many biographies of friends and other exalted characters, several histories of enterprises of which he approved, a number of edition of texts in various fields – and he left behind extensive unpublished diaries (now largely held by the Royal Geographical Society). He thought nothing of regularly writing two books in a year, books totalling 1,000 pages in print. But in the Victorian period such higher journalism as Markham's often involved original and even scientifically useful accounts of remote places or historical persons, involving research into relatively inaccessible sources of information. At the time, Markham's writings certainly appear to have been appreciated, and in a number of respects taken very seriously.[2] As for his career, starting in quite lowly posts he rose to become a prominent administrator, performing valuable and even uniquely important tasks, albeit sometimes, it would seem, at the expense of personal relations with colleagues. Yet while he is perhaps remembered today as the obstinate and quarrelsome old man who set Captain Scott on his Antarctic voyages, as a youth and throughout his life he made many friends, with one of whom, a spirited girl met in Peru, he was to correspond for some fifty years, without ever seeing

---

appreciated Markham's energy as administrator and editor, while as a former engineer in India he may have also have appreciated Markham's activities in relation to that country.

[1] It must be appreciated that beyond his early schooling at Cheam and in the Navy, Markham had no further formal education. The translations in his Hakluyt Society editions have been commented on in the following articles: Bailey W. Diffie and H. Bernstein, 'A Markham contribution to the *Leyenda Negra*', *Hispanic American Historical Review* [hereafter *HAHR*], 16, 1936, pp. 96–103; Bailey W. Diffie, 'Sir Clements R. Markham as a translator', *HAHR*, 17, 1937, pp. 546–57; Samuel E. Morison, 'Journal of Columbus's First Voyage', *HAHR*, 19, 1939, 251–3; William Foster, 'The Hakluyt Society. A Retrospect: 1846–1946', in E. Lynam, ed., *Richard Hakluyt & and his Successors*, London, 1946 (HS 2/93), p. 156; Robert Graves, 'The Isles of Unwisdom', London, 1950, p. xii; Celsus Kelly, 'The narrative of Pedro Fernandez de Quiros: MS. description, authorship, history, printed text and translation', *Historical Studies: Australia and New Zealand*, 9, 1959–61, pp. 189–90; G. R. Crone, '"Jewells of Antiquitie": the work of the Hakluyt Society', *Geographical Journal*, 128, 1962, pp. 322–3. See also the comment cited in the text below, on p. 185.

[2] Since the writings dealt with so many regions and subjects, it has not yet been possible to ascertain in detail how they stand up to modern scholarship.

her again. The essay that follows limits itself to sketching the background to Markham's role in the Hakluyt Society, by surveying, in summary from a wider study at present in progress, his remarkable career and major interests.

Peru and the Arctic

'Peru was his first love, Polar exploration his second; and to both he remained constant to the end.'[1] So Markham's biographer observed when summing up his cousin's life and work. The portrait of Clements Markham as an old man which hangs in the House of the Royal Geographical Society symbolises these ruling passions. Above Markham's right hand is a framed picture of the Cinchona plant, which he collected in Peru for the relief of malaria in India. Below that, on a stand, is painted a silver model of a loaded sledge and manhauling figure. This model was presented to Markham by the officers of the 'Discovery' and 'Morning', when they all met again on 7 November 1904, in the Royal Albert Hall, to hear Captain R. F. Scott lecture on the National Antarctic Expedition of 1901 to 1904, of which he had been commander. Scott was to call one of the grandest peaks bordering the Ross Ice Shelf, Mount Markham, after 'the Father of the Expedition and its most constant friend'.[2]

Born in 1830 the son of a Yorkshire clergyman,[3] Markham joined the Royal Navy as a cadet in 1844 at the age of fourteen, and served first on the Pacific station.[4] As well as receiving instruction in navigation and other naval arts, like the other youngsters Markham was taught Spanish and French, the former a language not only useful during the four years of the his ship's visits to ports in Chile and Peru but one which helped to shape Markham's later intellectual interests.[5] He wrote his

[1] Albert H. Markham, *The Life of Sir Clements R. Markham, K.C.B., F.R.S.* ... , London, 1917, p. 362. This, the only biography, is readable and contains much information regarding Markham's personal relations and movements but in considering his larger activities has the limitations of a study written by a close relative immediately after the subject's death.

[2] R. F. Scott, *The Voyages of the 'Discovery'*, London, 1905, 'Dedication'.

[3] Markham edited a handful of books between 1854 and 1904 on the history of the Markhams and he published a *Memoir of Archbishop Markham, 1719–1807*, Oxford, 1906, the archbishop having been his great-grandfather. Towards the end of his life, he compiled an MS. volume of 'Early Reminiscences' covering the years 1832–42 and thus in part on his schooldays. The MS. is in private hands.

[4] Markham's shipmates included Sherard Osborn, who later became one of the 'Arctic Officers' of the navy, and James Goodenough, another life-long friend, whose biography Markham was eventually to write: C. R. Markham, *Commodore J. G. Goodenough. A Brief Memoir*, Portsmouth, 1876.

[5] Clements Markham, *The Incas of Peru*, London, 1910, p. vi.

first extant diary, which is full of lively descriptions of people and places, and it is clear that he already found writing an easy pursuit. In 1850, through the good offices of a friend, he joined the Arctic Squadron whose aim was to find the lost Franklin expedition. His diaries for 1850–1851, a day-by-day sledging diary written up later into a private journal, indicate his fascination with the northern region. He wrote of the Whale Fish Islands on the west coast of Greenland as follows.

> In these islands, the bold granite cliff, the myriads of water fowl enjoying their short lives, the sense of solitude caused by the profound stillness, the towering ice bergs, the sun at midnight, the wonderful mirages, and deep blue of the heavens, all is grand, majestic, awe-inspiring; all too is pleasant and delightful; all save man.[1]

Although good geographical work was accomplished, the main object of the expedition was not achieved.

> Much has been done by the travelling parties, many severe hardships endured, hundreds of miles of new coast discovered, hundreds of miles of old coast has been searched, but not a trace of the missing expedition to be found in any direction. It is indeed a strange mystery.[2]

But the young midshipman found the experience invigorating. Confined to a tent by a storm, he 'Read Pickwick aloud, ate, drank, slept and read Johnson's life of Pope, alternately. Had a duck and sandpipers stewed in green pea soup, for dinner'.[3] Nevertheless, on the passage home he wrote a letter to his parents announcing his intention to leave the Navy, for 'to plod along in it, in a station below mediocrity would be misery to me . . . my wishes, hopes and aspirations are entirely apart from the Navy . . . I hope to carve out my own way in the world – deo volente'.[4] While he maintained a lifelong respect for the Navy, his short career in it had included a number of episodes when he clashed with his superiors, a foreshadowing of future occasions when a set determination, a product of warm sympathies and bright intellect, produced a stormy course.[5] His first independent action was to write an account of the 1850–1851 expedition. Significantly, in respect of his later Hakluyt

---

[1] MS, London, Royal Geographical Society Archives [hereafter RGSA], CRM 3. The final reference was to the local Eskimo, of whom Markham gave an unflattering picture.
[2] RGSA, CRM 3, p. 65.
[3] Ibid., CRM 4, entry for 7 July 1851.
[4] Ibid., CRM 36/2.
[5] The episodes are described in A. H. Markham, *Sir Clements Markham*, chapters IV–VI. In later life, however, Markham's early naval career disposed him to favour, for expeditions and explorations, naval officers such as Scott (and to be at times unfair to others): Ian Cameron, *The History of the Royal Geographical Society. To the Farthest Ends of the Earth*, London, 1980, p. 142.

'INCA PALACE OF LIMATAMBO'
Original drawing by Clements Markham in his diary of travels in Peru, 1853.
Reproduced by permission of the Wellcome Institute Library, London.

Society interest, it included a history of the earlier voyages in search of the North-West Passage. This, his first published book, appeared in 1853.[1]

During the Arctic winter Markham began to study the Quechua language of Peru (and he wrote a tragedy in blank verse on the fate of the last of the Incas). Once free from the Navy, in 1852 he sailed for Peru, but via New York, in order to call on W. H. Prescott, whose renowned history, *The Conquest of Peru*, had recently appeared.[2] Markham's travels in Peru produced a book published in 1856 which concluded thus.

> The writer of the preceding pages, undertaking a journey to Peru solely with a view to the examination of its antiquities, and the enjoyment of its magnificent scenery, soon found that the unaffected kindness of its warm-hearted inhabitants was even more attractive than the deeply interesting history of the Incas; and in conclusion he can only say that a journey through the land of the Children of the Sun is one of the most enjoyable expeditions that can possibly be undertaken.[3]

---

[1] Clements R. Markham, *Franklin's Footsteps: A Sketch of Greenland, along the Shores of which his Expedition passed, and of the Parry Isles, where the Last Traces of it were found*, London, 1853.

[2] This part of the career is dealt with in A. H. Markham, *Sir Clements Markham*, pp. 123–33.

[3] Clements R. Markham, *Cuzco: A Journey to the Ancient Capital of Peru; with an Account of the History, Language, Literature and Antiquities of the Incas. And Lima: A Visit to the Capital and Provinces of modern Peru, with a Sketch of the Vice-Regal Government, History of*

A manuscript account of the same travels, apparently written up in part from diaries now lost, was eventually published in 1991, as *Markham in Peru*.[1] One extract will suffice. Crossing the Andes with a guide in February 1853, and ascending the pass from Tambillo through rain clouds, towards dusk they approached black cliffs in which was situated a cave known to the guide where they proposed to shelter for the night.

> But to our horror we found it full of water and streams dripping from thee roof. The ground all round was covered with large tufts of grass a foot high charged with snow, making it uninviting to lie down. The snow was still falling and our matches had got wet. Agustin apologised by saying that he had never crossed in this season before and never thought it possible to be like what we saw and felt. In these very depressing circumstances Agustin Carpio, my guide, friend, and coun-cillor, bowed his head on the mule's neck and announced that he was moribund. There was no help for it but to wait standing until daylight. I wrapped my poncho round and laid my head on the Bdellium's neck, who kept fairly quiet during the night. As morning dawned it ceased to snow and things began to look more cheerful.[2]

Patently the traveller enjoyed moments of physical challenge, as, in later life, he did the recording of them.

Markham was particularly keen to visit Cuzco, since he believed (in fact wrongly) that no English traveller had left an account of that ancient city of the Incas and perhaps none had been there, but he also travelled widely in the region, mainly on foot with two mules. He seems to have entered into the life of Peru – attending mass, or going to parties and festivals with the families which offered him hospitality. Very many characters from all levels of society cross the pages of his journal. His meetings and conversations with the *curas* or priests were particularly informative, as these men were often learned in Quechua and the traditions of the Incas. An old *cura* of Lares, a descendant of the Incas, who owned what was said to be the best version of the Quechua drama of 'Apu Ollantay', allowed Markham to copy the text, which in

---

the Republic, and a Review of the Literature and Society of Peru, 1856, p. 387; German version (part), Leipzig, 1865. The comprehensive title of this work shows its didactic intent.

[1] Peter Blanchard, ed., *Markham in Peru*, Austin, Texas, 1991. The manuscript, entitled 'Travels in Peru in 1853', is now in the Wellcome Institute, London (American MS 126). It was written between 1908 and 1912, with subsequent amendments, and illustrated with maps, sketches, and watercolours, loose or pasted down, probably for the most part contemporary with his 1852–53 journeys. The 1991 edition reproduces only a proportion of the illustrations, some of the charm and interest of the original being thereby lost.

[2] Blanchard, *Markham in Peru*, pp. 57–8. Bdellium is a a resin used as a perfume, hence here a reference to the smell of the mule.

1871 he published in a line-for-line translation.[1] Markham measured
and described many Inca and other ruins, for example those at Ollan-
taytambo, which he considered 'the most interesting ruin in Peru
whether from a historical or a legendary point of view'.[2] For the rest of
his life Markham was to publish and correspond on Inca and Peruvian
subjects.[3] Many volumes of Spanish texts translated and edited for the
Hakluyt Society testify to this enduring interest. Outside the House of
the Royal Geographical Society in London is a bust of Markham, with
the following inscription underneath.

> This monument to the memory of Sir Clements Markham, K.C.B.,
> F.R.S., and for twelve years President of the Royal Geographical Society
> was erected in the year 1921 by the PERUVIAN NATION in gratitude
> for his services as Historian of their country.[4]

Quinine for India

On his return from Peru, Markham needed to help in supporting his
mother and sister, his father having died, and he obtained clerical posts
in the civil service, from 1858 as a clerk in the Correspondence Section
of the newly-established India Office. He was to continue at the India
Office in positions of increasing responsibility until a noisy dispute
with his superiors led to his resignation in 1877, with some notable
consequent bitterness on his part.[5] His capabilities and ambitions must,
however, have soon been recognised, since in 1859 he was selected not
only to superintend the collection in South America of medicinal plants
and seeds, but also to arrange for their transport and planting in parts of
India and Ceylon, where they might be expected to flourish. The
project was apparently proposed by Markham himself and derived
from his humane desire to combat the scourge of malaria in India, by
making more available the quinine obtained from the cinchona trees he

---

[1] C. R. Markham, *Ollanta. An ancient Ynca Drama*, London, 1871; Spanish version,
Buenos Aires, 1883. A free translation also appeared as an appendix to Markham, *Incas of
Peru*, pp. 321–407, and was separately reprinted at Lima in 1964.

[2] Blanchard, *Markham in Peru*, p. 102.

[3] His interest in Peru extended to its modern politics, hence Clements R. Markham,
The War between Peru and Chile, 1879–1882, London, 1882; 2nd ed. 1921, Spanish version,
Ciudad de Los Reyes, 1922.

[4] His major work in this category was Clements R. Markham, *A History of Peru*,
Chicago, 1892, reprinted New York, 1968; Spanish version, Lima, 1895, 1941, 1952.

[5] Markham's biographer omitted all mention of the India Office service and in his post-
1877 papers Markham himself mentioned it only in relation to his pension. His later
Hakluyt Society editions made no use of India Office sources, and his unfriendly attitude
to Foster, the later Honorary Secretary of the Society, may have been in part because of
the latter's post at the India Office.

had seen when in Peru.[1] Once for a second time in that country, he supervised the collecting of plants, sometimes surreptitiously in view of the hostility of some landowners, and with difficulty because of the terrain. On the last day of his collecting he wrote in his diary the following thoughts.

> I feel most deeply grateful to the all ruling Providence who has guarded me through so many dangers and difficulties, and has up to this time, crowned this important service with complete success. May its final issue be for the welfare and amelioration of the condition of my fellow men, to the praise and glory of God's holy name.[2]

In two books, published in 1862 and 1880, he described the perils of the operation and complained of the shabby subsequent treatment by the British government of his fellow collectors, one of them a botanist of considerable repute.[3] While in Peru he persuaded an aged priest to check his Quechua dictionary, and he published the result in 1864.[4] The tricky job of carrying the plants to the coast by mule and then transporting them by sea to India exercised Markham's patience and the accompanying gardener's skill. Sadly, those with which he was most closely concerned did not survive. Fortunately, other cinchona plants did reach both India and Kew.

In India, Markham surveyed suitable sites in the hill regions for cinchona plantations, and in 1865 he returned there, to report to the India Office on cultivation. He commented on the destruction of wild

---

[1] On the project and Markham's part in it, see Donovan Williams, 'Clements Robert Markham and the introduction of the cinchona tree into British India, 1861', *Geographical Journal*, 128, 1962, pp. 431–42. Markham tended to use the Spanish form of the term, 'chinchona'. Note his *A Memoir of the Lady Ana de Osorio, Countess of Chinchón and Vice-Queen of Peru (A.D. 1629–39). With a Plea for the Correct Spelling of the Chinchona Genus*, London, 1874.

[2] RGSA, CRM 5, 'Diary in Peru and India', p. 269.

[3] C. R. Markham, *Travels in Peru and India while superintending the Collection of Chinchona Plants and Seeds in South America, and their Introduction into India*, London, 1862; German version (of part), Leipzig, 1874; Clements R. Markham, *Peruvian Bark. A Popular Account of the Introduction of Chinchona Cultivation into British India*, London, 1880. His 'Private Journal' of his travels, trials and tribulations in the Caravaya region of southern Peru and in India is RGSA, CRM 5, 51, 52, 67, 68, 69.

[4] Clements R. Markham, *Contributions towards a Grammar and Dictionary of Quichua, the language of the Yncas of Peru*, London, 1864, reprinted Osnabrück, 1964. He later published *Vocabularies of the General Language of the Incas of Peru or Runa Simi (called Quichua by the Spanish Grammarians)*, London, 1908. While expressing his sorrow in the 1862 narrative at the likely extinction of the 'richest form of all the American group of languages', together with 'all the traditions which yet remain of the old glory of the Incas, all the elegies, love-songs, and poems which stamp the character of a once powerful, but always gentle and amiable race', he also regretted that 'unlike the English in India, the half-Spanish races of Peru have paid little attention to the history and languages of the aborigines within the present century' (Markham, *Travels*, p. 188).

forest for cultivated crops, but claimed that cinchona plantations would be 'as useful as the trees they have supplanted, in preventing evaporation, regulating drainage, and receiving the moisture which is wrung out of the passing clouds'.[1] The good intentions of the cinchona project were eventually realised, according to the Superintendent of the Royal Botanic Garden at Calcutta.

> We have at last compassed the end which Govt. set before itself in introducing Cinchona into India . . . viz., to put Quinine within the reach of the poorest native. Now anybody in Bengal who possesses a farthing (the equivalent of a *pice*) can buy for himself at any post-office in Bengal a dose of 5 grains of perfectly unadulterated Quinine![2]

Markham was awarded a grant of £3,000 for his services in Peru and India.[3]

Abyssinia

Having travelled in America and Asia, Markham next tackled Africa. In 1867 a British military expedition was launched against the ruler of Abyssinia (Ethiopia), Theodore. Troops from India and Britain, under the overall command of Sir Robert Napier, whose engineers enabled the inhospitable terrain to be crossed, in 1868 captured Theodore's mountain stronghold of Magdala. The official account of the campaign has this to say of Markham.

> Mr Clements Markham, Assistant Secretary of the Public Works Department in the India Office, and Secretary to the Royal Geographical Society, was appointed as Geographer to the Force in October 1867, and landed at Zeila on the 12th December. He accompanied the head-quarters during the march and until the capture of Magdala, making observations for latitude, variation and elevation above the sea, and also keeping a meteorological journal, and recording observations on the physical characteristics of the country. The results of his labours are comprised in three maps of the region traversed, and eight geographical memoirs, which

---

[1] Clements R. Markham, *A Memoir on the India Surveys*, India Office, London, 1871, p, 271, enlarged 2nd ed., 1878, reprinted Amsterdam, 1968, p. 373, citing C. R. Markham, 'On the effects of the destruction of forests in the western ghauts of India, on the water supply', *Journal of the Royal Geographical Society* [hereafter *JRGS*], 36, 1866, pp. 180–95.
[2] Cited in Leonard Huxley, ed., *Life and Letters of Joseph Dalton Hooker*, 2 vols, London, 1918, II, p. 5.
[3] Markham also played a small but significant part in another botanical transfer, that of the later transplanting of rubber from Brazil: this has been described in detail in Austin Coates, *The Commerce in Rubber: the first 200 years*, Singapore, 1987.

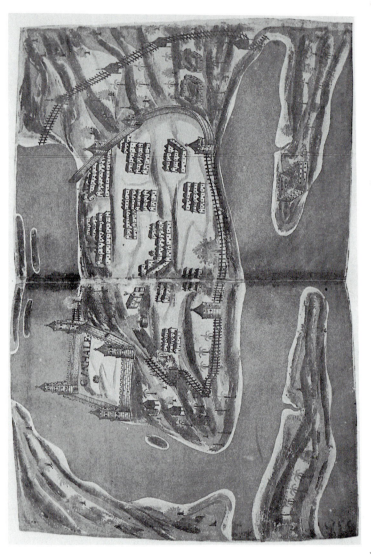

'KOTTEKKAL, THE TOWN AND FORTRESS OF KUNHALÍ, THE MALABAR CORSAIR'
From Barretto de Resende, 'Livro do Estado da India' (British Library, Sloane 197).
Reproduced in the edition of the voyage of Pyrard de Laval 1607–1611: HS 80 of 1890.

174

have since been published in the journal of the Royal Geographical Society for 1868.[1]

Markham had become a Joint Honorary Secretary of the Royal Geographical Society in 1863, and this responsibility, taken together with his India Office post, no doubt qualified him for the overseas excursion – one he must have welcomed. An archaeologist, a meteorologist, a zoologist and a geologist also accompanied the expedition at public expense, Abyssinia being so little known to the outside world.

Markham must have kept a diary of the campaign, but if extant it is untraced. He wrote a relatively objective account of the operation, which he published one year before the official report.[2] It included a lengthy introduction concerning the history of Abyssinia as well as a prefatory 'Note on the spelling, accentuation, and pronunciation of certain Abyssinian words', with frequent allusions to the travels of earlier Europeans in Ethiopia, Álvares, Lobo, Bruce, and Beke. The book gives a vivid and interesting account of the Ethiopian peoples, the landscape and the distinctive local churches,[3] and is even to some extent sympathetic to Theodore. Its beginning, however, breathed the spirit of the times.

> The march of an English army for several hundred miles into the heart of Abyssinia – a march which was looked upon as hazardous and almost impossible by the guides of public opinion, and which passed over a country so little known as actually to involve geographical discovery – was highly calculated to attract the attention and interest the imagination of Europe. There was something in it that recalled the exploits of that heroic age when dawning science enabled men who were still actuated by the spirit of knight errantry to achieve apparent impossibilities.

Following the fall of Magdala, refugees were to be found camped in hundreds of black tents. Markham observed.

> We came upon many forms of human misery – men in cruel pain with undressed wounds, helpless old people stripped by robbers on the road and exhausted by the fatigues of the march, children crying for food, their mothers with no means of satisfying their hunger. . . . In the English

---

[1] Trevenen J. Holland and Henry Montague Hozier, *Record of the Expedition to Abyssinia*, 2 vols, London, 1870, II, p. 371; C. R. Markham, 'Geographical results of the Abyssinian expedition', *JRGS*, 38, 1868, pp. 12–49 (but none of the three maps bears Markham's name). This article is preceded by another by Markham, 'The Portuguese expeditions to Abyssinia in the fifteenth, sixteenth and seventeenth centuries' (pp. 1–12).
[2] Clements R. Markham. *A History of the Abyssinian Expedition*, London, 1869.
[3] For instance, he made a ground plan of the ancient ruined church near Agula, which he believed to have been mentioned by the early Portuguese missionary and priest, Francisco Álvares (ibid., p. 236 and the facing plate).

camp there was no misery save such as was caused by rather tough beef and the absence of grog.[1]

After his travels with mules in Peru, Markham was well qualified to comment on the poor design of the pack saddle used on the 16,000 army mules. 'Instead of procuring pack-saddles from mule countries, they were made from patterns at Woolwich, Suez or India' – one of these being 'a structure between a hatchway-ladder and a hen coop', likely to 'kill any mule that was tortured with it'.[2] He made other criticisms but approved in general of the campaign. Once more he had travelled in the high hills and had found them to his liking. On his return to England, Markham received the campaign medal, and later, in May 1871, for his services in Abyssinia and in India, was made a Companion of the Bath.

The India Office

Although not mentioned by his biographer, one of Markham's most notable achievements was the reconstitution of the Geographical Department of the India Office between the years 1867 and 1877. A modern scholar has summed up this episode as follows.

> It was a poignant story of achievement laced with frustrated ambition, impatience and lack of restraint, played against the background of change and tension in the newly created India Office. It provides the measure both of [Markham's] ability as an organizer and idealist dedicated to the dissemination of geographical knowledge, and of his weakness in the form of undisciplined impulse which brought to a premature close a promising career in Whitehall.[3]

From 1858 to 1861 Markham worked in the Revenue Department and from 1861 to 1863 was Private Secretary to the Parliamentary Under-Secretary of State for India.[4] During the compilation of memoranda and reports he became more and more conscious of the lack of easily accessible geographical information, the Geographical Department being merely a minor and neglected division of the Revenue Department. By producing memoirs on various subjects, he attempted to

---

[1] Cited in A. H. Markham, *Sir Clements Markham*, p. 221, which gives no reference.
[2] Markham, *Abyssinian Expedition*, p. 213.
[3] Donovan Williams, 'Clements Robert Markham and the Geographical Department of the India Office 1867–77', *Geographical Journal*, 134, 1968, pp. 343–52, quotation on p. 343.
[4] Ibid., p. 344.

alleviate the deficiency.[1] In 1866, and again in 1867, he pointed out this sorry state of affairs to those senior to him, with the result that he was given charge of the geographical work. However, his position was anomalous in that up to 1875 he was provided with paid assistants but received no additional remuneration.

On taking over responsibility in 1868, he found the condition of records in the Geographical Department even worse than he had expected. The old correspondence books were destroyed, the invaluable collection of maps and geographical documents lay in a heap in a corner of a passage. Markham's final account of the scene of desolation, and how in ten years he brought order out of chaos, is admittedly a partial one, written in 1877 after his more or less enforced resignation.[2] But in 1871 he had already reported as follows.

> Since 1836 all geographical and kindred subjects had been deprived of separate departmental supervision, and the maps, journals, and other records had been cast aside to rot and perish. Those which were not lost were frayed and dust-stained, and finally a quantity were sold as waste paper. Ancient journals of great navigators, abstracts of which alone exist in the Pilgrims of Purchas, have disappeared; and many of the later memoirs and surveys of the time of Colin Mackenzie, and even a volume of the Great Trigonometrical Survey Series, are missing.[3]

Markham set about righting the situation – the additional staff included a map cataloguer and a map cleaner and mounter – and in 1877 he claimed, apparently with much justification, that 'the work of the Geographical Department is now organized and efficiently run'.[4] The present-day guide to the India Office maps notes that

> Markham, with Trelawney Saunders [his colleague and successor], was responsible for the complete reorganisation of the surviving geographical materials, and for the publication in 1878 of a catalogue of maps in the collection. This is the earliest date from which one can normally trace the continuous history of the maps.[5]

Markham's lengthy *Memoir on the Indian Surveys* of 1871, with a second

---

[1] It was apparently the writing of memoirs on various geographical areas which led him to produce *A General Sketch of the History of Persia*, London, 1874.

[2] *Report on the Geographical Department of the India Office, 1867 to 1877*, London, 1877. This booklet appears to have been printed privately, perhaps for the India Office files: the India Office Library copy is inscribed 'Trelawney Saunders (c) Private and Confidential'. However, part of the report was incorporated into the chapter entitled 'The Geographical Department of the India Office', as it appeared in the 1878 second edition of the *Memoir* (on pp. 399–423).

[3] Markham. *Memoir*, 1871, p. 284; 1878, p. 409.

[4] Markham, *Report on the Geographical Department*, p. 58.

[5] *Map Collections in the India Office Records*, British Library, [1988], p. 4.

edition in 1878, an impressive compilation and assessment, testified to his sound and wide knowledge of the surviving survey records and of the work progressing in India.[1]

Among the valuable earlier records which were brought to light by his reorganization were accounts of certain seventeenth-century voyages to the East Indies and also a record of a 1606 voyage to seek the North-West Passage. These were edited by Markham for the Hakluyt Society, together with narratives of the voyages of Sir James Lancaster reprinted from Hakluyt and Purchas. An appendix supplied a calendar of the 'ships' journals' of East India voyages of the seventeenth century preserved in the India Office, plus a list of the ships.[2] Markham also edited, for the India Office, an account of the missions to Tibet of Bogle in 1774 and Manning in 1811.[3] His interest in historical perspective led him in the *Memoir* to describe the establishment and duties of the Spanish Cosmographer of the Indies, and he also referred to the great names in the geography of India, Rennell, Dalrymple and others.[4] He further noted that, almost at the same time as the incorporation of the East India Company in 1599, Richard Hakluyt – whom Markham somewhat rhetorically described as the 'illustrious founder of the East India Geographical Department' – was at work

> preparing memoranda of the chief places where sundry sorts of spices do grow, gathered out of the best and latest authors; of the prices of precious stones and spices; of what is good to bring from the Indies by him that is skilful and trusty; of certain commodities of good request gathered out of

---

[1] In the *Memoir* he saw the work of the Geographical Department as encompassing the Great Trigonometrical Survey, the Topographical Surveys, the Revenue Survey, the Marine Survey, the Archaeological Survey, and the Meteorological Surveys, as well as more routine office work. His moving tribute to the surveyors of the Great Trigonometrical Survey is worth citing. 'It is, and has been, a very noble band, that body of surveyors who have been trained and worked under Lambton, Everest, Waugh, and Walker. . . . These men must combine the knowledge and habits of thought of a Cambridge rambler with the energy, resource, and presence of mind of an explorer or backwoodsman, and they must add to this the gallantry and devotion which inspire the leader of a forlorn hope. The danger of service in the jungles and swamps of India, with the attendant anxiety and incessant work, is greater than that encountered on a battle field; the percentage of deaths is larger; while the sort of courage which is required is of a far higher order. The story of the Great Trigonometrical Survey, when fitly told, will form one of the proudest pages in the history of English domination in the East' (*Memoir*, p. 146).

[2] Clements R. Markham, *The Voyages of Sir James Lancaster . . .*, London, 1877 (HS 56).

[3] Clements R. Markham, ed., *Narratives of the Mission of George Bogle to Tibet, and of the Journey of Thomas Manning to Lhasa*, London, 1876; 2nd ed., 1879; German version, Leipzig, 1909.

[4] See in the *Memoir* the section on 'The Geographical Department of the India Office' (pp. 275–89, 2nd. ed. pp. 399–423). Markham was to publish a biography of Rennell: C. R. Markham, *Major James Rennell and the Rise of Modern English Geography*, London, 1895 and 1901.

authors that have lived and trafficked in those parts; and of other information of a like nature.

He was quoting from the Society's edition of Hakluyt's *Divers Voyages*.[1]

In 1872, Markham took charge of the India Office's annual report to
Parliament, but increasingly felt dissatisfied in that he was passed over
for promotion. It seems that both his periodic absences – in Peru, India
and Abyssinia – and his extensive outside activities made him vulner-
able to criticism.[2] Attention was of course drawn to both by his string
of publications – in the relevant ten years he had published a dozen
books, many of them geographical yet only distantly (if at all) related to
his work at the India Office. In the spring of 1875 a special committee
was, nevertheless, appointed to consider his status. 'At this vital junc-
ture, when prudence and restraint were necessary to strengthen his
case, Markham committed an act of professional folly.'[3] He sailed off to
Greenland on the first leg of the 1875–1876 North Polar expedition and
exceeded his allowance of leave by one month. He appears to have kept
his superiors in ignorance of his forthcoming excursion and to have left
a subordinate to compile the next India Office annual report. The
Secretary of State for India was soon minuted that 'some very decisive
measure will be necessary, if anything like discipline or decency is to be
maintained in the office . . . and the time has come when he must be
told very distinctly that he must obey orders – comply with official
rules, or go.'[4] Markham went, albeit with a pension.

The Arctic again, and the Antarctic

Despite his work in the India Office, his journeys in Peru and India and
his excursion to Abyssinia, Markham retained his interest in the Arctic
regions. The tragic fate of the lost Franklin expedition of 1845–48 had

---

[1] Markham, *Memoir*, 1871, p. 275; 1878, p. 400; John Winter Jones, ed., *Divers Voyages
. . . Collected . . . by Richard Hakluyt*, London, 1850 (HS 7), pp. 151, 158, 160, 164. The
phrases quoted are not in fact from *Divers Voyages*. Markham was quoting and abbreviat-
ing the heads of notes produced by Hakluyt in 1601, which Jones included in his edition
as an appendix: Markham was perhaps unaware, as Jones certainly was, that the notes
were actually produced for the East India Company (E. G. R. Taylor, ed., *The Original
Writings and Correspondence of the two Richard Hakluyts*, 2 vols, single pag., London, 1935
(HS 2/76–77), p. 476). At the end of his 1871 preface Markham referred to Hakluyt as 'the
ancestor of the Geographical Department of the India Office'. Williams mysteriously
dated Hakluyt's comment on spices to 1661 (Williams, 'The Geographical Department',
p. 343).
[2] Williams, 'The Geographical Department', pp. 347–9.
[3] Ibid., p. 349.
[4] Ibid., p. 351.

been at last ascertained.[1] But after the Franklin tragedy, and the expense of the searching expeditions which followed, the British government was reluctant to sanction another naval voyage to explore the Arctic regions. However, papers given at the Royal Geographical Society in the 1860s and early 1870s urged the renewal of Arctic exploration.[2] At a time when the RGS was being associated with exciting and often dangerous exploring journeys to other parts of the world (notably in the search for the sources of the Nile), it is easy to understand why its President, Sir Roderick Murchison, and Markham, its Joint Honorary Secretary, were insistent in pressing the case for a new venture to the north. Gladstone disregarded a report from a committee of which Markham was a member, but in 1874 Disraeli agreed to an expedition. One of Markham's contributions to the approval of the project was the publication of a book outlining the history of Arctic exploration.[3] Popular imagination had seen the expedition as an assault on the North Pole, but Markham demurred.

> The North Pole is merely a spot where the sun's altitude is equal to its declination, and where bearings must be obtained by reference to time and not to the magnet. It will doubtless be reached in the course of exploration, and there is something which takes the imagination of ignorant and uncultivated persons in the idea of standing upon it. But this will not be the main or even a principal result of the Expedition. The objects in view are the discovery of the conditions of land and sea within the unknown area, and the investigation of all the phenomena in that region. These results can only be obtained by facing difficulties, perils and hardships of no ordinary character; but their vast importance, owing to the additions they will make to the sum of human knowledge, will be ample recompense.[4]

The book advocated Smith Sound as the best route towards a high latitude.

Markham sailed as far as Greenland in one of the ships whose second-in-command was his cousin and future biographer. As usual his diary includes lively descriptions of people and places, and describes a moment of danger when the supply ship 'Valorous' grounded off the

---

[1] Largely by McClintock, the subject of Clements Markham, *The Life of Sir Leopold McClintock . . . by an old Messmate*, London, 1909.

[2] Papers given by Markham's friend and former shipmate, Sherard Osborn.

[3] C. R. Markham, *The Threshold of the Unknown Region*, London, 1873, 2nd ed. 1873, 3rd (popular) ed. 1875, 4th enlarged ed., 1876; French version, Paris, 1875. He also published a useful historical compilation, Clements R. Markham, *The Arctic Navy list; or, A century of Arctic and Antarctic Officers, 1773–1873. . . Attempted by Clements R. Markham*, London, 1875, reprinted 1992.

[4] Markham, *Unknown Region*, 3rd ed., p. 325.

coast of Greenland.[1] He was away for three months; the whole expedition returned, after only one year, because of an outbreak of scurvy aboard the ships.[2] There was some disappointment at home as a result, although Markham's cousin had sledged to within 400 miles of the Pole and one ship had attained the highest latitude to date.[3] The commander of the expedition was blamed for the outbreak of scurvy and Markham wrote in his defence.[4] Having revisited the Arctic, it must have been with particular enthusiasm that Markham set to work to collect and edit for the Hakluyt Society *The Voyages of William Baffin*.[5] This 1881 publication had a sequel in a visit the next year to northern Spain, harpooners from the Basque region having accompanied the first English whalers to the Arctic.[6]

Markham never returned to the Arctic but in the last decades of the century he reflected on the need for further exploration of the Polar regions. According to the tribute he wrote after Robert Falcon Scott's death in 1912, Markham first met the future Antarctic explorer in the West Indies in 1887, when the young midshipman won a cutter race and Markham immediately marked him out for later deployment.[7] In 1896 Markham was present in Christiania (Oslo) to welcome home the Norwegian explorer Fridtjof Nansen and his vessel, the 'Fram'. Nansen had made the first crossing of the Greenland ice cap before organising the North Pole expedition of 1893–96. Markham's thoughts were, however, turning to the South. At this date the south polar regions

[1] RGSA, CRM 8/1–2.

[2] The scurvy issue is discussed in Ann Savours and Margaret Deacon, 'Nutritional aspects of the British Arctic (Nares) Expedition of 1875–76 and its predecessors', in James Watt et al., eds., *Starving Sailors: The Influence of Nutrition upon Naval and Maritime History*, National Maritime Museum, London, 1981, pp. 131–61, 203–05.

[3] G. S. Nares, *A Narrative of a Voyage to the Polar Sea during 1875–6*, 2 vols, London, 1878; A. H. Markham, *The Great Frozen Sea: A Personal Narrative of the Voyage of the 'Alert' during the Arctic Expedition of 1875–6*, 4th ed., London, 1880. For a summary and critical account of the expedition by one familiar with the area of operation, see Geoffrey Hattersley-Smith, 'The British Arctic Expedition, 1875–76', *Polar Record*, 18, 1976, pp. 117–26.

[4] Clements R. Markham, *A Refutation of the Report of the Scurvy Committee*, Portsmouth, 1877. The commander's account of the expedition (Nares, *Narrative*) does not mention Markham's part in it, probably because he went by private invitation of the officers. A contemporary map, however, shows 'Clements Markham Inlet', on the northern shores of what is now known as Ellesmere Island. After the return of the expedition, Markham presented to the RGS an oil painting by R. B. Beechey of the 'furthest north encampment'.

[5] Clements R. Markham, ed., *The Voyages of William Baffin, 1612–1622*, London, 1881 (HS 63).

[6] The diary of the visit shows Markham pursuing one of his other interests, heraldry (RGSA, CRM 48). He had earlier addressed the Zoological Society of London 'On the whale fishery of the Basque provinces of Spain' (published *Nature*, 25, 1882, pp. 365–8).

[7] *Geographical Journal*, 41, 1913, p. 217.

were scarcely better known than they had been in the 1840s. Owing to the unexpected resignation of his predecessor, Markham was elected President of the Royal Geographical Society in 1893 and was thus in an admirable position to campaign for the despatch of an expedition to the Antarctic. At his first Council meeting an Antarctic steering committee was appointed.[1] Thereafter Markham campaigned ceaselessly to gain the interest in his proposals of Government, geographers, scientists and the general public. There was much disagreement among the experts, and some plotting behind the scenes,[2] but funds were eventually raised and a special ship, the 'Discovery', was built.[3] The Government would not sanction a naval expedition, but was willing to help with the secondment of naval officers and ratings, so that the practical organisation of the National Antarctic ('Discovery') Expedition fell into the hands of Captain Scott.

The achievements of the 1901–1904 expedition in the Antarctic and the value of the published scientific results were very considerable. As stated earlier, Scott named a mountain, 'a monster of unsurpassed eminence and dignity', Mount Markham.[4] Markham's responsibilities were by no means over when the 'Discovery' left the British Isles. His principal task was to raise funds for the purchase and despatch of a relief ship, the 'Morning'. Markham became the 'Managing Owner' of the 'Morning' as he was of the 'Discovery', while the vessels actually belonged to the Royal Geographical Society. Markham met the 'Discovery' on her return to England in September 1904 and sailed from Spithead up the Thames to her berth in the East India Dock. Markham, Scott, and Ernest Shackleton (who had been invalided home at the end of the first year), dined together and had 'a very jolly evening'.[5] Markham later received the silver sledge, mentioned earlier in this essay, from the officers and men of the 'Discovery'. Scott found a welcome retreat at the Markhams' house, 21 Eccleston Square, in which to write

---

[1] John Murray, 'The renewal of Antarctic exploration', *Geographical Journal*, 3, 1894, pp. 1–42, map p. 80.

[2] The Royal Society was involved – Markham had become a Fellow in the 1870s – but his views prevailed over those of the Royal Society's representatives. For varying interpretations of these events, from different viewpoints, see H. R. Mill, *The Record of the Royal Geographical Society*, London, 1930, pp. 133–68; Cameron, *History of the RGS*, pp. 137–8; Clive Holland, ed., *Clements Markham: Antarctic Obsession*, Aldburgh, 1986, pp. 6–7; and Ann Savours, *The Voyages of the 'Discovery'*, London, 1992, 2nd. ed., 1994, pp. 1–102, which discusses the expedition, its origins and previous interpretations.

[3] Built and now berthed at Dundee, she was launched by Markham's wife, Minna.

[4] For details of the expedition, see Savours, *The Voyages of the 'Discovery'*, pp. 22–92.

[5] RGSA, CRM 1/15.

his narrative of the expedition.[1] There can be no doubt that the 1901–1904 Antarctic expedition was a triumph for Markham, a proof of his organising ability in combining practical, geographical and scientific considerations, and the most notable achievement of his long life.[2]

The early years of the twentieth century have been called the 'heroic age of Antarctic exploration', when, by their inland journeys, men pitted themselves against the unforgiving climate, terrain and isolation of the frozen continent. Markham's call in the 1890s for the renewal of Antarctic exploration, which was supported by the International Geographical Congress of 1895 held in London which he chaired, resulted not only in the British expedition of 1901–1904, but also in expeditions from Germany, Scotland, France, Belgium and Sweden.[3] Further British expeditions followed, but Markham's part in these was limited. Although he had earlier spoken highly of Shackleton, the latter's independent resolve to lead an expedition to the Ross Sea in 1907–1909 earned Markham's bitter disapproval, despite the South Magnetic Pole being reached and a party sledging to within 97 miles of the South Pole itself. Markham did, however, help in an advisory capacity with the planning of what became known as 'Scott's last expedition'. Before Scott left in June 1910 Markham had stood as godfather to Scott's baby son, Peter Markham Scott. The last entry in Markham's last diary, made on 18 January 1916, reads as follows: 'Sturdy little Peter Scott came and walked with us in the square garden. I often think of his dear father and the men he has trained to fight his country's battles.'[4]

The Royal Geographical Society and the Hakluyt Society

After his departure from the India Office in 1877, Markham continued as a Joint Honorary Secretary of the Royal Geographical Society and as Honorary Secretary of the Hakluyt Society for twelve and nine years respectively; and his later periods as president of each allowed him still to exercise considerable influence on their subsequent activities. His role in shaping the society was probably even greater in the former than in the latter. In the early 1870s, dissatisfied with the RGS's journal

---

[1] R. F. Scott, The Voyage of the 'Discovery', 2 vols, London, 1905.

[2] Cameron, History of the RGS, pp. 137–41. However, Markham's involvement with Antarctic exploration has been denigrated in Roland Huntford, Scott and Amundsen, London, 1979, and Shackleton, London, 1985, in the present writer's view unfairly.

[3] Markham however did not approve of foreigners 'poaching in our preserves ... Foreigners, anyhow, never get much beyond the Antarctic Circle' (Cameron, History of the RGS, p. 143). Nevertheless, the 1901–1904 expedition worked in scientific concert with the Germans, in the 'Gauss', between 1901 and 1903.

[4] A. H. Markham, Sir Clements Markham, p. 361.

(which was 'dull and over-formal' and lacked illustrations, for instance), Markham started up a rival journal, *Our Ocean Highways*. The RGS was eventually obliged to buy him out and incorporate the more progressive features of Markham's journal in the Society's own.[1] In 1881 he produced a short history of the first fifty years of the RGS.[2] He ceased to hold office in the Society only in 1905. A recent historian of the Society has summed up one aspect of his role, thus.

> For more than forty years Markham had championed the cause of exploration ... In Africa he had helped to promote the work of men like Livingstone, Burton, Speke and Stanley; in Asia of men like Rawlinson, Trotter, Montgomerie and Hooker; and now in the Antarctic it was his protegé Scott who had opened up a new world and ushered in a new era of scientific investigation. Markham was now 74 and he chose the hour of his triumph to hand over the helm to a younger man.[3]

The recollections of a Librarian of the Society throw light on Markham's activities within the institution and on certain sides of his character.

> Sir Clements Markham, as President, overflowing with enthusiasm like a boy, used to stage a series of brilliant evening meetings to commemorate the deeds of Prince Henry the Navigator, Columbus, Franklin and others on appropriate occasions. The annual dinners, where Cabinet Ministers, great ambassadors, poets and social lions of every kind did honour to the Society ... were at first the glory of the year ... I soon realized that the external brilliance was not produced without a vast amount of internal friction and toil ... During Markham's long reign as President, the Council was filled up by his nominees and the policy of the Society was dictated by him, reflecting the impulses and prejudices of his impetuous enthusiasm ....[4]

The historian quoted above concludes his assessment of Markham thus: 'for all his idiosyncrasies', he was, in the annals of the RGS, 'a star of the first magnitude'.[5]

---

[1] Cameron, *History of the RGS*, p. 203.

[2] Clements R. Markham, *Fifty Years' Work of the Royal Geographical Society*, RGS, London, 1881. Several of Markham's judgements in this work are cited in a later history, Cameron, *History of the RGS*, pp. 21, 54, 73, 107.

[3] Cameron, *History of the RGS*, pp. 141–2.

[4] H. R. Mill, *An Autobiography*, London, 1951, pp. 88–9, 96.

[5] Cameron, *History of the RGS*, pp. 156–7. Markham's publications were, when 'geographical' at all, largely in the field of historical geography or the history of geography, and few were scientific descriptions of contemporary localities. His achievements at the RGS therefore involved administration, public education and planning of surveys and expeditions, rather than academic contributions to the discipline as then understood. But it is arguable that it was then understood too narrowly and that Markham's interest in culture and historical context was ahead of his time.

By 1877 Markham had already produced nine editions for the Hakluyt Society and he went on to produce a further fifteen. A later Honorary Secretary noted that 'fewer volumes edited with greater care would have served his reputation better. A text to him was a narrative to be translated freely and published as soon as possible.'[1] His editions were largely of translations from the Spanish and most of these were on South America; in this field, 'his wide-ranging knowledge of South American history and ethnography, his acquaintance with scholars in the field and his personal enthusiasms' went some way to compensating for a degree of unscholarly haste.[2] A more recent judgement reads as follows. 'Markham's many translations for the Hakluyt Society do provide an easily accessible corpus of material, and his style, a little archaic, ... [as another scholar has said,] "has given us a story of singular charm and sustained dramatic quality ... with some passages it would be difficult to improve on"; but where there is anything directional or numerical, he is excessively careless. Nor is he always objective, as any reader of his works on Peruvian history will see at once.'[3]

In 1896, the year he was knighted 'in recognition of his great service to geographical science', Markham celebrated the first fifty years of the Hakluyt Society with an address on the subject of Richard Hakluyt's life and work.[4] The address, as revised on the occasion of the society's sixty-fifth anniversary in 1911, begins as follows:

The Hakluyt Society is an institution which has been doing steady work for sixty-five years, without much stir, without attracting any large share of attention; but diligently, usefully, and successfully. During these years the Society has issued volumes bearing on their sides that famous ship *Victoria*, which was the first to circumnavigate the globe, and usually containing the texts, the very words of travellers and voyagers in all parts of the world, which were previously inedited, untranslated, or unknown.

[1] Crone, '"Jewells of Antiquitie"', p. 322. The number of Hakluyt Society volumes Markham produced is higher than the number of Markham editions, not because he normally published in editions of more than one volume but because he brought out translated sections of the same original under different titles.
[2] Loc. cit. His other HS editions related to Spanish texts on Columbus, the Canaries, the Pacific and medieval geographical knowledge, an Italian text on Vespucci, and English texts on East Indian, American, North-West and Bay of Biscay voyages. In respect of Spanish texts on South America, 'his greatest achievement was to appreciate the importance of Pedro de Cieza de Léon, by far the finest and most important of the chroniclers of Peru, five volumes of whose writings Markham translated' (p.c. Dr John Hemming, 9.10.1995).
[3] O. H. K. Spate, *The Spanish Lake*, Canberra, 1979, p. 318 – the internal quotation being from Celsus Kelly, 'Quiros' (see p. 166 note 1).
[4] Clements Markham, *Richard Hakluyt, his Life and Work. With a Short Account of the Aims and Achievements of the Hakluyt Society*, Hakluyt Society, London, 1896 (OB 1).

One fifth of the HS volumes published up to the writing of these words carried on their title pages Markham's name.

Although it is by no means clear what the post of Honorary Secretary actually involved during the many years Markham held it – and given his other activities it may be suspected that the duties were not too arduous or time-consuming – nevertheless his administrative capacities were clearly trusted by the Council and membership, so that the claim that from the 1860s to the 1880s 'the Society was kept together largely through the enthusiasms and energy of Clements Markham' seems well justified.[1] Certainly his flow of editions, which typically began with two in one year (1859), made up such a substantial part of the total HS output that it is difficult to see how the Society could have survived in this period without him. The later Honorary Secretary summed up his judgement by awarding a back-handed compliment: 'his great achievement was to establish the Society as a going concern, in a position ultimately to publish works of sound scholarship'.[2] His contribution in his later life was less notable. During the period of his campaigning for Antarctic exploration a gap occurs in his HS publications (and even his general output slowed down), but he resumed intense literary activity after 1905, producing for the HS particularly editions on South America. At the age of eighty, in 1910, he resigned as President of the Hakluyt Society and left its Council, of which he had been a member for fifty-one years. Seven years after his death the Society thought it worthwhile to publish a further edition he had prepared.[3]

All the posts in both Societies were honorary and unpaid, hence, after he left the India Office, writing and publishing must have provided a good part of his income. In an age of prolific writers he was one of the most prolific. Several of his many and various other books have been noted above. His biographies included ones of Richard III and Edward VI, Columbus and John Davis and 'The Fighting Veres'. He wrote a history of *The Conquest of New Granada* (1912, reprinted 1971). He edited two volumes for the Navy Records Society. His more popular works included *Famous Sailors of Former Times* and a novel, *The Paladins of Edwin the Great*. He supplied introductions, prefaces and 'assistance' to many works by others, his name always appearing on the title page, and he contributed numerous articles to learned journals. When he was eighty he published *The Incas of Peru* in which he confessed that he had 'abandoned the idea of completing a detailed history ... once entertained',

---

[1] Crone, '"Jewells of Antiquitie"', p. 322.
[2] Loc. cit. But the judgement is unfair if it implies that no works of scholarship were published before or during Markham's period as Honorary Secretary.
[3] See p. 187 note 4 below.

although he had kept abreast of research on the Incas through correspondence, books and pamphlets.[1] Instead, therefore, of a *magnum opus*,
he was publishing a series of essays – 'the results of the studies of a
lifetime'. As one of the appendices, he published a revised, free translation of the drama of Ollantay, the text of which he had copied in 1853
and from which he had earlier made his 'first very faulty line-for-line
translation' of 1871. In the preface, he listed the works he had translated
and edited for the Hakluyt Society over a period of some fifty years.
Another feature of the book was the folding map of South Peru and
North Bolivia, whose compilation and drawing by the Map Curator
and the draughtsman of the Royal Geographical Society had occupied
two years. 'Even at the time of his death he was actually correcting the
proof-sheets of a couple of volumes that he had translated and edited.'[2]
A history of polar exploration which he had been writing was completed from his extensive draft by another scholar and published in 1921
under the title, *The Lands of Silence*.[3] Yet another translation from the
Spanish was found in his desk and the introduction was published by
the Hakluyt Society in 1920.[4]

Even in his later years, Markham was not always desk-bound,
however. By invitation of his cousin, who was its Commodore, he
several times sailed with the Naval Training Squadron in the West
Indies, delighting in the company of the officers and midshipmen. He
and his wife spent holidays in Norway and southern Europe, especially
Portugal.[5] The outbreak of war in Europe did not persuade the Markhams to abandon their seaborne visits to Portugal and they even went
as far as Madeira, despite the menace of submarines. In January 1916
they were back in London. On 29 January Markham was in bed
suffering from one of his recurrent attacks of gout and reading an early
Portuguese printed book. Under an electric light bulb not switched on,

[1] Markham, *The Incas of Peru*, pp. ix–xi.

[2] A. H. Markham, *Sir Clements Markham*, p. 275.

[3] Clements R. Markham, completed by F. H. H. Guillemard, *The Lands of Silence: a History of Arctic and Antarctic Exploration*, Cambridge, 1921.

[4] Philip Ainsworth Means, trans. and ed., *Memorias antiguas historiales del Peru*, with an introduction 'by the late Sir Clements R. Markham', London, 1920 (HS 2/48). Means agreed that, from the text left behind by Markham, the introduction should replace his own. In 1923 a final edition by Markham was published (HS 2/54), this being a continua-tion of his previous translations of Cieza de Léon. The title-page, unlike the 1920 one, did not describe him as 'the late', perhaps implying that the edition had been in the hands of the Society before his death, and the volume offered no explanation of the delay in publication.

[5] Hence Clements R. Markham, *The Story of Majorca and Minorca*, London, 1908. Estoril, on the coast of Portugal, became a favourite winter resort for the elderly couple, hence, *List of Plants collected round Estoril during Three Seasons by Lady Markham and her Friends, with an Introduction by Sir Clements Markham, K.C.B., etc.*, Lisbon, 1910.

he read by candle-light – as he had done as a midshipman in his hammock. Perhaps he nodded off for a moment and the flame caught his bedclothes. Although his calls for assistance were instantly met and the fire extinguished, the shock caused him to lose consciousness and he died peacefully after some twenty hours.[1]

Eighty years after his death, many of Markham's books are still in use and several have been recently reprinted. But above all, two British learned societies – both with an international membership – now approach the twenty-first century in full intellectual vigour, and with considerable achievements during the present century, thanks in no small part to the career and devoted attentions of Clements Markham.

---

[1] A. H. Markham, *Sir Clements Markham*, p. 361; Mill, *Record of the RGS*, p. 168.

Part III

THE TWENTIETH-CENTURY:
RECOLLECTED FIGURES

William Foster and the Records of the India Office

R. A. Skelton of the Map Room

Esmond S. de Beer: Scholar and Benefactor

'THE SHOGUN IYEYASU'
From a painting by Kāno Tanyū.
Reproduced as the frontispiece of the edition of an account of the 1613 English
voyage to Japan: HS 2/5 of 1900.

WILLIAM FOSTER

AND THE RECORDS OF THE INDIA OFFICE

C. F. Beckingham

In his long, uneventful and very productive life Sir William Foster was associated with three institutions above all, the India Office, the Hakluyt Society, and the Worshipful Company of Coopers.[1]

Foster was born at Southsea on 18 November 1863, the son of an Inland Revenue official, after whom he was named. While he was still a child the family moved to London, where he lived for the rest of his life, in his last years at West Heath Road in Hampstead. From 1874 to 1880 he was a pupil at the Coopers' School and was then apprenticed to a chemist. In 1882 he succeeded in an open competition for the Civil Service and became a second-class clerk in the India Office, where his entire career was to be spent. He worked for F. C. Danvers, then an assistant in the Statistics and Commerce Department, with special responsibility for the custody of the records.

In 1884 a separate Registry and Records Department was established with Danvers as its head. Foster enjoyed and exploited the new opportunities this afforded him, although he considered that the investigations Danvers was enabled to make in Portugal and in the Netherlands had no relevance to the work that needed to be done in the India Office. He also disliked what he regarded as Danvers's propensity to self-advertisement. He enrolled at what was then the Birkbeck Institute and acquired an external degree in History at London University. In 1898 he doubtless welcomed the appointment of A. N. Wollaston to succeed Danvers. Three years later Foster was made Assistant Registrar, and in 1907 he succeeded Wollaston. When he retired from his previous duties in 1923 the post of Historiographer, which had been in abeyance for many years, was revived for him, and he continued in that capacity till

---

[1] I am greatly indebted to Anthony Farrington's pamphlet, *Sir William Foster, 1863–1951: a Bibliography*, India Office Library and Records Occasional Publications No. 1, London, 1972. I am also grateful to Richard J. Perrin, Honorary Curator of the Worshipful Company of Coopers, for the trouble he took to answer several questions.

1927. Appointed Companion of the Order of the Indian Empire in 1911, he was knighted in 1925. In 1911 he had married Jessie Winifred, daughter of the Reverend H. W. Holland and Headmistress of the Coopers' Girls' School, who gave him constant and invaluable support in a very happy marriage. Foster died on 11 May 1951; Lady Foster died in 1969 at the age of 94.

In 1893 Clements Markham, then President of the Hakluyt Society, invited Foster to become Secretary in place of E. Delmar Morgan with whom Markham had quarrelled. Foster continued as Secretary till 1902, when he resigned because of pressure of work at the India Office. In 1928, on the death of Sir Albert Gray, he became President of the Society and he remained in office until he resigned at the end of the Second World War, after which he served as a Vice-President till his death. In 1886 he had been admitted to the Livery of the Coopers' Company 'by servitude on testimony of his Master'. He served on the Council of the Company, was Master in 1918 and again in 1935, and Chairman of the Governors of the Coopers' School, his old school, from 1928 to 1938. He became a Fellow of the Royal Geographical Society in 1899 and of the Royal Asiatic Society in 1909 and served on the Councils of both.

Foster's work at the India Office was concerned primarily with two projects of major importance. The first, *Letters Received by the East India Company*, consisted of six volumes of which Danvers edited the first and Foster the other five, Volume I appearing in 1896, volume VI in 1902.[1] The letters covered the period from the foundation of the Company to 1617. This project was followed by the great series *The English Factories in India*, a calendar of documents published between 1906 and 1927 of which Foster edited the first thirteen volumes, covering the period from 1618 to 1669.[2] The series was then continued in less detail by Sir Charles Fawcett, who was responsible for another four volumes dealing with the years 1670 to 1684.[3] Together the two series provide the historian with a superb collection of source material, and Foster's volumes were presented with the lucidity, accuracy and unpretentious helpfulness to readers which characterised all his editorial work. He also wrote the introductions and notes to the first eight volumes, covering the years from 1635 to 1670, of E. B. Sainsbury's calendar of the East India Company minutes, and he assisted Sir George Birdwood to edit

---

[1] F. C. Danvers and W. Foster, ed., *Letters Received by the East India Company from its Servants in the East*, 6 vols, London, 1896–1902.

[2] William Foster, ed., *The English Factories in India: a Collection of Documents in the India Office, British Museum and Public Record Office*, 13 vols, Oxford, 1906–27.

[3] C. Fawcett, ed., *The English Factories in India*, 4 vols, Oxford, 1936–55.

the company's register of letters.[1] Additionally, he compiled a descriptive catalogue of the paintings, statues, and framed prints in the India Office which went through five editions, and he wrote a guide to the India Office records.[2]

In a work published in 1921 he selected, edited and annotated the accounts of seven early English travellers in India: Fitch, Mildenhall, Hawkins, Finch, Withington, Coryat and Terry.[3] Apart, however, from the *Letters* and the *English Factories*, his most important editions were those he undertook for the Hakluyt Society. These were often of accounts among the India Office records. In all he was responsible for nine of the Society's volumes, the first of these being *The Embassy of Sir Thomas Roe to the Court of the Great Mogul, 1615–1619*, published in 1899.[4] All but one of the nine Hakluyt Society volumes are concerned with the records and exploits of individual travellers: Sir Thomas Roe, John Jourdain, John Sanderson, Thomas Best, Nicholas Downton, Sir James Lancaster, Sir Henry Middleton.[5] The exception is his final edition for the Society, published in 1949, a collection of narratives describing the countries adjacent to the Red Sea at about the end of the seventeenth century.[6] None of these books is simply an edition of a single narrative, as so many of the Society's publications have been. If the principal part of the book has been reproduced from a journal or from the works of Hakluyt or Purchas, it is always accompanied by relevant documents, correspondence, and extracts from other narratives or illustrative sources. Foster had a strong sense of what seemed to

---

[1] E. B. Sainsbury, ed., *Calendar of the Court Minutes etc. of the East India Company*, 11 vols, Oxford, 1907–138 (vols 1–8, 1907–29): G. Birdwood, ed., *The Register of Letters &c. of the Governour and Company of Merchants of London Trading into the East Indies, 1600–1619*, London, 1893, 2nd ed., London, 1965.

[2] William Foster, *A Descriptive Catalogue of the Paintings, Statues, and Framed Prints in the India Office*, London, 1893, 1902, 1906, 1914, 1924; *A Guide to the India Office Records, 1600–1858*, London, 1919.

[3] W. Foster, ed., *Early Travels in India 1583–1619*, London, 1921, 2nd ed., Delhi, 1968.

[4] William Foster, ed., *The Embassy of Sir Thomas Roe to the Court of the Great Mogul, 1615–1619, as Narrated in his Journal and Correspondence*, 2 vols, London, 1899 (HS 2/1–2). A revised edition was later independently published under a slightly different title, *The Embassy of Sir Thomas Roe to India, 1615–1619*, ed. William Foster, London, 1926.

[5] William Foster, ed., *The Journal of John Jourdain, describing his Experiences in Arabia, India, and the Malay Archipelago*, London, 1905 (HS 2/16); *The Travels of John Sanderson in the Levant 1584–1602. With his Autobiography and Selections from his Correspondence*, London, 1931 (HS 2/67); *The Voyage of Thomas Best to the East Indies 1612–1614*, London, 1934 (HS 2/75); *The Voyage of Nicholas Downton to the East Indies 1614–15. As Recorded in Contemporary Narratives and Letters*, London, 1939 (HS 2/82); *The Voyages of Sir James Lancaster to Brazil and the East Indies 1591–1603*, London, 1940 (HS 2/85); *The Voyage of Sir Henry Middleton to the Moluccas 1604–1606*, London, 1943 (HS 2/88).

[6] William Foster, ed., *The Red Sea and adjacent Countries at the Close of the Seventeenth Century as Described by Joseph Pitts, William Daniel, and Charles Jacques Poncet*, London, 1949 (HS 2/100).

him to be relevant. In the Red Sea volume he omitted a large and interesting part of Pitts's book, retaining only what relates to the pilgrim journey from and back to Cairo. In choosing ancillary matter his practice could vary. At times he discarded passages which were repetitive. In his edition of the Downton voyage he included a letter to the Company from William Edwards at Ahmadabad but excised from it the passages recounting Richard Steel's activities in Persia, referring the reader to the complete text in *Letters Received*.[1] In the same book he reproduced a 1633 pamphlet by Christopher Farewell but discarded the preliminary and supplementary addresses to the reader, as well as an addendum about the writer's experiences in Spain. In the body of the text he suppressed extensive Biblical quotations exemplifying 'rejoicings with music'. His edition of Jourdain's journal noted that 'some entries made at sea, recording merely the course of the vessel, the state of the weather, the direction of the wind, etc., have been omitted as being of no general interest.'[2] When he came to edit Best, however, he included many pages which contain nothing but such particulars. Apart from his editions, Foster contributed to two other volumes published by the Hakluyt Society. One was *Bombay in the Days of Queen Anne*, annotated by others but with his introduction.[3] The other was the Centenary volume of 1946 to which he contributed important articles on Purchas and on the history of the Society.[4]

In addition to all the work he did for the Hakluyt Society, and the work on early English travellers in India noted above, Foster edited Downing's 1737 history of the 'Indian Wars' and Hamilton's 1727 two-volume account of the East Indies, and he was responsible for an abridgement of Herbert's 1634 *Travels in Persia*.[5] He contributed a chapter on 'The East India Company, 1660–1740' to the fourth volume of the *Cambridge History of the British Empire*.[6] From 1893 until the year

---

[1] See Foster, *Downton*, p. 169, note.

[2] Foster, *Jourdain*, p. xi.

[3] Samuel T. Sheppard, ed., *Bombay in the Days of Queen Anne Being an Account of the Settlement written by John Burnell* [with additional notes by E. Cotton and L. M. Anstey], London, 1933 (HS 2/72).

[4] William Foster, 'Samuel Purchas' and 'The Hakluyt Society. A Retrospect: 1846–1946', in E. Lynam, ed., *Richard Hakluyt & his Successors*, London, 1946 (HS 2/93), pp. 47–61, 141–70. The second article was also published separately as a pamphlet.

[5] Clement Downing, *A History of the Indian Wars*, ed. William Foster, London, 1926; Alexander Hamilton, *A New Account of the East Indies*, ed. William Foster, London, 1930; Thomas Herbert, *Travels in Persia, 1627–9*, ed. William Foster, London, 1928.

[6] H. H. Dodwell, ed., *British India, 1497–1858*, Cambridge History of the British Empire vol. IV, Cambridge, 1929, pp. 76–116. This also constituted a chapter in the fifth volume of the *Cambridge History of India*.

'TERNATE'

From Valentijn's *Oude en Nieuw Oost-Indiën*, 1724–1726.
Reproduced in the edition of an account of the 1604–1606 English voyage to the East: HS 2/88 of 1943.

before his death he contributed articles, brief notes, comments and reviews to numerous journals.[1]

Apart from all his editions and articles Foster wrote four books based on historical research. The most important was *England's Quest for Eastern Trade*, published in the Pioneer Histories series in 1933.[2] He told me that he received about £6 for writing it, but had welcomed the opportunity. It is a masterly survey of the subject during the sixteenth and the first half of the seventeenth centuries by someone with a unique knowledge of the sources. He also published histories of the East India Company and its House, and of the Coopers' Company.[3] All four of these books, even to some extent the first, are not so much continuous narratives as collections of essays in which each essay is devoted to a separate, clearly-defined topic and can be read independently of the others.

All Foster's vast editorial work was distinguished by meticulous accuracy. It is very unusual to find a factual mistake in anything he wrote; if one does, it can nearly always be attributed to an over-confident scholar whom he had consulted. He made no claim to be a linguist but it is obvious he was able to read the principal Romance and Teutonic languages, though he was careful to check his work with experts. Confronted with the need to explain words or phrases in oriental languages, he had recourse to colleagues at the India Office or to London University, where he often, and on one notorious occasion unwisely, relied on Sir Denison Ross. When he came to annotate Poncet's narrative about Ethiopia in *The Red Sea and Adjacent Countries*, I was able to put him in touch with a retired Indian Army officer, Lieutenant-Colonel J. I. Eadie, who was a 1st Class Interpreter in Amharic.[4] Foster was as much concerned with precision as with accuracy. If anyone filled a significant role in the narrative he would endeavour to find out when and where he was born, his parentage, where he was educated, what occupation he had followed, even what wages he had been paid. In the same way, if he was concerned with a building

---

[1] The journals included *The Athenaeum*, *Bengal Past and Present*, *The English Historical Review*, *Geographical Journal*, *The Indian Antiquary*, *The Journal of the Royal Asiatic Society*, *The Journal of the Royal Society of Arts*, *The London Topographical Record*, *Notes and Queries*, *The Scottish Historical Review*, *Transactions of the Royal Historical Society*, and *The Walpole Society*. A topic discussed in 1900 was followed up by further thoughts on the same in 1950 (*Notes and Queries*, 9th ser., 6, 1900, pp. 41–2; 195, 1950, pp. 44–5).

[2] William Foster, *England's Quest for Eastern Trade*, London, 1933; German version, Leipzig, 1938.

[3] William Foster, *The East India House, its History and Associations*, London, 1924; *John Company*, London, 1926; *A Short History of the Worshipful Company of Coopers of London*, London, 1944.

[4] Eadie was author of *An Amharic Reader*, Cambridge, 1924.

of importance in the story, a private house, fort, factory, or church, he tried to determine its exact location and whether any parts of it survived, and if so which parts they were. He brought to such researches a very extensive knowledge of the historical topography of inner London and of its archives, its parish records and the records of the Livery Companies. A note in the Lancaster volume is characteristic of his standards. He reproduced the contents of an anonymous pamphlet of which only a copy in the Bodleian Library was known to survive. He states: 'Included in the pamphlet is a folding sheet with a woodcut of a ship. From the lavish display of the royal flag it is evidently a vessel of the royal navy, and we may infer that the publisher used an old block which had really no reference to the subject. The illustration has therefore been omitted.'[1]

He was a very modest man. He once told me that he was not a scholar, only an archivist. Anthony Farrington would prefer to call him a historiographer rather than an archivist for he was more interested in the facts yielded by the records than in their categorisation.[2] Personally, and in his writings, he was a man of impeccable courtesy. This is exemplified in the discreet way in which he corrected the errors of others, as in the amendments, in his own editions, of errors in previous editions of the same texts, notably in Bolton Corney's edition of the Middleton voyage and Markham's edition of the voyages of Lancaster.[3] When he was Secretary to the Hakluyt Society he had been 'furious' (his own word) at the arrogant discourtesy shown him by Markham as President. In commenting on the work of so prolific and so careless an editor he could easily have taken condign revenge, but in the chapter on the history of the Society he contributed to the Centenary volume he wrote about Markham with admirable discrimination. While recognising that, with Markham, 'difficulties in translation were solved by Gordian methods, and evidence was not always sifted with due care', Foster concluded that 'not only in his length of service but in his massive literary contribution, he was by far the most outstanding figure in the history of the Society'.[4]

Though his portrait suggests a rather austere personality, Foster was a sociable man, and in company that he found congenial, he talked freely, even volubly. His sense of humour, rarely indulged in his

[1] Foster, *Lancaster*, p. 144, n. 1.
[2] For Farrington's bibliography of Foster, see p. 191, note 1.
[3] Bolton Corney, ed., *The Voyage of Sir Henry Middleton to Bantam and the Maluco islands* ..., London, 1854 (HS 19); Clements R. Markham, ed., *The Voyages of Sir James Lancaster, Kt., to the East Indies* ..., London, 1877 (HS 56).
[4] Foster, 'A Retrospect', p. 16.

editorial annotations, was dry but acute. His observation of the drawing of a sea fight, reproduced in the Lancaster volume, is characteristic
in tone: 'The wind is obligingly blowing from all quarters at once.'[1] He
enjoyed relating how, when taking the chair at a lecture on a recondite
topic (if I remember rightly it was Tibetan translations of lost Sanskrit
Buddhist texts) the speaker had asked for the lights to be extinguished
while he showed a few slides. This was done but when the lights were
switched on again, it was found that the entire, small audience had left
under cover of darkness.

Perhaps the greatest service Foster rendered to the Hakluyt Society
was the example he gave to editors. His experience of annotating was
enormous and his practice exemplary. Too often editors of the
Society's volumes had either supplied virtually no notes at all, as did
Lord Stanley of Alderley in his edition of Alvarez's account of the
Portuguese in Ethiopia, or had overwhelmed the text with information
that was irrelevant, or, at best, available in readily accessible standard
works, as did G. P. Badger in editing J. W. Jones's translation of
Varthema.[2] Foster's notes were invariably helpful, concise, lucid and
pertinent. He never retailed information merely to display his own
erudition, but neither did he fail to give the reader any assistance he
might need. In the edition of the Downton voyage an observer remarks
of the country near the Cape of Good Hope that it 'seemeth to be very
fertill and good, if it were well manuered.' The last word carries a note:
'In the now obsolete sense of "cultivated"'. In the same book, on the
last word of the phrase, 'their manner of fighting with us and successe',
he comments: 'This was really a colourless word meaning simply the
outcome, whether good or bad'.[3] So when Best refers to 'being
boarded by 3 Flemish shippes' the reader is reminded that the primary
meaning of 'board' was 'to come up close to'.[4] He was sparing in
passing judgment on the character, conduct or capacity of men whose
exploits he examined. In general he was content to ensure that the
reader could understand the documents, which he left to speak for
themselves.

In his old age his vast knowledge of the India Office records was
always at his command and at the disposal of anyone who sought his

---

[1] Foster, *Lancaster*, p. viii.
[2] Lord Stanley of Alderley, ed., *Narrative of the Portuguese Embassy to Abyssinia during the Years 1520–1527, by Father Francisco Alvarez*, London, 1881 (HS 64); *The Travels of Ludovico de Varthema in Egypt, Syria, Arabia Deserta and Arabia Felix, in Persia, India, and Ethiopia, A.D. 1503 to 1508. Translated . . . by John Winter Jones . . . and Edited . . . by George Percy Badger . . .*, London, 1863 (HS 32).
[3] Foster, *Downton*, pp. 57, 185.
[4] Foster, *Best*, p. 94.

help. In the last year of his life he gave an excellent public lecture. In the spring of 1951 I wrote to ask him about early English knowledge of the Kathiawar coast. I received a long, exceedingly helpful and very prompt reply. Not long afterwards I came to realise that he must have written it on his deathbed.

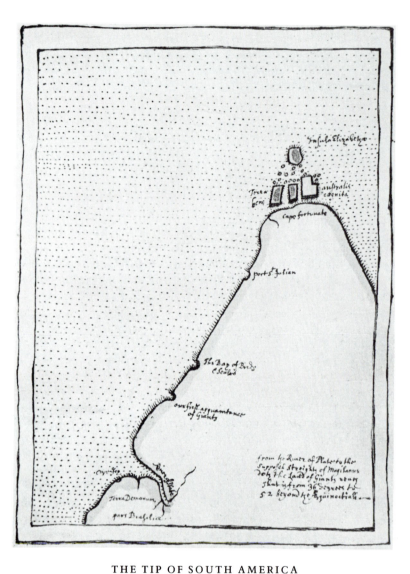

Insula Elizabeth:

Terra Australis incognita
bene

Cape fortunate

port St Julian

The Bay of Body
C Scaled

our first aquaintance
of Giants

from the River of Plate to the
Supposed Streight of Magilanus
doth the Lands of Giants reach
that is from 36 Degrees to
52 beyond the Equinoctiall

Cap: Joy

Terra Demonum:
pars Brasilica

THE TIP OF SOUTH AMERICA
Copy of a sketch map by Francis Fletcher, chaplain on the second
circumnavigation, 1577–1580.
The original in British Library, Sloane 61.
Reproduced in *New Light on Drake*: HS 2/34 of 1914.

R. A. SKELTON

OF THE MAP ROOM

D. B. Quinn

During the war years 1939–1945, Edward Lynam, Superintendent of the British Museum Map Room and Honorary Secretary of the Hakluyt Society since 1931, contrived, in spite of many of other commitments, to keep the Society's publications appearing regularly. In 1945 he was fortunate in having assigned to him, as his number two, Raleigh Ashlin Skelton (who, despite his baptismal forename, was always known to family and friends as 'Peter', his registered forename).[1] Skelton had served in the Royal Artillery and latterly in the Archives Branch of the Allied High Commission in Austria. As an Assistant Keeper in the Printed Books section of the British Museum before 1939 he had had the task of re-cataloguing the Museum's collection of post-Purchas travel collections and had come to know their texts and maps very well. It is therefore not surprising that he was promptly brought into the work of the Society. Indeed, when Lynam became President in 1945, Skelton soon succeeded him as Honorary Secretary – as he was to succeeed him as Superintendent of the Map Room a few years later – a position in the Society he was to occupy for twenty years.[2]

He was fortunate in his early years in that several old hands, Sir William Foster and H. A. R. Gibb among them, were ready with volumes for publication. This allowed him to concentrate on Frank Debenham's two volumes on the Bellingshausen voyage to the Antarctic (published 1945),[3] which drew his attention not only to the Antarctic but also to the Pacific Ocean, on whose exploration and mapping he was eventually to become an established authority. He soon established a practice of learning very rapidly the background of the areas covered

---

[1] For further biographical details, see the entry in *DNB 1961–1970*, Oxford, 1981.

[2] Lynam's immediate successor as Honorary Secretary was G. R. Crone, but Crone resigned after six months, and Skelton took up the office in March 1946.

[3] Frank Debenham, ed., *The Voyage of Captain Bellingshausen to the Antarctic Seas 1819–1821*, 2 vols, single pag., London, 1945 (HS 2/91–2).

by the volumes he was editing, while all the time building up his knowledge of their historical mapping. He showed his acquaintance with voyage-collections in a contribution, jointly with Gerald Crone, to the Society's centenary volume of 1946, the article becoming a standard reference.[1] The three volumes of the 1947–1948 edition of Abbé Carré's travels in India[2] shifted his interest to India and the East, but he had not yet run up against any considerable editorial problems. It was different when he came to deal with the third volume of English voyages to Spanish America offered by the formidable Irene A. Wright. She wanted her own way about detail, suffered unwillingly a few improvements to her translations and notes, and, finally, produced an index which covered only the introduction, admittedly a very full one, but did not extend to the texts. Even the title was in dispute, the final one being my suggestion.[3] Production was too far advanced to allow for a full index to be compiled so she got away with her partial one.

This was the first of several instances where Skelton, as general editor for the Society, had to make – or attempt to make – his own views prevail where they conflicted with those of the editor of a particular edition. His dealings later on with another eminent scholar, E. G. R. Taylor, in respect of her edition of the 1582–1583 Fenton voyage,[4] were not dissimilar. There were problems of selection among a mass of documents, questions about the correctness of transcripts, and other disputatious issues. Fortunately, by this time he had been joined in the Map Room by Helen Wallis, who took on a good deal of the necessary transcription and re-transcription, and other such clarifications. In the end the volume was an illuminating one; nevertheless it had to be later supplemented by Elizabeth Story Donno's diary of Richard Madox, which went over part of the story in greater detail.[5] In the case of the distinguished historian J. A. Williamson, whose health was failing, a great deal of help was needed to allow him to revise an earlier work (not published by the Society) so that he could concentrate on his introduction to the John Day letter (a document which L.A. Vigneras had recently brought to light). I was enlisted by Peter to produce texts of

[1] G. R. Crone and R. A. Skelton, 'English Collections of Voyages and Travels 1625–1846', in Edward Lynam, ed., *Richard Hakluyt & his Successors*, London, 1946 (HS 2/93), pp. 63–140.

[2] Charles Fawcett, ed., *The Travels of Abbé Carré in India and the Near East 1672 to 1674*, 3 vols, single pag., London, 1947–48 (HS 2/95–7).

[3] Irene A. Wright, ed., *Further English Voyages to Spanish America, 1583–1594*, London, 1951 (HS 2/99).

[4] E. G. R. Taylor, ed., *The Troublesome Voyage of Captain Edward Fenton, 1582–1583*, Cambridge, 1959 (HS 2/113).

[5] E. S. Donno, ed., *An Elizabethan in 1582: the Diary of Richard Madox*, London, 1976 (HS 2/147).

some additional documents while he himself added an important appendix on the cartography, with the result that in the end Williamson's edition of the Cabot and Bristol voyages could appear in 1962 in an effective form.[1] The volume has been of lasting value although it has been supplemented by later discoveries of material by Alwyn Ruddock and to some extent myself.

This has been to anticipate chronologically. By the early 1950s Peter's knowledge and judgement had become so highly regarded by the Council that he exercised a great deal of authority in the working of the Society. He came to regard the character and method of production of the Society's volumes as in need of substantial revision. MacLehose was printing very well but it was felt that not enough attention was being paid by the then publishers to the distribution and marketing of the volumes. With expert advice he drew up a new set of rules for editors and selected a more up-to-date type-face, while he transferred the printing and publication of the volumes to the Cambridge University Press, under whose imprint they were to appear for some years (until a problem about commission arose which led the Society to become its own publisher). The new arrangement was tried out on my *Roanoake Voyages* (1955),[2] a complex production in which Peter's help proved invaluable. The new arrangement was most useful for the Society on account of the worldwide connections and reputation which Cambridge enjoyed. This helped greatly to expand the range of interest in the Society and hence to enlarge its membership, while it also meant that its volumes were reviewed more widely than previously.

He was to have successes and problems in later years. Charles Boxer's *South China in the Sixteenth Century* (1953) opened up a new field for the Society and helped Peter to carry on a long struggle to make available to the western world a significant Chinese text about voyages in the Indian Ocean, Ma Huan's *The Overall Survey of the Ocean's Shores*.[3] The elderly editor, J. V. C. Mills, had repeatedly promised the volume and had sent in various segments from time to time; but although Peter got some way forward with it, it did not in fact appear, in the Extra Series, until 1970, the year of Peter's death. A notable innovation was the publication of a facsimile reprint of the neglected first edition of

---

[1] James A. Williamson, ed., *The Cabot Voyages and Bristol Discovery under Henry VII . . . with the Cartography of the Voyages by R. A. Skelton*, Cambridge, 1961 (HS 2/120).

[2] David Beers Quinn, ed., *The Roanoake Voyages 1584–1590 . . .*, Cambridge, 1954–5 (HS 2/104–5).

[3] C. R. Boxer, ed., *South China in the Sixteenth Century . . .*, London, 1953 (HS 2/106); J. V. G. Mills, ed., *Ma Huan, Ying-Yai Sheng-Lang. 'The Overall Survey of the Ocean's Shores'*, Cambridge, 1970 (HS Extra 42).

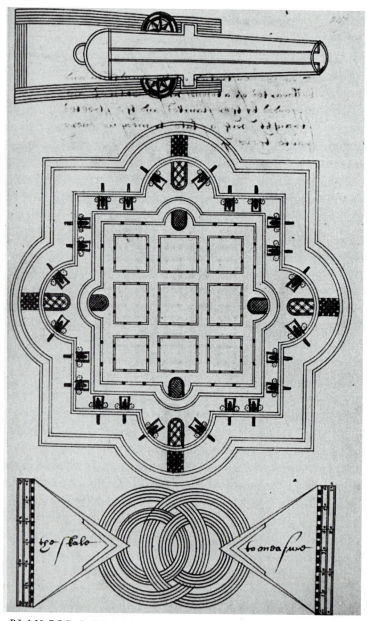

PLAN FOR A COLONIAL TOWN IN NORTH AMERICA,
BY GEORGE WAYMOUTH, 1604
Original in British Library, Additional MS 19889.
Reproduced in HS 2/161 of 1983.

Hakluyt's *Principall Navigations*.[1] Peter, together with myself and Alison Quinn, supplied the fairly extensive scholarly apparatus. He contributed largely to the bibliographical introduction and especially to the listing of surviving copies. This 1965 publication brought a new facet to the Extra Series. He also planned a *Hakluyt Handbook*, but it had advanced only a few stages when he retired from the secretaryship. It did not appear until 1974 and then under my editorship, but one of the contributions, his essay on maps, was a memorial to his initiative.[2] On the way he had obtained from the ageing but indefatiguable Irene Wright a further instalment of her translations from the Spanish on English voyages to the Caribbean which she did not wish to take responsibility for editing. He persuaded her to confide the task to Kenneth Andrews, whose *English Privateering Voyages to the West Indies, 1588–1595* of 1959 was to be followed in 1972 by a volume on the last voyage of Drake and Hawkins.[3] This left only the final few years of the Spanish War still uncovered by the Society.

It was, however, the Pacific which was to involve him most closely for much of his later time as Secretary. Hugh Carrington's *Discovery of Tahiti* opened up the field as early as 1948, but it was not until 1964 that R. E. Gallagher produced his edition of Byron's circumnavigation journal, and this was followed the next year by a two-volume edition on Carteret's similar voyage, edited by Skelton's colleague, Helen Wallis.[4] These however were minor involvements compared with his gradual submersion in a long and triumphant association with J. C. Beaglehole in the evolution of the great edition of Captain Cook's *Journals*, the major addition to the Extra Series in the twentieth century. Starting with an extensive correspondence between London and Wellington, it developed into complete absorption on Peter's part when John Beaglehole was able to get to England, so much so that the Society was obliged to appoint a second secretary-editor to share the work of producing the Ordinary Series volumes. This brought about the long involvement of Eila Campbell in the Society's publications. The Cook project expanded as it developed. The first volume appeared in 1955,

---

[1] David Beers Quinn and Raleigh Ashlin Skelton, eds., *The Principall Navigations . . . of the English Nation by Richard Hakluyt*, 2 vols, Cambridge, 1965 (HS Extra 39).

[2] R. A. Skelton, 'Hakluyt's maps', in D. B. Quinn, ed., *The Hakluyt Handbook*, 2 vols, single pag., London, 1974 (HS 2/144–5), pp. 48–69.

[3] Kenneth R. Andrews, ed., *English Privateering Voyages to the West Indies, 1588–1595*, Cambridge, 1959 (HS 2/111); *The Last Voyage of Drake & Hawkins*, Cambridge, 1972 (HS 2/142).

[4] Hugh Carrington, ed., *The Discovery of Tahiti*, London, 1948 (HS 2/198); Robert E. Gallagher, ed., *Byron's Journal of his Circumnavigation*, Cambridge, 1964 (HS 2/122); Helen Wallis, ed., *Carteret's Voyage Round the World*, 2 vols, Cambridge, 1965 (HS 2/124–5).

the second in 1961 and the third in two vast volumes in 1967.[1] The first volume was accompanied by a portfolio of 88 maps and views, selected by Peter. In the preface to the first volume John Beaglehole said of Peter that 'without his labours ... my own work would have been impossible', and he could have echoed this sentiment until the documentation of all three of Cook's voyages had been published. It was tragic that Peter Skelton and John Beaglehole died within a year of each other, neither at a great age.

Peter wrote fast and thought faster. His capacity for concentration was such that he was rarely seen, in train or bus, or in rest periods, without a set of proofs or a writing pad on his knee. At the same time he was always helpful and considerate to inquirers, whether on Map Room or Hakluyt Society business, treating everyone with a serious informality which made him many friends. He could be a hard taskmaster if he felt that some job had to be done urgently or was being done badly and he was inclined to form opinions on a topic rapidly and to prove sometimes unwilling to change them when new evidence or new insights were laid before him. But these were traits that appeared only occasionally. His positive characteristics helped to make him rapidly a world authority in the history of cartography and his international reputation in the field was even by the mid-1950s very high. He played an active part in a series of international cartographic conferences and also in the rescue of *Imago Mundi* after Leo Bagrow's death, arranging for its continued publication as a truly international journal. He rewrote and developed Bagrow's *History of Cartography*, so that Bagrow–Skelton has remained the standard work in this field.[2] He played a major part in the preparation of the English version of the text (and to some extent in the editing of the cartographic content) of *Portugaliae Monumenta Cartographica*, edited by Armando Cortesão and Avelino Teixeira da Mota – probably the most elaborate and comprehensive publication of any nation's overseas maps produced during the Age of Discovery.[3] In the early 1960s he also became involved in the

---

[1] J. C. Beaglehole, ed., *The Journals of Captain Cook on his Voyages of Discovery*, vol. 1 *The Voyage of the Endeavour, 1768–1771*, with a separate portfolio of maps and views by R. A. Skelton, Cambridge, 1955, revised 1968 (HS Extra 34a, 34b); volume 2 *The Voyage of the Resolution and Adventure, 1772–1775*, Cambridge, 1961, revised 1969 (HS Extra 35); volume 3 in two parts, *The Voyage of the Resolution and Discovery, 1776–1780*, Cambridge, 1967 (HS Extra 36a, 36b). See also J. C. Beaglehole, *The Life of Captain James Cook*, London, 1974 (HS Extra 37), which was completed after Beaglehole's death by his son and by members of the Society: copies in the Society's binding were purchased from the commercial publisher and added to the *Journal*, to make a set of six items.

[2] Leo Bagrow and R. A. Skelton, *History of Cartography*, London, 1964.

[3] A. Cortesão and A. Teixeira da Mota, *Portugaliae Monumenta Cartographica*, 6 vols, Lisbon, 1960–62.

famous, or infamous, Vinland Map issue. He did pioneering work on the early cartography of the North and much of this appeared in *The Vinland Map and Tartar Relation* (1965), which created such a stir at the time.[1] He was strongly inclined (mistakenly as it appeared after his death) to accept the map's authenticity, although he always maintained that only the scientific analysis of the material of the map, an analysis which it eventually received, could establish certainty either way. While he was Secretary for the Society he not only pursued the other commitments mentioned above but he also poured out a string of scholarly papers on a wide range of mainly cartographic topics, and furthermore he contributed a series of popular articles to the *Geographical Magazine* which eventually formed his widely-read book, *Explorers' Maps* (1959).[2]

He retired a few years earlier than necessary from his post as Deputy Keeper in the British Museum, and shortly afterwards, in 1966, retired from the Society's secretaryship, in order to devote himself to a host of planned projects and publications. These were cut short when, in December 1970, his car was rammed as he returned home from the Ordnance Survey Office at Southampton. Badly injured, he insisted on correcting proofs in his hospital bed until he was carried off by sudden heart failure a few days after his accident. His career as Secretary of the Society and as chief custodian of the map collections of the British Museum (which he did much to enlarge and enhance) can be seen as high points in the history of both institutions during the present century.

---

[1] T. E. Marston, R. A. Skelton and G. D. Painter, *The Vinland Map and the Tartar Relation*, New Haven, 1965.

[2] R. A. Skelton, *Explorers' Maps: Chapters in the Cartographical Record of Geographical Discovery*, London, 1958.

PORTRAIT HEADS OF MAORIS
Drawn on Cook's second voyage to the Pacific 1772–1775.
The original crayon drawings in the Commonwealth National Library, Canberra.
Reproduced in HS Extra 35 of 1961.

ESMOND S. de BEER

SCHOLAR AND BENEFACTOR

Michael Strachan

Esmond de Beer (1895–1990) was a great scholar whose definitive editions of *The Diary of John Evelyn* and *The Correspondence of John Locke* demonstrated a new standard of editing. He was enormously knowledgeable about history, particularly that of the seventeenth century, literature, art, music, and indeed about many other subjects. The reason for including a biographical essay in the present volume is that he was President of the Hakluyt Society from 1972 to 1978 and a Trustee from 1978 to 1988, having first joined the Society in 1946 and become a member of its Council in 1950. He was a very generous benefactor to learned societies, libraries, museums and art galleries. Not least among those with whom he shared his knowledge, and his wealth, was the Hakluyt Society, with which he was so actively associated for over forty years.[1]

He was able to devote his long life to scholarship, independent of any academic institution, and to make so many extremely valuable benefactions, owing to the commercial success of his maternal grandfather, Bendix Hallenstein (1835–1905). Bendix was the youngest of three Jewish brothers born in Brunswick, Germany, who all migrated to Melbourne, Australia, and ran a store to supply miners during the Victoria gold-rush. In Melbourne Bendix met his future wife, Mary Mountain, who was of Lincolnshire farming stock and had taken a position as housekeeper to the three brothers. When the Victoria gold-rush subsided Bendix decided to try his luck in New Zealand. With the financial support of his brothers he set up a store in Queenstown at the

---

[1] This essay is a much abbreviated and modified version of Michael Strachan, *Esmond S. de Beer (1895–1990): Scholar and Benefactor. A Personal Memoir, with a Bibliography by J. S. G. Simmons*, Norwich, 1995. Many details have been obtained from members of E. S. de B.'s extended family, notably the late Dr Charles Brasch, Dr Francesca Cianchi, Professor Walter Elkan and Mr Tim Thompson, also from Mr H. O. Allen, the proprietor of Stoke House where he spent his last years, and from E. S. de B.'s letters to me for which I have given as a reference 'Letter(s) [date(s)]'.

southern end of South Island. The town was started in 1860 and went ahead when there was a gold-rush in 1863. After a few years Bendix and his family moved to nearby Dunedin, where in 1873 he established a clothing factory and a store which developed into a chain of stores throughout New Zealand. Hallenstein Brothers Ltd was to be the main source of the family's wealth.

Bendix and Mary had four children, all daughters. The second, Emily (1864–1930), married Isidore Samuel de Beer (1860–1934), who came from Melbourne in the late eighties to join Hallenstein's, of which he became a director. Financially astute, he specialised in buildings and the design and layout of shops. Despite exhaustive research Esmond was unable to trace his paternal ancestry beyond his father's father, Samuel, but he thought that the de Beer family probably came from Portugal. Esmond was born in Dunedin on 15 September 1895, the youngest of four children. His elder brother was killed in action in 1917: his two sisters, Mary (1890–1981) and Dora (1891–1982), were to play an important part in his life and in his benefactions.

Esmond's passion for books and for reading began very early. At the age of six he would rather sit reading Shakespeare than go out to play with other children.[1] From 1903 to 1910 he attended a small private school in Dunedin. It was attached to Selwyn College, an Anglican foundation, which at that time housed the Shoults collection of books, now in the University of Otago Library. Despite his tender years Esmond was allowed access to this collection. 'At Selwyn I handled older books. With no instruction or guidance I could learn little about them, but I acquired freedom of approach to them and awareness that some of them invited study of a kind which I learnt later to know as bibliography.'[2] The family moved to London when Isidore de Beer was appointed to run Hallenstein's office there, and in 1910 Esmond and his brother became boarders at Mill Hill School.[3] In the autumn of 1914 he went up to New College, Oxford, as a commoner. Here he was much influenced by the teaching of Sir Charles Firth, the Regius Professor of Modern History, who specialised in British seventeenth-century history

---

[1] 'We had a good number of books in my parents' house, and there were more in that of my uncle Willi Fels [a director of Hallenstein's married to Esmond's mother's elder sister] so that I was acquainted with a good range of nineteenth century-books' – a passage in a 1974 letter from E. S. de B. to Dan and Winnie Davin read at a Memorial Gathering on 6 December 1990. (Copies of the readings and addresses on that occasion, collected in typescript or photocopy, were subsequently deposited in British copyright libraries and the archives of the Hakluyt Society.)

[2] Ibid.

[3] Esmond won prizes for French, German, General Knowledge and Essay: *Mill Hill School Register*.

and campaigned for more use of original documents in history teaching and examination. Esmond studied at Oxford for two full academic years. Thereafter he served for some time in the ranks of the Oxfordshire and Buckinghamshire Light Infantry, before receiving a temporary commission in the Indian Army in March 1918 and being appointed to the 2nd Battalion 35th Sikhs, a unit which saw action in the Third Afghan War of 1919.[1]

On demobilization Esmond did not return to Oxford; the University awarded him a BA War Degree, accorded to those who had been unable to complete their full course. He might have returned to New Zealand and taken up the position of his dead brother who had joined Hallenstein's in 1912. Fortunately for the world of learning he instead decided to follow in the footsteps of Sir Charles Firth. From 1920 to 1925 he studied at University College, London, and the newly founded Institute of Historical Research. In 1923 he was awarded an MA degree for a thesis on the development of parties in Danby's ministry of 1675–1678, based on archive and printed sources including John Evelyn's *Diary*. He then offered to work as Firth's voluntary assistant and moved to Oxford, renting a flat and employing a daily housekeeper, but working mainly in Firth's house and in the Bodleian. An acquaintance of those days has described him as being of medium height (5 feet 9 inches according to his passport) with a strong forehead and large, powerful head, set close upon broad shoulders which disguised his thinness. He wore a moustache which was then dark and square, but in later life became wider, grizzled, and always clipped short. He was invariably very correct and polite, spoke slowly pausing between words and phrases, emphasizing a point by taking off his pince-nez and gesturing with them; his voice thick and a little throaty. Food was important to him and he enjoyed good wine in moderation (this throughout his life). He used as much deliberation in eating as in speaking, so conversation during meals was extremely protracted since he commonly managed only one word at a time, each word being followed by a silence for prolonged mastication. He seemed 'middle-aged, or of no age, but not young, though he was only thirty-two'.[2]

---

[1] Ibid; E. S. Craig and W. M. Gibson, *Oxford University Roll of Service*, Oxford, 1920, p. 191; letter of 28 January 1994 to M. S. from the National Army Museum.

[2] Charles Brasch, *Indirections*, Wellington, 1980, pp. 148–9. When I first knew him over thirty years later conversation at meal-times was much easier. He invited me to dine at the Athenaeum in January 1961; he had a good sense of humour: chuckled rather than laughed. He now wore conventional horn-rimmed spectacles, a sober single-breasted suit, well polished shoes. He was always neat, like his handwriting and, like his literary style, never flashy. During dinner he gave me a list of books of none of which I had ever

In the thirties Esmond and his sisters, already comfortably off, inherited the shares of both parents in the Hallenstein business. They decided to set up house together at 11 Sussex Place, a large leased house, part of one of the Nash terraces that encircle Regent's Park – *the* Regent's Park as Esmond always said. Here there was room to house their rapidly growing collections of books, pictures and artefacts. Mary and Dora lived with Esmond harmoniously and mutually supportively for the rest of their lives; all were unmarried, all became nonagenarians. The de Beer household made minimal concessions to the dwindling availability of domestic staff. Long after the end of the Second World War the front door was opened by a uniformed parlourmaid, and besides a resident cook there was at least one housemaid.[1] Esmond, and to a large extent his sisters, resisted another social change which occurred during their lifetime: the supplanting of the horse by the automobile. Nobody seems to remember Esmond owning or driving a car, though he did hold a driving licence in the twenties. In the thirties he rode with Dora in Rotten Row, and he was a redoubtable walker and hillclimber, but not an expert mountaineer as Dora was.

In September 1931 the Delegates of the Clarendon Press invited him to prepare and edit the first full edition of John Evelyn's *Diary*. Pursuing Evelyn, he travelled extensively in Italy, France, Belgium and the Netherlands until the outbreak of the Second World War. His enthusiasm for travel, for visiting art galleries, museums, libraries, historic sites and buildings, for walking and hill climbing continued long after that war was over.[2] He and his sisters revisited Italy in 1962; he flew to New Zealand the following year, returning by ship, and made the last return to his roots to attend the Hallenstein centenary celebrations in 1973. On a visit to the USA in 1965 he took the opportunity of visiting one or two of what he called 'the great editorial factories' and came away feeling that pre-eminent scholars such as Scaliger and Bentley had done their work – like Esmond himself, though he was too modest to say so – without research assistants, and also that 'card indexes can grow too large altogether. The products will be very good but in a

---

heard, but precisely those needed to help answer the questions I was trying to resolve; author, title, date, all given out of his head.

[1] They were considerate employers; to the end of his life Esmond sent a large Army and Navy Stores hamper at Christmas to former servants. Seven of them received a legacy of £1,000 each in his will.

[2] Esmond and his sisters had a particular affection for Raasay, the long narrow island between Skye and the Scottish mainland, which reminded them so much of New Zealand. They returned summer after summer, accompanied by friends, to walk, climb, read, and in Esmond's case, to work.

secretary's rather than a scholarly way.'[1] During the later seventies and early eighties he ranged less far, but still enjoyed holidays in Scotland, Herefordshire and Cornwall. His breadth of interests and knowledge were reflected in his reading of English, French, German, Italian, Dutch and Latin. This was not confined to scholarly works. He had a comprehensive knowledge of English novels from the earliest to modern times, with a particular affection for those of the nineteenth century, and a weakness for crime fiction which he called 'tecs'.

When war came in 1939 Esmond volunteered as an Air-Raid Precautions warden. Mary became a volunteer telephone operator at a fire brigade station in the City, Dora took on various commitments including work at the New Zealand soldiers' club and at the Red Cross prisoner of war department. Esmond soon found that sitting up most of the night with not an enemy plane in the sky was a waste of time. He resigned as an ARP warden and embarked on two more congenial tasks at the Historical Association and the Institute of Historical Research. From 1940 until 1945 he was the Honorary Acting Librarian of the Institute. Almost single-handed he not only edited its publications and kept the cataloguing of books and periodicals up to date but masterminded the moving of over 60,000 volumes from the library's permanent home in the University of London's Senate House, when that was requisitioned by the Ministry of Information, into temporary accommodation in the British Medical Association's building in Tavistock Square. At the same time he was helping to keep alive the Historical Association which had likewise been left without any professional staff. He knew Firth would have approved – he had been a founder of the Association in 1906 and its first president.

After the war Esmond was again able to devote most of his time to Evelyn. The *Diary* in six volumes (priced at fifteen guineas for the set) was not published until 1955, but the main body of the text and commentary was complete and ready some years earlier.[2] The work was immediately acclaimed as a masterpiece. He had added 250,000 words to the previous published text and enriched the whole with more than 12,000 notes 'based on an exceptional command over the most recondite sources (many of which de Beer had in his own library) [and

---

[1] He was in New York when a power failure lasting twelve hours started at rush hour on 9 November 1965: he wrote – 'New York seems to me to be the greatest of all manifestations of human energy, but energy for its own sake; magnificent but with its ugly side. And the products are apt to be measured too much in cash ... The black-out was a puncture in the American way of life. Such things will do for London, etc ... The newspapers were slightly surprised that there was no increase in crime ... ' (Letters 22 November, 19 December 1965).

[2] E. S. de Beer, ed., *The Diary of John Evelyn*, 6 vols, Oxford, 1955.

these] illuminated the dark places while refusing to lavish superfluous enlightenment on the obvious'.[1] Furthermore –

> He was not simply the prince of textual editors, he was also the king of indexers. The six hundred pages of the index volume ... are surely unique amongst the whole collection of books published in English. You can explore any topic touched on in the diary under any head you like, recover any detail you please, and you can do it easily, as an interesting pursuit in itself. Computerized indexing is simply not in the same class.[2]

Before completing the index Esmond had characteristically made a careful investigation of the problems involved, and no less characteristically he transmitted his knowledge and experience to others by publishing an article on the subject.[3]

Esmond was sixty when *Evelyn* was published. It was his first major work, so he might be thought of as a late developer. But it was such a gigantic achievement based on such width of knowledge that from now on there were many requests for his services, and he was accorded many academic honours, which he never overtly sought but gratefully acknowledged by substantial bequests in his will. In January 1957 Oxford University conferred upon him the honorary degree of D.Litt. The Public Orator spoke of *Evelyn* and of Esmond's work for the Institute of Historical Research during the war. His last sentence was (in translation from the Latin) as follows. 'No one, I think, does more to help and encourage fellow-students in various ways and to promote their interests.'[4] Many can bear witness to the accuracy of that statement. For instance, he was enormously helpful to me. I sent him some draft chapters and he responded with six pages of notes and a long covering letter.

> I am glad my notes are proving useful. They are a product not of learning [a grotesquely modest disavowal] but of a combination of inquisitiveness ('What does that mean?') and scepticism ('What is your authority for that?' or 'How do you know that?') and some special knowledge; and the circumstance, fortunate for myself, that I have had most of my time free to give to scholarship.[5]

His very extensive library contained many rare books, and he was prepared to lend the rarest, if he thought they would be used in a good cause: 'I can lend you Gölnitz's *Ulysses* [1631] and Thomas's *History of*

[1] J. S. G. Simmons, in *The Times*, 15 October 1990.
[2] P. Laslett, in *The Guardian*, 8 October 1990.
[3] E. S. de Beer, 'The large index', *Journal of Documentation*, 12, 1956, pp. 1–14.
[4] D. G. Vaisey, address at the Memorial Gathering (see p. 210 note 1).
[5] Letter 18 May 1961.

Italy [1549]. I would rather not send them through the post.'[1] He explained his generosity very simply:

> You must not be unduly lavish in acknowledgments to me. Long before I heard of the Republic of Letters I became acquainted with its more agreeable habits; and it would be a poor response to what my teachers did for me not to try to help other scholars in my turn. It is always a pleasure to assist at the birth of a good book.[2]

Many researchers may have remained unaware of the origins of their good fortune. For example, he much admired the work of the Director of the Warburg Institute, Fritz Saxl. Soon after Saxl's death in 1948 he and his sisters founded the Saxl Fund, to which for the rest of their lives they were the most regular contributors. The fund has provided grants for research and publication, as well as fellowships to both junior and senior scholars, who have come from Argentina, Czechoslovakia, France, East and West Germany, Hungary, Italy, Israel, Poland, Russia, USA and elsewhere.

Soon after publication of *Evelyn* he accepted an invitation to collect and edit John Locke's correspondence as part of the Clarendon Edition of Locke's works. This proved to be another vast task that occupied much of the rest of his working life. Tracking down hitherto unpublished or unknown material, letters to Locke as well as those from him, involved scores of investigations.[3] Esmond's letters to me in the sixties and early seventies provide a commentary on the chase and how he tackled the results.

15 August 1962 My latest guess is 8,000 working hours for Locke before he reaches the printer ... [this proved to be a considerable underestimate]. He has recently been concerned with Carolina, the Bahamas and Barbados. *9 December 1962* I find I go on working on Locke until towards eleven at night, and by then am too tired for much except looking at a few scraps, small pieces of bibliography and so on. *26 February 1963* You are frequently on the barriers of knowledge ... If there were just a little more information so much would be clear. The only thing to do is after a reasonable effort to give in, which is always hateful. *26 April 1964* I am getting entangled in the East Indies ... *19 December 1965* [I am] preparing a review of the catalogue of Locke's library. Of his known 3,641 books

---

[1] Ibid.

[2] Letter 8 November 1961.

[3] Esmond told me that while exploring Locke's family tree he had come across a nineteenth-century descendant, who, he surmised, might have inherited some of Locke's papers. He discovered that the man had died in Belgium and that relatives still lived there. They invited him to their farmhouse and there in a loft he found a number of hitherto unrecorded items. This piece of detective work gave him great satisfaction.

215

195 were voyages and travels and another eighty were geography. *5 January 1967* The letters of the last two or three years of Locke's life are important for the rise of the London stock market. As a result of decent government finance and commercial expansion it became possible to have an income derived from investments ... The development in social terms means a great increase of the leisured class. Wayside flowers of this kind are apt to be a nuisance: I have neither the knowledge nor the energy to deal with them adequately, and yet dislike leaving them to the desert air. *14 April 1969* Revision of Locke is going tolerably. For every hole that I stop two new ones appear, but the means of filling them are usually at hand. *3 December 1970* I am completing and revising my notes for Locke, and finding a good many I don't like the looks of: statements are apt to be wrong or irrelevant, or just plain incompetent. The trouble is that it's easy to take a jaundiced view. The things I have to deal with now are generally the more and most difficult, and so produce a continuing depression. Which is I suppose a salutary state of mind, but I hope you don't have much of it. *1 April 1972* I have been ... reading and testing the biographical statements made about Locke by my predecessors and contemporaries, and trying to plan an article about them ... in some cases it will be difficult to be explicit without being offensive. No one likes being told he is saying a thing which is not. They do it frequently ...[1]

The first seven volumes of *Locke* were published between 1976 and 1981. Then there was long gap. Esmond in his middle eighties was going blind and had to give up work. The eighth volume appeared at last in 1989; the index volume is still in preparation.[2] The eight volumes, totalling over 6,000 pages, contain 3,655 letters, all but seven transcribed and nearly all annotated by Esmond: 'a piece of scholarship beyond praise'.[3]

There are good reasons why Esmond should have devoted so much time over so many years to the affairs of the Hakluyt Society. When he became a member in 1946 he was interested in the work of another New Zealand scholar, J. C. Beaglehole, who was editing for the Society the journals of Captain James Cook. He had great admiration

---

[1] He continued with perceptive comments on the period. 'I have a notion that Locke's readership was a new element in the population, administrative, professional, financial and mercantile, all greatly expanded from earlier times, and needing a new structure of thought in harmony with the great accumulation of new knowledge of the sixteenth century and the following years. I do not know how to state this adequately. [He attempted to do so very briefly in 'The Literature of Travel in the Seventeenth Century' referred to below]. A better astronomy was wanted for the oceanic voyages ... that infected thought about other subjects ... The oceanic voyages required larger organisations at home ... I think that there is need of a new synthesis beyond the study of each activity more or less in isolation.'

[2] E. S. de Beer, *The Correspondence of John Locke*, 8 vols, Oxford, 1976–89.

[3] H. G. Nicholas, in *The Daily Telegraph*, 13 October 1990.

for Beaglehole's work, which in thoroughness and scale was comparable to editing Evelyn. After prolonged gestation the first part was published in 1955, the fourth and last, a biography of Cook, in 1974.[1] The work might never have been published but for the quiet determination of de Beer, and the generosity of Esmond and his two sisters. All three contributed unstintingly to the publication costs of the entire work.[2]

Esmond's innate appetite for inquisitive travel was sharpened and widened by his historical studies and in particular by his special interest in Evelyn and Locke. Both were polymathic travellers; both in varying degrees, albeit Locke more than Evelyn, influenced thought about travel in relation to trade. Evelyn's treatise on navigation and commerce was published in 1674; Locke's government appointments gave him many fertile insights into overseas trade. So Esmond found himself very much in sympathy with the Society's objects: 'to advance education by the publication of records of voyages, travels, naval expeditions, and other geographical matter'. His service on the Society's Council in the fifties and sixties made him conversant with its problems. The Society has always aimed to publish works to the highest standards of accuracy, scholarship and book production, but relies on unpaid editors and authors, who usually have to devote much of their time to earning a living, and cannot be put under too much pressure to meet deadlines. De Beer outlined some of the problems in letters of 1961–1962.

> The Society has got badly behind with the issue of its volumes . . . it got into arrears during the war, and the devaluation of the pound added to its troubles . . . I think that many of the learned societies have been in trouble with their publications ever since the last war. They can give only small orders and they want highly skilled printing; the authors and editors are not always considerate when they provide their copy, and sometimes want many expensive corrections . . . I have had to report on a proposed work for the Hakluyt Society – the editor's work won't do; she knows her stuff but has a messy mind . . . the Hakluyt Society is constantly in difficulties with its printers . . . I think that the Hakluyt Secretary [at that time R.A. Skelton] does his best to secure good copy. But in this case it is Cambridge University Press that is at fault.[3]

When de Beer became President of the Society in 1972 he inherited a

---

[1] Forming all told five volumes (HS Extra 34–7). A portfolio of charts prepared by R. A. Skelton accompanied the first volume.
[2] E. M. J. Campbell in *Annual Report* [for 1990], Hakluyt Society, London.
[3] Letters 18 May 1961, 9 and 12 December 1962.

number of these problems, particularly what he, and others, considered to be inadequate editing.

In editing *Evelyn* and *Locke* he himself had spared no effort and no expense in going back to the contemporary sources; he was sternly critical of inadequate research, slipshod writing or muddled thinking, whether he found such shortcomings in those sources, sensed them when revising his own work, or encountered them elsewhere. It was not unnatural that he should have applied the same principles to the editing of Hakluyt Society publications; but his definition of his role as President differed from that of his immediate predecessors and successors. As his successor, Professor Glyndwr Williams has written to me:

> He seemed to feel that he was personally responsible for every word which appeared in the Society's volumes scheduled for his term of office. And this strong sense of duty was allied to a quiet but unrelenting insistence in stamping his own imprint of what was, stylistically, right and wrong, on the editorial introductions. I trod warily round these problems most of which had been cleared by the time I took over; and personally I found de Beer unfailingly courteous.

But the result was that not a single volume was published during his presidency 1972–1978, and the membership, who had expected at least one annual volume in return for their subscriptions, became somewhat disenchanted. However, the backlog of nine volumes was cleared by 1982; the Society's high standards were upheld and 'many editors have reason to be grateful . . . His scholarship made a great deal of difference to their final texts, although it delayed (but rightly so) their publication.'[1]

Several Hakluyt Society volumes thus include his anonymous help, and the Society did publish the text of a talk he gave at the 1975 Annual General Meeting entitled 'The Literature of Travel in the Seventeenth Century'.[2] The talk included this passage:

> In 1600 the western world was backward looking. The world had been deteriorating ever since the Creation and was now hastening to its end. Thought was bound by dogma . . . In 1700 . . . the idea of deterioration

---

[1] Campbell, *Annual Report*, p. 17. It may be added that de Beer was much respected by the Society's officers, as the following anecdote indicates. During his presidency the Society's patron, the Duke of Gloucester, died and de Beer was invited at short notice to attend a memorial service at Windsor. His wardrobe did not include the required morning suit. To meet this crisis he sought the aid of the Society's Administrative Assistant, Mrs Alexa Barrow (daughter of a former Honorary Secretary, R. A. Skelton), who rushed to London, measured him somewhat to his embarrassment, hired the correct clothes. and ordered a chauffeur-driven car. He was deeply grateful and relished the ceremonial.

[2] The talk appeared in *Annual Report* [1975], Hakluyt Society, London.

was giving way to the idea of progress. Scripture, the Fathers, and the classical heritage were still revered but were no longer sacrosanct; dogma was challenged by what men called reason. Some part of the change was due to the enlargement of human experience provided by the travellers and their writings.

The passage provides another clue to the reasons why Esmond found the literature of travel so significant – reasons which he justified practically by continuing substantial support for the Society's further Cook publications. Lieutenant Commander Andrew David was working on a definitive folio edition of Cook's charts and views.[1] Esmond gave £4,000 towards the publication costs of the first volume which appeared in 1988, and in his will left the Society a further £4,000. He did not specify how the money was to be spent, but let it be known that he hoped it would be used towards meeting the costs of the second volume. Both volumes have been acclaimed and widely acquired.[2]

After the lease of 11 Sussex Place ran out Esmond and his sisters bought 31 Brompton Square which was large enough to house their collections, particularly his very large library. They lived there from 1964; Mary and Dora died soon after one another in 1981 and 1982, leaving their estates, including their books, pictures and artefacts, to Esmond. He decided that the great house must be given up and its contents dispersed. He did this through the Friends of the National Libraries and the National Art Collections Fund (both of which he had served for many years), giving advice on which institutions would benefit most from the vast range of treasures.[3] Some of Esmond's early guidebooks went to the University of Otago Library, some to the British Library.[4]

Esmond and his sisters always regarded Dunedin as their real home and London as their second home. They wished to enhance the collections of Dunedin's institutions: the University of Otago Library, the Otago Museum and Dunedin Public Art Gallery. During the seventies they had given individual works to the Gallery, including the quattrocento Florentine 'Virgin and Child' by Zanobi Machiavelli which was

---

[1] Andrew David et al., eds, *The Charts and Coastal Views of Captain Cook's Voyages* (HS Extra 43, 44), 1988, 1992 – a final volume will appear probably in 1997.

[2] At the time of writing Andrew David has nearly completed the third and final volume.

[3] Space does not permit any detailed discussion of Esmond's great knowledge of art. He was a trustee of the National Portrait Gallery 1959–1967 and a member of the government's Reviewing Committee on the Export of Works of Art 1965–1970. For his services to the Reviewing Committee he was appointed CBE.

[4] Part of Mary's large collection of modern English poetry was given to Edinburgh University and the Alpine Club received Dora's collection of mountaineering books.

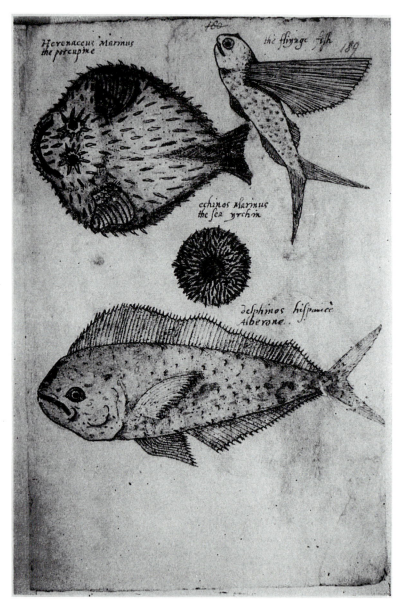

FISHES AT SIERRA LEONE
Drawn by chaplain Madox in 1582.
Original in British Library, Cotton MSS, Titus B VIII.
Reproduced in HS 2/147 of 1976.

subsequently reproduced on a New Zealand postage stamp. The Gallery now received its most important donation ever. Outstanding among the paintings were Claude's 'Hagar and the Angel', the first work by this artist to go to New Zealand, and Monet's 'La Débâcle', showing the frozen Seine melting after the exceptionally severe winter of 1879–1880. The de Beer collection included prints by Dürer, Van Dyck, Hollar, Rembrandt, Callot, Canaletto and Piranesi. More modern works included French and English watercolours and drawings by Boudin, Signac, Lear, David Roberts, Muirhead Bone and Wilson Steer. The gift was enhanced by a large collection of Japanese wood block prints by Hokusai, Hiroshige, Utamaro and Toyokuni. In all, the Gallery received more than one hundred items.[1] The de Beers contributions to the Museum were spread over many years and included textiles, jewellery, ceramics, silver, items from Japan, ancient Egypt and Greece, in all over one thousand first-class objects which 'helped to build the Otago Museum's collections into an outstanding resource of international significance'.[2] The Library had already received about 2,000 volumes and in 1984 was given those books he had used in editing Locke. Esmond's residual estate amounted to over £1 million from which all three institutions received substantial legacies.

Esmond moved to a flat in St John's Wood but in 1984, going deaf as well as blind and suffering from the beginnings of Parkinson's disease, he was persuaded to move to Stoke House, a residential home for the elderly in Buckinghamshire. After a Hakluyt Society Council meeting in 1985 some of us who were present recorded messages of gratitude and congratulation on his ninetieth birthday. Maybe this recording was allowed to surmount his barrier against modern technology. He scorned cassette players, television, radio and gramophone throughout his life. His considerable knowledge and love of music, particularly opera, seems to have been acquired solely from attending live performances. He told the chaplain at Stoke House that he was an atheist, and expressed the wish that his ashes should be scattered, no matter where, without ceremony. This is why a Memorial Gathering took place at the Warburg Institute (of which he had been an Honorary Fellow) on 6 December 1990, when addresses were read by representatives of the institutions, including the Hakluyt Society, which had especially benefited from his and his sisters' generosity.

[1] See *Dunedin Public Art Gallery Annual Report, 1982*, pp. 3–9; Peter Entwistle, *Treasures of the Dunedin Public Art Gallery*, Dunedin, 1990; Robyn Notman, 'Esmond de Beer, Patron of the Arts' in *Bulletin of New Zealand Art History*, 15, 1994, pp. 33–54.
[2] Letter of 19 November 1990 from Richard Cassels, Director of the Otago Museum (Memorial Gathering – see p. 210 note 1).

A preliminary bibliography compiled and published by his friend, Dr J. S. G. Simmons of All Souls College, Oxford, records one hundred and fifty items, and Simmons has since added more.[1] De Beer's name appears in the preliminaries of numerous Hakluyt Society volumes and is carved on the great marble slab at the top of the staircase leading to Duke Humfrey's Library in the Bodleian, only the forty-ninth in a list of major benefactors that begins with Duke Humfrey of Gloucester himself in 1439. Among the very few possessions that Esmond retained to the last was one of his undergraduate essays on which Sir Charles Firth had written a sharp criticism ending – 'Life demands completed work; the world will never set much value on what you do unless you show a finished result to the best of your ability'. De Beer did that in *Evelyn* and *Locke*, which are enduring monuments.

---

[1] J. S. G. Simmons, *Esmond Samuel de Beer (1885–1990), Obituary Notices and a Bibliography*, Oxford, 1990. Apart from the six volumes of *Evelyn* and the eight volumes of *Locke*, the list includes many articles in learned journals, many book reviews, and his biographies of Evelyn and Locke in the 1969 edition of the *Encyclopaedia Britannica*.

Part IV

EPILOGUE

The Hakluyt Society and World History

MACQUARIE ISLAND IN THE ANTARCTIC, WITH RUSSIAN VESSELS

EPILOGUE

THE HAKLUYT SOCIETY AND WORLD HISTORY

R. C. Bridges and P. E. H. Hair

The discovery of America, and that of a passage to the East Indies by the Cape of Good Hope, are the two greatest and most important events recorded in the history of mankind.

Adam Smith, *The Wealth of Nations*, Book IV, Chapter VII, Part III

The Hakluyt Society has a record of one hundred and fifty years devoted to the scholarly understanding of overseas 'Voyages and Travels'. This notable history is now being appropriately celebrated. But it is also appropriate to assess that history. We may ask, not only how the scholarly understanding of previous travels and encounters has changed over the period, but also where the Society has stood as an institution – an institution within British society which, by its very existence and form, has to some extent participated in the interplay of cultural relations between Europe and the rest of the world. In the present volume both themes are considered. The essays above speak for themselves, but in this Epilogue we attempt an overview and deal especially with the historical context of the institution in the period up to the First World War.

★   ★   ★

Geoffrey Scammell, a distinguished historian of European overseas out-thrust and a former member of the Council of the Hakluyt Society, writing on the period approximately from the births of Columbus and Vasco da Gama to that of Adam Smith, has thought it wise to begin by reminding his readers of a prevalent common view about the eventual historical consequences of that period.

Europe's prosperity in the expansive years of the nineteenth and twentieth

225

centuries was founded on the exploitation of the rest of the globe, thereby condemning much of it to underdevelopment and dependency.[1]

The view of Adam Smith in 1776 and this present-day view, albeit opposed to each other in underlying moral implication, have more in common than a touch of generalising rhetoric in each. Each presupposes the predominant importance to humanity of economic advance. More relevantly for this volume, by stressing the role of European overseas activity each makes a global appraisal of the latterday history of mankind. Yet the most significant term in the passage from Adam Smith is 'recorded'. For without records there can be no world history to be applauded or deplored.

Understanding of the history of mankind has progressively matured since 1776, and particularly has done so in the present century. The first 'empire on which the sun never sets' was not the one proclaimed in the 1890s, but the conjoint Portuguese-Spanish empire of the Felipes three centuries earlier. The European out-thrust of the fifteenth and sixteenth centuries may have owed much to the crusty individualism of Columbus and da Gama, but the marine movement had roots in much earlier European overseas activities, as Geoffrey Scammell showed in a previous study of European overseas expansion, and as Felipe Fernández-Armesto, a present member of the Council of the Hakluyt Society, has confirmed in his *Before Columbus* (1989). Again, while the out-thrust from Europe was on a global scale not known before – and so encompassing as unlikely to be matched again in any foreseeable future – wide imperial expansions had existed earlier, not merely the empires of Greece and Rome but those of non-Europeans such as the Mongols, Inca and Manding. True, Europeans were the first to circumnavigate, the first to link up all the continents, and the first to spread their genes around the world; but other peoples have committed themselves to major migrations, by sea like the Polynesians, by land like the Arabians and (over much longer periods) the peoples termed Bantu and Amerindian. Nor would modern historians share the confidence of Adam Smith that the most important events in the history of mankind can be limited to imperial out-thrusts and aggressive economic expansions.

Nevertheless, it is difficult to live at the present moment anywhere on the globe and not share the conviction that the One-World apparently in train is the product of progressive cultural unification over

---

[1] Geoffrey Scammell, *The First Imperial Age: European Overseas Expansion c.1400–1715*, 1988, Introduction. As regards explanations of 'underdevelopment', note an influential polemic, Walter Rodney, *How Europe Underdeveloped Africa*, London/Dar es Salaam, 1972.

many centuries. The records of that process are varyingly incomplete. Preliteracy has robbed history of detailed knowledge of most cultural encounters in the past, while the modern economic hegemony of western Europe and its North American god-child has to date paid for history writing which concentrated on initial encounter resulting from marine enterprise, with the insular British leading the pack.[1] Richard Hakluyt would not have disagreed with Adam Smith about the supreme role of Columbus and da Gama in mankind's secular progress, as evident by his anxiety to expand English influence to the Outer Continents.[2] Three centuries later, the second Honorary Secretary of the Hakluyt Society no doubt gave considerable satisfaction to fellow Victorians by exalting the role in the European out-thrust of a Portuguese prince who had an English mother.[3] Inevitably some of the editions of the Hakluyt Society have implied a belief that world unification is all for the best, provided it be conducted under the aegis of the English-speaking establishment. The inconvenient fact that the English were slow coaches in global adventure led Hakluyt, in search for records of traditional outward-looking, back through Macham and Mandeville and Madoc to scrape the early-medieval barrel with equally implausible Britons and Anglo-Saxons. Yet whatever the limitations of the views of Hakluyt and Adam Smith, the potency of the European out-thrust in shaping the world order of today – although perhaps not that of the coming century – cannot be overlooked, any more than can the fact that the language generated in a small, damp, off-shore island is today the major language of global communication.

When the history of the world is thus taken to be shaped by cultural encounter, then the documentation of those encounters that are recorded becomes the essential study material of the world historian. For while the records of the past are not limited to the extant documentation, some, for instance, being represented by the genes of today's populations, written sources are unequalled in detailing for the historian the more subtle aspects of human endeavour. And this applies not least to those primary sources dealing with the initial and early stages of

---

[1] For discussion of the out-thrust from Muscovy/Russia, a movement noted by Richard Hakluyt but largely neglected by historians of European expansion, because of their concentration on 'overseas' at the expense of 'overland' expansion, see Terence Armstrong, 'Russian penetration into Siberia up to 1800', in Cecil H. Clough and P. E. H Hair, eds, *The European Outthrust: The First Phase c.1400–c.1700* , Liverpool, 1994, pp. 119–40, and also pp. 62–4.

[2] But the Reverend Richard Hakluyt would not have given these secular events quite the moral weight implied by the Enlightenment savant.

[3] P. E. Russell, *Portugal, Spain and the African Atlantic, 1343–1490*, Aldershot, 1995, item XI, pp. 4–5; item XV, pp. 8–9. Professor Russell points out, however, that, much earlier, Purchas had noted Henry's English connection.

cultural encounter, the records of exploratory 'Voyages and Travels'. The Hakluyt Society has existed for one hundred and fifty years to publish, in critical editions, and to make more accessible in a world language, precisely those records.

★   ★   ★

The present volume attempts to see the Hakluyt Society as an institution contributing to both national and international history. It does so in part through a study of the Society's publications and in part through biographical essays on leading figures in its past. We hope that this represents a first step towards assessing the development of the Society within a global context. Little has previously been written about the Society as an institution, even in relation merely to the history of the British, at home and overseas. Earlier commemorations presented a historical perspective, heart-felt and well-intentioned no doubt, but somewhat myopic. In the published address that Sir Clements Markham, as President, produced in 1896 to mark the fiftieth anniversary of the Society, while ignoring the actual founder of the Society (as noted in Bridges' essay above), he concentrated on the merits of the work of Richard Hakluyt, in order to reach the conclusion that 'there was the same danger as in Hakluyt's time that the glorious deeds of our explorers by sea and land would pass into oblivion . . . [with] all the precious information they collected for the use of posterity'.[1] After briefly reviewing the regional scope of the Society's publications in its first fifty years, a useful exercise, Markham further reflected that the contemplation of the 'heroic deeds of explorers' and the knowledge they imparted was 'ennobling to those who are under its influence', and hence that the existence of the Society was a sign of 'healthy tendencies of thought and of healthy aspirations among the peoples who speak the English language.'[2] The range of the remarks uttered at the time of the tercentenary of Hakluyt's death in 1916 by the then President, Sir Albert Gray, ran little wider or deeper. Speaking in a year of national crisis, he emphasised that the outward thrust of Elizabethan England, which Hakluyt's writings had helped to generate, had led to 'two of the dominant factors in the modern world, the British Empire and the great American Republic.'[3] Like Markham in 1896, Gray in 1916 had more to

---

[1] C. R. Markham, *Richard Hakluyt. His Life and Work*, London, 1896, p. 10.

[2] Ibid., pp. 15–17.

[3] Albert Gray, *An Address on the Occasion of the Tercentenary of the Death of Richard Hakluyt 23rd November 1916*, London, 1917, pp. 5, 11–12. No doubt Gray was influenced

say about Hakluyt and his time than about the history of the Hakluyt Society.

On the centenary of the foundation of the Society, in 1946, a commemorative volume was produced. It is not surprising that a Society whose editions and interests had related mainly to the early modern period should have had this emphasis reflected in the contents of the volume, three of its five essays dealing with pre-1846 topics.[1] J. A. Williamson, the notable imperial historian, wrote an attractive essay on Richard Hakluyt and his influence. In so far as he considered the Society, he appeared to judge its importance to lie in the realm of catering to the growing interest of the educated public in reading about 'voyages and travels' for pleasure.[2] In contrast, Sir William Foster's 'Retrospect' did indeed deal with the history of the Society. Foster provided the best account up to that time of the Society's foundation and he described its subsequent activity with succinct and just verdicts on previous Honorary Secretaries and Presidents.[3] It was left, however, to Edward Lynam, the then President, to sketch the wider historical context of the institution, at least at its foundation. His essay, when referring to 1846, noted Britain's maritime ascendancy, the 'birth of a new democratic spirit', and the effects of the Industrial Revolution, including social unrest. 'The bold irregularity of the English' was still to be seen in emigration schemes and these were compared to the overseas initiatives of Hakluyt's day. Increased interest in overseas affairs in the early nineteenth century had generated a demand for accounts of exploration, and it was because the Royal Geographical Society could not fully meet this demand that the Hakluyt Society had appeared. Lynam had thus linked the foundation and, by implication, the development of the Society to the imperial interests of Britain and the contemporary condition of geographical enquiry. He did not,

---

by current affairs: the British Empire was two years into a destructive war which it was not yet winning; the U.S.A. was moving towards allying with the Empire, which it did four months later.

[1] E. Lynam, ed., *Richard Hakluyt & his Successors. A Volume Issued to Commemorate the Centenary of the Hakluyt Society*, Hakluyt Society, London, 1946 (HS 2/93). The pre-1846 contributions included an overview, by R. A. Skelton and G. R. Crone, the Honorary Secretary and his predecessor, of English collections of voyages and travels in the period between Hakluyt's immediate successor, Purchas, and the foundation of the Hakluyt Society. This not only provided an historical perspective on the publication of travel literature but drew attention to the occasional elements of scholarly editorial practice in earlier material, for instance, those of the anonymous editor of Astley's *Collection of Voyages and Travels*, which foreshadowed the editorial requirements of the Hakluyt Society.

[2] J. A. Williamson, 'Richard Hakluyt', in ibid., pp. 9–46.

[3] W. Foster, 'The Hakluyt Society. A Retrospect: 1846–1946', in ibid., pp. 141–70.

however, pursue these perceptive lines of argument very far and in the end stated that the Society's foundation was 'as much the result of a revival in the study of history'.[1]

Four decades on from the Centenary volume, the Council became more aware of the Society's archives and asked Mrs Dorothy Middleton to make a survey of them. This resulted in an article which pointed the way forward in several important respects, in particular because it not only provided pen-portraits of past officers but also drew attention to their wider careers.[2]

The biographical essays in the present volume have taken this contextualisation rather further. It cannot as yet be claimed that we have anything like a clear picture of the role of the Society even within British society. Research remains to be done on the subscription membership over the whole period.[3] Until this is done we have little idea why individuals joined, and hence what use, if any, they made of the volumes they obtained. The membership of the Council, both active and honorary, equally calls for further investigation. Generalisations about the role of the Society in British overseas activity, as yet attempted by few historians, are therefore likely to be premature and little more than speculative. It may be instructive to consider one such attempt.

★   ★   ★

The modern biographer of Sir Roderick Murchison, first President of the Society from 1847 until his death in 1871, has argued that the Hakluyt Society served to emphasise the 'causal links between exploration and global power'.[4] The Society fitted into Murchison's schemes for making imperial advance respectable and science its handmaiden, because he saw it as 'an historical intelligence bureau, delving into British and foreign archives for "lost" information concerning trade

---

[1] E. Lynam, 'The Present and the Future', in ibid., pp. 171–89, especially pp. 178–83.

[2] D. Middleton, 'The Hakluyt Society 1846–1923' in *Annual Report* [for 1984], Hakluyt Society, pp. 12–23; also published in a slightly different form, the beginning date amended to 1847, in *Geographical Journal*, 152, 1986, pp. 217–24. A brief reference to the history of the Society had already been provided in 1962 by G. R. Crone ('"Jewells of Antiquitie": the work of the Hakluyt Society', *Geographical Journal*, 128, 1962, pp. 321–4), but the article concentrated on the range and quality of the editions produced.

[3] Of the kind recently carried out by Professor Fage on the foundation membership of the African Society: J. D. Fage, 'When the African Society was founded, who were the Africanists?', *African Affairs*, 94, 1995, pp. 369–81.

[4] R. Stafford, *Scientist of Empire. Sir Roderick Murchison, Scientific Exploration and Victorian Imperialism*, Cambridge, 1989, p. 24.

routes, mines, and native products discovered by ancient civilisations and early European navigators'. As proof of this view, the following passage from Murchison's 1857 presidential address to the Royal Geographical Society is cited.

These early narratives not only charm us by the quaint and nervous language in which the manly exploits of our ancestors are related, but frequently record discoveries or assert important truths which, from those distant times, lie dormant or are regarded as fictions, until accident or science unfolds anew, to the adventurer of the present day, the secret of their existence.[1]

Murchison proceeded to give as an example of the commercial use of early overseas narratives the reference in a Hakluyt Society publication to Drake's belief that gold and silver would be found in New Albion, 'and it was not till 1848 that the whole world was astonished by the discovery of the Californian goldfields'.

The example is weak and unconvincing, since it was standard practice for every Renaissance explorer to try to impress his monarch or patron with tales of possible gold and silver. Moreover, there is little evidence that nineteenth-century explorers and adventurers were influenced in respect of where to go and what to look for by their historical forbears.[2] And for that matter, there is also little evidence that the production of particular Hakluyt Society volumes was ever determined by specific contemporary needs, what was produced depending in the main upon what editors happened to offer and how soon a text could be made ready. The historian concerned did not investigate the Hakluyt Society itself, and the archives of the Society suggest that in actuality Murchison did not take a close and active personal interest in its proceedings, serving more as a figurehead.[3] A great accumulator of decorations and presidencies, he was almost certainly appointed and maintained as President of the Hakluyt Society to make it respectable and

---

[1] R. I. Murchison, 'Anniversary Address to the Royal Geographical Society, 25th May 1857', *Journal of the Royal Geographical Society*, 27, 1857, pp. xciv–cxcviii, clxxxix. The quotation from the 1896 address by Markham given above (p. 228) followed much the same line, by referring to the 'precious information' collected by early explorers.

[2] As Cooley was to learn in his post-Hakluyt Society career as an 'armchair geographer' (R. C. Bridges, 'W. D. Cooley, the RGS and African Geography in the Nineteenth Century, Part I', *Geographical Journal*, 142, 1976, pp. 27–47).

[3] The standard nineteenth-century biography of Murchison actually makes no mention of the Hakluyt Society (Archibald Geikie, *Life of Sir Roderick I. Murchison*, 2 vols, London, 1875). Murchison's lack of close and continuous involvement in the Society's affairs, plus the existence of Stafford's recent and valuable biography, are the reasons why the present volume does not include an essay on the first President of the Hakluyt Society.

perhaps also to keep it orientated towards exalting the British element in overseas exploration (as argued by Bridges elsewhere in the present volume). It is, moreover, likely that the passage cited above was not written by Murchison but provided for him by the Honorary Secretary, Major. All in all, therefore, the claim that the Society was an 'intelligence bureau' serving as an agency of imperial advance must be regarded, on the evidence presented, as 'not proven'. Nevertheless, a connection between the Society and British overseas expansion – but a more subtle one than that outlined above – is plausible and deserves future investigation, perhaps on the lines of the following hypothesis. While the Hakluyt Society was devoted to scholarship for its own sake, very occasionally in a conscious way but more often unconsciously, it served the needs and validated the preoccupations of subscribers, a number of whom either took a close interest in contemporary British overseas activity or were themselves directly involved in enterprises in the wider world.

★   ★   ★

The biographical essays provide some clues regarding these broader issues. A feature of much of the history of the Society has been a tension – perhaps a healthy tension – between the rival claims of 'British heritage' and international enterprise. At the very beginning of the Society, there was momentary dispute as to whether it should be named after Columbus or Hakluyt (see the essay by Bridges). If the Englishman won – and Hakluyt's great work was the *Principall Navigations, Voiages & Discoveries of the English Nation* – nevertheless, shortly after the name of the Society was fixed, the logo of the Society, appearing on every volume since (and on our 1996 Appeal literature), was allowed to be a foreign vessel, Magellan's 'Victoria'. This was a victory for internationalism and comprehensiveness, subsequently confirmed by the fact that only one third of the Society's publications since 1847 have dealt with English or British sources. And if in the high noon of expansion Markham's presidential language, as cited above, was patriotic, nationalist, and imperialistic, he himself actually worked almost solely on non-British, mainly Spanish sources (see the essay by Savours). Nevertheless it cannot be gainsaid that the attitudes of Victorian editors, who were almost exclusively British, tended to be 'sturdily patriotic'.[1] Editing in an age of confident British expansion overseas,

---

[1] Crone, '"Jewells of Antiquitie"', p. 322.

their attitude could hardly have been otherwise. Only in the later twentieth century has the Society become less British and more international in its range of editors (see the essay by Hair). For instance, the great 1950s and 1960s edition of the journals of Cook was edited, and its publication in part subsidised, by scholars born, not in Britain, but in New Zealand (see the essays by Quinn and Strachan). Yet 'international' does not yet mean global: only a few non-European sources (or even non-west-European sources) have to date been edited and there have been hardly any editors from Asia, Africa or Latin America.

The personal experiences and interests, in geographical terms, of the subjects of the biographical essays were varying, but virtually global. As such, they reflected the worldwide influence of Britain, up to 1914 concomitant with the 'imperialism of free trade'. Cooley, Major, and Foster did not travel outside Europe, but Cooley studied European overseas activity in general as well as central Africa in particular, Major edited material on Virginia, India, Russia, Australia and Greenland, and Foster devoted a lifetime of research to India and neighbouring parts. Markham travelled in the Arctic, Peru, India and Ethiopia; he edited material on Peru, the Pacific, the Canary Islands, the East Indies, and the Polar approaches. Yule worked in India and Burma as a canal and railway engineer, then wrote on central Asia and China. Skelton, as general editor for the Society, supervised editions relating to most parts of the world and contributed cartographical material to many of the editions. De Beer was a noble benefactor to New Zealand, his birthplace there being regarded as his 'real home' (see the essay by Strachan). It is hardly surprising that several figures were closely connected with the Royal Geographical Society: Cooley founded the Hakluyt Society to some extent in defiance of the RGS, Major and Markham served the RGS for long periods as officers. In particular, Markham was the driving force behind many RGS explorations, as well as some independent ones, especially in Africa and the Antarctic, his final enterprise being the first Scott expedition. Inevitably, however, the range of languages in which the major sources studied by these scholars were originally written was far less than global. English, Spanish, Italian, and Latin – in that order – were the principal languages represented.

One aspect of the intellectual contribution of these men to British society was their respect for individual effort, as displayed by the historical characters they wrote about, or, especially in Victorian times, as manifested by themselves. The Society was named after a single individual, and voyages were regularly defined in terms of a commander, as the titles of volumes show. Major's quasi-invention of 'Henry the Navigator', so that a complex process was attributed to the genius of a single person, was a typical product of the era of Carlyle's *Heroes, Hero Worship, and the Heroic in History*. Markham's adulation of physical prowess, often awarded high moral commendation, especially the man-hauling of sledges, has led one historian to argue that the 1912 British disaster in the Antarctic was due to a prejudice against replacing men with dogs (an interpretation not, however, generally accepted). These men did not spare themselves: the individual literary output of Major, Markham, Yule, Foster and de Beer was extraordinary. In the case of Markham so persistent was *cacoëthes scribendi* that one ventures a psychological explanation: at first a mere clerk from the India Office, confronted on the one hand by the aristocratic and High-Establishment members of Council, and on the other by graduate colleagues at the Office and in the Society, he needed to prove himself by excess vigour. Be that as it may, his enthusiasm and ambition were soon matched by a steely determination to have his own way. Yule, on the other hand, was a man in authority before he joined the Society, and he appears to have been somewhat casual when at the top. With the indulgence of wealth, de Beer pursued his own narrow set path throughout life, with utter devotion, no ostentation, a kindly disposition and a cloistered personal existence.

As the essays below detail, all the leading figures in the Society discussed in the present volume were born into a middle-class family, either a long-standing one, such as that of Yule, or a recently-attained one, such as that of de Beer. During life all were comfortably off, in varying degrees, although all except de Beer had to take remunerative work. The Victorian figures, although not related to the landed aristocracy, found it useful to have social relations with individual members; while most of them eventually succeeded in gaining personal honours, either from the national establishment or elsewhere, for their lifetimes of merit. As with many other national institutions, the Hakluyt Society was an area of activity and devotion for a newly empowered middle class, or rather for a particular section of that class. Bridges has elsewhere referred to a 'service class' of administrators and other military, naval, and colonial officials working overseas. Certain members of this class were associated with the foundation of the Royal Geographical Society in 1830, although the Society's Council continued to include members drawn from the landed aristocracy. Something of a similar character appears to have been true of the Hakluyt Society, for much longer than its initial period. This pattern seems to reflect a more general tendency in the social order which certain recent historians have identified in relation to the economy of the early Victorian decades, whereby the landed aristocracy was no longer able to dominate, on its

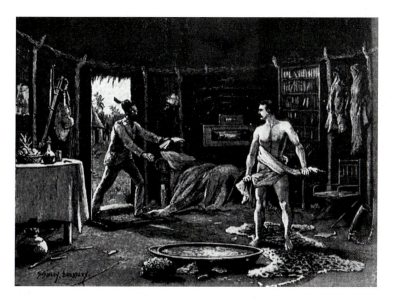

'NEWS FROM STANLEY AT LAST!'
Illustration from a work of 1890.
Reproduced in HS Extra 40 of 1969.

own, the financial and service enterprises based on the City of London, and had to be joined by men without significant landed interests in creating what has been termed 'gentlemanly capitalism'. It is further suggested that this domestic 'gentlemanly order' was paralleled by a 'gentlemanly diaspora', that is, a renewed interest in overseas expansion.[1]

Although direct links between the personnel of the Hakluyt Society – the officers, Council members, editors and subscribers – and the national economy, not only in the founding period but up to at least 1914, appear to have been limited, a large number of the more active individuals, who might well be described as of the gentlemanly order, had served overseas, or at least had been, or still were, involved in overseas affairs. No doubt these men regarded both their overseas and their Hakluyt Society activities as serving national advance and global progress, as they saw those causes. On a less ideal view, as members of a directing 'officer class' they were anxious to recall the exploits of those

---

[1] R. C. Bridges, 'Europeans and East Africans in the Age of Exploration', *Geographical Journal*, 139, 1973, pp. 220–32; P. Cain and A. G. Hopkins, *British Imperialism: Innovation and Expansion 1688–1914*, London/New York, 1993, pp. 22ff., 44–5, 55, 81–3, 99–100. Cain and Hopkins suggest that 'the imperial mission was the export version of the gentlemanly order'.

whom they considered (perhaps unhistorically) their predecessors in that class, and it can be argued that this at times affected judgement when it came to selecting and editing publications. History was 'from above'; the poorly-recorded masses deserved little detailed or intimate attention and collective forces tended to be ignored. Nevertheless, these individuals aimed to increase knowledge of Europe's past encounters with the rest of the world, a worthwhile and progressive aim, by collecting, ordering, and making more easily available the necessary materials for the study; and it is difficult to deny their successful and often devoted pursuit of this aim.

In the extension of intellectual learning and the mobilisation of learning resources, the leading figures discussed in this volume did not limit themselves, as influential middle-class patrons, to serving only the Hakluyt Society. Lynam perceptively drew attention to the rise of organs of historical scholarship in the early nineteenth century. The foundation of the Hakluyt Society may be considered as of a piece with the setting up of the Camden Society in 1837, the opening of the Public Record Office in the following year, and the creation of other public and private organisations intent on publishing historical records, such as the Bannatyne Club and the Spalding Club in Scotland. The reorganisation and re-cataloguing of historical material at the British Museum and Royal Geographical Society directly or indirectly masterminded by Major, and undertaken at the India Office by Markham and Foster, fit into this pattern. And to some extent so do the services of Major in relation to the Society of Antiquaries and the Royal Society of Literature, to Yule in relation to the Royal Asiatic Society, and to de Beer in relation to Friends of the National Libraries and the National Arts Collections Fund – on all of which bodies the individual served as a member of the executive council.[1] A fair number of the Society's past editors also prepared editions for other societies, and many of them served these societies in other ways. It can be argued that this 'heritage' activity tended to engender respect for and acceptance of the current forms of British socio-political institutions, such as Parliament and the courts of law. By drawing attention to the exploits of previous explorers and adventurers, the Hakluyt Society fulfilled an analogous purpose: we repeat that to some degree it validated and justified European exploration and commercial exploitation of the resources of overseas areas of the world.

★   ★   ★

[1] There might be added the services of an important figure in the early years of the Society, Admiral Malcolm, in setting up the Bombay Geographical Society.

Inasmuch as the Society for long concentrated on the 'Hakluyt period', the texts in English were at intervals recommended to the readership for their literary quality, as prime examples of Elizabethan or Jacobean prose (see the essay by Hair). If the founding of the Hakluyt Society thus had something in common with the contemporary founding of several societies devoted to the publication and study of early English texts, it was also related to contemporary pre-occupations with travel and exploration, and hence with 'travel literature', not least because of the Hakluyt Society's descent from the Royal Geographical Society. Travel as a particularly commendable form of human activity ('broadening the mind'), and hence the literature of travel, have always provided an interest drawing a number of subscribers to the Society and many readers to its volumes. Yet a distinction can be made between travel and exploration, a distinction which tends to separate the Hakluyt Society from its parent body, the Royal Geographical Society. That body was given its inception in 1830 by members of the Raleigh Travellers Club, founded three years earlier, essentially a dining club to which members brought choice viands from the parts of the world they had visited. Such a club bore witness to the continuing strength of the notion of the 'grand tour' as part of the education of men of the upper classes. Travel literature, while noting the exotic, was (and still is) concerned as much with the subjective experience of the traveller as with the region visited; the effects on individual sensibilities of the new environment and the new peoples encountered tending to take prominence. Thus, in the early nineteenth century topographical descriptions could be fitted into contemporary notions of the Sublime and the Picturesque.[1]

Some of the conflict between opposing views of the aim of travel, subjective reward or objective description, comes through in a passage from an address to the Royal Geographical Society in 1838 by a notable traveller.

> But the real geographer becomes at once an ardent traveller, indifferent whether he plunges into the burning heats of tropical deserts, plains, or swamps, launches his boat on the unknown stream, or endures the hardships of an Arctic climate, amidst perpetual snows and ice, or scales the almost inaccessible heights of the Chimborazo or the Himálaya. Buoyed up in his greatest difficulties by the consciousness that he is labouring for the good of his fellow creatures, he feels delight that he is upon ground untrodden by man, that every step he makes will serve to

[1] Beau Riffenburgh, *The Myth of the Explorer*, London, 1993, pp. 9–14. An early Honorary Secretary of the RGS produced a paper on 'Picturesque descriptions' (C. R. Markham, *The Fifty Years' Work of the Royal Geographical Society*, London, 1881, p. 39).

enlarge the sphere of human knowledge, and that he is laying up for himself a store of gratitude and fame.[1]

In practice, from the start the RGS was under constant pressure to be 'scientific' and produce useful objective results. It thus had to encourage 'exploration' rather than 'travel'. Although disputes about the proper activities for those who called themselves geographers, as reflected in their lectures and publications, rumbled on till the 1890s, exploration won the day.[2] It came to be required that a visitor to a little known area should take astronomical observations to determine his position and in other ways conform to best scientific practice. In contrast, the Hakluyt Society remained more of a haven for those interested in travel in the older and more romantic sense. The Society's nineteenth-century editors rarely included dull lists of places with their latitudes and longitudes. Texts did not necessarily have contemporary utility (although claims were occasionally made that they assisted explorers); rather it was generally expected that they should have a measure of literary merit, even if translations, and preferably make exciting reading. If, on the one hand, the Society thus tended to avoid the more scientific, but sometimes more Gradgrinderish aspects of the RGS, on the other hand its declared concern with exploration saved it from veering away totally from objective description and merely providing reading fodder for scenic voyeurism and tourism. Travel in the past, as described and interpreted, was thought to yield returns in the area of cultural under-standing – even although this was seldom proclaimed explicitly and never in this terminology. Probably because the approach was histori-cal and not 'scientific' (in the narrow sense of the term general in the nineteenth century), the Hakluyt Society was, in fact, helping Euro-peans, and particularly the British, to move towards a new understand-ing of the world and appreciation of its peoples.

Future research on the Society might well include a focus on the nature of that appreciation, as fostered by the choice of texts to be published and the way the texts were introduced. Edward Said and his disciples have recently argued that interest of the kind displayed by the Society was part of an intellectual apparatus deployed to produce a particular notion of the 'Orient', the term by extension referring to all non-European regions. This 'Orientalism', it is claimed, was a 'Western

---

[1] 1836 anniversary address to the RGS by W. R. Hamilton, as quoted in Markham, *Fifty Years' Work*, p. 37.

[2] Probably it was the tradition of travel that made exploration a fit occupation for gentlemen, this being perhaps analogous to the way other sciences were made respectable in the mid nineteenth century. See J. Morell and A. Thackray, *Gentlemen of Science. The Early Years of the British Association for the Advancement of Science*, Oxford, 1981.

style for dominating, restructuring and having authority over the Orient'.[1] But both the historical reality of the encounter between Europeans and non-Europeans, spread over many centuries, and the understanding of it by a body such as the Hakluyt Society, appear to have been far more complex than such an easy verdict would imply. It can be argued, for instance, that to some extent there was a counter-current of 'restructuring', the Orient influencing and changing the West. Further, we have seen that there was only limited association between the Society and imperial pursuits. Nevertheless, it is consistent with the argument of this essay that the Hakluyt Society emerged and developed at a period of self-confident British expansion, economic, territorial and cultural, and was concerned to advance the study of the history of European expansion. That being so, it will be proper in the future to examine more closely the possible connections, explicit and implicit, between prevailing British relationships with the non-European world and the intellectual, financial and emotional pre-occupations of the Hakluyt Society members, officers and editors. And this should cover not merely the period of imperial advance and enthusiasm up to, say, 1914, but also the period of imperial decline and gradual victory of anti-imperial sentiment thereafter.

★   ★   ★

It would, however, be wrong to conclude other than by taking the widest overview of all. Historians, including editors, may examine and use records from varying angles at different periods, and their own viewpoints are worth later critical assessment. But without records there can be no interpretations, valid or otherwise, indeed no serious history. Whether or not there are 'lessons from the past', humanity and scholarship equally demand that such records as survive the irreversible depredations of time be brought to light and made available for study. In respect of a fundamental category of records of world history, the written texts of initial and early encounter, the Hakluyt Society has done just that, for one hundred and fifty years. It seems set to continue as successfully. Because the texts it has published are now in the light and accessible in a world language, interpretations may proceed.

---

[1] Edward Said, *Orientalism*, London, 1978, p. 3. For a critique of the work of Said and those who have accepted his basic stance, and a more balanced view of the subject, see John MacKenzie, *Orientalism. History, Theory and the Arts*, Manchester, 1995. However, neither of these studies nor, as far as we are aware, any others in the same area have mentioned the Hakluyt Society.

Appendices

A Listing of Hakluyt Society Publications 1847–1995

An Index to the Listing

A List of Officers of the Hakluyt Society 1846–1996

Contributors to the Volume

PUBLICATIONS OF
THE HAKLUYT SOCIETY 1847–1995

A listing compiled by

P. E. H. Hair

EXPLANATION OF THE LISTING

Previous lists

1. This listing updates, enlarges, revises and restyles a series of lists of HS volumes. From the 1850s onwards, cumulative lists of titles, with names of editors and limited other details, appeared in occasional volumes (in the additional sections of supplementary material at the front or rear devoted to Society affairs), the final list appearing in 1931 (HS 2/166). These lists had also appeared in a brochure entitled 'Prospectus' which was prepared and issued at intervals from at least the 1910s; and updated lists continued to be issued after 1931 in this form. These lists have the particular disadvantage that they progressively updated the titles and honorifics of still-living past editors. A revised list prepared by R. A. Skelton and printed in the Centenary commemorative volume of 1946 (HS 2/93), pp. vi–xxv, updated and added more details: in turn this list was updated, presumably also by Skelton, in later prospectuses and finally in the 1956 Prospectus (HS OB/6). A further updated list, prepared by E. L. C. Mullins and printed in *The Hakluyt Handbook* of 1974 (HS 2/144–5), pp. 611–48, was compiled somewhat differently, adding summary descriptions of the content of volumes but omitting certain details of the earlier lists, notably the pagination of volumes. As far as the earlier lists advanced chronologically, the present listing takes its details of pagination, maps and illustrations mainly from the Skelton lists, while the summary descriptions of contents of volumes are mainly from the Mullins list. Comparable information on post-1973 volumes is the work of the present compiler, or in a few instances is borrowed from an updating of the Mullins list prepared by Professor Loren Pennington. The present listing adds information about the supplementary material (see below) which forms part of certain volumes.

2. The present listing differs from previous lists in that it attempts to represent more closely the information on the title-page and the contemporary editorial presentation. Editorial and typographic practice has inevitably changed over a period of a century and a half, hence the present list achieves a measure of historical accuracy at the expense of total consistency in bibliographical presentation.

Title-pages

3. The present listing copies in full the title-page of each volume in respect of the information supplied regarding the contents and the editor(s). Repetitions of this information between volumes of a single edition are, however, omitted and indicated by three dots (...). The verses and other literary dedications which very occasionally appeared in early editions are not copied. The present listing adds emphasis, in the form of *italics* for the title, and **bold** print for the name(s) of editor(s) and translator(s).

4. The original punctuation is followed. Occasionally in the nineteenth century and increasingly thereafter until it became the rule, normal punctuation was replaced in the main title, and at times elsewhere on the title-page, by lining. When lining replaces necessary punctuation, the lining is indicated (/).

5. Consistently up to the 1920s and commonly thereafter, editorial practice was to set the whole title-page in upper case letters. In the present listing, lower case letters are introduced, initial capitals being retained, either according to the consistent usage on other title-pages of the period, or else according to current editorial practice. From the 1940s, however, initial capitals were frequently reduced, at times to normal prose usage, especially on sub-titles, and this has been followed, despite the inconsistency with previous titles.

6. Personal titles of editors and honorifics after their names are given, but for any individual only on first appearance in any specific form, repetition thereafter being omitted and indicated by three dots (...).

Numbering and dates

7. Originally volumes were not numbered. Within lists of previous publications appearing in the supplementary material in certain volumes (for supplementary material see 10–14 below), the numbering of items was not introduced until 1861 (HS 28). The number of a volume, indicated on its half-title page, was introduced in 1874 (HS 51) and has continued since.

8. Some volumes carry two dates, the subscription or issue year, and the imprint or publication year. On occasions these dates differ. The issue year date was shown on the half-title page between 1905 (HS 2/12) and 1982 (HS 2/152), this page having before 1905 shown the publication year date. The early annual reports, which lack a month of publication, are vague about which volumes were assigned to particular subscription years, but in 1861 the list of previous publications, as well as having numbered items, also supplied for all earlier items a subscription year ('Issued in 1847', etc). This was presumably the work of the Honorary Secretary at the time, Clements Markham, but it is not clear how he obtained the information and not all the issue year dates he assigned to early volumes would seem to be correct, since some are later than the publication date. (The Mullins and Skelton lists avoided the issue, the former supplying only issue dates, the latter only publication dates.)

9. The listing below supplies the publication date, and if the issue date was different this is added in brackets. The annual reports and the British Museum date stamps on volumes suggest that occasionally the stated publication year may have preceded the actual year of release and distribution, but more research is required on this problem.

Supplementary material

10. Apart from a list of officers and members of Council which has appeared in all Hakluyt Society volumes to date, normally before the title page, and which is included in the regular pagination, separately-paginated supplementary material relating to the Society was included in most Hakluyt Society volumes from publication dates 1849 up to 1931 (HS 4 – HS 2/66), intermittently but generally in any single-volume edition or the first volume of a multi-volume edition.

11. This supplementary material always included, separately paginated and of increasing length and contents (in 1925 it reached 45 pages), what might be termed a prospectus of the Society, beginning with a statement of aims. It continued with lists of various features (previous publications, works in progress, works suggested, subscriber membership, agents), and for long concluded with 'Laws of the Society'. The 1904 material is in thin blue paper covers and perhaps copies were always distributed separately in this brochure form too; certainly at intervals from at least the 1920s up to 1956 a brochure entitled 'Prospectus' containing such material was separately issued.

12. The supplementary material could include, separately paginated,

the annual report. This appeared, in only one volume each issue year, between publication dates 1849 and 1894 (HS 5 – HS 91), and again in 1902 and 1903 (HS 2/9, 15), its length normally three or four pages. The reports for 1853, 1874–1877, 1881 and 1883 are, however, lacking in the sets of volumes examined. Whether before 1895 the annual report was published separately as well as within volumes is not known; after 1894, other than in 1902–1903, it was only published separately, as is the case today.

13. Normally the annual report preceded the remaining supplementary material, and all the material appeared at the front of volumes up to the 1880s, and thereafter at the rear of volumes. The pagination(s) of the supplementary material are distinguished in the listing by being in *italic numbers*.

14. It must be added that the Liverpool University and Aberdeen University sets do not exactly match as regards the supplementary material, mainly in respect of whether the material is at the front or the rear of volumes but occasionally in respect of material totally missing from specific volumes in either set. This is most likely the result of errors in collation at the printers (or binders) when the volumes were being made up, and it raises the possibility that other sets may have different dispositions of this material.

Pagination

15. Over the period conventions in respect of inserting page numbers have changed, as have bibliographical conventions in respect of the count of page numbers. The count in the listing below does not always agree with that in previous lists (whose conventions were unexplained). Here the pagination count represents numbered pages, as indicated by the highest printed number. It does not include the unnumbered blank verso page which often appears after the last numbered page of a section, but it adds one to the highest printed number where a printed but unnumbered page occurs after the last numbered page of a section, as happens occasionally. Where pagination runs on to a second or third volume, the starting page-number for the later text is given as the actual page-number of the first page of text, whether printed or not.

Illustrations

16. The count of illustrations requires explanation. The earlier volumes had no lists of illustrations, and subsequent lists were variously and inconsistently titled, while the Mullins overall list did not include a

count of illustrations. Skelton, following the earlier lists, supplied a count of illustrations distinguished, by categories of form of production, between 'maps' and 'plates', that is, (normally) fold-out maps and full-page plates. With the increasing use of maps reproduced on photographic plates and of in-text illustrations these distinctions are impossible to maintain. The count in the present listing therefore attempts to categorise solely by form of content, distinguishing 'maps' (including charts, plans, sketch maps, etc) from 'illustrations', i.e. all other illustrations. This has led to recounting for the earlier volumes, but it needs to be understood that the distinction is not always clear (for instance, are birds' eye views of harbours 'maps' or 'illustrations'?). Nor do my totals always agree with Skelton's, perhaps because of different interpretations of what constitutes a separate map or illustration. Hence the distribution between the two categories is suggestive and approximate only. Skelton provided, in the same volume, a separate list of 'the most important maps' in earlier editions (pp. xxvii–xxxiv), with an index, and in the 1956 Prospectus (HS OB/6) the list and index were updated to 1955: it is regretted that it has not proved possible to update further this useful list.

Publisher and place of publication

17. The place of publication has always been London, except between HS 2/108 of 1957 and HS 2/143 of 1973 when it was Cambridge, and except in the single case of HS 2/59 of 1927, which for an unstated reason was published at Oxford. London is not noted in the listing, but the exceptional places are noted. The publisher's name is not noted in the listing. From 1847 to 1954 the wording was 'London / Printed for the Hakluyt Society', and in 1955 'London / For the Hakluyt Society'. Between 1957 and 1973 it read 'Cambridge / Published for the Hakluyt Society / At the University Press'. Since then it has read 'The Hakluyt Society / London'.

Other publishers

18. Extra Series nos 1–12, 14–33, 37 and 38 appeared in commercial editions by other publishers. Only volumes whose binding bears the name of the Society were issued under its auspices.

Reprints

19. Since the 1960s most volumes of the First and Second Series and a few of the Extra Series have been reissued by various reprint publishers,

on licence from the Society, and microfiche and microform reproductions have more recently become available. Details appear in the Society's annual List of Publications in Print.

FIRST SERIES

1. *The Observations of Sir Richard Hawkins, Knt., in his Voyage into the South Sea in the Year 1593. Reprinted from the Edition of 1622.* Edited by **C. R. Drinkwater Bethune**, Captain R.N.

    1847. Pages xvi, 246.

    The text edited 'with only such slight alterations as were necessary where the sense of the author had been obviously marred by a misprint'. Original index only. For a second edition see First Series 57 below.

2. *Select Letters of Christopher Columbus, with other Original Documents, relating to his Four Voyages to the New World.* Translated and Edited by **R. H. Major**, Esq., of the British Museum.

    1847. Pages xc, 240.

    Five letters by Columbus describing his first, third, and fourth voyages; another by Dr Chanca, physician, descriptive of the second voyage; and an extract from the will of Diego Mendez, one of Columbus's officers on the fourth voyage. With Spanish texts. Two copies of this edition were printed in vellum and one presented to the British Museum. For a second edition see First Series 43 below; for a third edition see Second Series 65 and 70 below.

3. *The Discovery of the Large, Rich, and Beautiful Empire of Guiana, with a Relation of the Great and Golden City of Manoa (which the Spaniards call El Dorado), etc. Performed in the Year 1595, by Sir W. Ralegh, Knt., Captain of Her Majesty's Guard, Lord Warden of the Stanneries, and Her Majesty's Lieutenant-General of the County of Cornwall. Reprinted from the Edition of 1596, with some Unpublished Documents relative to that Country.* Edited, with Copious Explanatory Notes and a Biographical Memoir, by Sir **Robert H. Schomburgk**, Ph.D., Knight of the Royal Prussian Order of the Red Eagle, of the Royal Saxon Order of Merit, of the French Order of the Legion of Honour, etc.

    1849 (1848). Pages lxxxv, 240 + 1 map.

    With Anon, 'Of the Voyage for Guiana', probably written in 1596, Ralegh's journal of the second voyage, 1617–18, and miscellaneous documents. Typographical errors of the 1596 text were corrected.

4. *Sir Francis Drake his Voyage, 1595, by Thomas Maynarde, together with*

the Spanish Account of Drake's Attack on Puerto Rico. Edited, from the Original Manuscripts, by **W. D. Cooley**.

1849 (1848). Pages *12*, viii, 65.

With a translation of the Spanish document. The volume is the first to include supplementary material on the Society, but the material does not include an annual report.

5. *Narratives of Voyages towards the North-West, in Search of a Passage to Cathay and India. 1496 to 1631. With Selections from the early Records of the Honourable the East India Company and from MSS. in the British Museum.* [Edited] By **Thomas Rundall**, Esq.

1849. Pages *8, 4*, xx, 260 + 2 maps.

Accounts of the voyages of Cabot, Davis, Frobisher, and others, drawn chiefly from the works of Hakluyt, Purchas, Harris and Foxe. The supplementary material includes the 1848 annual report.

6. *The Historie of Travaile into Virginia Britannia; expressing the Cosmographie and Comodities of the Country, together with the Manners and Customes of the People. Gathered and observed as well by those who went first thither as collected by William Strachey, Gent., the first Secretary of the Colony.* Now First Edited, from the Original Manuscript, in the British Museum, by **R. H. Major**, of the British Museum.

1849. Pages xxxvi, 203 + 1 map, 6 illustrations.

From British Library, Sloane MS 1622.

7. *Divers Voyages touching the Discovery of America and the Islands adjacent. Collected and published by Richard Hakluyt, Prebendary of Bristol, in the Year 1582.* Edited, with Notes and an Introduction, by **John Winter Jones** of the British Museum.

1850 (1849). Pages cxi, 171, 6, *8* + 2 maps, 1 illustration.

The original printed text. The edition described as prepared 'for the subscribers of 1849' and as the third volume of 1849 in the report in the next volume.

8. *Memorials of the Empire of Japon in the XVI and XVII Centuries.* Edited, with Notes, by **Thomas Rundall**.

1850. Pages *4, 8*, xxxviii, 187 + 1 map, 5 illustrations.

Documents, including a description of Japan in the sixteenth century and the letters of William Adams, 1611–17. The supplementary material includes the 1849 annual report.

9. *The Discovery and Conquest of Terra Florida, by Don Ferdinando de Soto and six hundred Spaniards his Followers, written by a Gentleman of Elvas, employed in all the Action, and translated out of Portuguese, by Richard Hakluyt. Reprinted from the Edition of 1611.* Edited, with Notes and an

Introduction and a Translation of a Narrative of the Expedition by Luis Hernandez de Biedma, Factor to the same, by **William B. Rye**, of the British Museum.

1851. Pages *4*, *8*, lxvii, 200, v + 1 map.

For Hakluyt's translation, see *The Hakluyt Handbook* (Second Series, 144–5 below), pp. 42, 252–5. The translation of Hernández de Biedma's narrative was made from Ternaux-Compans, *Recueil de pièces sur la Floride*, Paris, 1841. The supplementary material includes the 1850 annual report.

10. *Notes upon Russia: Being a Translation of the earliest Account of that Country, entitled Rerum Muscoviticarum commentarii, by the Baron Sigismund von Herberstein, Ambassador from the Court of Germany to the Grand Prince Vasiley Ivanovich, in the years 1517 and 1526.* Translated and Edited, with Notes and an Introduction, by **R. H. Major**, ...

Volume I. 1851. Pages *8*, clxii, 116, errata slip + 2 illustrations.

The first edition of the *Commentarii* appeared in Vienna in 1549, but it is not clear which edition was used for this translation. Continued in First Series 12 below.

11. *The Geography of Hudson's Bay: Being the Remarks of Captain W. Coats, in many Voyages to that Locality, between the Years 1727 and 1751. With an Appendix containing Extracts from the Log of Capt. Middleton on his Voyage for the Discovery of the North-West Passage in H.M.S. "Furnace," in 1741–2.* Edited by **John Barrow**, Esq., F.R.S., F.S.A.

1852 (1851). Pages x, 147, *8*.

Fuller documentation of the Middleton and related voyages to Hudson's Bay is supplied in Second Series 177 and 181 below. This edition described in the 1851 annual report as 'delivered to 1851 Members'.

12. *Notes upon Russia* . . . .

Volume II. 1852. Pages *4*, iv, 266 + 2 maps, 1 illustration.

With an appendix of documents, translated and in part collected by Richard Eden and printed from the 1577 edition of his *History of Travayle in the West and East Indies*, revised by Richard Willes. The supplementary material consists of the 1851 annual report.

13. *A true Description of three Voyages by the North-East towards Cathay and China, undertaken by the Dutch in the Years 1594, 1595, and 1596, by Gerrit de Veer. Published at Amsterdam in the Year 1598, and in 1609 translated into English by William Phillip.* Edited by **Charles T. Beke**, Phil.D., F.S.A.

1853. Pages *8*, cxlii, 291 + 4 maps, 12 illustrations.

With an appendix of documents printed by Hakluyt and Purchas. Revised in First Series 54 below.

14. *The History of the great and mighty Kingdom of China and the Situation Thereof. Compiled by the Padre Juan Gonzalez de Mendoza, and now Reprinted from the early Translation of R. Parke.* Edited by Sir **George T. Staunton**, Bart. With an Introduction by **R. H. Major**, Esq., of the British Museum, Honorary Secretary of the Hakluyt Society.
[Volume 1]. 1853 (1854 [sic]). Pages *4, 8,* lxxxiii, 172.
From the 1588 black-letter edition, after the 1586 Madrid edition. The supplementary material includes the 1852 annual report.

15. *The History of the great and mighty Kingdom of China . . . .* Volume II. 1854. Pages *8,* 350.

16. *The World Encompassed by Sir Francis Drake; being his next voyage to that to Nombre de Dios. Collated with an unpublished manuscript of Francis Fletcher, chaplain to the expedition.* [Edited] with Appendices illustrative of the Same Voyage, and Introduction, by **William Sandys Wright Vaux**.
1854 (1855 [sic]). Pages *8,* xl, 295 + 1 map.
From the 1628 edition 'collected out of the notes of Master Francis Fletcher', collated with British Library, Sloane MS 61.

17. *History of the two Tartar Conquerors of China, including the two Journeys into Tartary of Father Ferdinand Verbiest in the Suite of the Emperor Kang-hi: From the French of Père Pierre Joseph d'Orléans, of the Company of Jesus. To which is added Father Pereira's Journey into Tartary in the Suite of the same Emperor, From the Dutch of Nicholaas Witsen.* Translated and Edited by the Earl of **Ellesmere**. With an Introduction by **R. H. Major**, ...
1854. Pages *4,* xv, vi, 153.
The first is from the 1688, Paris, edition; the narrative of Father Pereira's journey and the text of two letters by Father Verbiest are from the 1692, Amsterdam, edition. The supplementary material consists of the 1854 annual report.

18. *A Collection of Documents on Spitzbergen & Greenland, comprising a translation from F. Martens'* Voyage to Spitzbergen: *a Translation from Isaac de la Peyrère's* Histoire du Groenland: *and God's Power and Providence in the Preservation of Eight Men in Greenland nine Months and twelve Dayes.* Edited by **Adam White**, Esq., of the British Museum.
1855 (1856 [sic]). Pages *4,* xvi, 288 + 2 maps.
The first is from an English collection published in 1694; the second from the *Relation du Groenland*, Paris, 1663; the third is the text of Edward Pelham's tract, London, 1631. The supplementary material consists of the 1855 annual report.

19. *The Voyage of Sir Henry Middleton to Bantam and the Maluco islands; being the Second Voyage set forth by the Governor and Company of Merchants of London trading into the East-Indies.* From the Edition of 1606. Annotated and Edited by **Bolton Corney**, M.R.S.L.

> 1855 (1856 [sic]). Pages 4, 8, xii, 83, 52, viii + 3 maps.
>
> The 1606 title-page begins: *The last East-Indian voyage.* The appendix includes commissions, letters of James I addressed to foreign rulers, and other documents. For a second edition, see Second Series 88 below. The supplementary material includes the 1856 annual report.

20. *Russia at the Close of the Sixteenth Century. Comprising the Treatise "Of the Russe Common Wealth," by Dr Giles Fletcher; and The Travels of Sir Jerome Horsey, Knt., now for the first time printed entire from his own Manuscript.* Edited by **Edward A. Bond**, Assistant Keeper of the Manuscripts in the British Museum.

> 1856 (1857 [sic]). Pages cxxxiv, 392.
>
> The first is a reprint of the London, 1591, edition; the second relates to the late sixteenth century. With additional documents descriptive of Russia and the missions of the two writers.

21. *History of the New World, by Girolamo Benzoni, of Milan. Shewing his Travels in America, from A.D. 1541 to 1556: with some Particulars of the Island of Canary.* Now First Translated, and Edited by Rear-Admiral **W. H. Smyth**, K.S.F., D.C.L., etc etc etc.

> 1857. Pages 4, iv, 280 + 19 illustrations.
>
> Text originally published at Venice, 1572. The supplementary material consists of the 1857 annual report.

22. *India in the Fifteenth Century. Being a Collection of Narratives of Voyages to India in the Century preceding the Portuguese Discovery of the Cape of Good Hope; from Latin, Persian, Russian, and Italian Sources, now first Translated into English.* Edited, with an introduction, by **R. H. Major**, Esq., F.S.A..

> 1857 (1558 [sic]). Pages xc, 49, 39, 32, 10, [8].
>
> The travels of Abd-er-Razzak, Nicolò Conti, Athanasius Nikitin, and Hieronimo di Santo Stefano.

23. *Narrative of a Voyage to the West Indies and Mexico in the years 1599–1602, With Maps and Illustrations. By Samuel Champlain.* Translated from the Original and Unpublished Manuscript, with a Biographical Notice and Notes, by **Alice Wilmere**. Edited by **Norton Shaw**.

> 1859 (1858). Pages 4, xcix, 48, 8 (loose) + 4 maps, 5 illustrations.
>
> Text written c. 1602 (now considered an invention). The supplementary material consists of the 1858 annual report.

24. *Expeditions into the Valley of the Amazons, 1539, 1540, 1639.* Translated and Edited, with Notes, by **Clements R. Markham**, F.R.G.S., Author of "Cuzco and Lima".

1859. Pages *4, 8,* lxiv, 190 + 1 map.

The expeditions of Gonzalo Pizarro, Francisco de Orellana, and Father Cristóbal de Acuña. With a 'List of the Principal Tribes of the Valley of the Amazons'. The supplementary material includes the 1859 annual report.

25. *Early Voyages to Terra Australis, now called Australia: a Collection of Documents, and Extracts from early Manuscript Maps, illustrative of the History of Discovery on the Coasts of that vast Island, from the Beginning of the Sixteenth Century to the Time of Captain Cook.* Edited, with an Introduction, by **R. H. Major**, ...

1859. Pages cxix, 200 + 5 maps.

From Spanish and Dutch sources and relating to Spanish and Dutch enterprises. A separate pamphlet dated 1861 and containing an article by Major on the discovery of Australia by the Portuguese in 1601, reprinted from *Archaeologia,* 38, 1860, was distributed 'for insertion as a Supplement' to HS 25.

26. *Narrative of the Embassy of Ruy Gonzalez de Clavijo to the Court of Timour, at Samarcand, A.D. 1403–6.* Translated, for the First Time, with Notes, a Preface, and an Introductory Life of Timour Beg, by **Clements R. Markham**, F.R.G.S.

1859 (1860 [sic]). Pages lvi, 200 + 1 map.

27. *Henry Hudson the Navigator: the Original Documents in which his Career is recorded.* Collected, partly Translated, and Annotated, with an Introduction, by **G. M. Asher**, LL.D.

1860. Pages *4, 8,* ccxviii, 292 + 2 maps.

The supplementary material includes the 1860 annual report.

28. *The Expedition of Pedro de Ursua & Lope de Aguirre in Search of El Dorado and Omagua in 1560–1.* Translated from Fray Pedro Simon's "*Sixth historical Notice of the Conquest of Tierra Firme*". By **William Bollaert**, Esq., F.R.G.S. With an Introduction by **Clements R. Markham**.

1861. Pages *4, 8,* lii, 237 + 1 map.

From the Spanish text, published at Cuenca, 1627. The supplementary material includes the 1861 annual report.

29. *The Life and Acts of Don Alonzo Enriquez de Guzman, a Knight of Seville, of the Order of Santiago, A.D. 1518 to 1543.* Translated from an Original and Inedited Manuscript in the National Library at Madrid; with Notes and an Introduction, by **Clements R. Markham**, F.S.A.,

F.R.G.S., Corr. Mem. of the University of Chile. Author of "Cuzco and Lima".

1862. Pages *3, 8*, xxv, 168 + 1 illustration.

Includes accounts of travel in Europe and Peru. The supplementary material includes the 1862 annual report.

30. *The Discoveries of the World, from their First Original unto the Year of Our Lord 1555, by Antonio Galvano, governor of Ternate. Corrected, Quoted and Published in England, by Richard Hakluyt, (1601).* Now Reprinted, With the Original Portuguese Text; and Edited by Vice-Admiral **Bethune**, C.B.

1862. Pages iv, viii, 242.

For the edition of António Galvão, *Tratado* . . . , used by Hakluyt and the edition here reprinted, see *The Hakluyt Handbook* (Second Series 144–5 below), pp. 41, 344, 603.

31. *Mirabilia Descripta. The Wonders of the East, by Friar Jordanus, of the Order of Preachers and Bishop of Columbum in India the Greater, (circa 1330).* Translated from the Latin Original, as published at Paris in 1839, in the *Recueil de Voyages et de mémoires*, of the Society of Geography, with the Addition of a Commentary, by Colonel **Henry Yule**, C.B., F.R.S.G., late of the Royal Engineers (Bengal).

1863 (1862). Pages *4, 8*, iv, xvii, 68.

The supplementary material includes the 1863 annual report.

32. *The travels of Ludovico de Varthema in Egypt, Syria, Arabia Deserta and Arabia Felix, in Persia, India, and Ethiopia, A.D. 1503 to 1508.* Translated from the Original Italian Edition of 1510, with a Preface, by **John Winter Jones**, Esq., F.S.A. And Edited, with Notes and an Introduction, by **George Percy Badger**, late Government Chaplain in the Presidency of Bombay, Author of "The Nestorians and their rituals," etc, etc, etc.

1863 (1864 [sic]). Pages cxxii, 321 + 2 maps.

33. *The Travels of Pedro de Cieza de León, A.D. 1532–50, contained in the First Part of his Chronicle of Peru.* Translated and Edited, with Notes and an Introduction, by **Clements R. Markham**, F.S.A., F.R.G.S., Author of "Cuzco and Lima," "Travels in Peru and India," and a "Quichua Grammar and Dictionary".

Volume I. 1864. Pages *4, 12*, xvi, lvii, 438.

From the 1554 Antwerp edition. Continued from another source in First Series 68 below. The supplementary material includes the 1864 annual report.

34. *Narrative of the Proceedings of Pedrarias Davila in the Provinces of Tierra*

Firme or Castilla del Oro, and of the Discovery of the South Sea and the Coasts of Peru and Nicaragua. Written by the Adelantado Pascual de Andagoya. Translated and Edited, with Notes and an Introduction, by **Clements R. Markham**.

1865. Pages *12, 4*, xxix, 88 + 1 map.

Text written c. 1514. The supplementary material includes the 1865 annual report.

35. *A Description of the Coasts of East Africa and Malabar in the Beginning of the Sixteenth Century, by Duarte Barbosa, a Portuguese*. Translated from an Early Spanish Manuscript in the Barcelona Library, with Notes and a Preface, by the Hon. **Henry E. J. Stanley**.

1866 (1865). Pages xi, 336 + 2 illustrations.

Text written c. 1514. Revised edition, Second Series 44, 49 below.

36. *Cathay and the Way Thither. Being a Collection of Medieval Notices of China*. Translated and Edited by Colonel **Henry Yule**, ... With a Preliminary Essay on the Intercourse between China and the Western Nations previous to the Discovery of the Cape Route.

Volume I. 1866. Pages *4, 15*, ccliii, 250, iii + 3 maps, 6 illustrations.

Containing the travels of Friar Odoric of Pordenone, 1316–30, and letters and reports from missionary friars from Cathay and India, 1292–1338, in English translation. With a list of 'illustrations from drawings by the author'. This and the following item have continuous main pagination. The supplementary material includes the 1866 annual report.

37. *Cathay and the way thither ....* .

Volume II. 1866. Pages 253–596, xcviii + 1 map, 3 illustrations.

Contemporary notices of Cathay under the Mongols, from Rashíduddín; Pegolotti's notices of the land route to Cathay and of Asiatic trade in the fourteenth century; Marignolli's recollections of eastern travel; Ibn Battūta's travels in Bengal and China; the journey of Benedict Goës from Agra to Cathay; all in English translation, with Latin and Italian texts of Odoric's narrative. For a revised version of the whole work, see Second Series 33, 37, 38, 41 below.

38. *The Three Voyages of Martin Frobisher, in search of a Passage to Cathaia and India by the North-West, A.D. 1576–8. Reprinted from the First Edition of Hakluyt's Voyages, with Selections from Manuscript Documents in the British Museum and State Paper Office*. By Rear-Admiral **Richard Collinson**, C.B.

1867. Pages *4, 16*, xxvi, 376 + 2 maps, 1 illustration.

With Edward Sellman's account of the third voyage, and a list of artefacts from Frobisher encampments, etc, found by C. F. Hall and deposited with the Royal Geographical Society. The additional documents relate to numerous aspects of the financing and fitting out of the expedition. According to the British Museum date stamp, despite the stated publication date, actual publication did not occur until 1869. The supplementary material includes the 1867 annual report.

39. *The Philippine Islands, Moluccas, Siam, Cambodia, Japan, and China, at the Close of the Sixteenth Century. By Antonio De Morga.* Translated from the Spanish, with Notes and a Preface, and a Letter from Luis Vaez de Torres describing his Voyage through the Torres Straits. By the Hon. **Henry E. J. Stanley**.

1868. Pages xxiv, 431 + 2 illustrations.

From a transcription of the 1609 Mexico edition. The appendix includes a brief continuation of the history of the Philippines to 1868, particularly with regard to government and commerce. Revised edition, Second Series 140 below.

40. *The Fifth Letter of Hernan Cortes to the Emperor Charles V, containing an Account of his Expedition to Honduras.* Translated from the Original Spanish by Don **Pascual de Gayangos** of the Spanish Academy; Corresponding Member of the Institute of France.

1868. Pages 3, xvi, 156.

The letter is dated 1526. The supplementary material consists of the 1868 annual report.

41. *First Part of the Royal Commentaries of the Yncas by the Ynca Garcillasso de la Vega.* Translated and Edited, with Notes and an Introduction, by **Clements R. Markham**. Volume I (Containing Books I, II, III, and IV).

1869. Pages xi, 359.

From the 1609 Lisbon edition. Continued in First Series 45 below.

42. *The Three Voyages of Vasco da Gama, and his Viceroyalty. From the Lendas da India of Gaspar Correa. Accompanied by Original Documents.* Translated from the Portuguese, with Notes and an Introduction, by the Hon. **Henry E. J. Stanley**.

1869. Pages 2, lxxx, 430, xxxvi + 3 illustrations.

The additional documents, mainly letters and reports to the king of Portugal, are in Portuguese. The supplementary material consists of the 1869 annual report.

43. *Select Letters of Christopher Columbus, with other Original Documents relating to this Four Voyages to the New World.* Translated and Edited by **R. H. Major**, ... , Keeper of the Department of Maps and Charts in the British Museum and Hon. Sec. of the Royal Geographical Society. Second Edition.

1870. Pages iv, cxlii, 254 + 3 maps, 1 illustration (in colour).

A revised translation of the documents in no. 2 above, with the editor's reply to J. A. Froude's strictures on the earlier edition in the *Westminster Review* (1852) and in his *Short Studies on Great Subjects*, vol. 2.

44. *History of the Imâms and Seyyids of 'Omân by Salîl-ibn-Razîk, from A.D. 661–1856.* Translated from the Original Arabic and Edited, with Notes, Appendices, and an Introduction, continuing the History down to 1870, by **George Percy Badger**, F.R.G.S., ...

1871. Pages cxxviii, 435 + 1 map.

45. *First Part of the Royal Commentaries of the Yncas . . . .* by **Clements R. Markham**, C.B. Volume II (Containing Books V, Vi, VII, VIII and IX).

1871. Pages 553.

Continued from 41 above.

46. *The Canarian, or, Book of the Conquest and Conversion of the Canarians in the Year 1402, by Messire Jean de Béthencourt, Kt., Lord of the Manors of Bethencourt, Reville, Gourret, and Grainville de Teinturière, Baron of St. Martin le Gaillard, Councillor and Chamberlain in Ordinary to Charles V and Charles VI, composed by Pierre Bontier, Monk, and Jean le Verrier, Priest.* Translated and Edited by **Richard Henry Major**, ...

1872. Pages 2, [2], 2, [2], lv, 229 + 1 map, 2 illustrations.

With the fifteenth-century French text. The supplementary material consists of the 1870 and 1871 annual reports.

47. *Reports on the Discovery of Peru. I. Report of Francisco de Xeres, Secretary to Francisco Pizarro. II. Report of Miguel de Astete on the Expedition to Pachacamac. III. Letter of Hernando Pizarro to the Royal Audience of Santo Domingo. IV. Report of Pedro Sancho on the Partition of the Ransom of Atahuallpa.* Translated and Edited, with Notes and an Introduction, by **Clements R. Markham**, ...

1872. Pages xxii, 143 + 1 map.

Documents of c. 1533.

48. *Narratives of the Rites and Laws of the Yncas.* Translated from the Original Spanish Manuscripts, and Edited, with Notes and an Introduction, by **Clements R. Markham**, ...

1873 (1872). Pages 4, 4, 12, xx, 220.

Accounts by Cristóbal de Molina, c. 1570–84, Juan de Santa Cruz (an Indian), c. 1620, Francisco de Avila, 1608, and Polo de Ondegardo, c. 1560. Indexes include one of Quichua vocabulary. The supplementary material includes the 1872 and 1873 annual reports.

49a. *Travels to Tana and Persia, by Josafa Barbaro and Ambrogio Contarini.*

Translated from the Italian by William Thomas, Clerk of the Council to Edward VI, and by **S. A. Roy**, Esq., And Edited, with an Introduction, by Lord **Stanley** of Alderley.
1873. Pages xi, 175.

49b. *A Narrative of Italian Travels in Persia in the Fifteenth and Sixteenth Centuries.* Translated and Edited by **Charles Grey**.
1873. Pages xvii, 231.
The two editions are bound together but separately paginated. The second contains accounts by Caterino Zeno, Giovan Maria Angiolello, Vincentio d'Alessandri, and an unknown merchant.

50. *The Voyages of the Venetian Brothers, Nicolò and Antonio Zeno, to the Northern Seas in the XIVth Century, comprising the latest known Accounts of the Lost Colony of Greenland; and of the Northmen in America before Columbus.* Translated and Edited, with Notes and an Introduction, by **Richard Henry Major**, ...
1873. Pages ciii, 64 + 4 maps.
The Italian text of the Zenos' narrative, and the Danish and Latin texts of Ivar Bardsen's description of Greenland in the fourteenth century, with English translation.

51. *The Captivity of Hans Stade of Hesse, in A.D. 1547–1555, among the Wild Tribes of Eastern Brazil.* Translated by **Albert Tootal**, Esq., of Rio de Janeiro, and annotated by **Richard F. Burton**.
1874. Pages *12*, xcvi, 169.
From the 1557 Marburg edition.

52. *The First Voyage Round the World, by Magellan.* Translated from the Accounts of Pigafetta, and other Contemporary Writers. Accompanied by Original Documents, with Notes and an Introduction, by Lord **Stanley** of Alderley.
1874. Pages lx, 257, xx + 2 maps, 5 illustrations.
Includes the log-book of Francisco Alvo or Alvaro, Pigafetta's treatise on navigation and his account of the voyage, Gaspar Correa's account, other anonymous narratives, and documents relating to the cost and other aspects of the expedition.

53. *The Commentaries of the great Afonso Dalboquerque, second Viceroy of India.* Translated from the Portuguese Edition of 1774, with Notes and an Introduction, by **Walter de Gray Birch**, F.R.S.L., Senior Assistant of the Department of Manuscripts in the British Museum; Honorary Secretary of the British Archaeological Association, etc.
Volume I. 1875. Pages lx, 256 + 2 maps, 1 illustration.
Continued in First Series 55, 62, and 69 below.

54. *The Three Voyages of William Barents to the Arctic Regions, 1594, 1595, and 1596, by Gerrit de Veer.* First Edition Edited by Charles T. Beke, Phil.D., F.S.A. 1853. Second Edition, with an Introduction, by Lieutenant **Koolemans Beynen** (Royal Netherlands Navy).
   1876. Pages clxxiv, 289 + 2 maps, 12 illustrations.
   Revised edition of 13 above. With a 'Postscript' of five unnumbered pages at the beginning of the text.

55. *The Commentaries of the great Afonso Dalboquerque* . . . . . . by **Walter de Gray Birch**, . . . , Honorary Librarian of the Royal Society of Literature.
   Volume II. 1877 (1875). Pages cxxxiv [error: cxxxvi], 242 + 1 map, 2 illustrations.
   Part ii of the 1774 edition.

56. *The Voyages of Sir James Lancaster, Kt., to the East Indies, with Abstracts of Journals of Voyages to the East Indies, during the Seventeenth Century, preserved in the India Office. And the Voyage of Captain John Knight (1606), to seek the North-West Passage.* Edited by **Clements R. Markham**, C.B., F.R.S.
   1877. Pages xxii, 314.
   The abstracts relate to the voyages of Keeling and Hawkins, Sharpie, Sir Henry Middleton, Thomas Love, Nicholas Downton, and Ralph Cross. With a calendar of ships' journals of the seventeenth century and a list of ships employed by the East India Company in the same period. For a revised edition of the Lancaster voyages, see Second Series 85 below.

57. *The Hawkins' Voyages during the Reigns of Henry VIII, Queen Elizabeth, and James I.* Edited, with an Introduction, by **Clements R. Markham**, ...
   1878 (1877). Pages 7, lii, 453 + 1 illustration.
   A revised edition of 1 above, with narratives of the voyages of Sir Richard Hawkins' grandfather William, of his father Sir John, and of his cousin William Hawkins, from manuscripts and printed editions. The supplementary material consists of the 1878 annual report.

58. *The Bondage and Travels of Johann Schiltberger, a Native of Bavaria, in Europe, Asia, and Africa, 1396–1427.* Translated from the Heidelberg MS edited in 1859 by Professor Karl Friedrich Neumann, by Commander **J. Buchan Telfer**, R.N., F.S.A., F.R.G.S. With Notes by Professor **P. Bruun** of the Imperial University of South Russia, at Odessa, and a Preface, Introduction and Notes by the Translator and Editor.
   1879 (1878). Pages xxxii, 263, 3 + 1 map.
   The supplementary material consists of the 1879 annual report.

59a. *The Voyages and Works of John Davis the Navigator.* Edited, with an Introduction and Notes, by **Albert Hastings Markham**, Captain R.N., F.R.G.S., Author of "A Whaling Cruise in Baffin's Bay," "The Great Northern Sea," and "Northward Ho!".

1880 (1878). Pages xcv, 392 + 2 maps, 15 illustrations.

Includes *The worldes hydrographical Discription* (1595), *The seamans secrets* (1607), a list of works on navigation available before and during the reign of Elizabeth, and her latters patent to Adrian Gilbert and others for the exploration of a North-West Passage.

59b. *The Map of the World, A.D. 1600, called by Shakspere "the new map, with the augmentation of the Indies".* To illustrate the Voyages of John Davis.

1880. Pages 16.

Bound separately, with notes by **C. H. Coote**.

60. *The Natural and Moral History of the Indies, by Father Joseph de Acosta. Reprinted from the English Translated Edition of Edward Grimston, 1604.* And Edited, with Notes and an Introduction, by **Clements R. Markham**, ... Volume I The Natural History (Books I, II, III, and IV).

1880 (1879). Pages xlv, 295.

Concerned chiefly with Mexico and Peru. The main pagination of this and the following volume is continuous.

61a. *The Natural and Moral History of the Indies* . . . . Volume II The Moral History (Books V, VI and VII).

1880 (1879). Pages xiii, 295 [sic]-551.

61b. *Map of Peru to illustrate the Travels of Cieza de León, in 1532–50; The Royal Commentaries of Garcilasso de la Vega (1609); and The Natural and Moral History of the Indies, by Father Joseph de Acosta (1608),* by **Clements R. Markham**, C.B.

n.d. 'To accompany Acosta, Natural and Moral History.'

Bound separately.

62. *The Commentaries of the great Afonso Dalboquerque* . . . .

Volume III. 1880. Pages 2, lvi, 308, errata slip + 3 maps, 3 illustrations.

Continued from 55 above. Part iii of the 1774 edition. With descriptions of Malacca and Goa translated from Pedro Barretto de Resende's *Livro do Estado da Índia Oriental.* The supplementary material consists of the 1880 annual report.

63. *The Voyages of William Baffin, 1612–1622.* Edited, with Notes and an Introduction by **Clements R. Markham**, ...

1881 (1880). Pages lix, 192 + 8 maps, 1 illustration.

From narratives and journals by John Gatonbe, Robert Fotherby, and others, with Baffin's letters, journals, and other observations, and various treatises on the probability of a North-West Passage.

64. *Narrative of the Portuguese Embassy to Abyssinia during the Years 1520–1527, by Father Francisco Alvarez.* Translated from the Portuguese, and Edited, with Notes and an Introduction, by Lord **Stanley** of Alderley. 1881. Pages xxviii, 416.
Revised edition, Second Series 114, 115.

65. *The Historye of the Bermudaes or Summer Islands.* Edited, from a MS. in the Sloane Collection, British Museum, by General Sir **J. Henry Lefroy**, R.A., C.B., K.C.M.G., F.R.S., etc. / formerly Governor of the Bermudas; Author of "Memorials of the Discovery and early Settlement of the Bermudas or Somers Islands".
1882 (1881). Pages xii, 327, *3* + 1 map, 3 illustrations.
The account relating to 1609–1622 by Nathaniel Butler. Additional documents include a note on constitutional procedure at the first General Assembly held at St George's, 1 August 1620. The supplementary material consists of the 1882 annual report.

66. *Diary of Richard Cocks, Cape-Merchant in the English Factory in Japan 1615–1622 with Correspondence.* Edited by **Edward Maunde Thompson**.
Volume I. 1883 (1882). Pages liv, 349.
Ends December 1617. Continued to 1622 in the following item, together with Cocks's correspondence with the East India Company and others.

67. *Diary of Richard Cocks . . . .*
Volume II. 1883 (1882). Pages 368.

68. *The Second Part of the Chronicle of Peru by Pedro de Cieza de León.* Translated and Edited, with Notes and an Introduction, by **Clements R. Markham**, ...
1883. Pages lx, 247.
Continues the narrative in First Series 33 above.

69. *The Commentaries of the great Afonso Dalboquerque . . . .*
Volume IV. 1884 (1883). Pages xxxv, 324 + 6 illustrations.
Continued from 62 above. Part iv of the 1774 edition. With Portuguese descriptions of places and fortresses in Portuguese India, and a pedigree of Albuquerque from British Library MSS. With an index to all four volumes.

70. *The Voyage of John Huyghen van Linschoten to the East Indies. From the Old English Translation of 1598. The First Book, containing his Description of the East. In Two Volumes.* Edited, the First Volume by the late

Arthur Coke Burnell, Ph.D., C.I.E., of the Madras Civil Service. The Second Volume by Mr **P. A. Tiele** of Utrecht.

Volume I. 1885 (1884). Pages lii, 307, *3*.

The supplementary material consists of the 1884 annual report.

71. *The Voyage of John Huyghen van Linschoten . . . .*
Volume II. 1885 (1884). Pages xv, 341, *16*.

The supplementary material does not include an annual report.

72. *Early Voyages and Travels to Russia and Persia by Anthony Jenkinson and other Englishmen. With some Account of the First Intercourse of the English with Russia and Central Asia by Way of the Caspian Sea.* Edited by **Edward Delmar Morgan**, Member of the Hakluyt Society, and **Charles Henry Coote**, of the British Museum.

Volume I. 1886 (1885). Pages clxii, 176. + 2 maps (one of parchment), 3 illustrations.

From the manuscript writings of Jenkinson and other agents of the Muscovy Company in the second half of the sixteenth century, and including correspondence between Elizabeth I and Ivan IV, and reports to Cecil and the Council. This and the following volume have continuous pagination.

73. *Early Voyages and Travels to Russia and Persia . . . .*
Volume II. 1886. Pages 177–496, *16*, *3* + 2 maps, 1 illustration.

The supplementary material includes the 1885 annual report.

74. *The Diary of William Hedges, Esq. (afterwards Sir William Hedges), during his Agency in Bengal; as well as on his Voyage Out and Return Overland (1681–1687). Volume I. The Diary, with Index.* Transcribed for the Press, with introductory Notes, etc. by **R. Barlow**, Esq., and illustrated by Copious Extracts from Unpublished Records, etc. by Colonel **Henry Yule**, R.E., C.B., Ll.D., President of the Hakluyt Society.

1887 (1886). Pages xii, 265, *3*.

Continued in First Series 75 and 78 below. The supplementary material consists of the 1886 annual report.

75. *The Diary of William Hedges, Esq. . . . . Volume II. Containing Notices regarding Sir William Hedges, documentary Memoirs of Job Charnock, and other biographical and miscellaneous Illustrations of the Time in India. . . . .*

1888 (1886). Pages *3*, ccclx, *16* + 13 illustrations.

The supplementary material includes the 1887 annual report.

76. *The Voyage of François Pyrard of Laval to the East Indies, the Maldives, the Moluccas, and Brazil.* Translated into English from the Third French edition of 1619, and Edited, with Notes, by **Albert Gray**, formerly of

the Ceylon Civil Service, assisted by **Harry Charles Purvis Bell**, of the Ceylon Civil Service.

Volume I. 1887. Pages lviii, 452 + 1 map, 11 illustrations.

This volume covers from 1601 to Pyrard's arrival at Goa in 1608. Continued in First Series 77 and 80 below.

77. *The Voyage of François Pyrard* . . . .
Volume II, Pt. 1. 1888 (1887). Pages xlvii, 287 + 7 illustrations.

From 1608 to Pyrard's departure from Goa in 1610. This volume has continuous main pagination with First Series 80 below.

78. *The diary of William Hedges, Esq* . . . . *Volume III. Containing Documentary Contributions to a Biography of Thomas Pitt, Governor of Fort St George; with Collections on the early History of the Company's Settlement in Bengal; and on early Charts and Topography of the Húglí River.* . . . .
1889 (1888). Pages 3, 19, cclxii + 1 map, 8 illustrations.

With pedigrees of Pitt of Blandford St Mary and Pitt of Stratfieldsay, and indexes to all three volumes. The supplementary material is the 1888 annual report.

79a. *Tractatus de globis et eorum usu. A Treatise descriptive of the Globes constructed by Emery Molyneux, and published in 1592. By Robert Hues.* Edited, with Annotated Indices and an Introduction, by **Clements R. Markham**, ...
1889 (1888). Pages l, 229 + 1 illustration.

79b. *Sailing Directions for the Circumnavigation of England, and for a Voyage to the Straits of Gibraltar, from a 15th Century MS.* Edited, with an Account of the MS., by **James Gairdner**; with a Glossary by **Edward Delmar Morgan**.
1889 (1888). Pages 37, 16 + 1 map.

The two bound together but separately paginated. The first contains the text of the 1638 English translation, *A learned treatise of globes* by John Chilmead (but 'usually attributed to Edmund Chilmead with apparent corrections'); the title-page of the Latin original is dated 1594.

80. *The Voyage of François Pyrard* . . . .
Volume II, Pt. 2. 1890 (1889). Pages 4, xii, 289–572, 16 + 2 maps.

Continued from 77 above. Covering 1610–1611, the return to France. With a treatise on animals, trees, and fruits, and advice upon the voyage to the East Indies. The supplementary material includes the 1889 annual report.

81. *The Conquest of the River Plate (1535–1555). I. Voyage of Ulrich Schmidt to the Rivers La Plata and Paraguai. From the Original German Edition, 1567. II. The Commentaries of Alvar Núñez Cabeza de Vaca, from the Original Spanish edition, 1555.* Translated for the Hakluyt Society.

With Notes and an Introduction, by **Luis L. Dominguez**, Minister Plenipotentiary of the Argentine Republic, Corresponding Member of the Argentine Geographical Institute and of the Royal Spanish Academy of History.

1891 (1889). Pages xxxix, 282 + 1 map.

The translator is not named.

82. *The Voyage of François Leguat of Bresse to Rodriguez, Mauritius, Java, and the Cape of Good Hope.* Transcribed from the First English Edition. Edited and annotated by Captain **Samuel Pasfield Oliver**, late Royal Artillery.

Volume I. 1889 (1890). Pages *4*, lxxxviii, 137, *16* + 6 maps, 4 illustrations.

The edition of 1708. This volume covering 1689–1693. The supplementary material includes the 1890 annual report.

83. *The Voyage of François Leguat . . . .*

Volume II. 1891 (1890). Pages xviii, 139–433 + 5 maps, 5 illustrations.

Covering 1693–1698.

84. *The Travels of Pietro della Valle in India. From the old English Translation of 1664, by G. Havers. In Two Volumes.* Edited, with a Life of the Author, an Introduction and Notes, by **Edward Grey** (late Bengal Civil Service).

Volume I. 1892 (1891). Pages *4*, lvi, 192 + 2 maps, 2 illustrations.

Letters 1–3, 1623. This and the following volume have continuous main pagination. The supplementary material consists of the 1891 annual report.

85. *The Travels of Pietro della Valle in India. . . . .*

Volume II. 1892 (1891), Pages xii, 193–455, *16*.

Letters 4–8, 1623–1624.

86. *The Journal of Christopher Columbus (during his First Voyage, 1492–93), and Documents relating to the Voyages of John Cabot and Gaspar Corte Real.* Translated, with Notes and an Introduction, by **Clements R. Markham**, . . . , President of the Hakluyt Society.

1893 (1892). Pages liv, 259, *16* + 3 maps, 1 illustration.

With Paolo Toscanelli's sailing directions in letters to Columbus, and documents relating to Sebastian Cabot.

87. *Early Voyages and Travels in the Levant. I.- The Diary of Master Thomas Dallam, 1599–1600. II.- Extracts from the Diaries of Dr John Covel, 1670–1679. With Some Account of the Levant Company of Turkey merchants.* Edited, with an Introduction and Notes, by **James Theodore Bent**, F.S.A., F.R.G.S.

1893 (1892). Pages *3*, xlv, 305, *16*.
The supplementary material consists of the 1892 annual report.

88. *The Voyages of Captain Luke Foxe of Hull, and Captain Thomas James of Bristol, in Search of a North-West Passage, in 1631–32; with Narratives of the earlier North-West Voyages of Frobisher, Davis, Weymouth, Hall, Knight, Hudson, Button, Gibbons, Bylot, Baffin, Hawkridge, and others.* Edited, with Notes and an Introduction, by **Miller Christy**, F.L.S.
Volume I. 1894 (1893). Pages *3*, ccxxxi, 259 + 2 maps, 2 illustrations.
Containing part of the text of *North-west Fox*, London, 1635. This and the following volume have continuous main pagination. The supplementary material consists of the 1893 annual report.

89. *The Voyages of Captain Luke Foxe of Hull, and Captain Thomas James of Bristol* . . . .
Volume II. 1894 (1893). Pages viii, 261–681 + 3 maps, 1 illustration.
The concluding part of *North-west Fox*, and the text of *The Strange and Dangerous Voyage of Captaine Thomas James*, London, 1633, with documents relating to early voyages to Hudson's Bay and the North-West.

90. *The Letters of Amerigo Vespucci and Other Documents illustrative of his Career.* Translated, with Notes and an Introduction, by **Clements R. Markham**, . . . , President of the Hakluyt Society.
1894. Pages xliv, 121, *16*.

91. *Narratives of the Voyages of Pedro Sarmiento de Gambóa to the Straits of Magellan.* Translated and Edited, with Notes and an Introduction, by **Clements R. Markham**, ... President of the Royal Geographical Society.
1895 (1894). Pages xxx, 401, *3*, *16*.
The voyages of 1579–1589. The supplementary material includes the 1894 annual report.

92. *The History and Description of Africa and of the Notable Things therein contained, written by Al-Hassan Ibn-Mohammed Al-Wezaz Al-Fasi, a Moor, baptised as Giovanni Leone, but better known as Leo Africanus. Done into English in the Year 1600, by John Pory.* And now Edited, with an Introduction and Notes, by Dr. **Robert Brown**.
Volume I. 1896 (1895). Pages viii, cxi, 224 + 4 maps.
Containing Book I of the original. This and the following two volumes have continuous pagination.

93. *The History and Description of Africa* . . . .
Volume II. 1896 (1895). Pages 225–698.
Containing Books II–IV.

94. *The history and Description of Africa* . . . .
Volume III. 1896 (1895). Pages 699–1119.
Containing Books V-IX and Pory's additions.

95. *The Chronicle of the Discovery and Conquest of Guinea. Written by Gomes Eannes de Azurara.* Now first done into English by **Charles Raymond Beazley**, M.A., F.R.G.S., late Fellow of Merton College, Oxford; Corresponding Member of the Lisbon Geographical Society, and **Edgar Prestage**, B.A., Oxon., Knight of the Most Noble Portuguese Order of S. Thiago, Corresponding Member of the Lisbon Royal Academy of Sciences, the Lisbon Geographical Society, etc. Volume I. (Chapters I-XL) With an Introduction on the Life and Writings of the Chronicler.
1896. Pages lxvii, 127, *16* + 4 maps, 1 illustration.
Written c. 1450. Continues in First Series 100 below.

96. *Danish Arctic Expeditions, 1605 to 1620. In Two Books. Book I.- The Danish Expeditions to Greenland in 1605, 1606, and 1607; to which is added Captain James Hall's Voyage to Greenland in 1612. Book II.- The Expedition of Captain Jens Munk to Hudson's Bay in Search of a North-West Passage in 1619–20.* Edited by **C. C. A. Gosch**.
Book I. 1897 (1896). Pages xvi, cxvii, 205 + 10 maps.

97. *Danish Arctic Expeditions* . . . .
Book II. 1897. Pages cxviii, 187 + 4 maps, 2 illustrations.

98. *ΚΟΣΜΑ ΑΙΓΥΠΤΙΟΥ ΜΟΝΑΧΟΥ ΧΡΙΣΙΑΝΙΚΗ ΤΟΠΟΓΡΑΦΑ / The Christian Topography of Cosmas, an Egyptian Monk.* Translated from the Greek, and Edited, with Notes and Introduction, by **John W. McCrindle**, M.A., M.R.A.S., F.R.G.S., late Principal of the Government College at Patna, and Fellow of Calcutta University; Author of a series of works on Ancient India, as described by the Classical Authors, including the "Indica" of Ctesias, Megásthenes, and Arrian; the "Periplus of the Erythraean Sea"; Ptolemy's "Geography of India"; and the "Invasion of India by Alexander the Great".
1897. Pages xii, xxvii, 398, *16* + 4 illustrations.

99. *A Journal of the First Voyage of Vasco da Gama, 1497–1499.* Translated and Edited, with Notes, an Introduction and Appendices. By **E. G. Ravenstein**, F.R.G.S., Corresponding Member of the Geographical Society of London.
1898. Pages xxxvi, 250, *16* + 8 maps, 23 illustrations.
With letters of King Manuel and Girolamo Sernigi, 1499, and early seventeenth-century Portuguese accounts of da Gama's first voyage.

100. *The Chronicle of the Discovery and conquest of Guinea . . . . Volume II (Chapters 41–97).* With an Introduction on the early History of African Exploration, Cartography, etc.
1899 (1898). Pages cl, 362, *20* + 5 maps.
Continued from 95 above.

SECOND SERIES

2/1. *The Embassy of Sir Thomas Roe to the Court of the Great Mogul, 1615–1619, as Narrated in his Journal and Correspondence.* Edited from Contemporary Records by **William Foster**, B.A., Editor of "Letters Received by the East India Company, 1615," Joint Editor of "The First Letter Book of the East India Company, 1600–1619," Honorary Secretary of the Hakluyt Society.
Volume I. 1899. Pages x, lxviii, 271 + 1 map, 3 illustrations.
The main pagination of this and the following volume is continuous. A revised edition independently issued, 1926.

2/2. *The embassy of Sir Thomas Roe . . . .*
Volume II. 1899. Pages viii, 273–586, *20* + 1 map, 3 illustrations.

2/3. *The Voyage of Sir Robert Dudley, afterwards styled Earl of Warwick and Leicester and Duke of Northumberland, to the West Indies, 1594–1595, narrated by Capt. Wyatt, by himself, and by Abram Kendall, Master.* Edited by **George F. Warner**, Assistant-Keeper of Manuscripts, British Museum.
1899. Pages lxvi, 104, *20* + 1 map, 2 illustrations.

2/4. *The Journey of William of Rubruck to the Eastern Parts of the World, 1253–55, as Narrated by Himself. With Two Accounts of the Earlier Journey of John of Pian de Caprine.* Translated from the Latin and Edited, with an Introductory Notice, by **William Woodville Rockhill**, Honorary Corresponding Member of the Royal Geographical Society.
1900. Pages lvi, 304, *20*.
For a later edition of the primary work, see 173 below.

2/5. *The Voyage of Captain John Saris to Japan, 1613.* Edited by Sir **Ernest Mason Satow**, K.C.M.G., Her Majesty's Envoy Extraordinary and Minister Plenipotentiary to China, and late Her Majesty's Envoy Extraordinary and Minister Plenipotentiary to Japan.
1900. Pages lxxxviii, 242, *20*.
Saris's journal, with two of his reports to the East India Company, a letter, and extracts from Purchas.

2/6. *The Strange Adventures of Andrew Battell of Leigh, in Angola and the Adjoining Regions. Reprinted from "Purchas his Pilgrimes."* Edited, with Notes and a Concise History of Kongo and Angola, by **E. G. Ravenstein**.

1901 (1900). Pages xx, 210, *20* + 2 maps.

Adventures between 1589 and 1607. With part of Anthony Knivet's account of his activities in the same countries, from the same source. The spine title incorrectly reads 'Andrew Battell in Guinea', a geographical blunder.

2/7. *The Discovery of the Solomon Islands by Alvaro de Mendaña in 1568. Translated from the Original Spanish Manuscripts.* Edited, with Introduction and Notes, by Lord **Amherst** of Hackney, and **Basil Thomson**.

Volume I. 1901. Pages lxxxvi, 191 + 3 maps, 17 illustrations.

Four narratives, two of them by or attributed to Mendaña's companions, Hernando Gallego and Pedro Sarmiento. This and the following volume have continuous pagination.

2/8. *The Discovery of the Solomon Islands . . . .*

Volume II. 1901. Pages 195–482, *20* + 2 maps, 16 illustrations.

Three further narratives, including one by Gomez Catoira.

2/9. *The Travels of Pedro Teixeira; with his "Kings of Harmuz", and Extracts from his "Kings of Persia."* Translated and Annotated by **William F. Sinclair**, Bombay Civil Service (Retd.), with Further Notes and an Introduction by **Donald Ferguson**.

1902 (1901). Pages cvii, 292, *4*, *24*.

Texts of c.1600. The first supplementary material appears to be the annual report for 1902 but the inner pages are misprinted with a repetition of pp. cxxx-cxxxi instead of the actual report.

2/10. *The Portuguese Expedition to Abyssinia in 1541–1543, as Narrated by Castanhoso, with Some Contemporary Letters, the Short Account of Bermudez, and Certain Extracts from Correa.* Translated and Edited by **R. S. Whiteway**, Bengal Civil Service (Retired).

1902. Pages cxxxii, 296, *24* + 1 map, 2 illustrations.

Including a bibliography of Abyssinia, pp. civ-cxxxii.

2/11. *Early Dutch and English Voyages to Spitsbergen in the Seventeenth Century, including Hessel Gerritsz. "Histoire du pays nommé Spitsberghe," 1613,* Translated into English, for the First Time, by **Basil H. Soulsby**, F.S.A., of the British Museum; *and Jacob Segersz. van der Brugge "Journael of dagh register,"* Amsterdam, *1634,* Translated into English, for the First Time, by **J. A. J. de Villiers**, of the British Museum. Edited, with Introduction and Notes, by Sir **W. Martin Conway**, F.S.A.

1904 (1902). Pages xvi, 191, *37* + 3 maps, 3 illustrations.

With affidavits by English merchants and seamen relating to happenings at Spitzbergen in 1618, and two documents telling of events there in 1634–5, taken from Public Record Office, State Papers Domestic. Including a bibliography of Spitzbergen, pp. ix–xiv.

2/12. *A Geographical Account of Countries round the Bay of Bengal, 1669 to 1679, by Thomas Bowrey* / Edited by Lt.-Col. Sir **Richard Carnac Temple**, Bart., C.I.E.

1905 (1903). Pages lvi, 387, *37* + 1 map, 19 illustrations.

2/13. *The Voyage of Captain Don Felipe Gonzalez in the Ship of the Line* San Lorenzo, *with the Frigate* Santa Rosalia *in Company, to Easter Island in 1770–1: Preceded by an Extract from Mynheer Jacob Roggeveen's Official Log of his Discovery and Visit to Easter Island in 1722.* Transcribed, Translated, and Edited by **Bolton Glanvill Corney**, Companion of the Imperial Service Order.

1908 (1903). Pages lxxvii, 176, *40* + 3 maps, 4 illustrations.

Journals, instructions, minutes, and despatches, with an extract from the 1825 journal of Lieut. George Peard, of H.M.S. *Blossom*. Preface by *Cyprian Bridge*. Includes a bibliography of 'Easter Island and the Pacific Ocean', pp. 147–58.

2/14. *The Voyages of Pedro Fernandez de Quiros, 1595 to 1606.* Translated and Edited by Sir **Clements Markham**, K.C.B., P.R.G.S., President of the Hakluyt Society.

Volume I. 1904. Pages xlviii, 320 + 3 maps.

Three narratives of voyages to the Pacific. The main pagination of this and the following volume is continuous.

2/15. *The Voyages of Pedro Fernandez de Quiros . . . .*

Volume II. 1904. Pages viii, 323–555, [4], *31* + 3 maps.

Two further narratives, including one by Torquemada, and an appendix of letters and memoranda addressed to Philip III. The supplementary material includes the annual report for 1903, bound in blue covers.

2/16. *The Journal of John Jourdain, 1608–1617, describing his Experiences in Arabia, India, and the Malay Archipelago* / Edited by **William Foster**, . . . , Editor of "The Embassy of Sir Thomas Roe to the Great Mogul," . . . , etc.

1905. Pages lxxxii, 394, *40* + 4 maps.

An account of the East India Company's fourth voyage; with an appendix containing William Revett's 1609 account of the Seychelles, and reports on other places by merchants and seamen of the same period.

2/17. *The Travels of Peter Mundy, in Europe and Asia, 1608–1667.* Edited by Lt.-Col. Sir **Richard Carnac Temple**, Bart., ... , Editor of 'A Geographical Account of Countries round the Bay of Bengal.' Vol. I: Travels in Europe, 1608–1628.

1907 (1905). Pages lxiii, 284 + 6 maps.

With an appendix of extracts from the writings of seventeenth-century travellers to the Levant. Continued in 35, 45, 46, 55, and 78 below.

2/18. *The East and West Indian Mirror, Being an Account of Joris van Speilbergen's Voyage Round the World (1614–1617), and the Australian Navigations of Jacob le Maire.* Translated and Edited, with Notes and an Introduction, by **John A. J. de Villiers**, ...

1906. Pages lxi, 272, *40* + 2 maps, 23 illustrations.

From the Dutch edition of 1619, with its illustrations, many of them birds'eye 'maps'.

2/19. *A New Account of East India and Persia. Being Nine Years' Travels, 1672–1681, by John Fryer.* Edited, with Notes and an Introduction, by **William Crooke**, formerly of the Bengal Civil Service.

Volume I. 1909. Pages xxxviii, 353, *35* + 1 map, 6 illustrations.

Composed in the form of letters and first published in 1698. This volume contains Letters I-III. Continued in 20 and 39 below.

2/20. *A new account of East India and Persia* ... .

Volume II. 1912. Pages 371 + 1 map.

Letters IV and part of V, with a chapter on Indian history and customs, and another on coins, weights, and precious stones.

2/21. *The Guanches of Tenerife / The Holy Image of Our Lady of Candelaria / and the Spanish Conquest and Settlement, by the Friar Alonso de Espinosa of the Order of Preachers.* Translated and Edited, with Notes and an Introduction, by Sir **Clements Markham**, ...

1907. Pages xxvi, 221 + 2 maps, 4 illustrations.

Written 1580–90, first published at Seville in 1594. The edition includes a bibliography of the Canary Islands, 1341–1907, pp. 187–203.

2/22a. *History of the Incas / by Pedro Sarmiento de Gamboa / and the Execution of the Inca Tupac Amaru / by Captain Baltasar de Ocampo /* Translated and Edited, with Notes and an Introduction, by Sir **Clements Markham**, ...

1907. Pages xxii, 395 + 2 maps, 2 illustrations.

The first text was dedicated to Philip II in 1572; the second was written in 1610. The edition includes a bibliography of Peru, pp. 341–58. Pagination of this and the following volume is continuous.

2/22b. *History of the Incas ... / With a Supplement: A Narrative of the Vice-Regal Embassy to Vilcabamba, 1571, and of the Execution of the Inca*

Tupac Amaru, December 1571, by Friar Gabriel de Oviedo, of Cuzco. 1573.
Translated by Sir **Clements Markham**.
1908 (1907). Pages 397–412.
Another eye-witness account. Internally stated to have been issued as a separate item, yet in fact bound within the previous item.

2/23. *The True History of the Conquest of New Spain. By Bernal Diaz del Castillo, One of its Conquerors. From the Exact Copy made of the Original Manuscript. Edited and published in Mexico by Genaro García.* Translated into English and Edited, with Introduction and Notes, by **Alfred Percival Maudslay**, M.A., Hon. Professor of Archaeology, National Museum, Mexico.
[Volume I.] 1908. Pages lxv, 396 + 3 maps, 15 illustrations.
Books I-IV (1517–19) concerning the discovery of Mexico and the expeditions of Francisco Hernández de Cordova and Hernan Cortés, the march inland, and the war in Tlaxcala. The edition includes a bibliography of Mexico, pp. 311–68. Continued in 24, 25, 30, and 40 below.

2/24. *The True History of the Conquest of New Spain . . . .*
Volume II. 1910. Pages xvi, 343 + 1 map, 13 illustrations.
Books V-IX (1519–20) concerning the march to Mexico, the stay there, the expedition against Narvaez, the flight from Mexico, and the halt at Tepeaca.

2/25. *The True History of the Conquest of New Spain . . . .*
Volume III. 1910. Pages 38 + 8 maps.
A box of maps and plans of the valley and city of Mexico, several reproduced from sixteenth-century originals.

2/26. *Storm van 's Gravesande / The Rise of British Guiana / Compiled from His Despatches /* By **C. A. Harris**, C.B., C.M.G., Chief Clerk, Colonial Office, and **J. A. J. de Villiers**, ...
Volume I. 1911. Pages 372 + 3 maps, 4 illustrations.
Extracts from despatches by Laurens Storm van 'sGravesande to the directors of the Zeeland Chamber of the Dutch West India Company, 1738–72, selected to illustrate the rise and expansion of the colony, with a detailed introduction. This volume ends with the despatch dated 15 March 1760. For May 1760 to September 1772, see the following volume, with which the pagination is continuous.

2/27. *Storm van 's Gravesande . . . .*
Volume II. 1911. Pages 373–704, *xxxvi* + 1 illustration.

2/28. *Early Spanish Voyages to the Strait of Magellan /* Translated and Edited, with a Preface, Introduction and Notes, by Sir **Clements Markham**, K.C.B., Vice-President of the Hakluyt Society.
1911. Pages xii, 288 + 12 maps.

Narratives of the second voyage through the strait, commanded by the Comendador Loaysa and Sebastián del Cano, 1524–6, the third voyage, under the command of Simón de Alcazaba, 1534–5, and the reconnaissance by Bartolomé and Gonzalo de Nodal, 1618–19; with a fragment relating to the expedition sent by the bishop of Plasencia under Alonso de Camargo, 1539–41.

2/29. *Book of the Knowledge of All the Kingdoms, Lands, and Lordships that are in the World, and the Arms and Devices of each Land and Lordship, or of the Kings and Lords who possess them. Written by a Spanish Franciscan in the Middle of the XIV Century. Published for the First Time / with Notes by Marcos Jiménez de la Espada, in 1877.* Translated and Edited by Sir **Clements Markham**, ...
1912. Pages xiii, 85, *xxxvi* + 20 illustrations.

2/30. *The True History of the Conquest of New Spain* . . . .
Volume IV. 1912. Pages xiv, 395 + 3 maps, 3 illustrations.
Continued from Second Series 25 above. Books X–XIII, relating the siege and capture of Mexico, 1521, and the ensuing settlement.

2/31. *The War of Quito / by Pedro de Cieza de León / and Inca Documents / * Translated and Edited by Sir **Clements R. Markham**, ...
1913. Pages xii, 212, *xxxvi*.
Book III (1543–44) of Cieza's 'Civil Wars of Peru'. The additional documents continue the narrative to c. 1568. For other sections of the same source, in volumes variously titled, see 42 and 54 below.

2/32. *The Quest and Occupation of Tahiti by Emissaries of Spain during the Years 1772–1776. Told in Despatches and other Contemporary Documents:* Translated into English and Compiled, with Notes and an Introduction, by **Bolton Glanvill Corney**, Companion of the Imperial Service Order.
Volume I. 1913. Pages lxxxviii, 363 + 3 maps, 8 illustrations.
Instructions, minutes, despatches, and other documents from Spanish and English archives, relating to exploration of the East Indies. Title should read 'Quest for and Occupation of . . .'. Continued in 36 and 43 below.

2/33. *Cathay and the Way Thither.* . . . . New Edition, Revised throughout in the Light of Recent Discoveries, by **Henri Cordier**, D.Litt., Hon. M.R.A.S., Hon. Cor. M.R.G.S., Hon. F.R.S.L., Member of the Institut de France, Professor at the École des Langues Orientales Vivantes, Paris. Volume II Odoric of Pordenone.
1913. Pages xiii, 367 + 1 map, 6 illustrations.
Volume I followed (38 below). A revised edition of First Series 36 (1866) and 37 (1866) above, whose title page was followed. The appendix contains a

Latin and an Italian text of Friar Odoric's travels in the early fourteenth century. Continued in 37 and 41 below.

2/34. *New Light on Drake / A Collection of Documents relating to his Voyage of Circumnavigation, / 1577–1580.* Translated and Edited by **Zelia Nuttall** / Illustrated by a Map and Plates.
1914. Pages lvi, 443, *xxxvi* + 3 maps, 14 illustrations.
Spanish official documents, depositions by prisoners, documents relating to Nuño da Silva, etc.

2/35. *The Travels of Peter Mundy . . . . Vol. II: Travels in Asia, 1628–1634.*
1914. Pages lxxix, 437 + 3 maps, 29 illustrations.
Continued from Second Series 17 above.

2/36. *The Quest and Occupation of Tahiti . . . .*
Volume II. 1915. Pages xlvii, 521 + 8 illustrations.
Continued from Second Series 32 above.

2/37. *Cathay and the Way Thither . . . . Vol. III: Missionary Friars – Rashíduddín – Pegolotti – Marignolli.*
1914. Pages xv, 270 + 1 map, 1 illustration.
Letters and reports of missionary friars from Cathay and India, 1292–1338; Cathay under the Mongols, from Rashiduddin's history, c. 1300–1307; Pegolotti's notices of the land route to Cathay, c. 1330–40; and John d'Marignolli's recollections of eastern travel, 1338–53, taken from his 'Chronicle of Bohemia'.

2/38. *Cathay and the Way Thither . . . . Vol. I: Preliminary Essay on the Intercourse between China and the Western Nations previous to the Discovery of the Cape Route.*
1915. Pages xxiii, 318, *xxxvi* + 1 map, 1 illustration.
With numerous supplementary extracts from writers of the first to the sixteenth century.

2/39. *A new account of East India and Persia . . . .*
Volume III. 1915. Pages viii, 271.
Continued from Second Series 20 above. Letter V (continued) – Letter VIII.

2/40. *The True History of the Conquest of New Spain . . . .*
Vol 5. 1916. Pages xv, 463, *xxxvi* + 3 maps (in pocket), 2 illustrations.
Continued from Second Series 30 above. Books XIV–XVII, relating the expedition to Honduras, the return to Mexico, the rule of the Audiencia there, and the record of the conquistadores, with an appendix including the fifth letter of Cortés to the Emperor Charles V, 1526.

2/41. *Cathay and the Way Thither* .... *Volume IV: Ibn Batuta – Benedict Goes – index.*

1916. Pages xii, 359 + 1 map, 1 illustration.

Volume I is 33 above. Ibn Baṭṭūṭa's travels in Bengal and China, c. 1347, and the journey of Goës from Agra to Cathay, 1602–7, with an index to all four volumes.

2/42. *Civil Wars of Peru / by Pedro de Cieza de León / (Part IV, Book II) / The War of Chupas /* Translated and Edited, with Notes and an Introduction, by Sir **Clements R. Markham**, ... , F.R.S., D.Sc. (Cambridge and Leeds).

1918 (1917). Pages xlvii, 386, *xxxix* + 2 maps, 2 illustrations.

This forms part of the original Book II of Cieza's 'Civil Wars of Peru'. For other sections of the same source, in volumes variously titled, see 2/31 above and 54 below.

2/43. *The Quest and Occupation of Tahiti* .... *Volume III. Containing the Diary of Maximo Rodríguez.*

1919 (1918). Pages xlix, 271 + 1 map, 7 illustrations.

Continued from Second Series 36 above. With the memorial submitted by Rodríguez to the viceroy of Peru, 1788.

2/44. *The Book of Duarte Barbosa. An Account of the Countries bordering on the Indian Ocean and their Inhabitants, Written by Duarte Barbosa, and Completed about the year 1518 A.D. Translated from the Portuguese Text First Published in 1812 A.D. by the Royal Academy of Sciences at Lisbon, in Vol. II of its Collection of Documents regarding the History and Geography of the Nations beyond the Seas,* and Edited and Annotated by **Mansel Longworth Dames**, Indian Civil Service (Retired); Vice-President Royal Asiatic Society and Royal Anthropological Institute; F.R.N.S., M.F.S. *Vol I. Including the Coasts of East Africa, Arabia, Persia and Western India as far as the Kingdom of Vijayanagar.*

1918. Pages lxxxv, 238, *xxxix* + 2 maps.

With a translation of chapter 2, the history of Rander, from Narmashankar's 'Principal events of Surat'. Continued in 49 below.

2/45. *The Travels of Peter Mundy* ... . *Vol. III, Part 1: Travels in England, Western India, Achin, Macao, and the Canton River, 1634–1637.*

1919. Pages l, 316 + 6 maps, 36 illustrations.

Continued from Second Series 35 above. Pagination of this and the following volume is continuous.

2/46. *The Travels of Peter Mundy* .... *Vol. III, Part 2: Travels in Achin, Mauritius, Madagascar, and St Helena, 1638.*

1919. Pages viii, 317–577, *xl* + 16 illustrations.

With his first appendix, consisting of notes on his China voyage, and additional documents, including papers connected with Courteen's Association, and Dutch and Portuguese accounts of the naval action off Goa, 1637.

2/47. *The Chronicle of Muntaner*. Translated from the Catalan by Lady **Goodenough**.
Volume I. 1920. Pages xc, 370 + 2 maps.
The text covers 1208–85. Continued to 1328 in 50 below, with which the the main pagination is continuous.

2/48. *Memorias antiguas historiales del Peru*. By *Fernando Montesinos*. Translated and Edited by **Philip Ainsworth Means**, M.A., with an Introduction by the late Sir **Clements R. Markham**, K.C.B., F.R.S.
1920. Pages li, 130, *xlii* + 10 illustrations.
Text written in the seventeenth century. Chronological tables added.

2/49. *The Book of Duarte Barbosa* .... *Volume II. Including the Coasts of Malabar, Eastern India, Further India, China, and the Indian Archipelago*.
1921. Pages xxxi, 286, *xlii* + 2 maps, 1 illustration.
Continued from Second Series 44 above. With translated extracts from João de Barros, *Decadas de Asia*.

2/50. *The Chronicle of Muntaner* ....
Volume II. 1921. Pages xxxiv, 371–759 + 1 map.

2/51. *Journal of the Travels and Labours of Father Samuel Fritz in the River of the Amazons between 1686 and 1723* / Translated from the Evora MS. and Edited by The Rev. Dr. **George Edmundson**
1922. Pages viii, 164, *xliii* + 2 maps.
With a translation of the Act of Possession of Pedro Teixeira, 1639, and of contemporary references in Portuguese sources to the work of Father Fritz in the Upper Amazon.

2/52. *The Journal of William Lockerby / Sandalwood Trader in the Fijian Islands during the Years 1808–1809: With an Introduction & Other Papers connected with the Earliest European Visitors to the Islands*. Edited by Sir **Everard Im Thurn**, K.C.M.G., K.B.E., C.B., and **Leonard C. Wharton**.
1925 (1922). Pages cxi, 250 + 3 maps, 3 illustrations.
The additional documents include Samuel Patterson's account of the wreck of the *Eliza*, 1808, the journal of the missionaries from the *Hibernia*, 1809, Captain Richard Siddon's experiences in Fiji in 1809–15, and extracts from periodical publications, 1804–15.

2/53. *The Life of the Icelander Jón Ólafsson / Traveller to India / Written by Himself and Completed about 1661 A.D. / with a Continuation, by Another*

Hand, up to his Death in 1679 / Translated from the Icelandic edition of Sigfús Blöndal, By **Bertha S. Phillpotts**, O.B.E., M.A., Litt.D., Mistress of Girton College, Cambridge; Author of *Kindred & Clan, The Elder Edda and Ancient Scandinavian Drama*, etc. / Volume I / Life and Travels: Iceland, England, Denmark, White Sea, Faroes, Spitzbergen, Norway / 1593–1622. Edited by the Translator.

1923. Pages xxxv, 238, *xliii* + 2 maps, 4 illustrations.

Continued, with two new editors, in 68 below.

2/54. *Civil Wars in Peru / The war of Las Salinas / by Pedro de Cieza de León* / Translated, with an Introduction, by Sir **Clements Markham**.

1923. Pages xxiv, 304.

Book I of Cieza's chronicle. For other sections of the same source, in volumes variously titled, see Second Series 31 and 42 above.

2/55. *The Travels of Peter Mundy . . . . Vol. IV: Travels in Europe 1639–1647*.

1925 (1924). Pages xlvi, 280, *xlv* + 4 maps, 17 illustrations.

Continued from Second Series 46 above. With Mundy's second appendix, including a note on English change-ringing.

2/56. *Colonising Expeditions to the West Indies and Guiana, 1623–1667*. Edited by **V. T. Harlow**, B.A., B.Litt., F.R.Hist.S., Sometime Scholar of Brasenose College, Oxford. Lecturer in Modern History at the University College, Southampton.

1925 (1924). Pages xcv, 262 + 6 maps, 2 illustrations.

Journals, narratives, and descriptions relating to British colonization in the islands of St Christopher, Nevis, Barbados, Tobago and Trinidad, and in Guiana, and to Admiral de Ruyter's raid in the West Indies, 1664–5.

2/57. *Francis Mortoft: his Book / Being his Travels through France and Italy 1658–1659*. Edited by **Malcolm Letts**, Author of "Bruges and its Past".

1925. Pages xxxiv, 216 + 2 maps, 1 illustration.

2/58. *The Papers of Thomas Bowrey / 1669–1713 / Discovered in 1913 by John Humphreys, M.A., F.S.A., and now in the possession of Lieut.-Colonel Henry Howard, F.S.A. / Part I. Diary of a Six Weeks' Tour in 1698 in Holland and Flanders / Part II. The Story of the Mary Galley, 1704–1710*. Edited by Lieut.-Colonel Sir **Richard Carnac Temple**, Bt., C.B., C.I.E., F.B.A., F.S.A.

1927 (1925). Pages xxx, 398 + 5 maps, 9 illustrations.

2/59. *Travels of Fray Sebastien Manrique 1629–1643*. A Translation of the *Itinerario de las Missiones Orientales* with Introduction and Notes by

Lieut.-Colonel **C. Eckford Luard**, C.I.E., M.A., assisted by Father **H. Hosten**, S.J. *Volume I, Arakan.*
Oxford, 1927 (1926). Pages lxvi, 450 + 6 maps, 3 illustrations.
Continued in 61 below.

2/60. *A Relation of a Voyage to Guiana by Robert Harcourt 1613 / With Purchas' Transcript of a Report made at Harcourt's Instance on the Marrawini District* / Edited / with Introduction and Notes / by Sir **C. Alexander Harris**, K.C.M.G., C.B., C.V.O.
1928 (1926). Pages xii, 191 + 3 maps, 1 illustration.

2/61. *Travels of Fray Sebastien Manrique . . . . Volume II: China, India, etc.*
1927 (1926). Pages xii, 481 + 13 maps, 3 illustrations.
The text was proof-read by Sir Richard Carnac and Miss L. M. Anstey.

2/62. *Spanish Documents concerning English Voyages to the Caribbean 1527–1568 / Selected from the Archives of the Indies at Seville* / by **Irene A. Wright**, B.A., F.R.Hist.S., Fellow of the Dutch Royal Historical Society, Utrecht.
1929 (1928). Pages x, 167, *xlvii* + 2 maps, 1 illustration.
In English translation. For further documents, see 71, 99 and 111 below.

2/63. *The Desert Route to India / Being the Journals of Four Travellers by the Great Desert Caravan Route between Aleppo and Basra / 1745–1751.* Edited by **Douglas Carruthers**.
1929 (1928). Pages xxxvi, 196 + 1 map, 6 illustrations.
The journals of William Beawes, Gaylard Roberts, Bartholomew Plaisted, and John Carmichael.

2/64. *New Light on the Discovery of Australia / as Revealed by the Journal of Captain Don Diego de Prado y Tovar* / Edited by **Henry N. Stevens**, M.A., F.A.G.S., Hon. Member Am. Antiq. Socy. With Annotated Translations from the Spanish by **George F. Barwick**, B.A., Keeper of Printed Books, British Museum 1914–1919.
1930 (1929). Pages xvi, 261 + 5 maps, 2 illustrations.
Spanish text, with English translation, of Prado's *Relación* of the voyage begun in company with Quirós and Torres in 1607, together with a report of the Spanish Council of State concerning Quirós, 1618, and letters of Torres and Prado, 1607–13.

2/65. *Select Documents illustrating the Four Voyages of Columbus / Including those contained in R. H. Major's Select Letters of Christopher Columbus / Translated and Edited / With Additional Material, an Introduction, and Notes* / by **Cecil Jane** / *Vol. I: The First and Second Voyages.*

1930 (1929). Pages clv, 188 + 3 maps, 1 illustration.
Enlarges on First Series 43 (1870). Continued in 70 below.

2/66. *Relations of Golconda in the Early Seventeenth Century.* Edited by
W. H. Moreland, C.S.I., C.I.E.
1931 (1930). Pages li, 109, *xlvii* + 2 maps.
William Methwold's 'Relation', reprinted from *Purchas his Pilgrimes* and two
other 'relations', one by Antony Schorer, translated from the Dutch.

2/67. *The Travels of John Sanderson in the Levant / 1584–1602 / With his
Autobiography and Selections from his Correspondence /* Edited by Sir **William Foster**, C.I.E.
1931 (1930). Pages xliv, 322 + 3 maps, 5 illustrations.

2/68. *The Life of the Icelander Jón Ólafsson . . . . Volume II / Life and
Travels: Denmark, England, The Cape, Madagascar, Comoro Is., Coromandel Coast, Tranquebar, St Helena, Ascension Is., Ireland, Iceland / 1618–
1679.* Edited by the late Sir **Richard Temple**, Bart, . . . , and **Lavinia
Mary Anstey**.
1932 (1931). Pages xxx, 290 + 1 map.
Continued from Second Series 53 above.

2/69. *A Brief Summe of Geographie / by Roger Barlow /* Edited with an
Introduction and Notes / by **E. G. R. Taylor**, D.Sc., F.R.G.S.
1932 (1931). Pages lvi, 210 + 1 map, 3 illustrations.
Transcript of the manuscript dedicated to Henry VIII, with a pedigree of
Barlow.

2/70. *Select Documents illustrating the Four Voyages of Columbus . . . . Vol.
II: The Third and Fourth Voyages.* With a Supplementary Introduction
by **E. G. R. Taylor**.
1933 (1932). Pages lxxxix, 164 + 3 maps, 1 illustration.
Continued from Second Series 65 above.

2/71. *Documents concerning English Voyages to the Spanish Main / 1569–
1580 / I Spanish Documents selected from the Archives of the Indies at Seville
/ II English Accounts / Sir Francis Drake revived, and Others Reprinted /* By
Irene A. Wright, . . . , Comendadora, Order of Afonso XII, ...
1932. Pages lxiv, 348 + 2 maps, 1 illustration.

2/72. *Bombay in the Days of Queen Anne / Being an Account of the
Settlement written by John Burnell /* With an Introduction and Notes by
Samuel T. Sheppard, late Editor of The Times of India / To which
is added Burnell's narrative of his adventures in Bengal / With an

Introduction by Sir **William Foster**, ... , and Notes by Sir **Evan Cotton**, C.I.E., and **L.M. Anstey**.
1933. Pp xxx, 192 + 3 maps.

2/73. *A New Voyage and Description of the Isthmus of America / by Lionel Wafer / Surgeon on Buccaneering Expeditions in Darien, the West Indies, and the Pacific / from 1680 to 1688 / With Wafer's Secret Report (1698), and Davis's Expedition to the Gold Mines (1704).* Edited, with Introduction, Notes and Appendices, by **L. E. Elliot Joyce**.
1934 (1933). Pages lxxi, 221 + 4 maps, 4 illustrations.
The text of the 1699 edition, with slight changes, and additional material.

2/74. *Peter Floris / his Voyage to the East Indies in the Globe / 1611–1615 / The Contemporary Translation of his Journal /* Edited by **W. H. Moreland**, ...
1934. Pages lxx, 164 + 3 maps.

2/75. *The Voyage of Thomas Best to the East Indies / 1612–14 /* Edited by Sir **William Foster**, ...
1934. Pages lvi, 316.
Journals, extracts from journals, and narratives, written on board the *Dragon* and *Hosiander* by Best and various other persons, with Best's correspondence and extracts from the Court minutes of the East India Company.

2/76. *The Original Writings & Correspondence of the Two Richard Hakluyts /* With an Introduction and Notes by **E. G. R. Taylor**, ... , Professor of Geography, University of London.
1935. Volume I. Pages xiv, 210 + 2 maps, 4 illustrations.
The main pagination of this and the following volume is continuous.

2/77. *The Original Writings ... of the Two Richard Hakluyts ... .*
Volume II. 1935. Pages xii, 211–516.

2/78. *The Travels of Peter Mundy ... . Vol. 5 / Travels in South-West England and Western India, with a Diary of Events in London, 1658–1663, and in Penryn, 1664–1667.* Edited by the late Sir **Richard Carnac Temple**, Bt., and **Lavinia Mary Anstey**.
1936. Pages xxvii, 226 + 1 map, 14 illustrations.
Continued from 55 above.

2/79. *Esmeraldo de situ orbis / By Duarte Pacheco Pereira /* Translated and Edited by **George H. T. Kimble**, M.A., Lecturer in Geography in the University of Reading.
1937 (1936). Pages xxxv, 193 + 4 maps, 7 illustrations.
A Portuguese account of the coasts of Africa and their discovery, written c.1505–1508.

2/80. *The Voyages of Cadamosto / And Other Documents on Western Africa in the Second Half of the Fifteenth Century* / Translated and Edited by **G. R. Crone**.
   1937. Pages xlv, 159 + 2 maps, 1 illustration.
   The additional documents, in translation, comprise a letter by Antoine Malfante, 1447, an account of the voyages of Diogo Gomes, c. 1456, and extracts from João de Barros, *Decadas de Asia*.

2/81. *The Voyage of Pedro Álvares Cabral to Brazil and India / From Contemporary Documents and Narratives* / Translated / with Introduction and Notes / by **William Brooks Greenlee**.
   1938 (1937). Pages lxix, 228 + 3 maps, 6 illustrations.
   Letters, narratives, and extracts from diaries, etc. of 1500–01, chiefly of Portuguese and Venetian origin, in translation.

2/82. *The Voyage of Nicholas Downton to the East Indies / 1614–15 / As Recorded in Contemporary Narratives and Letters* / Edited by Sir **William Foster**, ... /
   1939 (1938). Pages xxxvii, 224 + 3 maps, 5 illustrations.

2/83. *The Voyages and Colonising Enterprises of Sir Humphrey Gilbert* / With an Introduction and Notes / by / **David Beers Quinn**, Ph.D., Lecturer in History, Queen's University, Belfast /
   Volume I. 1940 (1938). Pages xxix, 238 + 1 map, 1 illustration.
   A collection of documents, chiefly from English sources, including a few relating to Ireland. The main pagination of this and the following volume is continuous.

2/84. *The Voyages ... of Sir Humphrey Gilbert* ... .
   Volume II. 1940 (1939). Pages xiv, 239–534 + 4 maps, 1 illustration.
   Includes documents relating to the Munster plantation scheme, 1569, and the Knollys piracy, 1579.

2/85. *The Voyages of Sir James Lancaster to Brazil and the East Indies / 1591–1603 /* A new edition / with Introduction and Notes / by Sir **William Foster**, ... /
   1940. Pages xl, 178 + 3 maps, 3 illustrations.
   Previous edition First Series 56 (1877) above. Contains three additional narratives and other documents and omits certain supplementary matter.

2/86. *Europeans in West Africa, 1540–1560 / Documents to illustrate the nature and scope of Portuguese enterprise in West Africa, the abortive attempt of Castilians to create an empire there, and the early English voyages to Barbary and Guinea* / Translated and Edited by **John William Blake**, M.A.
   Volume I. 1942 (1941). Pp xxxvi, 246 + 2 maps.

Dealing with Portuguese and Castilian enterprise. The main pagination of this and the following volume is continuous.

2/87. *Europeans in West Africa* . . . .
Volume II. 1942. Pages xi, 249–461 + 1 map.
Documents relating to early English voyages.

2/88. *The Voyage of Sir Henry Middleton to the Moluccas / 1604–1606.* A new and enlarged edition, with an Introduction and Notes by / Sir **William Foster**, . . . /
1943. Pages xliv, 209 + 2 maps, 2 illustrations.
Previous edition First Series 19 (1854) above. The additional material includes an account by Edmund Scott of events at Bantam, 1603–05, and his description of Java.

2/89. *The Suma Oriental of Tomé Pires / An Account of the East, from the Red Sea to Japan, written in Malacca and India in 1512–1515 / and The Book of Francisco Rodrigues / Rutter of a Voyage in the Red Sea, Nautical Rules, Almanack and Maps, Written and Drawn in the East before 1515* / Translated from the Portuguese MS in the Bibliothèque de la Chambre des Deputés, Paris, and Edited by **Armando Cortesão**.
Volume I. 1944. Pages xcvi, 228 + 14 maps, 13 illustrations.
Containing the translated Books I–V of the *Suma Oriental*. The main pagination of this and the following volume is continuous.

2/90. *The Suma Oriental* . . . .
Volume II. 1944. Pages 229–578 + 10 maps, 5 illustrations.
Book VI of the *Suma Oriental*, together with a translation of Rodrigues' 'Book', the entire Portuguese texts, and a letter from Pires to King Manuel, 1516. The translations in both volumes are by the editor.

2/91. *The Voyage of Captain Bellingshausen to the Antarctic Seas / 1819–1821 / Translated from the Russian /* Edited by **Frank Debenham**, O.B.E., M.A., Director of the Scott Polar Institute, Cambridge.
Volume I. 1945. Pages xxx, 259 + 5 maps, 24 illustrations.
Various translators, especially Edward Bullough and N. Volkov. The pagination of this and the following volume is continuous.

2/92. *The Voyage of Captain Bellingshausen* . . . .
Volume II. 1945. Pages *viii*, 261–474 + 9 maps, 12 illustrations.
An additional section entitled 'Short notes on the colonies of New South Wales' is included.

2/93. *Richard Hakluyt & his Successors / A Volume Issued to Commemorate the Centenary of the Hakluyt Society /* Edited by **Edward Lynam**, D.Litt., M.R.I.A., F.S.A.

1946. Pages lxviii, 192 + 8 illustrations.

Containing: (i) 'Richard Hakluyt, by J. A. Williamson, D.Lit.', (ii) 'Samuel Purchas, by Sir William Foster, C.I.E.' (iii) 'English Collections of Voyages and Travels 1625–1846, by G. R. Crone and R. A. Skelton', (iv) 'The Hakluyt Society. A Retrospect 1846–1946, by Sir William Foster, C.I.E.' [on the Contents page 'The Hakluyt Society, 1846–1946. A Retrospect'] (v) 'The Present and the Future [of the Society], by Edward Lynam, D. Litt.' Also a prospectus with lists of publications, select maps, and members, the Laws of the Hakluyt Society, and an 'Index to the Society's publications, 1847–1946'.

2/94. *The Pilgrimage of Arnold von Harff / Knight / from Cologne, through Italy, Syria, Egypt, Arabia, Ethiopia, Nubia, Palestine, Turkey, France and Spain, which he Accomplished in the years 1496–1499 /* Translated from the German and edited with notes and an introduction / by **Malcolm Letts**.

1946. Pages xxxv, 325.

2/95. *The Travels of the Abbé Carré in India and the Near East / 1672 to 1674 /* Translated from the manuscript journal of his travels in the India Office by Lady **Fawcett**, and Edited by Sir **Charles Fawcett** with the assistance of Sir **Richard Burn** / *Volume One / From France through Syria, Iraq and the Persian Gulf to Surat, Goa, and Bijapur, with an account of his grave illness.*

1947. Pages lvi, 315 + 3 maps, 2 illustrations.

The main pagination of this and the two following volumes is continuous, but each has its own Introduction.

2/96. *The Travels of the Abbé Carré . . . / Volume Two / From Bijapur to Madras and St Thomé. Account of the capture of Trincomalee Bay and St Thomé by De la Haye, and of the siege of St Thomé by the Golconda army and hostilities with the Dutch.*

1947. Pages xxiv, 317–675 + 3 maps, 1 illustration.

2/97. *The Travels of the Abbé Carré . . . / Volume Three / Return Journey to France / with an account of the Sicilian revolt against Spanish rule at Messina.*

1948. Pages xxiii, 677–984 + 3 maps, 3 illustrations.

2/98. *The Discovery of Tahiti / A Journal of the Second Voyage of H.M.S.* Dolphin *Round the World, under the Command of Captain Wallis, R.N., in the Years 1766, 1767, and 1768 / Written by her Master / George Robertson* / Edited by **Hugh Carrington** /

1948. Pages xvii, 292 + 6 maps, 4 illustrations.

2/99. *Further English Voyages to Spanish America / 1583–1594 / Documents from the Archives of the Indies at Seville illustrating English Voyages to the*

Caribbean, the Spanish Main, Florida, and Virginia / Translated and Edited by **Irene A. Wright**, ... , Gold Medallist of the Society of Women Geographers of America /
1951 (1949). Pages xciii, 314 + 8 maps.

2/100. *The Red Sea and adjacent Countries at the Close of the Seventeenth Century / As described by Joseph Pitts / William Daniel / and Charles Jacques Poncet* / Edited by Sir **William Foster**, . . . /
1949. Pages xl, 192 + 2 maps, 1 illustration.
With additional documents. The first narrative is from Pitts's *Religion and Manners of the Mahometans* (3rd Edition, 1731); Daniel's journal was printed in 1702, Poncet's in 1709.

2/101. *Mandeville's Travels* / Texts and Translations / By **Malcolm Letts**, F.S.A.
Volume I. 1953 (1950). Pages lxiii, 223 + 2 maps, 1 illustration.
The text of British Library Egerton MS 1982, with an essay on the cosmographical ideas of Mandeville's day by **E. G. R. Taylor**. The main pagination of this and the following volume is continuous.

2/102. *Mandeville's Travels* . . . .
Volume II. 1953 (1950). Pages xii, 226–554 + 3 illustrations.
The Paris text (French, with translation), the Bodleian text, and extracts from other versions.

2/103. *The Historie of Travell into Virginia Britania (1612)* / by *William Strachey, gent.* Edited by **Louis B. Wright** and **Virginia Freund**.
1953 (1951). Pages xxxii, 221 + 3 maps, 1 illustration.
New edition of 6 (1849). Transcript of the Princeton MS, with Strachey's vocabulary of an Algonkian dialect and an essay on the same by **James A. Geary**.

2/104. *The Roanoke Voyages / 1584–1590 / Documents to illustrate / the English Voyages to North America / under the Patent granted / to Walter Raleigh / in 1584* / Edited by **David Beers Quinn** / Professor of History in the University College of Swansea / (University of Wales)
Volume I. 1955 (1952). Pages xxxv, 496 + 6 maps, 2 illustrations.
Texts from Hakluyt's *Principall Navigations* (1589), together with the items added by him in 1600 and much additional material, a few documents in summary form. This volume takes the narrative to January 1586/7 and includes a descriptive list of John White's drawings of the first colony; the narrative is continued to 1590 and later in the following volume, with which the main pagination is continuous.

2/105. *The Roanoke Voyages* . . . .
Volume II. 1955 (1952). Pages vi, 497–1004 + 2 maps, 2 illustrations.

Appended is an article on the language of the Carolina Algonkian tribes by James A. Geary, with a word-list; a chapter on the archaeology of the Roanoke settlements; a detailed account of the MS and printed sources; and (in pocket) a map of Ralegh's Virginia. Incorrectly numbered 104 on half-title.

2/106. *South China in the Sixteenth Century / Being the narratives of Galeote Pereira / Fr. Gaspar da Cruz, O.P. / Fr. Martin de Rada, O.E.S.A. / (1550–1575) /* Edited by **C. R. Boxer**, ... /
1953. Pages xci, 388 + 10 maps, 10 illustrations.
Translations, the first based largely on that in Richard Willes, *History of Travayle in the West and East Indies* (1577), the second derived from *Purchas his Pilgrimes* (1624), the third by the editor from three sixteenth-century Spanish versions. With appendices on various matters, including a Chinese glossary and a table of Chinese dynasties and emperors.

2/107. *Some Records of Ethiopia / 1593–1646 / Being Extracts from* The History of High Ethiopia or Abassia *by Manoel de Almeida / Together with Bahrey's* History of the Galla / Translated and Edited by **C. F. Beckingham** and **G. W. B. Huntingford** /
1954. Pages xcviii, 267 + 5 maps, 5 illustrations.
The selections from Almeida describe the country and its people and the journeys of Jesuit missionaries attempting to enter or leave Ethiopia.

2/108. *The Travels of Leo of Rozmital / through Germany, Flanders, England, France, Spain, Portugal and Italy / 1465–1467 /* Translated from the German and Latin and Edited by **Malcolm Letts**, ... /
Cambridge, 1957 (1955). Pages xv, 196 + 2 maps, 5 illustrations.
From the German account by Gabriel Tetzel, with supplementary passages from the Latin versions (printed in 1577, 1843 and 1951) of the lost account in Czech by Václav Šašek, both having been Rozmital's companions.

2/109. *Ethiopian Itineraries circa 1400–1524 / Including those Collected by Alessandro Zorzi at Venice in the Years 1519–24 /* Edited by **O. G. S. Crawford**, C.B.E., Litt.D., F.B.A.
Cambridge, 1958 (1955). Pages xxix, 232 + 22 maps, 1 illustration.
Zorzi's Italian text with translation by C. A. Ralegh Radford. Includes a gazetteer for Fra Mauro's map.

2/110. *The Travels of Ibn Baṭṭūṭa / A.D. 1325–1354 /* Translated with revisions and notes, from the Arabic Text Edited by C. Defrémery and B. R. Sanguinetti / by **H. A. R. Gibb** /
Volume I. Cambridge, 1958 (1956). Pages xvii, 269 + 4 maps, 3 illustrations.
Covers travels in North-West Africa, Egypt, Syria, and to Mecca. Continued

in 117, 141, and 178 below (and the final volume to follow). The main pagination of all the volumes is continuous.

2/111. *English Privateering Voyages to the West Indies / 1588–1595 / Documents relating to English voyages to the West Indies, from the defeat of the Armada to the last voyage of Sir Francis Drake, including Spanish documents contributed by Irene A. Wright /* Edited by **Kenneth R. Andrews /** Cambridge, 1959 (1956). Pages xxvii, 421 + 6 maps, 3 illustrations.

Documents, some summarized entirely or in part, relating to twenty-five voyages, drawn mainly from the records of the High Court of Admiralty, with selections from narratives printed by Hakluyt and from a quantity of translations by **I. A. Wright** of originals (1593–5) in the Archivo General de Indias in Seville intended for a further volume on English West Indies Voyages (see Second Series 66, 71 and 99 above). The Introduction gives an account of the Court itself and of privateering during the Spanish war and in the West Indies.

2/112. *The Tragic History of the Sea / 1589–1622 / Narratives of the shipwrecks of the Portuguese East Indiamen* São Thomé *(1589),* Santo Alberto *(1593),* São João Baptista *(1622) and the journeys of the survivors in South East Africa.* Edited from the original Portuguese by **C. R. Boxer**, Camoens Professor of Portuguese, University of London, King's College /
Cambridge, 1959 (1957). Pages xiv, 297 + 9 maps, 7 illustrations.

The narratives by Diogo do Couto, João Baptista Lavanha and Francisco Vaz d'Almada, translated from the original editions of accounts which were subsequently included in the *História Trágico-Marítima* edited by Bernardo Gomes de Brito at Lisbon in 1735–6. The introduction and appendices discuss the 'Carreira da Índia'. For a further selection from the same source, see 132 below.

2/113. *The Troublesome Voyage of Captain Edward Fenton / 1582–1583 /* Narratives & Documents Edited by **E. G. R. Taylor**, Emeritus Professor of Geography in the University of London.
Cambridge, 1959 (1957). Pages lvii, 333 + 9 maps, 12 illustrations.

Transcripts of certain surviving records of the voyage for Cathay sponsored by the Privy Council and intended to establish the first English trading base in the Far East. Includes Fenton's own sea journal and extracts from the official narrative of Richard Madox, for which see 147 below.

2/114. *The Prester John of the Indies / A True Relation of the Lands of the Prester John / being the narrative of the Portuguese Embassy to Ethiopia in 1520 / written by Father Francisco Alvares /* The translation of Lord Stanley of Alderley (1881) / revised and edited with additional material by **C. F. Beckingham** and **G. W. B. Huntingford /**

Volume I. Cambridge, 1961 (1958). Pages xvi, 321 + 8 maps, 41 illustrations.

The first 88 chapters, representing the mission of Dom Rodrigo de Lima, from his landing at Massawa on the west coast of the Red Sea in April 1520 to his re-embarking there six years later, the first European embassy known to have reached the Ethiopian court and returned in safety. Continued in the following volume, with which the main pagination is continuous.

2/115. *The Prester John of the Indies . . . /*
Volume II. Cambridge, 1961 (1958). Pages vi, 323–617 + 2 maps, 8 illustrations.

Chapters 89–142 of Álvares, with the narrative of the return to Portugal, a translation of a seventeenth-century Ethiopian description of Aksum, and accounts of the rock-cut churches at Lalibala and certain other matters.

2/116. *The History of the Tahitian Mission / 1799–1830 / Written by John Davies, Missionary to the South Sea Islands / With Supplementary Papers of the Missionaries /* Edited by **C. W. Newbury** /
Cambridge, 1961 (1959). Pages liv, 392 + 3 maps, 18 illustrations.

Chapters 6–12 and 14–20 of Davies's unpublished 'History', chapter 13 omitted as already in print (see pp. 119–60 of Second Series 52 above). The editor's 'Epilogue', continuing the history of the mission to 1860, includes part of Davies's 'Conclusion' and supplementary correspondence. Appendices discuss the Pomare dynasty and missionary codes of law for eastern Polynesia.

2/117. *The Travels of Ibn Baṭṭūṭa . . . /*
Volume II. Cambridge, 1962 (1959). Pages xii, 271–537 + 5 maps, 1 illustration.

Continued from Second Series 110 above. Covering southern Persia, Iraq, southern Arabia, East Africa, the Persian Gulf, Asia Minor and South Russia.

2/118. *The Travels and Controversies of Friar Domingo Navarrete / 1616–1686 /* Edited from Manuscript and Printed Sources by **J. S. Cummins** /
Volume I. Cambridge, 1962 (1960). Pages cxx, 163 + 3 maps, 7 illustrations.

A translation of the autobiographical portions of the *Tratados Historicos*, with interpolations from his unpublished 'Controversias' and other works. Describes travels in China and the outward and homeward journeys. The origin and nature of the Jesuit-Dominican controversy over the Chinese rites are summarized in the editor's Introduction. The main pagination of this and the following volume is continuous.

2/119. *The Travels and Controversies of Friar Domingo Navarrete . . . /*
Volume II. Cambridge, 1962 (1960). Pages x, 165–475 + 3 maps, 10 illustrations.

Includes Navarrete's account of the island of Santo Domingo (1679) and appendices on various matters such as the detention of the missionaries in Canton, 1666–70, and Navarrete's relations with Richard Cony, governor of St Helena.

2/120. *The Cabot Voyages and Bristol Discovery under Henry VII* / by **James A. Williamson** / with the Cartography of the Voyages by **R. A. Skelton** /
Cambridge, 1962 (1961). Pages xvi, 332 + 18 maps, 2 illustrations.
Documents from English, Portuguese, and Spanish archives, transcribed or in translation, and from printed sources, relating to the Atlantic voyages out of Bristol between 1480 and 1508–9; including the voyages of John and Sebastian Cabot.

2/121. *A Regiment for the Sea* / *and other Writings on Navigation* / by *William Bourne of Gravesend, a Gunner (c. 1535–1582)* / Edited by **E. G. R. Taylor**, ... /
Cambridge, 1963 (1961). Pages xxxv, 464 + 7 maps, 9 illustrations.
Reprints Bourne's two almanacks and the *Regiment* (1574). Appended are the surviving portion of John Dee's navigational tables, the wills of Bourne and his wife, and a bibliographical description of Bourne's manuscript and printed works by **D. W. Waters** and **R. A. Skelton**.

2/122. *Byron's Journal of his Circumnavigation* / *1764–1766* / Edited by **Robert E. Gallagher** /
Cambridge, 1964 (1962). Pages lxxxii, 230 + 12 maps, 8 illustrations.
The voyage of the *Dolphin*. Includes the secret instructions by the Admiralty, a list of the crew, and transcripts of documents relating to the voyage. The appendix, on the Patagonians, includes 'The Patagonian giants' by **Helen Wallis**.

2/123. *Missions to the Niger* / *Volume I* / *The Journal of Friedrich Horneman's Travels from Cairo to Murzuk in the Years 1797–98* / *The Letters of Major Alexander Gordon Laing, 1824–26* / Edited by **E. W. Bovill** /
Cambridge, 1964 (1962). Pages xii, 406 + 8 maps, 4 illustrations.
With Laing's letters are included his 'Cursory remarks on the course and termination of the great river Niger', his 'Notes on Gadamis', his only surviving letter to his wife, and the newspaper report of his death. Continued in 128–130 below.

2/124. *Carteret's Voyage Round the World* / *1766–1769* / Edited by **Helen Wallis** /
Volume I. Cambridge, 1965 (1963). Pages xii, 273 + 16 maps, 4 illustrations.
Derived from the abstract retained by Philip Carteret after his voyage and the journal he compiled from it and other papers in about 1773. The main pagination of this and the following volume is continuous.

2/125. *Carteret's Voyage round the world* . . . /
Volume II. Cambridge, 1965 (1963). Pages vi, 275–564 + 2 maps, 3 illustrations.

A collection of documents, 1756–1811, relating to the preparations, to the voyage itself, and to its aftermath.

2/126. *La Austrialia del Espíritu Santo / The Journal of Fray Martin de Munilla O.F.M. / and other documents relating to The Voyage of Pedro Fernández de Quirós / to the South Sea (1605–1606) / and / the Franciscan missionary plan / (1617–1627) /* Translated and Edited by **Celsus Kelly** O.F.M. / With ethnological introduction, appendix, and other contributions by **G. S. Parsonson**.
Volume I. Cambridge, 1966 (1964). Pages xvii, 270 + 8 maps, 4 illustrations.

The 'Relación' of Munilla, chaplain and vicar of the royal fleet and commissary of the Franciscans in the Quirós expedition, with an extensive introduction. Continued in 127 below, with which the main pagination is continuous.

2/127. *La Austrialia del Espíritu Santo* . . . .
Volume II. Cambridge, 1966. Pages xv, 273–446 + 1 map, 3 illustrations.

The 'Sumario Breve' of Juan de Iturbe, followed by documents bearing on the preparations for the expedition, the voyage of Quirós, Quirós in New Spain, negotiations for another expedition, and the missionary plan. Two appendices, one by G. S. Parsonson.

2/128. *Missions to the Niger / Volume II / The Bornu Mission 1822–25 / Part I* . . . /
Cambridge, 1966 (1965). Pages xiv, 306.

Continued from Second Series 123 above. This and the following volumes reprint most of the *Narrative of Travels and Discoveries in Northern and Central Africa in the years 1822, 1823, and 1824 by Major Denham, Captain Clapperton and the late Doctor Oudney* (2nd edition, 1826). This volume begins Denham's narrative. Includes previously unpublished documents relating to the mission. Each volume contains a glossary of Arabic terms. The main pagination of this and the two following volumes is continuous.

2/129. *Missions to the Niger / Volume III / The Bornu mission 1822–25 / Part 2* . . . /
Cambridge, 1966 (1965). Pages xii, 309–595 + 7 maps, 30 illustrations.

Continues Denham's narrative, with additional documents.

2/130. *Missions to the Niger / Volume IV / The Bornu mission 1822–25 / Part 3* . . . /

Cambridge, 1966. Pages x, 599–798 + 6 maps, 3 illustrations.
Clapperton's narrative, with the appendix of documents translated from
Arabic, and additional documents.

2/131. *The Journal and Letters of Captain Charles Bishop on the North-West
Coast of America, in the Pacific, and in New South Wales 1794–1799* /
Edited by **Michael Roe** /
Cambridge, 1967 (1966). Pages lvi, 342 + 6 maps, 1 illustration.
Recording the voyage of the *Ruby* from Bristol to Amboyna and the voyage
of the *Nautilus* from Amboyna to Macao.

2/132. *Further Selections from the Tragic History of the Sea / 1559–1565 /
Narratives of the Shipwrecks of the Portuguese East Indiamen* Aguia and
Garça *(1559),* / São Paulo *(1561) and the Misadventures of the Brazil-ship*
Santo Antonio *(1565)* / Translated and Edited from the Original Portu-
guese by **C. R. Boxer** /
Cambridge, 1968 (1967). Pages x, 170 + 4 maps, 11 illustrations.
The narratives of Diogo do Couto, Henrique Dias and Afonso Luis. For a
previous selection from the same source, see Second Series 112 above.

2/133. *The letters of F. W. Ludwig Leichhardt* / Collected and newly
translated by **M. Aurousseau** /
Volume I. Cambridge, 1968 (1967). Pages xvi, 423 + 4 maps.
Full texts of all letters, together with translations of those in German, French
and Italian. This volume contains the letters written while in Germany,
1832–7, and between 1837 and Leichardt's departure for Sydney in 1841.
Continued in the following volumes, with which the main pagination is
continuous.

2/134. *The letters of F. W. Ludwig Leichhardt* ... /
Volume II. Cambridge, 1968. Pages v, 425–819 + 5 maps.
The years of scientific reconnaissance in Australia, 1842–4, around Sydney
and Newcastle, in the Hunter-Goulburn valley, and to the Moreton Bay
district.

2/135. *The letters of F. W. Ludwig Leichhardt* ... /
Volume III. Cambridge, 1968. Pages v, 821–1175 + 2 maps.
Leichardt's major exploration, from 1844 until his disappearance in 1848,
with a table of subsequent events.

2/136. *The Jamestown Voyages under the First Charter / 1606–1609. Documents relating to the Foundation of Jamestown and the History of the Jamestown Colony up to the Departure of Captain John Smith, last President of the
Council in Virginia under the First Charter, early in October, 1609* / Edited
by **Philip L. Barbour** /

Volume I. Cambridge, 1969. Pages xxviii, 247 + 6 maps, 2 illustrations.

Includes a combined list of names of the original planters up to about 1 October 1608. The main pagination of this and the following volume is continuous.

2/137. *The Jamestown Voyages . . . /*
Volume II. Cambridge, 1969. Pages viii, 249–524.

2/138. *Russian Embassies to the Georgian Kings (1589–1605) / Volume I /* Edited with Introduction, Additional Notes, Commentaries and Bibliography by **W. E. D. Allen** / Texts translated by **Anthony Mango** / Cambridge, 1970. Pages xxxii, 368 + 6 maps, 11 illustrations.

Documents and commentaries relating to the embassy of Zvenigorodski and Antonov, 1589–90. The main pagination is continuous with the next volume.

2/139. *Russian embassies . . . / Volume II . . . /*
Cambridge, 1970. Pages ix, 369–640 + 2 maps, 7 illustrations.

The embassy of Tatishchev and Ivanov, 1604–05, with supplementary documents from the embassy of Sovin and Polukhanov, 1596–9, and genealogical notes and tables.

2/140. *Sucesos de las Islas Filipinas / by Antonio de Morga /* Translated and Edited by **J. S. Cummins**, Reader in Spanish, University College, London /
Cambridge, 1971. Pages xi, 347 + 2 maps, 3 illustrations.

From the first edition, Mexico, 1609. A new edition of First Series 39 above.

2/141. *The Travels of Ibn Baṭṭūṭa A.D. 1325–1354 . . . /*
Volume III. Cambridge, 1971. Pages xii, 539–772 + 3 maps, 5 illustrations.

Continued from Second Series 117 above. Covering Turkestan, Khurasan, Sind, north-western India and Delhi, including an account of the reign of Sultan Muhammad ibn Tughluq.

2/142. *The Last Voyage of Drake & Hawkins /* Edited by **Kenneth R. Andrews** /
Cambridge, 1972. Pages xiv, 283 + 4 maps, 8 illustrations.

Transcripts or translations of documents, mainly from manuscripts and including many from the archives at Seville. With an appendix on the art of navigation in the age of Drake, by **D. W. Waters**.

2/143. *To the Pacific and Arctic with Beechey / The Journal of Lieutenant George Peard of H.M.S. 'Blossom' 1823–8 /* Edited by **Barry M. Gough** /
Cambridge, 1973 (1972). Pages x, 272 + 5 maps, 3 illustrations.

From British Library Additional MS 35141.

2/144. *The Hakluyt Handbook* / Edited by **D. B. Quinn** / Volume I. 1974. Pages xxvi, 331 + 6 maps, 11 illustrations.

Essays by various hands, (a) on aspects of Hakluyt's achievement, including essays on Hakluyt's maps (by **R. A. Skelton**), on the conveyance of material from Hakluyt to Purchas (by **C. R. Steele**), and on Hakluyt's reputation (by **D. B. Quinn**); (b) on Hakluyt's use of material, by twelve world regions. Also a Hakluyt chronology (by **D. B.** and **A. M. Quinn**). The main pagination of this and the following volume is continuous.

2/145. *The Hakluyt Handbook* ... / Volume II. 1974. Pages xiii, 335–707 + 37 illustrations.

A listing of the contents of Hakluyt's works, a primary Hakluyt bibliography, an essay discussing secondary works on Hakluyt (by **L. E. Pennington**), a listing of all Hakluyt Society works to date (by **E. L. C. Mullins**), and indexes (by **A. M. Quinn**).

2/146. *Yermak's Campaign in Siberia* / A selection of documents translated from the Russian by **Tatiana Minorsky** and **David Wileman**, and edited, with an introduction and notes, by **Terence Armstrong** / 1975 (1974). Pages x, 315 + 2 maps, 155 illustrations.

The Siberian chronicles documenting Yermak's campaign in the 1580: the Stroganov, Yesipov, Remezov, and New chronicles are reproduced in translation, together with the 154 pen and ink drawings illustrating the Remezov chronicle of c.1700. Includes seven charters and letters of Ivan IV relating to the advance across the Urals.

2/147. *An Elizabethan in 1582* / *The Diary of Richard Madox, Fellow of All Souls* / [Edited] by **Elizabeth Story Donno** / 1976 (1976, slip corrects to 1974). Pages xvi, 365 + 5 maps, 13 illustrations.

Completes publication of the diaries of the two chaplains on the Fenton expedition intended for Cathay, replacing the extracts from one diary in Second Series 113 above. The localities mainly described are Sierra Leone and Brazil.

2/148. *Sir Francis Drake's West Indian Voyage* / *1585–86* / Edited by **Mary Frear Keeler** / 1981 (1975). Pages xiv, 358 + 3 maps, 11 illustrations.

Documents published and unpublished, particularly journals kept aboard the ships, including the newly-discovered *Leicester* journal, with drawings of episodes made by the voyage's artist.

2/149. *François Valentijn's Description of Ceylon* / Edited by **Sinnappah Arasaratnam** / 1978 (1975). Pages xv, 395 + 7 maps, 12 illustrations.

The first twelve chapters on Ceylon in Valentijn's *Oud en Nieuw Oost-Indien* (Dordrecht, 1724–6).

2/150. *The Travel Journal of Antonio de Beatis / Germany, Switzerland, the Low Countries, France and Italy, 1517–1518 /* Translated from the Italian by **J. R. Hale** and **J. M. A. Lindon** / Edited by **J. R. Hale** / 1979 (1976). Pages xii, 206 + 1 map, 2 illustrations.
Translated from the Italian text published in 1905, with an introduction discussing Renaissance travel accounts.

2/151. *The Periplus of the Erythraean Sea / by an unknown author / With some extracts from Agatharkhides 'On the Erythraean Sea' /* Translated and edited by **G. W. B. Huntingford**.
1980 (1976). Pages xiv, 225 + 11 maps, 10 illustrations.
A trader's guide to the Red Sea and neighbouring Indian Ocean coasts, anonymous, written probably between 95 and 130 A.D.: here in translation. Appendices discuss the topography, the history and contemporary commerce of the area, and other matters. For a fuller edition of Agatharkhides, see 172 below.

2/152. *The* Resolution *Journal of Johann Reinhold Forster / 1772–1775 /* Edited by **Michael E. Hoare** /
Volume I. 1982. Pages xvii, 182 + 2 maps, 6 illustrations.
The previously unpublished journal of the principal naturalist on Cook's second voyage. The introduction discusses Forster's career. The main pagination of this volume and the following three volumes is continuous.

2/153. *The* Resolution *Journal* . . . /
Volume II. 1982. Pages viii, 183–370 + 5 maps, 7 illustrations.

2/154. *The* Resolution *Journal* . . . /
Volume III. 1982. Pages viii, 371–554 + 5 maps, 8 illustrations.

2/155. *The* Resolution *Journal* . . . /
Volume IV. 1982. Pages viii, 555–831 + 6 maps, 6 illustrations.
Includes a list of George Forster's plant drawings from Cook's second voyage.

2/156. *The Three Voyages of Edmond Halley in the* Paramore */ 1698–1701 /* Edited by **Norman J. W. Thrower** /
Volume I. 1982. Pages 392 + 6 maps, 9 illustrations.
The journals published in full from manuscripts now in the British Library.

2/157. [*The Three Voyages of Edmond Halley* . . . /]
Volume II. 1982.
No title-page and actually a portfolio of facsimiles of Halley's Atlantic and Channel charts.

2/158. *The Expedition of the* St Jean-Baptiste *to the Pacific / 1769–1770 /*

From Journals of Jean de Surville and Guillaume Labé. Translated and edited by **John Dunmore** /
1981. Pages x, 310 + 8 maps, 14 illustrations.
Translation of manuscript shipboard journals in French, with an account of the voyage.

2/159. *The Voyage of Semen Dezhnev in 1648: Bering's Precursor / With selected documents* / [Edited] by **Raymond H. Fisher** /
1981. Pages xiv, 326 + 23 maps, 3 illustrations.
Dezhnev was the first European to sail round the north-eastern tip of Asia. Translation of published Russian documents, with an extensive critical exposition of their significance.

2/160. *Newfoundland Discovered / English Attempts at Colonisation, 1610–1630* / edited by **Gillian T. Cell** /
1982. Pages xviii, 310 + 3 maps, 2 illustrations.
Documents, mainly unpublished and from British archives.

2/161. *The English New England Voyages / 1602–1608* / Edited by **David B. Quinn** and **Alison M. Quinn** /
1983. Pages xxiv, 580 + 20 maps, 16 illustrations.
Documents published and unpublished, with appendices, including one on maps of New England 1606–1610, and one (by Philip L. Barbour) on an early vocabulary of an Algonkian language.

2/162. *The* Itinerario *of Jerónimo Lobo* / Translated by / **Donald M. Lockhart** / From the Portuguese Text Established and Edited by M. G. Da Costa / With an Introduction and Notes by **C. F. Beckingham** /
1983. Pages xxxvi, 417 + 4 maps, 9 illustrations.
Lobo, a Portuguese Jesuit, served in Ethiopia 1625–1634. He also describes a famous 1635–1636 shipwreck on the coast of Natal. A French summary version of his account was published in 1728 but the complete manuscript was only discovered in 1947.

2/163. *George Vancouver / A Voyage of Discovery to the North Pacific Ocean and Round the World / 1791–1795* / With an Introduction and Appendices / Volume I / Edited by **W. Kaye Lamb** /
1984. Pages xx, 442 + 5 maps, 14 illustrations.
Book 1, the voyage to Australia and Tahiti, of a new and annotated edition of *A Voyage of Discovery* . . . (London, 1798). The main pagination of this and the following three volumes is continuous.

2/164. *The Voyage of George Vancouver . . . / Volume II / . . . /*
1984. Pages ix, 443–786 + 5 maps, 14 illustrations.
Book 2 and part of Book 3, the voyage to Hawaii and the North American coast.

2/165. *The Voyage of George Vancouver ... / Volume III / ... /*
1984. Pages viii, 787–1230 + 4 maps, 5 illustrations.
Remainder of Book 3, all Book 4, part of Book 5, voyage on the Pacific coast
of North America and return to Hawaii.

2/166. *The Voyage of George Vancouver ... / Volume IV / ... /*
1984. Pages viii, 1231–1752 + 2 maps, 6 illustrations.
Remainder of Book 5, on the coast of North America. Appendices include
documents relating to the voyage and a list of the ships' company.

2/167. *Jerusalem Pilgrimage / 1099–1185 /* [Edited by] **John Wilkinson**
with **Joyce Hill** and **W. F. Ryan** /
1988. Pages xi, 372 + 24 maps.
Edition of previously published translations of texts in Latin, Greek, Arabic
and other languages, and new translations of texts in Icelandic and Russian.

2/168. *The Iceland Journal of Henry Holland / 1810 /* Edited by **Andrew
Wawn** /
1987. Pages xvii, 342 + 11 maps, 19 illustrations.
Holland's manuscript, part of which was used in George Mackenzie's *Travels
in Iceland ...* (Edinburgh, 1811), is here published in full. The maps are
mostly Holland's own sketch maps. Appendices include tables of population
and commerce, a list of parishes, a page from a parish register, and a register
of weather.

2/169. *The Journal of Rochfort Maguire / 1852–1854 / Two years at Point
Barrow, Alaska, aboard H.M.S. Plover in the search for Sir John Franklin /
Volume I /* Edited by **John Bockstoce** /
1988. Pages xiv, 318 + 5 maps, 6 illustrations.
In particular, concerning the encounter and relations with the local 'Eski-
mos'. The main pagination of this and the following volume is continuous.

2/170. *The Journal of Rochfort Maguire ... / Volume II / ... /*
1988. Pages vi, 319–584 + 1 map, 2 illustrations.
Appendices include accounts of boat expeditions along the coast and an essay
on the Inuit of south-eastern Alaska, by the ship's surgeon, John Simpson.

2/171. *English and Irish Settlement on the River Amazon / 1550–1646 /*
Edited by **Joyce Lorimer** /
1989. Pages xxvi, 499 + 10 maps.
Documents, many from manuscripts in English, Irish, Dutch, Spanish and
Portuguese archives.

2/172. *Agatharchides of Cnidus / On the Erythraean Sea /* Translated and
edited by **Stanley M. Burstein** /
1990. Pages xi, 202 + 1 map.
Written 'sometime before 100 B.C.' and thought to have been an appendix

to a larger historical work not extant. A translation of the abridgements found in later Greek writers. Completes the extracts in Second Series 151 above.

2/173. *The Mission of Friar William of Rubruck / His Journey to the court of the Great Khan Möngke / 1253–1255 /* Translated by **Peter Jackson /** Introduction, notes and appendices by **Peter Jackson** with **David Morgan /**
1990. Pages xv, 312 + 4 maps, 1 illustration.
An extended revision of Second Series 4 above. With a genealogical table of the Mongol imperial family and nine appendices on detailed matters.

2/174. *Prutky's Travels in Ethiopia and Other Countries /* Translated and edited by **J. H. Arrowsmith-Brown /** and annotated by **Richard Pankhurst /**
1991. Pages xxviii, 546 + 4 maps, 1 illustration.
Václav Prutky, a Bohemian doctor of medicine and a Franciscan missionary, worked in Ethiopia 1752–1753. His account in Latin includes material on the Middle East and India, but material on Syria and Palestine is not included in this translation. An appendix documents Prutky's mission to Russia in 1766–1769.

2/175. *Barbot on Guinea / The writings of Jean Barbot / on West Africa 1678–1712 /* Edited by **P. E. H. Hair**, **Adam Jones** and **Robin Law /** Volume I. 1992 Pages cxxv, 327 + 8 maps, 18 illustrations.
An edition of the original material in a manuscript account of the Guinea coast written in French in the 1680s and deriving in part from Barbot's two trading voyages to Guinea, in translation; together with additional original material from an enlarged version of the account written in English and eventually published in 1732. Sources of derived material are noted. Barbot's own drawings include the earliest set of illustrations of European forts in Guinea. This volume covers the coast from Senegal to Gold Coast. The main pagination of this and the following volume is continuous.

2/176. *Barbot on Guinea ... /*
Volume II. 1992. Pages vii, 331–916 + 4 maps, 26 illustrations.
The coast from River Volta to Cape Lopez.

2/177. *Voyages to Hudson Bay in Search of a Northwest Passage / 1741–1747 / Volume I / The Voyage of Christopher Middleton / 1741–1742 /* Edited by **William Barr** and **Glyndwr Williams /**
1994. Pages xii, 333 + 8 maps, 3 illustrations.
Documents from British and Canadian archives, including Middleton's journal of the voyage, and his printed *Vindication*. Continued in 181 below.

2/178. *The Travels of Ibn Baṭṭūṭa / A.D. 1325–1354 ... / Volume IV /* The translation completed with annotations by **C. F. Beckingham /**

1994. Pages xvi, 773–983 + 5 illustrations.

Continued from Second Series 141 above. Covering South India, South-East Asia, China, Morocco, Spain and West Africa.

2/179. *The Journal of Jean-François de Galaup de la Pérouse / 1785–1788 / Volume I /* Translated and edited by **John Dunmore** /

1994. Pages ccxl, 232 + 8 maps, 3 illustrations.

A translation of the journal, published with abridgements in 1797, in full in 1985. The introduction discusses the background to the voyage and its achievement, despite the final disaster. This volume covers the voyage to Australia, the Pacific coast of North America, and Macao. The main pagination of this and the following volume is continuous.

2/180. *The Journal of Jean-François de Galaup de la Pérouse ... / Volume II ... /*

1995. Pages vi, 233–613 + 17 maps, 4 illustrations.

The voyage between the Philippines and Kamchatka, then to Australia. The appendices include related correspondence and the muster rolls of the ships.

2/181. *Voyages to Hudson Bay ... / Volume II / The Voyage of William Moor and Francis Smith / 1746–1747 / ... /*

1995. Pages xv, 393 + 13 maps, 7 illustrations.

Continued from 177 above. Extracts from printed accounts, with related documents from British and Canadian archives. One appendix discusses the Fonte letter.

EXTRA SERIES

Extra

[1–12] *The Principal / Navigations Voyages / Traffiques & Discoveries / of the English Nation / Made by Sea or Over-land to the Remote and Farthest Distant Quarters of the Earth at any Time within the Compasse of these 1600 Yeeres / By Richard Hakluyt / Preacher, and sometime Student of Christ-Church in Oxford /*

12 vols, I–III, 1903; IV–XI, 1904; XII, 1905.

Reprint of the 1598–1600 edition, slightly modified in spelling, with contemporary maps, plans and charts in facsimile and, in vol. XII, an essay by **Walter Raleigh** on the life and work of Hakluyt and a new index by **Marie Michon** and **Elizabeth Carmont**. Published by MacLehose, Glasgow, and without mention of the Hakluyt Society. A limited number of sets were taken over by the Society and bound in HS binding.

Extra

[13] *The Texts and Versions of John de Plano Carpini and William de Rubruquis / as printed for the first time by Hakluyt in 1598 / together with some shorter pieces.* Edited by **C. Raymond Beazley**, M.A., F.R.G.S. / Fellow of Merton College, Oxford.

1903. Pages xx, 345.

A reprint of the texts and versions, Latin and English, and of shorter pieces, especially the voyages of Ohthere and Wulfstan, which open *Principal Navigations*, with critical and explanatory commentary. The title-page does not mention the Extra Series.

Extra

[14–33] *Hakluytus Posthumus / or / Purchas His Pilgrimes / Contayning a History of the World in Sea Voyages and Lande Travells by Englishmen and others / By Samuel Purchas, B.D.*

20 vols, I-X, 1905; XI-XIX, 1906; XX, 1907.

Reprint of the 1625 edition, slightly modified in spelling, with the addition of a new index by **Marie Michon**. Published by MacLehose, Glasgow, without mention of the Hakluyt Society. A limited number of sets were taken over by the Society and bound in HS binding.

Extra

34a. *The Journals of Captain James Cook on his Voyages of Discovery / The Voyage of the* Endeavour *1768–1771* / Edited by **J. C. Beaglehole** /

1955. Reprinted, with addenda and corrigenda, 1968. Pages cclxxxiv, 684/696 + 20 maps, 25 illustrations.

Admiralty instructions and the journal of the First Voyage, with many appendices.

Extra

34b. *The Journals of Captain James Cook . . . / Charts & Views / Drawn by Cook and his Officers and Reproduced from the Original Manuscripts* / edited by **R. A. Skelton** /

1955, second edition 1969. Pages viii + 58 loose maps, charts, plans, profiles, views and other illustrations.

A separate and unnumbered portfolio containing reproductions of charts and views drawn on the three voyages, with a list.

Extra

35. *The Journals of Captain James Cook . . . / The Voyage of the* Resolution *and* Adventure *1772–1775 / . . . /*

1961. Reprinted, with addenda and corrigenda, 1969. Pages clxx, 1021/1028 + 19 maps, 63 illustrations.

Half-title gives II as number within the set. Admiralty instructions and the journal of the Second Voyage, with many appendices.

Extra

36a. *The Journals of Captain James Cook* ... / *The Voyage of the* Resolution *and* Discovery *1776–1780 /* ... / *Part One /*
  1967. Reprinted, with addenda and corrigenda, 1969. Pages ccxxiv,
  718 + 17 maps, 64 illustrations.
  Half-title gives III as number within set. Admiralty instructions and the
  journal of the Third Voyage, with supplementary extracts from journals or
  logs by James King, Charles Clerke, James Burney, Richard Gilbert, Thomas Edgar. The main pagination of this and the following volume is continuous. For a separate addendum, see Occasional Booklet 8 below.

Extra

36b. *The Journals of Captain James Cook* ... *1776–1780 / Part Two /*
  1967. Reprinted, with addenda and corrigenda, 1969. Pages viii, 723–
  1647 + 2 maps, 10 illustrations.
  Half-title gives III as number within set. Appendices containing the journals
  of William Anderson and David Samwell; extracts from other journals; rolls
  of the ships' companies, and a calendar of documents, 1774–1791. A separate
  pamphlet, *Cook and the Russians,* consisting of six documents translated from
  Russian sources, edited by J. C. Beaglehole, was published in 1973 as an
  addendum to this volume.

Extra

37. *The Life of Captain James Cook* / by **J. C. Beaglehole** /
  1974. Pages xi, 760 + 11 maps, 38 illustrations.
  First separately published by A. and C. Black, 1974, then for the Hakluyt
  Society.

Extra

38. *The Journal of Christopher Columbus* / Translated by **Cecil Jane** /
revised and annotated by **L. A. Vigneras** / with an Appendix by **R. A.
Skelton** / Ninety illustrations from prints and maps of the period /
  1960. Pages xii, 227 + 16 maps, 74 illustrations.
  A revision of Second Series 65 above. From the transcription by Cesare de
  Lollis and Julian Paz for the *Raccolta Colombiana* (1892). Includes Columbus's
  letter, February-March 1493, describing the results of his first voyage. The
  appendix is concerned with the cartography of the first voyage. Published by
  a commercial publisher, Anthony Blond & The Orion Press, and not in the
  standard Hakluyt Society binding. The Society took over a number of sets
  with a separate title page.

Extra

39a. *The Principall Navigations / Voiages and Discoveries / of the English
Nation / by Richard Hakluyt / Imprinted at London, 1589 / ★* [i.e. vol I] / A
Photo-lithographic Facsimile with an Introduction by **David Beers**

Quinn and **Raleigh Ashlin Skelton** and with a new Index by **Alison Quinn** /
1965. Pages lx, 501.
Hakluyt's preliminaries, map, first and second parts, and the editors' introduction. Pagination of this and the following volume is continuous.

Extra
39b. *The Principall Navigations . . .* / ★★ [i.e. vol. II] / . . . /
1965. Pages 506–975.
The 'Third and Last Part', including the unnumbered Drake leaves, the 'table alphabeticall', and the new index.

Extra
40. *The Diary of A. J. Mounteney Jephson / Emin Pasha Relief Expedition 1887–1889.* Edited by **Dorothy Middleton** / With Preface, Prologue and Epilogue compiled by the Editor in Collaboration with **Maurice Denham Jephson** /
1969. Pages xii, 456 + 2 maps, 16 illustrations.
Two-thirds of the complete diary, the omissions supplied by editorial narrative.

Extra
41. *The Journals and Letters of Sir Alexander Mackenzie* / Edited by **W. Kaye Lamb** /
1970. Pages viii, 552 + 6 maps, 3 illustrations
Mackenzie's 'general history' of the fur trade 'from Canada to the North-West' and his journal of his expedition from Fort Chipewyan to the Pacific in 1793, reprinted from the 1801 edition, together with his unpublished journal of his expedition from Fort Chipewyan to the Arctic in 1789 and all his known letters or fragments of letters.

Extra
42. *Ma Huan / Ying-Yai Sheng-Lang / 'The Overall Survey of the Ocean's Shores' / [1433]* / Translated from the Chinese Text Edited by Feng Ch'eng-Chün / with Introduction, Notes and Appendices by **J. V. G. Mills**, formerly Puisne Judge / Straits Settlement /
1970. Pages xix, 393 + 5 maps, 6 illustrations.
The fullest account of China's overseas expansion in the early fifteenth century. Appendices discuss various matters such as southern Asian place-names known to the Chinese in 1433, the Mao K'un map, four Chinese stellar diagrams, and the earliest European rutter of the voyage from Malacca to China.

Extra
43. *The Charts & Coastal Views of Captain Cook's Voyages / Volume One / The Voyage of the* Endeavour */ 1768–1771 / With a Descriptive Catalogue*

of all the known original surveys and coastal views and the original engravings associated with them / Together with original drawings of the Endeavour *and her boats /* Chief Editor / **Andrew David** / Assistant Editors for the Views / **Rüdiger Joppien** and **Bernard Smith** /

1988. Pages lxiv, 328 + colour frontispiece, 480 half-tone plates.

Published in association with the Australian Academy of the Humanities.

Extra

44. *The Charts & Coastal Views of Captain Cook's Voyages / Volume Two / The Voyage of the* Resolution *and* Adventure */ 1772–1775 / ... /*

1992. Pages c, 332 + colour frontispiece, 23 colour plates, 320 half-tone plates.

Extra

45. *A Particuler Discourse Concerning the Greate Necessitie and Manifolde Commodyties that are like to Growe to this Realm of Englande by the Westerne Discoueries lately Attempted, Written in the Yere 1584. By Richarde Hackluyt of Oxforde / Known as / Discourse of Western Planting /* Edited by **David B. Quinn** and **Alison M. Quinn** /

1993. Pages xxxi, 229 + 69 half tone plates, 6 other illustrations.

Includes a facsimile of the manuscript and a line for line transcription, with a commentary, bibliography, and index, preceded by a general introduction.

OCCASIONAL BOOKLETS

(OB/1–4 and 6 apparently published for sale as well as distribution to members)

OB

1. *Richard Hakluyt: his life and work. With a short account of the aims and achievements of the Hakluyt Society.* An address delivered by Sir Clements Markham, K.C.B., F.R.S. (President), on the occasion of the fiftieth anniversary of the foundation of the society, London, 1896. Pages 19.

2. *Address by Sir Clements R. Markham K.C.B. on the fiftieth anniversary of the foundation of the society, December 15th, 1896. Revised on the occasion of the sixty-fifth anniversary, 1911,* London, 1911. Pages 16.

3. *A reproduction of the tablet erected in Bristol Cathedral to the memory of Richard Hakluyt, 1911.,* [1911].

4. *An address on the occasion of the tercentenary of the death of Richard Hakluyt 23 November, 1916 with a note on the Hakluyt family.* By Albert

Gray, C.B., K.C., President of the Hakluyt Society, London, 1917. Pages 19.

5. *Guide for Editors of the Hakluyt Society's Publications*, 1929, revised 1958, 2nd edition [with a Preface by E. S. de Beer], 1975. Pages (1975) 34.

6. *The Hakluyt Society: A Retrospect.* By Sir William Foster, C.I.E., 1946 [a reprint of the essay in 2/93].

7. *Prospectus of the Hakluyt Society with List of Publications and Maps*, 1956 [also contains indexes and Laws of the Society, as revised 1950: the final and fullest of a series of 'Prospectus' issued since at least the 1910s, many untraced], pp. lvi.

8. *Cook and the Russians* An addendum to the Hakluyt Society's edition of the *The voyage of the* Resolution *and* Discovery, *1776–1780.* Edited by J. C. Beaglehole. 1973. Pages 9.

TALKS IN ANNUAL REPORTS

The 'Annual Report', a paginated brochure which included statements of accounts and the Council's report, was issued to all subscribers from an uncertain date, but at least from the 1890s. From 1972, talks given at the Annual General Meeting were published in this brochure, sometimes in a revised version and with annotation. The brochures carry no publication date but appeared in the year after the date of the Annual Report. The year of the Annual Report and the pagination of the talk are given below.

D. B. Quinn, 'Richard Hakluyt and his followers', 1972, pages 1–11
E. S. de Beer, 'The literature of travel in the seventeenth century', 1975, pages 1–6
T. E. Armstrong, 'Editing the Siberian Chronicles', 1976, pages 1–6
R. C. Bridges, 'The documentation of David Livingstone: some new materials', 1977, pages 1–8 + 4 illustrations
C. R. Boxer, 'Some second thoughts on "The Tragic History of the Sea, 1550–1650"', 1978, pages 1–9 + 4 maps
C. F. Beckingham, 'Arabic texts and the Hakluyt Society', 1979, pages 1–13 + 1 illustration
Dorothy Middleton, 'Travel literature in the Victorian and Edwardian eras', 1980, pages 1–10

G. V. Scammell, 'The great age of discovery, 1400–1650', 1981, pages 1–9

P. J. Marshall, 'Thomas Hyde: *Stupor Mundi*', 1982, pages 1–11

H. C. Porter, 'The Tudors and the North American Indians', 1983, pages 1–13

K. R. Andrews, 'The coastal profiles relating too Drake's last voyage', 1984, pages 10–11

Dorothy Middleton, 'The Hakluyt Society 1846–1923', 1984, pages 12–23

Not an AGM talk but an account researched at the request of the Council.

J. S. Cummins, 'Las Casas goes East', 1985, pages 10–22

Ann Savours, 'Discovering the *Discovery*', 1986, pages 13–25

Andrew David, 'The charts and coastal views of Captain Cook's voyages', 1987, pages 11–20

Glyndwr Williams, 'From Dampier to Cook: English perceptions of Australia', 1988, pages 12–25 + 4 maps

Derek Howse, 'A buccaneer's atlas: Basil Ringrose's atlas of the Pacific coast of the Americas', 1989, pages 10–22 + 7 maps

G. S. P. Freeman-Grenville, 'Travellers to Christ's tomb', 1990, pages 14–28 + 6 plates of illustrations

P. E. H. Hair, '"An accomplish'd traveller will take draughts": Barbot's illustrations of Guinea', 1991, pages 12–20 + 4 illustrations

Anthony Farrington, 'The English in Japan 1613–1623', 1992, pages 10–18 + 4 illustrations

Roy Bridges, 'James Augustus Grant's visual record of East Africa', 1993, pages 12–24 + 7 illustrations

Peter Jackson, 'Early missions to the Mongol empire: Carpini and contemporaries', 1994, pages 14–32 + 2 maps, 4 illustrations

Wendy James, 'Re-discovering Schuver's Africa', 1995, pages 1–17 + 1 map, 8 illustrations

INDEX

TO THE LISTING

1. Although individual HS volumes have always contained indexes, the Society has, regrettably, never issued cumulative indexes to all preceding volumes. Even if it were practical, conflating today the three hundred or so volume indexes would have limited value, inasmuch as individual indexes were prepared by separate editors without standard instructions and are therefore highly inconsistent in their selection of items and coverage. However, in 1904, within the section of supplementary material in HS 2/11, the Society provided 'a short Index to Countries, Places, Authors, Editors, etc for the First and Second Series of the Society's Publications' (p. 3). This was essentially a cumulative index of the personal and place names found within titles. At intervals thereafter, up to 1930, and finally in the Centenary volume of 1946 (Edward Lynam, ed., *Richard Hakluyt & his Successors*, London, 1946, HS 2/93), the Society provided, within volumes, a similar cumulative title-page index, updated. These indexes also appeared in various prospectuses separately issued by the Society, and a final updating to 1949 appeared in the 'Prospectus' of 1956 (OB/7). Latterly the indexes were somewhat misleadingly entitled 'Index to the Society's Publications, 1847–'.

2. The present index resumes this tradition, the names indexed being taken from the listing of HS volumes above. It therefore includes both names appearing on title-pages and names within the summary descriptions of contents of each volume. It will be appreciated that the title-page information and the descriptions of contents supply only a small part of the total of personal names and places mentioned within the editions, and the index can therefore only provide a preliminary guide to the volumes.

3. Other limitations of the index are these.

(i) The index being based on the listing, personal and place names are given in the form (e.g. spelling) listed within the titles or in the descriptions of contents of each volume. However, forenames of HS editors given on title-pages only as initials are here presented in full, whenever full names can be traced, the extension shown within square brackets.

(ii) Since not all particulars of the later volumes of a single edition are repeated in the listing, an index reference may be only to the first volume of the edition.

(iii) Where editors in their self-descriptions on title-pages include titles of their other writings, names within these are not indexed. Places of publication supplied within descriptions of contents are also not indexed.

4. PERSONAL NAMES are listed as those of either WRITERS or VOYAGERS AND TRAVELLERS. The first category includes both writers of early travel accounts and related documents, and the editors, translators and other contributors to HS volumes, the names of the latter being signalled in italics. The second category includes, as well as voyagers and travellers, all other mentioned persons. Since many voyagers and travellers were also writers of accounts, the categories to some extent overlap, but individuals are to be found in only one category. In general, an individual who might be in either category is allocated to the one on which the title lays emphasis, by referring either to his travels or to his account. But because of uncertainties about authorship of accounts the allocation is at times arbitrary. An individual not found in one category should therefore be sought in the other.

5. PLACE NAMES are only those given in the listing. Many titles do not list all the regions mentioned in the edition, let alone the lesser place names: some titles fail to mention any region. Descriptions of content sometimes supply more information but are also far from comprehensive in this respect.

6. NUMBERS The numbers given in the index are the volume or item numbers. The second series of volumes is distinguished by initial 2/, and the Extra Series by Ex/. Items of Occasional Booklets are signalled as OB/, and items within the unnumbered series of Talks in Annual Reports by T/ and the date of the report.

WRITERS

Acosta, Joseph de 60
Adams, William 8
Africanus, Leo 92
Agatharchides/Agatharkhides of Cnidus
    2/151, 2/172
Al-Hassan Ibn-Mohammed Al-Wezaz Al-
    Fasi 92
Alessandri, Vincentio d' 49
Allen, W[illiam]. E[dward]. D[avid]. 2/138
Almeida, Manoel de 2/107
Álvares, Francisco 2/114, 2/115
Alvarez, Francisco 64
Alvo/Alvaro, Francisco 52
Amherst, [William Amhurst Tyssen] [Lord]
    2/7
Andagoy, Pascual de 34
Anderson, William Ex/36
Andrews, Kenneth R[aymond]. 2/111,
    2/142, T/1984
Angiolello, Giovan Maria 49
Anstey, Lavinia Mary 2/61, 2/68, 2/72,
    2/78
Arasaratnam, Sinnappah 2/149
Armstrong, Terence [Edward] 2/146,
    T/1976
Arrowsmith-Brown, J.H. 2/174
Asher, G[eorge]. M[ichael]. 27
Astete, Miguel de 47
Aurousseau, M[arcel]. 2/133
Avila, Francisco de 48
Azurara, Gomes Eannes de 95

Badger, George Percy 32, 44
Bahrey 2/107
Barbaro, Josafa 49
Barbosa, Duarte 35, 2/44, 2/49
Barbot, Jean 2/176, T/1991
Barbour, Philip L. 2/136, 2/161
Barlow, Roger 74, 2/69
Barr, William 2/177
Barretto, Pedro de Resende 62

Barros, João de 2/49, 2/80
Barrow, John 11
Barwick, George F[rederick]. 2/64
Battell, Andrew 2/6
Ibn Baṭṭūṭa 37, 2/41, 2/110, 2/117, 2/141,
    2/178
Beatis, Antonio de 2/150
Beawes, William 2/63
Beaglehole, J[ohn]. C[awte]. Ex/34–37
Beazley, C[harles]. Raymond 95, Ex/13
Beckingham, C[harles]. F[raser]. 2/107,
    2/114, 2/162, 2/178, T/1979
Beer, E[smond]. S[amuel]. de T/1975
Beke, Charles T[ilstone]. 13, 54
Bell, Harry Charles Purvis 76
Bent, James Theodore 87
Benzoni, Girolamo 21
Bermudez 2/10
Bethencourt, Jean de 46
Bethune, C[harles]. R[amsay]. Drinkwater
    1, 30
Beynen, Koolemans 54
Birch, Walter de Gray 53, 55
Bishop, Charles 2/131
Blake, John W[illiam]. 2/86
Blöndal, Sigfús 2/53
Bockstoce, John 2/169
Bollaert, William 28
Bond, Edward A[ugustus]. 20
Bontier, Pierre 46
Bourne, William 2/121
Bovill, E[dward]. W[illiam]. 2/123
Bowrey, Thomas 2/12, 2/58
Boxer, C[harles]. R[alph]. 2/106, 2/112,
    2/132, T/1978
Bridge, Cyprian 2/13
Bridges, R[oy]. C. T/1977, T/1993
Brown, Robert 92
Bruun, P. 58
Bullough, Edward 2/91
Burn, Richard 2/95

305

VOYAGERS AND TRAVELLERS

AND ALL OTHER PERSONS

PLACES

OFFICERS OF THE HAKLUYT SOCIETY 1846–1996

Note that the dates relate to the Society's year which runs from one AGM to the next and therefore covers two calendar-year dates. Individuals may have resigned, retired or died in the course of their final Society year, hence in some instances in the calendar year previous to the date shown below.

Honorary Secretary		*President*	
W. D. Cooley	1847–1849	R. Murchison	1847–1871
R. H. Major	1849–1858	D. Dundas	1871–1877
C. R. Markham	1858–1887	H. Yule	1877–1889
E. D. Morgan	1887–1893	C. R. Markham	1889–1909
W. Foster	1893–1902		
B. H. Soulsby	1902–1909		
J. A. J. de Villiers	1909–1923	A. Gray	1909–1928
T. A. Joyce	1923–1926	W. Foster	1928–1945
F. P. Sprent	1926–1931		
E. D. Lynam	1931–1945		
G. R. Crone	1945–1946	E. D. Lynam	1945–1950
R. A. Skelton	1946–1966	M. Letts	1950–1954
and		J. N. L. Baker	1955–1959
E. M. J. Campbell	1962–1983	A. Burns	1959–1964
and		G. Laithwaite	1964–1969
T. E. Armstrong	1966–1990	C. F. Beckingham	1969–1972
and		E. S. de Beer	1972–1978
S. J. Tyacke	1983–1995	G. Williams	1978–1982
and		D. B. Quinn	1982–1987
W. F. Ryan	1990–1995	H. Smedley	1987–1992
		P. E. H. Hair	1992–

A. P. Payne	1995–
(*Honorary Secretary*)	
S. J. Tyacke	1995–
and	
W. F. Ryan	1995–
(*Honorary Series Editors*)	

OFFICERS OF THE HAKLUYT SOCIETY 1846–1996

317

CONTRIBUTORS TO THE VOLUME

C. H. Beckingham: FBA, formerly Professor of Islamic Studies, University of London

R. J. Bingle: formerly Curator (Archivist), Oriental and India Office Collections, British Library

R. C. Bridges: Professor of History, University of Aberdeen

Tony Campbell: Map Librarian, British Library

P. E. H. Hair: formerly Professor of Modern History, University of Liverpool

D. B. Quinn: Hon. FBA, formerly Professor of Modern History, University of Liverpool

Ann Savours (Mrs Ann Shirley): formerly on the curatorial staff, Scott Polar Institute, Cambridge, and National Maritime Museum, Greenwich

Michael Strachan: CBE, chairman, Ben Line 1970–1982, author of 'Sir Thomas Roe (1581–1644): A Life' (1989), etc.

GENERAL INDEX

The following lists relate only to the essays (pp. 6–239). For an index to the Listing of HS Publications, see pp. 303–315 above.

The lists below index references **within the text** to the names of all Persons, to the names of all Places, Peoples and Languages, and to certain Select Subjects. Significant references **within footnotes**, other than bibliographical citations, are added in instances where the item is not mentioned in the text of the specific page. Footnote references are indicated by page numbers in *italics*.

PERSONS

Note that the index to the Listing of HS Publications (pp. 305–311 above) supplies fuller names for certain individuals. If only surnames are given in the essays, forenames or forename initials, whenever these can be ascertained, are supplied below, in square brackets.

PLACES, PEOPLES, and LANGUAGES

For places named in the Listing of HS Publications, see the index on pp. 312–315 above. The following items are not listed below: England/English, British, London, street names.

Abyssinia/Abyssinian 26, 100, 173, 175, 176, 179
Addiscombe 145, 147, 148
Aden 145, 146, 152
Africa/African 16, 18, 20, 30, 32, 34, 35, 38, 39, 56–61, 71, 75, 77, 110, 130, 133, 159, 173, 184, 233
Africa, Central 55, 56, 233
Africa/African, East 34, 57, 58, 60, 75, 77
Africa, Nilotic 35
Africa/African, North 16, 39
Africa, North East 16, 41
Africa, South 16, 34, 71
Africa, West 30, 58
Africa, West Central 56
Agula 175
Ahmadabad 194
Alaska 32
Alderley Park 90
Algiers 84, 85
Allahabad 152
Amarapura 151
Amazon, [River] 35
America/American 9, 11, 24, 32, 38, 41, 44, 60, 108, 114, 115, 117, 119, 171, 173, 185, 186, 202, 225, 227, 228, 233
America, Central 33
America, Latin 32, 233
America/American, North 9, 11, 18, 24, 32, 38, 41, 121, 204, 227
America, South 24, 98, 171, 185, 186, 200
America, Spanish 202
Americas 32
Amerindian 226
Amharic 196
An, River 150
Andes 18, 35, 170
Anglo-Saxons 227
Angola 31
Antarctic/Antarctica 20, 31, 32, 35, 166,

167, 179, 181–184, 186, 201, 224, 233, 234
Antwerp 113, 118
Arab 39
Arabian 226
Arabic 12, 34, 39, 58, 144
Arakan 150
Ararat, [Mount] 63
Arctic 20, 32, 164, 167–169, 179–181, 233, 237
Argentinian 20, 38
Armenian 13
Asia/Asian/Asiatic 18, 26, 32, 34, 35, 38, 146, 157, 160, 173, 184, 192, 233, 236
Asia, Central 15, 32, 34, 157, 233
Asia, Further 35
Assam 146
Atlantic 114, 119, 120
Atlantic, North 114
Australasia 32, 35
Australia 87, 98, 99, 108, 110, 113, 114, 116–121, 136, 139, 209, 233
Ava 151, 154

Bahamas 215
Bantu 60, 226
Barbados 215
Barrow, Point 19
Basque 181
Belgium 183, 212, 215
Benares 152
Bengal 143–147, 158, 159, 173
Berlin 101
Biscay, Bay of 185
Bolivia 187
Bombay 71, 145–147, 194
Brahmaputra, [River] 149
Brazil 28, 35, 121, 173
Bristol 203
Brunswick 209

SELECT SUBJECTS

Note the following sub-headings: **Books and Journals; Ships; Societies, Associations and Clubs.**

Afghan War, First/Third 148, 211
'Apu Ollantay' 170
Arctic Officers *167*

Bengal Army 143
Bengal Civil Service 144
Bengal Engineers 144, 147, 159
Bengal Pilot Service *158*
Biblical research *134*
Birkbeck Institute 191
Bodleian Library 197, 211, 222
Bombay Marine 71

Books and Journals

Titles in the text only, in the form given: author or HS editor added.

Apothegms of Alee [W. Yule] 144
Athenaeum, The 61–64, 67, 73, 77, 97, 112, 133, 135
Before Columbus [Fernández-Armesto] 226
Biography of R. H. Major, F. S. A. &c [J. H.] 138
Bombay in the Days of Queen Anne [Foster] 194
Book of Ser Marco Polo [Yule] 143, 155
Calendar of State Papers 9
Cambridge History of the British Empire 194
Catalogue of the Map Room of the Royal Geographical Society, The 112
Cathay and the Way Thither [Yule] 22, 28, 154, 155, 157, 162
Claudius Ptolemy and the Nile [Cooley] 78
Columbus Letters [Major] 89–91, 96, 97, 101, 105, 109, 113, 114, 132, 139
Conquest of New Granada, The [Markham] 186
Conquest of Peru, The [Prescott] 169
Cook's Journals [Beaglehole] 205
Correspondence of John Locke [De Beer] 209

Diary of John Evelyn/Diary/Evelyn [De Beer] 209, 211–215, 217, 218, 222
Dictionary of National Biography/DNB 53, 81, 137, 138
Discoveries of the World [Galvão] 91
Discovery of Tahiti [Carrington] 205
Divers Voyages [Hakluyt] 12, 89, 179
Edinburgh Review 56, 57
Embassy of Sir Thomas Roe to the Court of the Great Mogul, 1615–1619 [Foster] 193
Encyclopedia Britannica 139
England's Quest for Eastern Trade [Foster] 196
English Factories in India/English Factories [Foster] 192, 193
English Privateering Voyages to the West Indies, 1588–1595 [Andrews] 205
Explorers' Maps [Skelton] 207
Famous Sailors of Former Times [Markham] 186
Geographical Magazine 207
Hakluyt Handbook [Quinn] 12, 22, 205
Hakluytus Posthumus [Putchas] 12
Hawkins Voyages [Markham] 22
Heroes, Hero Worship, and the Heroic in History [Carlyle] 234
History of Cartography [Skelton/Bagrow] 81, 115, 116, 121, 126, 206
History of Maritime and Inland Discovery/ Maritime and Inland Discovery [Cooley] 50, 56, 60, 67
History of the New World [Benzoni] 91
Hobson-Jobson: being a Glossary of Anglo-Indian colloquial Words and Phrases/ Hobson-Jobson [Yule] 143, 160, 162
Illustrated London News 137
Imago Mundi 206
Incas of Peru, The [Markham] 186
Inner Africa Laid Open [Cooley] 75
Journal of the Asiatic Society of Bengal 146
Lands of Silence, The [Markham] 187